Python Machine Learning

Second Edition

Machine Learning and Deep Learning with Python, scikit-learn, and TensorFlow

Sebastian Raschka

Vahid Mirjalili

BIRMINGHAM - MUMBAI

Python Machine Learning
Second Edition

First published: September 2015

Second edition: September 2017

Revision log for the second edition:

First release: 14-09-2017

Second release: 15-09-2017

Third release: 23-10-2017

Fourth release: 04-09-2018

Published by Packt Publishing Ltd.
Livery Place
35 Livery Street
Birmingham B3 2PB, UK.

ISBN 978-1-78712-593-3

www.packtpub.com

Credits

Authors
Sebastian Raschka
Vahid Mirjalili

Reviewers
Jared Huffman
Huai-En, Sun (Ryan Sun)

Acquisition Editor
Frank Pohlmann

Content Development Editor
Chris Nelson

Project Editor
Monika Sangwan

Technical Editors
Bhagyashree Rai
Nidhisha Shetty

Copy Editor
Safis Editing

Project Coordinator
Suzanne Coutinho

Proofreader
Safis Editing

Indexer
Tejal Daruwale Soni

Graphics
Kirk D'Penha

Production Coordinator
Arvindkumar Gupta

About the Authors

Sebastian Raschka, the author of the bestselling book, *Python Machine Learning*, has many years of experience with coding in Python, and he has given several seminars on the practical applications of data science, machine learning, and deep learning including a machine learning tutorial at SciPy — the leading conference for scientific computing in Python.

While Sebastian's academic research projects are mainly centered around problem-solving in computational biology, he loves to write and talk about data science, machine learning, and Python in general, and he is motivated to help people develop data-driven solutions without necessarily requiring a machine learning background.

His work and contributions have recently been recognized by the departmental outstanding graduate student award 2016-2017 as well as the ACM Computing Reviews' Best of 2016 award. In his free time, Sebastian loves to contribute to open source projects, and the methods that he has implemented are now successfully used in machine learning competitions, such as Kaggle.

I would like to take this opportunity to thank the great Python community and developers of open source packages who helped me create the perfect environment for scientific research and data science. Also, I want to thank my parents who always encouraged and supported me in pursuing the path and career that I was so passionate about.

Special thanks to the core developers of scikit-learn. As a contributor to this project, I had the pleasure to work with great people who are not only very knowledgeable when it comes to machine learning but are also excellent programmers. Lastly, I'd like to thank Elie Kawerk, who volunteered to review the book and provided valuable feedback on the new chapters.

Vahid Mirjalili obtained his PhD in mechanical engineering working on novel methods for large-scale, computational simulations of molecular structures. Currently, he is focusing his research efforts on applications of machine learning in various computer vision projects at the department of computer science and engineering at Michigan State University.

Vahid picked Python as his number-one choice of programming language, and throughout his academic and research career he has gained tremendous experience with coding in Python. He taught Python programming to the engineering class at Michigan State University, which gave him a chance to help students understand different data structures and develop efficient code in Python.

While Vahid's broad research interests focus on deep learning and computer vision applications, he is especially interested in leveraging deep learning techniques to extend privacy in biometric data such as face images so that information is not revealed beyond what users intend to reveal. Furthermore, he also collaborates with a team of engineers working on self-driving cars, where he designs neural network models for the fusion of multispectral images for pedestrian detection.

I would like to thank my PhD advisor, Dr. Arun Ross, for giving me the opportunity to work on novel problems in his research lab. I also like to thank Dr. Vishnu Boddeti for inspiring my interests in deep learning and demystifying its core concepts.

About the Reviewers

Jared Huffman is an entrepreneur, gamer, storyteller, machine learning fanatic, and database aficionado. He has dedicated the past 10 years to developing software and analyzing data. His previous work has spanned a variety of topics, including network security, financial systems, and business intelligence, as well as web services, developer tools, and business strategy. Most recently, he was the founder of the data science team at Minecraft, with a focus on big data and machine learning. When not working, you can typically find him gaming or enjoying the beautiful Pacific Northwest with friends and family.

> I'd like to thank Packt for giving me the opportunity to work on such a great book, my wife for the constant encouragement, and my daughter for sleeping through most of the late nights while I was reviewing and debugging code.

Huai-En, Sun (Ryan Sun) holds a master's degree in statistics from the National Chiao Tung University. He is currently working as a data scientist for analyzing the production line at PEGATRON. Machine learning and deep learning are his main areas of research.

www.PacktPub.com

eBooks, discount offers, and more

Did you know that Packt offers eBook versions of every book published, with PDF and ePub files available? You can upgrade to the eBook version at www.PacktPub.com and as a print book customer, you are entitled to a discount on the eBook copy. Get in touch with us at customercare@packtpub.com for more details.

At www.PacktPub.com, you can also read a collection of free technical articles, sign up for a range of free newsletters and receive exclusive discounts and offers on Packt books and eBooks.

https://www.packtpub.com/mapt

Get the most in-demand software skills with Mapt. Mapt gives you full access to all Packt books and video courses, as well as industry-leading tools to help you plan your personal development and advance your career.

Why subscribe?

- Fully searchable across every book published by Packt
- Copy and paste, print, and bookmark content
- On demand and accessible via a web browser

Packt is Searching for Authors Like You

If you're interested in becoming an author for Packt, please visit authors.packtpub. com and apply today. We have worked with thousands of developers and tech professionals, just like you, to help them share their insight with the global tech community. You can make a general application, apply for a specifi c hot topic that we are recruiting an author for, or submit your own idea.

Table of Contents

Preface

Through exposure to the news and social media, you are probably aware of the fact that machine learning has become one of the most exciting technologies of our time and age. Large companies, such as Google, Facebook, Apple, Amazon, and IBM, heavily invest in machine learning research and applications for good reasons. While it may seem that machine learning has become the buzzword of our time and age, it is certainly not a fad. This exciting field opens the way to new possibilities and has become indispensable to our daily lives. This is evident in talking to the voice assistant on our smartphones, recommending the right product for our customers, preventing credit card fraud, filtering out spam from our email inboxes, detecting and diagnosing medical diseases, the list goes on and on.

If you want to become a machine learning practitioner, a better problem solver, or maybe even consider a career in machine learning research, then this book is for you. However, for a novice, the theoretical concepts behind machine learning can be quite overwhelming. Many practical books have been published in recent years that will help you get started in machine learning by implementing powerful learning algorithms.

Getting exposed to practical code examples and working through example applications of machine learning are a great way to dive into this field. Concrete examples help illustrate the broader concepts by putting the learned material directly into action. However, remember that with great power comes great responsibility! In addition to offering a hands-on experience with machine learning using the Python programming languages and Python-based machine learning libraries, this book introduces the mathematical concepts behind machine learning algorithms, which is essential for using machine learning successfully. Thus, this book is different from a purely practical book; it is a book that discusses the necessary details regarding machine learning concepts and offers intuitive yet informative explanations of how machine learning algorithms work, how to use them, and most importantly, how to avoid the most common pitfalls.

Currently, if you type "machine learning" as a search term in Google Scholar, it returns an overwhelmingly large number of publications — 1,800,000. Of course, we cannot discuss the nitty-gritty of all the different algorithms and applications that have emerged in the last 60 years. However, in this book, we will embark on an exciting journey that covers all the essential topics and concepts to give you a head start in this field. If you find that your thirst for knowledge is not satisfied, this book references many useful resources that can be used to follow up on the essential breakthroughs in this field.

If you have already studied machine learning theory in detail, this book will show you how to put your knowledge into practice. If you have used machine learning techniques before and want to gain more insight into how machine learning actually works, this book is for you. Don't worry if you are completely new to the machine learning field; you have even more reason to be excited. Here is a promise that machine learning will change the way you think about the problems you want to solve and will show you how to tackle them by unlocking the power of data.

Before we dive deeper into the machine learning field, let's answer your most important question, "Why Python?" The answer is simple: it is powerful yet very accessible. Python has become the most popular programming language for data science because it allows us to forget about the tedious parts of programming and offers us an environment where we can quickly jot down our ideas and put concepts directly into action.

We, the authors, can truly say that the study of machine learning has made us better scientists, thinkers, and problem solvers. In this book, we want to share this knowledge with you. Knowledge is gained by learning. The key is our enthusiasm, and the real mastery of skills can only be achieved by practice. The road ahead may be bumpy on occasions and some topics may be more challenging than others, but we hope that you will embrace this opportunity and focus on the reward. Remember that we are on this journey together, and throughout this book, we will add many powerful techniques to your arsenal that will help us solve even the toughest problems the data-driven way.

What this book covers

Chapter 1, Giving Computers the Ability to Learn from Data, introduces you to the main subareas of machine learning in order to tackle various problem tasks. In addition, it discusses the essential steps for creating a typical machine learning model by building a pipeline that will guide us through the following chapters.

Chapter 2, Training Simple Machine Learning Algorithms for Classification, goes back to the origins of machine learning and introduces binary perceptron classifiers and adaptive linear neurons. This chapter is a gentle introduction to the fundamentals of pattern classification and focuses on the interplay of optimization algorithms and machine learning.

Chapter 3, A Tour of Machine Learning Classifiers Using scikit-learn, describes the essential machine learning algorithms for classification and provides practical examples using one of the most popular and comprehensive open source machine learning libraries: scikit-learn.

Chapter 4, Building Good Training Sets – Data Preprocessing, discusses how to deal with the most common problems in unprocessed datasets, such as missing data. It also discusses several approaches to identify the most informative features in datasets and teaches you how to prepare variables of different types as proper input for machine learning algorithms.

Chapter 5, Compressing Data via Dimensionality Reduction, describes the essential techniques to reduce the number of features in a dataset to smaller sets while retaining most of their useful and discriminatory information. It discusses the standard approach to dimensionality reduction via principal component analysis and compares it to supervised and nonlinear transformation techniques.

Chapter 6, Learning Best Practices for Model Evaluation and Hyperparameter Tuning, discusses the dos and don'ts for estimating the performances of predictive models. Moreover, it discusses different metrics for measuring the performance of our models and techniques to fine-tune machine learning algorithms.

Chapter 7, Combining Different Models for Ensemble Learning, introduces you to the different concepts of combining multiple learning algorithms effectively. It teaches you how to build ensembles of experts to overcome the weaknesses of individual learners, resulting in more accurate and reliable predictions.

Chapter 8, Applying Machine Learning to Sentiment Analysis, discusses the essential steps to transform textual data into meaningful representations for machine learning algorithms to predict the opinions of people based on their writing.

Chapter 9, Embedding a Machine Learning Model into a Web Application, continues with the predictive model from the previous chapter and walks you through the essential steps of developing web applications with embedded machine learning models.

Chapter 10, Predicting Continuous Target Variables with Regression Analysis, discusses the essential techniques for modeling linear relationships between target and response variables to make predictions on a continuous scale. After introducing different linear models, it also talks about polynomial regression and tree-based approaches.

Chapter 11, Working with Unlabeled Data – Clustering Analysis, shifts the focus to a different subarea of machine learning, unsupervised learning. We apply algorithms from three fundamental families of clustering algorithms to find groups of objects that share a certain degree of similarity.

Chapter 12, Implementing a Multilayer Artificial Neural Network from Scratch, extends the concept of gradient-based optimization, which we first introduced in *Chapter 2, Training Simple Machine Learning Algorithms for Classification*, to build powerful, multilayer neural networks based on the popular backpropagation algorithm in Python.

Chapter 13, Parallelizing Neural Network Training with TensorFlow, builds upon the knowledge from the previous chapter to provide you with a practical guide for training neural networks more efficiently. The focus of this chapter is on TensorFlow, an open source Python library that allows us to utilize multiple cores of modern GPUs.

Chapter 14, Going Deeper – The Mechanics of TensorFlow, covers TensorFlow in greater detail explaining its core concepts of computational graphs and sessions. In addition, this chapter covers topics such as saving and visualizing neural network graphs, which will come in very handy during the remaining chapters of this book.

Chapter 15, Classifying Images with Deep Convolutional Neural Networks, discusses deep neural network architectures that have become the new standard in computer vision and image recognition fields—convolutional neural networks. This chapter will discuss the main concepts between convolutional layers as a feature extractor and apply convolutional neural network architectures to an image classification task to achieve almost perfect classification accuracy.

Chapter 16, Modeling Sequential Data Using Recurrent Neural Networks, introduces another popular neural network architecture for deep learning that is especially well suited for working with sequential data and time series data. In this chapter, we will apply different recurrent neural network architectures to text data. We will start with a sentiment analysis task as a warm-up exercise and will learn how to generate entirely new text.

What you need for this book

The execution of the code examples provided in this book requires an installation of Python 3.6.0 or newer on macOS, Linux, or Microsoft Windows. We will make frequent use of Python's essential libraries for scientific computing throughout this book, including SciPy, NumPy, scikit-learn, Matplotlib, and pandas.

The first chapter will provide you with instructions and useful tips to set up your Python environment and these core libraries. We will add additional libraries to our repertoire; moreover, installation instructions are provided in the respective chapters: the NLTK library for natural language processing (*Chapter 8, Applying Machine Learning to Sentiment Analysis*), the Flask web framework (*Chapter 9, Embedding a Machine Learning Model into a Web Application*), the Seaborn library for statistical data visualization (*Chapter 10, Predicting Continuous Target Variables with Regression Analysis*), and TensorFlow for efficient neural network training on graphical processing units (*Chapters 13 to 16*).

Who this book is for

If you want to find out how to use Python to start answering critical questions of your data, pick up *Python Machine Learning, Second Edition* — whether you want to start from scratch or extend your data science knowledge, this is an essential and unmissable resource.

Conventions

In this book, you will find a number of text styles that distinguish between different kinds of information. Here are some examples of these styles and an explanation of their meaning.

Code words in text, database table names, folder names, filenames, file extensions, pathnames, dummy URLs, user input, and Twitter handles are shown as follows: "Using the `out_file=None` setting, we directly assigned the dot data to a `dot_data` variable, instead of writing an intermediate `tree.dot` file to disk."

A block of code is set as follows:

```
>>> from sklearn.neighbors import KNeighborsClassifier
>>> knn = KNeighborsClassifier(n_neighbors=5, p=2,
...                            metric='minkowski')
>>> knn.fit(X_train_std, y_train)
>>> plot_decision_regions(X_combined_std, y_combined,
...                       classifier=knn, test_idx=range(105,150))
>>> plt.xlabel('petal length [standardized]')
>>> plt.ylabel('petal width [standardized]')
>>> plt.show()
```

Any command-line input or output is written as follows:

`pip3 install graphviz`

New terms and **important words** are shown in bold. Words that you see on the screen, for example, in menus or dialog boxes, appear in the text like this: "After we click on the **Dashboard** button in the top-right corner, we have access to the control panel shown at the top of the page."

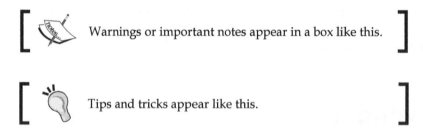

> Warnings or important notes appear in a box like this.

> Tips and tricks appear like this.

Reader feedback

Feedback from our readers is always welcome. Let us know what you think about this book—what you liked or disliked. Reader feedback is important for us as it helps us develop titles that you will really get the most out of.

To send us general feedback, simply email feedback@packtpub.com, and mention the book's title in the subject of your message.

If there is a topic that you have expertise in and you are interested in either writing or contributing to a book, see our author guide at www.packtpub.com/authors.

Customer support

Now that you are the proud owner of a Packt book, we have a number of things to help you to get the most from your purchase.

Downloading the example code

You can download the example code files for this book from your account at `http://www.packtpub.com`. If you purchased this book elsewhere, you can visit `http://www.packtpub.com/support` and register to have the files emailed directly to you.

You can download the code files by following these steps:

1. Log in or register to our website using your email address and password.
2. Hover the mouse pointer on the **SUPPORT** tab at the top.
3. Click on **Code Downloads & Errata**.
4. Enter the name of the book in the **Search** box.
5. Select the book for which you're looking to download the code files.
6. Choose from the drop-down menu where you purchased this book from.
7. Click on **Code Download**.

You can also download the code files by clicking on the **Code Files** button on the book's web page at the Packt Publishing website. This page can be accessed by entering the book's name in the **Search** box. Please note that you need to be logged in to your Packt account.

Once the file is downloaded, please make sure that you unzip or extract the folder using the latest version of:

- WinRAR / 7-Zip for Windows
- Zipeg / iZip / UnRarX for Mac
- 7-Zip / PeaZip for Linux

The code bundle for the book is also hosted on GitHub at `https://github.com/PacktPublishing/Python-Machine-Learning-Second-Edition`. We also have other code bundles from our rich catalog of books and videos available at `https://github.com/PacktPublishing/`. Check them out!

Downloading the color images of this book

We also provide you with a PDF file that has color images of the screenshots/diagrams used in this book. The color images will help you better understand the changes in the output. You can download this file from http://www.packtpub.com/sites/default/files/downloads/PythonMachineLearningSecondEdition_ColorImages.pdf. In addition, lower resolution color images are embedded in the code notebooks of this book that come bundled with the example code files.

Errata

Although we have taken every care to ensure the accuracy of our content, mistakes do happen. If you find a mistake in one of our books—maybe a mistake in the text or the code—we would be grateful if you could report this to us. By doing so, you can save other readers from frustration and help us improve subsequent versions of this book. If you find any errata, please report them by visiting http://www.packtpub.com/submit-errata, selecting your book, clicking on the **Errata Submission Form** link, and entering the details of your errata. Once your errata are verified, your submission will be accepted and the errata will be uploaded to our website or added to any list of existing errata under the Errata section of that title.

To view the previously submitted errata, go to https://www.packtpub.com/books/content/support and enter the name of the book in the search field. The required information will appear under the **Errata** section.

Piracy

Piracy of copyrighted material on the Internet is an ongoing problem across all media. At Packt, we take the protection of our copyright and licenses very seriously. If you come across any illegal copies of our works in any form on the Internet, please provide us with the location address or website name immediately so that we can pursue a remedy.

Please contact us at copyright@packtpub.com with a link to the suspected pirated material.

We appreciate your help in protecting our authors and our ability to bring you valuable content.

Questions

If you have a problem with any aspect of this book, you can contact us at questions@packtpub.com, and we will do our best to address the problem.

1
Giving Computers the Ability to Learn from Data

In my opinion, **machine learning**, the application and science of algorithms that make sense of data, is the most exciting field of all the computer sciences! We are living in an age where data comes in abundance; using self-learning algorithms from the field of machine learning, we can turn this data into knowledge. Thanks to the many powerful open source libraries that have been developed in recent years, there has probably never been a better time to break into the machine learning field and learn how to utilize powerful algorithms to spot patterns in data and make predictions about future events.

In this chapter, you will learn about the main concepts and different types of machine learning. Together with a basic introduction to the relevant terminology, we will lay the groundwork for successfully using machine learning techniques for practical problem solving.

In this chapter, we will cover the following topics:

- The general concepts of machine learning
- The three types of learning and basic terminology
- The building blocks for successfully designing machine learning systems
- Installing and setting up Python for data analysis and machine learning

Building intelligent machines to transform data into knowledge

In this age of modern technology, there is one resource that we have in abundance: a large amount of structured and unstructured data. In the second half of the twentieth century, machine learning evolved as a subfield of **Artificial Intelligence (AI)** that involved self-learning algorithms that derived knowledge from data in order to make predictions. Instead of requiring humans to manually derive rules and build models from analyzing large amounts of data, machine learning offers a more efficient alternative for capturing the knowledge in data to gradually improve the performance of predictive models and make data-driven decisions. Not only is machine learning becoming increasingly important in computer science research, but it also plays an ever greater role in our everyday lives. Thanks to machine learning, we enjoy robust email spam filters, convenient text and voice recognition software, reliable web search engines, challenging chess-playing programs, and, hopefully soon, safe and efficient self-driving cars.

The three different types of machine learning

In this section, we will take a look at the three types of machine learning: **supervised learning**, **unsupervised learning**, and **reinforcement learning**. We will learn about the fundamental differences between the three different learning types and, using conceptual examples, we will develop an intuition for the practical problem domains where these can be applied:

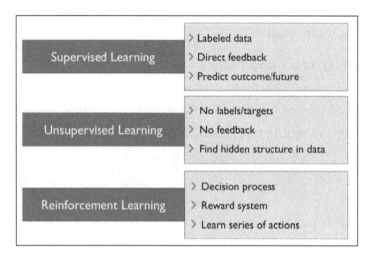

Making predictions about the future with supervised learning

The main goal in supervised learning is to learn a model from labeled training data that allows us to make predictions about unseen or future data. Here, the term **supervised** refers to a set of samples where the desired output signals (labels) are already known.

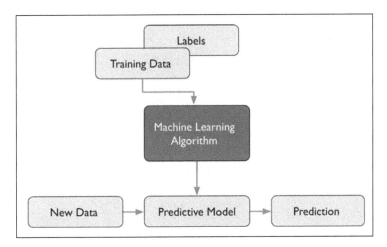

Considering the example of email spam filtering, we can train a model using a supervised machine learning algorithm on a corpus of labeled emails, emails that are correctly marked as spam or not-spam, to predict whether a new email belongs to either of the two categories. A supervised learning task with discrete class labels, such as in the previous email spam filtering example, is also called a **classification task**. Another subcategory of supervised learning is **regression**, where the outcome signal is a continuous value:

Classification for predicting class labels

Classification is a subcategory of supervised learning where the goal is to predict the categorical class labels of new instances, based on past observations. Those class labels are discrete, unordered values that can be understood as the group memberships of the instances. The previously mentioned example of email spam detection represents a typical example of a binary classification task, where the machine learning algorithm learns a set of rules in order to distinguish between two possible classes: spam and non-spam emails.

However, the set of class labels does not have to be of a binary nature. The predictive model learned by a supervised learning algorithm can assign any class label that was presented in the training dataset to a new, unlabeled instance. A typical example of a **multiclass classification** task is handwritten character recognition. Here, we could collect a training dataset that consists of multiple handwritten examples of each letter in the alphabet. Now, if a user provides a new handwritten character via an input device, our predictive model will be able to predict the correct letter in the alphabet with certain accuracy. However, our machine learning system would be unable to correctly recognize any of the digits zero to nine, for example, if they were not part of our training dataset.

The following figure illustrates the concept of a binary classification task given 30 training samples; 15 training samples are labeled as negative class (minus signs) and 15 training samples are labeled as positive class (plus signs). In this scenario, our dataset is two-dimensional, which means that each sample has two values associated with it: x_1 and x_2. Now, we can use a supervised machine learning algorithm to learn a rule — the decision boundary represented as a dashed line — that can separate those two classes and classify new data into each of those two categories given its x_1 and x_2 values:

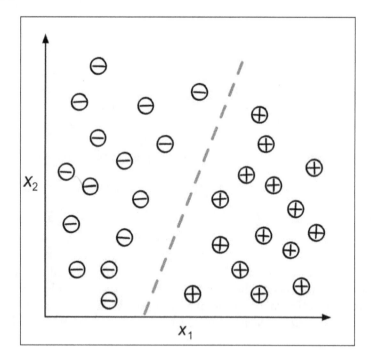

Regression for predicting continuous outcomes

We learned in the previous section that the task of classification is to assign categorical, unordered labels to instances. A second type of supervised learning is the prediction of continuous outcomes, which is also called **regression analysis**. In regression analysis, we are given a number of predictor (**explanatory**) variables and a continuous response variable (**outcome** or **target**), and we try to find a relationship between those variables that allows us to predict an outcome.

For example, let's assume that we are interested in predicting the math SAT scores of our students. If there is a relationship between the time spent studying for the test and the final scores, we could use it as training data to learn a model that uses the study time to predict the test scores of future students who are planning to take this test.

 The term *regression* was devised by Francis Galton in his article *Regression towards Mediocrity in Hereditary Stature* in 1886. Galton described the biological phenomenon that the variance of height in a population does not increase over time. He observed that the height of parents is not passed on to their children, but instead the children's height is regressing towards the population mean.

The following figure illustrates the concept of linear regression. Given a predictor variable *x* and a response variable *y*, we fit a straight line to this data that minimizes the distance—most commonly the average squared distance—between the sample points and the fitted line. We can now use the intercept and slope learned from this data to predict the outcome variable of new data:

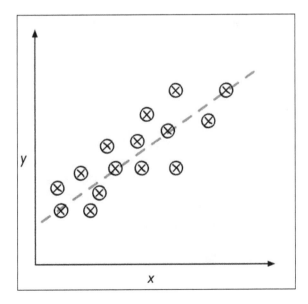

Solving interactive problems with reinforcement learning

Another type of machine learning is **reinforcement learning**. In reinforcement learning, the goal is to develop a system (**agent**) that improves its performance based on interactions with the environment. Since the information about the current state of the environment typically also includes a so-called **reward signal**, we can think of reinforcement learning as a field related to supervised learning. However, in reinforcement learning this feedback is not the correct ground truth label or value, but a measure of how well the action was measured by a reward function. Through its interaction with the environment, an agent can then use reinforcement learning to learn a series of actions that maximizes this reward via an exploratory trial-and-error approach or deliberative planning.

A popular example of reinforcement learning is a chess engine. Here, the agent decides upon a series of moves depending on the state of the board (the environment), and the reward can be defined as **win** or **lose** at the end of the game:

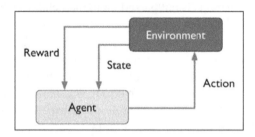

There are many different subtypes of reinforcement learning. However, a general scheme is that the agent in reinforcement learning tries to maximize the reward by a series of interactions with the environment. Each state can be associated with a positive or negative reward, and a reward can be defined as accomplishing an overall goal, such as winning or losing a game of chess. For instance, in chess the outcome of each move can be thought of as a different state of the environment. To explore the chess example further, let's think of visiting certain locations on the chess board as being associated with a positive event—for instance, removing an opponent's chess piece from the board or threatening the queen. Other positions, however, are associated with a negative event, such as losing a chess piece to the opponent in the following turn. Now, not every turn results in the removal of a chess piece, and reinforcement learning is concerned with learning the series of steps by maximizing a reward based on immediate and delayed feedback.

While this section provides a basic overview of reinforcement learning, please note that applications of reinforcement learning are beyond the scope of this book, which primarily focusses on classification, regression analysis, and clustering.

Discovering hidden structures with unsupervised learning

In supervised learning, we know the right answer beforehand when we train our model, and in reinforcement learning, we define a measure of reward for particular actions by the agent. In unsupervised learning, however, we are dealing with unlabeled data or data of unknown structure. Using unsupervised learning techniques, we are able to explore the structure of our data to extract meaningful information without the guidance of a known outcome variable or reward function.

Finding subgroups with clustering

Clustering is an exploratory data analysis technique that allows us to organize a pile of information into meaningful subgroups (**clusters**) without having any prior knowledge of their group memberships. Each cluster that arises during the analysis defines a group of objects that share a certain degree of similarity but are more dissimilar to objects in other clusters, which is why clustering is also sometimes called **unsupervised classification**. Clustering is a great technique for structuring information and deriving meaningful relationships from data. For example, it allows marketers to discover customer groups based on their interests, in order to develop distinct marketing programs.

The following figure illustrates how clustering can be applied to organizing unlabeled data into three distinct groups based on the similarity of their features x_1 and x_2:

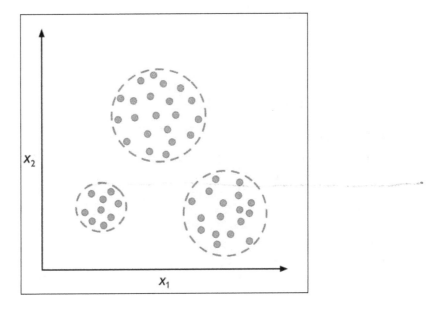

Dimensionality reduction for data compression

Another subfield of unsupervised learning is **dimensionality reduction**. Often we are working with data of high dimensionality—each observation comes with a high number of measurements—that can present a challenge for limited storage space and the computational performance of machine learning algorithms. Unsupervised dimensionality reduction is a commonly used approach in feature preprocessing to remove noise from data, which can also degrade the predictive performance of certain algorithms, and compress the data onto a smaller dimensional subspace while retaining most of the relevant information.

Sometimes, dimensionality reduction can also be useful for visualizing data, for example, a high-dimensional feature set can be projected onto one-, two-, or three-dimensional feature spaces in order to visualize it via 3D or 2D scatterplots or histograms. The following figure shows an example where nonlinear dimensionality reduction was applied to compress a 3D Swiss Roll onto a new 2D feature subspace:

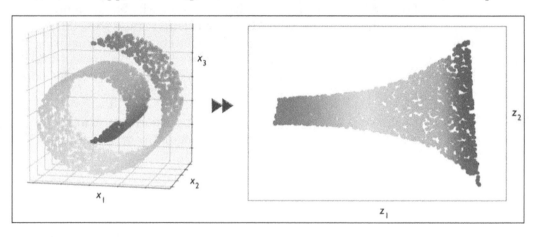

Introduction to the basic terminology and notations

Now that we have discussed the three broad categories of machine learning—supervised, unsupervised, and reinforcement learning—let us have a look at the basic terminology that we will be using throughout the book. The following table depicts an excerpt of the Iris dataset, which is a classic example in the field of machine learning. The Iris dataset contains the measurements of 150 Iris flowers from three different species—Setosa, Versicolor, and Virginica. Here, each flower sample represents one row in our dataset, and the flower measurements in centimeters are stored as columns, which we also call the **features** of the dataset:

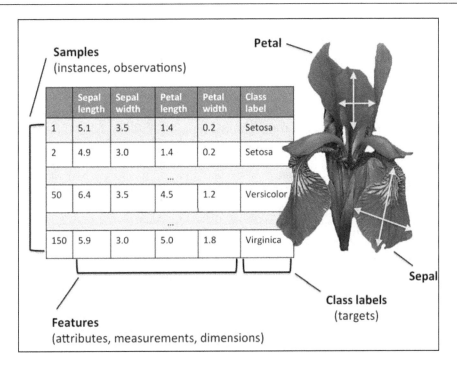

To keep the notation and implementation simple yet efficient, we will make use of some of the basics of linear algebra. In the following chapters, we will use a matrix and vector notation to refer to our data. We will follow the common convention to represent each sample as a separate row in a feature matrix **X**, where each feature is stored as a separate column.

The Iris dataset consisting of 150 samples and four features can then be written as a 150×4 matrix $X \in \mathbb{R}^{150\times4}$:

$$
\begin{bmatrix}
x_1^{(1)} & x_2^{(1)} & x_3^{(1)} & x_4^{(1)} \\
x_1^{(2)} & x_2^{(2)} & x_3^{(2)} & x_4^{(2)} \\
\vdots & \vdots & \vdots & \vdots \\
x_1^{(150)} & x_2^{(150)} & x_3^{(150)} & x_4^{(150)}
\end{bmatrix}
$$

For the rest of this book, unless noted otherwise, we will use the superscript i to refer to the ith training sample, and the subscript j to refer to the jth dimension of the training dataset.

We use lowercase, bold-face letters to refer to vectors $\left(x \in \mathbb{R}^{n \times 1}\right)$ and uppercase, bold-face letters to refer to matrices $\left(X \in \mathbb{R}^{n \times m}\right)$. To refer to single elements in a vector or matrix, we write the letters in italics $(x^{(n)}$ or $x_{(m)}^{(n)}$, respectively).

For example, x_1^{150} refers to the first dimension of flower sample 150, the *sepal length*. Thus, each row in this feature matrix represents one flower instance and can be written as a four-dimensional row vector $x^{(i)} \in \mathbb{R}^{1 \times 4}$:

$$x^{(i)} = \begin{bmatrix} x_1^{(i)} & x_2^{(i)} & x_3^{(i)} & x_4^{(i)} \end{bmatrix}$$

And each feature dimension is a 150-dimensional column vector $x_j \in \mathbb{R}^{150 \times 1}$. For example:

$$x_j = \begin{bmatrix} x_j^{(1)} \\ x_j^{(2)} \\ \vdots \\ x_j^{(150)} \end{bmatrix}$$

Similarly, we store the target variables (here, class labels) as a 150-dimensional column vector:

$$y = \begin{bmatrix} y^{(1)} \\ \dots \\ y^{(150)} \end{bmatrix} \left(y \in \{\text{Setosa, Versicolor, Virginica}\}\right)$$

A roadmap for building machine learning systems

In previous sections, we discussed the basic concepts of machine learning and the three different types of learning. In this section, we will discuss the other important parts of a machine learning system accompanying the learning algorithm. The following diagram shows a typical workflow for using machine learning in predictive modeling, which we will discuss in the following subsections:

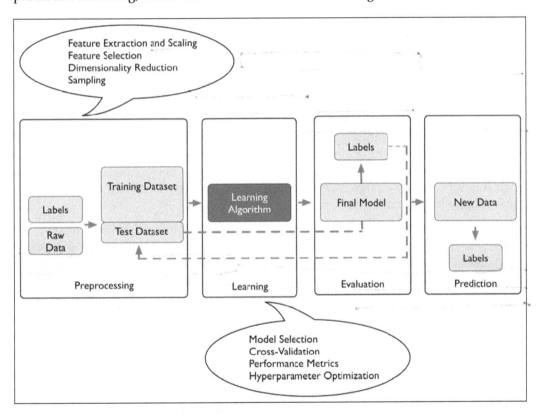

Preprocessing – getting data into shape

Let's begin with discussing the roadmap for building machine learning systems. Raw data rarely comes in the form and shape that is necessary for the optimal performance of a learning algorithm. Thus, the preprocessing of the data is one of the most crucial steps in any machine learning application. If we take the Iris flower dataset from the previous section as an example, we can think of the raw data as a series of flower images from which we want to extract meaningful features. Useful features could be the color, the hue, the intensity of the flowers, the height, and the flower lengths and widths. Many machine learning algorithms also require that the selected features are on the same scale for optimal performance, which is often achieved by transforming the features in the range [0, 1] or a standard normal distribution with zero mean and unit variance, as we will see in later chapters.

Some of the selected features may be highly correlated and therefore redundant to a certain degree. In those cases, dimensionality reduction techniques are useful for compressing the features onto a lower dimensional subspace. Reducing the dimensionality of our feature space has the advantage that less storage space is required, and the learning algorithm can run much faster. In certain cases, dimensionality reduction can also improve the predictive performance of a model if the dataset contains a large number of irrelevant features (or noise), that is, if the dataset has a low signal-to-noise ratio.

To determine whether our machine learning algorithm not only performs well on the training set but also generalizes well to new data, we also want to randomly divide the dataset into a separate training and test set. We use the training set to train and optimize our machine learning model, while we keep the test set until the very end to evaluate the final model.

Training and selecting a predictive model

As we will see in later chapters, many different machine learning algorithms have been developed to solve different problem tasks. An important point that can be summarized from David Wolpert's famous *No free lunch theorems* is that we can't get learning "for free" (*The Lack of A Priori Distinctions Between Learning Algorithms*, D.H. Wolpert 1996; *No free lunch theorems for optimization*, D.H. Wolpert and W.G. Macready, 1997). Intuitively, we can relate this concept to the popular saying, *I suppose it is tempting, if the only tool you have is a hammer, to treat everything as if it were a nail* (Abraham Maslow, 1966). For example, each classification algorithm has its inherent biases, and no single classification model enjoys superiority if we don't make any assumptions about the task. In practice, it is therefore essential to compare at least a handful of different algorithms in order to train and select the best performing model. But before we can compare different models, we first have to decide upon a metric to measure performance. One commonly used metric is classification accuracy, which is defined as the proportion of correctly classified instances.

One legitimate question to ask is this: *how do we know which model performs well on the final test dataset and real-world data if we don't use this test set for the model selection, but keep it for the final model evaluation?* In order to address the issue embedded in this question, different cross-validation techniques can be used where the training dataset is further divided into training and validation subsets in order to estimate the generalization performance of the model. Finally, we also cannot expect that the default parameters of the different learning algorithms provided by software libraries are optimal for our specific problem task. Therefore, we will make frequent use of hyperparameter optimization techniques that help us to fine-tune the performance of our model in later chapters. Intuitively, we can think of those hyperparameters as parameters that are not learned from the data but represent the knobs of a model that we can turn to improve its performance. This will become much clearer in later chapters when we see actual examples.

Evaluating models and predicting unseen data instances

After we have selected a model that has been fitted on the training dataset, we can use the test dataset to estimate how well it performs on this unseen data to estimate the generalization error. If we are satisfied with its performance, we can now use this model to predict new, future data. It is important to note that the parameters for the previously mentioned procedures, such as feature scaling and dimensionality reduction, are solely obtained from the training dataset, and the same parameters are later reapplied to transform the test dataset, as well as any new data samples – the performance measured on the test data may be overly optimistic otherwise.

Using Python for machine learning

Python is one of the most popular programming languages for data science and therefore enjoys a large number of useful add-on libraries developed by its great developer and open-source community.

Although the performance of interpreted languages, such as Python, for computation-intensive tasks is inferior to lower-level programming languages, extension libraries such as NumPy and SciPy have been developed that build upon lower-layer Fortran and C implementations for fast and vectorized operations on multidimensional arrays.

For machine learning programming tasks, we will mostly refer to the scikit-learn library, which is currently one of the most popular and accessible open source machine learning libraries.

Installing Python and packages from the Python Package Index

Python is available for all three major operating systems—Microsoft Windows, macOS, and Linux—and the installer, as well as the documentation, can be downloaded from the official Python website: `https://www.python.org`.

This book is written for Python version 3.5.2 or higher, and it is recommended you use the most recent version of Python 3 that is currently available, although most of the code examples may also be compatible with Python 2.7.13 or higher. If you decide to use Python 2.7 to execute the code examples, please make sure that you know about the major differences between the two Python versions. A good summary of the differences between Python 3.5 and 2.7 can be found at `https://wiki.python.org/moin/Python2orPython3`.

The additional packages that we will be using throughout this book can be installed via the `pip` installer program, which has been part of the Python standard library since Python 3.3. More information about `pip` can be found at `https://docs.python.org/3/installing/index.html`.

After we have successfully installed Python, we can execute `pip` from the Terminal to install additional Python packages:

```
pip install SomePackage
```

Already installed packages can be updated via the `--upgrade` flag:

```
pip install SomePackage --upgrade
```

Using the Anaconda Python distribution and package manager

A highly recommended alternative Python distribution for scientific computing is Anaconda by Continuum Analytics. Anaconda is a free—including for commercial use—enterprise-ready Python distribution that bundles all the essential Python packages for data science, math, and engineering in one user-friendly cross-platform distribution. The Anaconda installer can be downloaded at `http://continuum.io/downloads`, and an Anaconda quick-start guide is available at `https://conda.io/docs/test-drive.html`.

After successfully installing Anaconda, we can install new Python packages using the following command:

```
conda install SomePackage
```

Existing packages can be updated using the following command:

```
conda update SomePackage
```

Packages for scientific computing, data science, and machine learning

Throughout this book, we will mainly use NumPy's multidimensional arrays to store and manipulate data. Occasionally, we will make use of pandas, which is a library built on top of NumPy that provides additional higher-level data manipulation tools that make working with tabular data even more convenient. To augment our learning experience and visualize quantitative data, which is often extremely useful to intuitively make sense of it, we will use the very customizable Matplotlib library.

The version numbers of the major Python packages that were used for writing this book are mentioned in the following list. Please make sure that the version numbers of your installed packages are equal to, or greater than, those version numbers to ensure the code examples run correctly:

- NumPy 1.12.1
- SciPy 0.19.0
- scikit-learn 0.18.1
- Matplotlib 2.0.2
- pandas 0.20.1

Summary

In this chapter, we explored machine learning at a very high level and familiarized ourselves with the big picture and major concepts that we are going to explore in the following chapters in more detail. We learned that supervised learning is composed of two important subfields: classification and regression. While classification models allow us to categorize objects into known classes, we can use regression analysis to predict the continuous outcomes of target variables. Unsupervised learning not only offers useful techniques for discovering structures in unlabeled data, but it can also be useful for data compression in feature preprocessing steps. We briefly went over the typical roadmap for applying machine learning to problem tasks, which we will use as a foundation for deeper discussions and hands-on examples in the following chapters. Eventually, we set up our Python environment and installed and updated the required packages to get ready to see machine learning in action.

Later in this book, in addition to machine learning itself, we will also introduce different techniques to preprocess our dataset, which will help us to get the best performance out of different machine learning algorithms. While we will cover classification algorithms quite extensively throughout the book, we will also explore different techniques for regression analysis and clustering.

We have an exciting journey ahead, covering many powerful techniques in the vast field of machine learning. However, we will approach machine learning one step at a time, building upon our knowledge gradually throughout the chapters of this book. In the following chapter, we will start this journey by implementing one of the earliest machine learning algorithms for classification, which will prepare us for *Chapter 3*, *A Tour of Machine Learning Classifiers Using scikit-learn*, where we cover more advanced machine learning algorithms using the scikit-learn open source machine learning library.

2
Training Simple Machine Learning Algorithms for Classification

In this chapter, we will make use of two of the first algorithmically described machine learning algorithms for classification, the perceptron and adaptive linear neurons. We will start by implementing a perceptron step by step in Python and training it to classify different flower species in the Iris dataset. This will help us understand the concept of machine learning algorithms for classification and how they can be efficiently implemented in Python.

Discussing the basics of optimization using adaptive linear neurons will then lay the groundwork for using more powerful classifiers via the scikit-learn machine learning library in *Chapter 3, A Tour of Machine Learning Classifiers Using scikit-learn*.

The topics that we will cover in this chapter are as follows:

- Building an intuition for machine learning algorithms
- Using pandas, NumPy, and Matplotlib to read in, process, and visualize data
- Implementing linear classification algorithms in Python

Artificial neurons – a brief glimpse into the early history of machine learning

Before we discuss the perceptron and related algorithms in more detail, let us take a brief tour through the early beginnings of machine learning. Trying to understand how the biological brain works, in order to design AI, Warren McCulloch and Walter Pitts published the first concept of a simplified brain cell, the so-called **McCulloch-Pitts (MCP)** neuron, in 1943 (*A Logical Calculus of the Ideas Immanent in Nervous Activity*, W. S. McCulloch and W. Pitts, *Bulletin of Mathematical Biophysics*, 5(4): 115-133, *1943*). Neurons are interconnected nerve cells in the brain that are involved in the processing and transmitting of chemical and electrical signals, which is illustrated in the following figure:

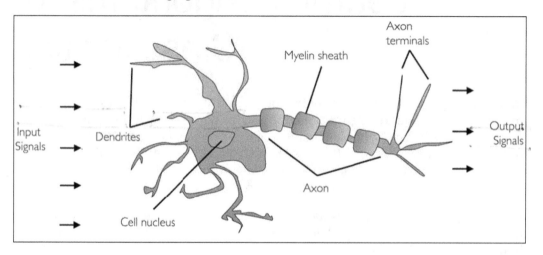

McCulloch and Pitts described such a nerve cell as a simple logic gate with binary outputs; multiple signals arrive at the dendrites, are then integrated into the cell body, and, if the accumulated signal exceeds a certain threshold, an output signal is generated that will be passed on by the axon.

Only a few years later, Frank Rosenblatt published the first concept of the perceptron learning rule based on the MCP neuron model (*The Perceptron: A Perceiving and Recognizing Automaton*, F. Rosenblatt, *Cornell Aeronautical Laboratory, 1957*). With his perceptron rule, Rosenblatt proposed an algorithm that would automatically learn the optimal weight coefficients that are then multiplied with the input features in order to make the decision of whether a neuron fires or not. In the context of supervised learning and classification, such an algorithm could then be used to predict if a sample belongs to one class or the other.

The formal definition of an artificial neuron

More formally, we can put the idea behind **artificial neurons** into the context of a binary classification task where we refer to our two classes as 1 (positive class) and -1 (negative class) for simplicity. We can then define a decision function ($\phi(z)$) that takes a linear combination of certain input values **x** and a corresponding weight vector **w**, where z is the so-called net input $z = w_1 x_1 + \ldots + w_m x_m$:

$$w = \begin{bmatrix} w_1 \\ \vdots \\ w_m \end{bmatrix}, \quad x = \begin{bmatrix} x_1 \\ \vdots \\ x_m \end{bmatrix}$$

Now, if the net input of a particular sample $x^{(i)}$ is greater than a defined threshold θ, we predict class 1, and class -1 otherwise. In the perceptron algorithm, the decision function $\phi(\cdot)$ is a variant of a **unit step function**:

$$\phi(z) = \begin{cases} 1 & \text{if } z \geq \theta \\ -1 & \text{otherwise} \end{cases}$$

For simplicity, we can bring the threshold θ to the left side of the equation and define a weight-zero as $w_0 = -\theta$ and $x_0 = 1$ so that we write z in a more compact form:

$$z = w_0 x_0 + w_1 x_1 + \ldots + w_m x_m = \mathbf{w}^T \mathbf{x}$$

And:

$$\phi(z) = \begin{cases} 1 & \text{if } z \geq 0 \\ -1 & \text{otherwise} \end{cases}$$

In machine learning literature, the negative threshold, or weight, $w_0 = -\theta$, is usually called the **bias unit**.

In the following sections, we will often make use of basic notations from linear algebra. For example, we will abbreviate the sum of the products of the values in $\mathbf{x}$ and $\mathbf{w}$ using a vector dot product, whereas superscript ^{T} stands for **transpose**, which is an operation that transforms a column vector into a row vector and vice versa:

$$z = w_0 x_0 + w_1 x_1 + \cdots + w_m x_m = \sum_{j=0}^{m} x_j w_j = \mathbf{w}^T \mathbf{x}$$

For example:

$$\begin{bmatrix} 1 & 2 & 3 \end{bmatrix} \times \begin{bmatrix} 4 \\ 5 \\ 6 \end{bmatrix} = 1 \times 4 + 2 \times 5 + 3 \times 6 = 32$$

Furthermore, the transpose operation can also be applied to matrices to reflect it over its diagonal, for example:

$$\begin{bmatrix} 1 & 2 \\ 3 & 4 \\ 5 & 6 \end{bmatrix}^T = \begin{bmatrix} 1 & 3 & 5 \\ 2 & 4 & 6 \end{bmatrix}$$

In this book, we will only use very basic concepts from linear algebra; however, if you need a quick refresher, please take a look at Zico Kolter's excellent *Linear Algebra Review and Reference*, which is freely available at http://www.cs.cmu.edu/~zkolter/course/linalg/linalg_notes.pdf.

The following figure illustrates how the net input $z = \mathbf{w}^T \mathbf{x}$ is squashed into a binary output (-1 or 1) by the decision function of the perceptron (left subfigure) and how it can be used to discriminate between two linearly separable classes (right subfigure):

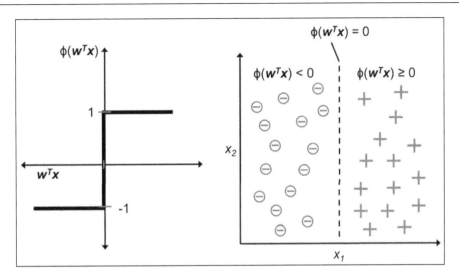

The perceptron learning rule

The whole idea behind the MCP neuron and Rosenblatt's *thresholded* perceptron model is to use a reductionist approach to mimic how a single neuron in the brain works: it either *fires* or it doesn't. Thus, Rosenblatt's initial perceptron rule is fairly simple and can be summarized by the following steps:

1. Initialize the weights to 0 or small random numbers.
2. For each training sample $x^{(i)}$:
    a. Compute the output value $\hat{y}$.
    b. Update the weights.

Here, the output value is the class label predicted by the unit step function that we defined earlier, and the simultaneous update of each weight w_j in the weight vector **w** can be more formally written as:

$$w_j := w_j + \Delta w_j$$

The value of Δw_j, which is used to update the weight w_j, is calculated by the perceptron learning rule:

$$\Delta w_j = \eta \left(y^{(i)} - \hat{y}^{(i)} \right) x_j^{(i)}$$

Where η is the **learning rate** (typically a constant between 0.0 and 1.0), $y^{(i)}$ is the **true class label** of the ith training sample, and $\hat{y}^{(i)}$ is the **predicted class label**. It is important to note that all weights in the weight vector are being updated simultaneously, which means that we don't recompute the $\hat{y}^{(i)}$ before all of the weights Δw_j are updated. Concretely, for a two-dimensional dataset, we would write the update as:

$$\Delta w_0 = \eta\left(y^{(i)} - output^{(i)}\right)$$

$$\Delta w_1 = \eta\left(y^{(i)} - output^{(i)}\right)x_1^{(i)}$$

$$\Delta w_2 = \eta\left(y^{(i)} - output^{(i)}\right)x_2^{(i)}$$

Before we implement the perceptron rule in Python, let us make a simple thought experiment to illustrate how beautifully simple this learning rule really is. In the two scenarios where the perceptron predicts the class label correctly, the weights remain unchanged:

$$\Delta w_j = \eta\left(-1-(-1)\right)x_j^{(i)} = 0$$

$$\Delta w_j = \eta\left(1-1\right)x_j^{(i)} = 0$$

However, in the case of a wrong prediction, the weights are being pushed towards the direction of the positive or negative target class:

$$\Delta w_j = \eta\left(1--1\right)x_j^{(i)} = \eta\left(2\right)x_j^{(i)}$$

$$\Delta w_j = \eta\left(-1-1\right)x_j^{(i)} = \eta\left(-2\right)x_j^{(i)}$$

To get a better intuition for the multiplicative factor $x_j^{(i)}$, let us go through another simple example, where:

$$\hat{y}^{(i)} = -1, \quad y^{(i)} = +1, \quad \eta = 1$$

Let's assume that $x_j^{(i)} = 0.5$, and we misclassify this sample as *-1*. In this case, we would increase the corresponding weight by 1 so that the net input $x_j^{(i)} \times w_j$ would be more positive the next time we encounter this sample, and thus be more likely to be above the threshold of the unit step function to classify the sample as *+1*:

$$\Delta w_j = (1 - -1)0.5 = (2)0.5 = 1$$

The weight update is proportional to the value of $x_j^{(i)}$. For example, if we have another sample $x_j^{(i)} = 2$ that is incorrectly classified as *-1*, we'd push the decision boundary by an even larger extent to classify this sample correctly the next time:

$$\Delta w_j = (1 - -1)2 = (2)2 = 4$$

It is important to note that the convergence of the perceptron is only guaranteed if the two classes are linearly separable and the learning rate is sufficiently small. If the two classes can't be separated by a linear decision boundary, we can set a maximum number of passes over the training dataset (**epochs**) and/or a threshold for the number of tolerated misclassifications—the perceptron would never stop updating the weights otherwise:

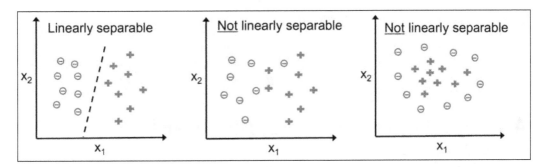

Now, before we jump into the implementation in the next section, let us summarize what we just learned in a simple diagram that illustrates the general concept of the perceptron:

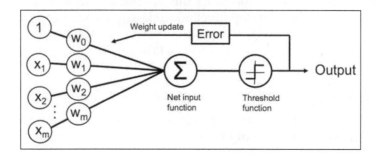

The preceding diagram illustrates how the perceptron receives the inputs of a sample **x** and combines them with the weights **w** to compute the net input. The net input is then passed on to the threshold function, which generates a binary output -1 or +1 — the predicted class label of the sample. During the learning phase, this output is used to calculate the error of the prediction and update the weights.

Implementing a perceptron learning algorithm in Python

In the previous section, we learned how the Rosenblatt's perceptron rule works; let us now go ahead and implement it in Python, and apply it to the Iris dataset that we introduced in *Chapter 1, Giving Computers the Ability to Learn from Data.*

An object-oriented perceptron API

We will take an object-oriented approach to define the perceptron interface as a Python class, which allows us to initialize new `Perceptron` objects that can learn from data via a `fit` method, and make predictions via a separate `predict` method. As a convention, we append an underscore (_) to attributes that are not being created upon the initialization of the object but by calling the object's other methods, for example, `self.w_`.

If you are not yet familiar with Python's scientific libraries or need a refresher, please see the following resources:

- **NumPy**: https://sebastianraschka.com/pdf/books/dlb/appendix_f_numpy-intro.pdf
- **pandas**: https://pandas.pydata.org/pandas-docs/stable/10min.html
- **Matplotlib**: http://matplotlib.org/users/beginner.html

The following is the implementation of a perceptron:

```python
import numpy as np

class Perceptron(object):
    """Perceptron classifier.

    Parameters
    ------------
    eta : float
      Learning rate (between 0.0 and 1.0)
    n_iter : int
      Passes over the training dataset.
    random_state : int
      Random number generator seed for random weight
      initialization.

    Attributes
    -----------
    w_ : 1d-array
      Weights after fitting.
    errors_ : list
      Number of misclassifications (updates) in each epoch.

    """
    def __init__(self, eta=0.01, n_iter=50, random_state=1):
        self.eta = eta
        self.n_iter = n_iter
        self.random_state = random_state

    def fit(self, X, y):
        """Fit training data.

        Parameters
```

```
    ----------
    X : {array-like}, shape = [n_samples, n_features]
      Training vectors, where n_samples is the number of
      samples and
      n_features is the number of features.
    y : array-like, shape = [n_samples]
      Target values.

    Returns
    -------
    self : object

    """
    rgen = np.random.RandomState(self.random_state)
    self.w_ = rgen.normal(loc=0.0, scale=0.01,
                          size=1 + X.shape[1])
    self.errors_ = []

    for _ in range(self.n_iter):
        errors = 0
        for xi, target in zip(X, y):
            update = self.eta * (target - self.predict(xi))
            self.w_[1:] += update * xi
            self.w_[0] += update
            errors += int(update != 0.0)
        self.errors_.append(errors)
    return self

def net_input(self, X):
    """Calculate net input"""
    return np.dot(X, self.w_[1:]) + self.w_[0]

def predict(self, X):
    """Return class label after unit step"""
    return np.where(self.net_input(X) >= 0.0, 1, -1)
```

Using this perceptron implementation, we can now initialize new `Perceptron` objects with a given learning rate `eta` and `n_iter`, which is the number of epochs (passes over the training set). Via the `fit` method, we initialize the weights in `self.w_` to a vector $\mathbb{R}^{m+1}$, where m stands for the number of dimensions (features) in the dataset, where we add *1* for the first element in this vector that represents the bias unit. Remember that the first element in this vector, `self.w_[0]`, represents the so-called bias unit that we discussed earlier.

Also notice that this vector contains small random numbers drawn from a normal distribution with standard deviation `0.01` via `rgen.normal(loc=0.0,` `scale=0.01, size=1 + X.shape[1])`, where `rgen` is a NumPy random number generator that we seeded with a user-specified random seed so that we can reproduce previous results if desired.

Now, the reason we don't initialize the weights to zero is that the learning rate η (`eta`) only has an effect on the classification outcome if the weights are initialized to non-zero values. If all the weights are initialized to zero, the learning rate parameter `eta` affects only the scale of the weight vector, not the direction. If you are familiar with trigonometry, consider a vector $v1 = \begin{bmatrix} 1 & 2 & 3 \end{bmatrix}$, where the angle between $v1$ and a vector $v2 = 0.5 \times v1$ would be exactly zero, as demonstrated by the following code snippet:

```
>>> v1 = np.array([1, 2, 3])
>>> v2 = 0.5 * v1
>>> np.arccos(v1.dot(v2) / (np.linalg.norm(v1) *
...             np.linalg.norm(v2)))
0.0
```

Here, `np.arccos` is the trigonometric inverse cosine and `np.linalg.norm` is a function that computes the length of a vector. (The reason why we have drawn the random numbers from a random normal distribution—for example, instead from a uniform distribution—and why we used a standard deviation of `0.01` was arbitrary; remember, we are just interested in small random values to avoid the properties of all-zero vectors as discussed earlier.)

 NumPy indexing for one-dimensional arrays works similarly to Python lists using the square-bracket (`[]`) notation. For two-dimensional arrays, the first indexer refers to the row number and the second indexer to the column number. For example, we would use `X[2, 3]` to select the third row and fourth column of a two-dimensional array `X`.

After the weights have been initialized, the `fit` method loops over all individual samples in the training set and updates the weights according to the perceptron learning rule that we discussed in the previous section. The class labels are predicted by the `predict` method, which is called in the `fit` method to predict the class label for the weight update, but `predict` can also be used to predict the class labels of new data after we have fitted our model. Furthermore, we also collect the number of misclassifications during each epoch in the `self.errors_` list so that we can later analyze how well our perceptron performed during the training. The `np.dot` function that is used in the `net_input` method simply calculates the vector dot product $w^T x$.

Instead of using NumPy to calculate the vector dot product between two arrays a and b via a.dot(b) or np.dot(a, b), we could also perform the calculation in pure Python via sum([i * j for i, j in zip(a, b)]). However, the advantage of using NumPy over classic Python for loop structures is that its arithmetic operations are vectorized. **Vectorization** means that an elemental arithmetic operation is automatically applied to all elements in an array. By formulating our arithmetic operations as a sequence of instructions on an array, rather than performing a set of operations for each element at the time, we can make better use of our modern CPU architectures with **Single Instruction, Multiple Data (SIMD)** support. Furthermore, NumPy uses highly optimized linear algebra libraries such as **Basic Linear Algebra Subprograms (BLAS)** and **Linear Algebra Package (LAPACK)** that have been written in C or Fortran. Lastly, NumPy also allows us to write our code in a more compact and intuitive way using the basics of linear algebra, such as vector and matrix dot products.

Training a perceptron model on the Iris dataset

To test our perceptron implementation, we will load the two flower classes Setosa and Versicolor from the Iris dataset. Although the perceptron rule is not restricted to two dimensions, we will only consider the two features sepal length and petal length for visualization purposes. Also, we only chose the two flower classes Setosa and Versicolor for practical reasons. However, the perceptron algorithm can be extended to multi-class classification — for example, the **One-versus-All (OvA)** technique.

OvA, or sometimes also called **One-versus-Rest (OvR)**, is a technique that allows us to extend a binary classifier to multi-class problems. Using OvA, we can train one classifier per class, where the particular class is treated as the positive class and the samples from all other classes are considered negative classes. If we were to classify a new data sample, we would use our n classifiers, where n is the number of class labels, and assign the class label with the highest confidence to the particular sample. In the case of the perceptron, we would use OvA to choose the class label that is associated with the largest absolute net input value.

First, we will use the `pandas` library to load the Iris dataset directly from the *UCI Machine Learning Repository* into a `DataFrame` object and print the last five lines via the `tail` method to check the data was loaded correctly:

```
>>> import pandas as pd
>>> df = pd.read_csv('https://archive.ics.uci.edu/ml/'
...                  'machine-learning-databases/iris/iris.data',
...                  header=None)
>>> df.tail()
```

	0	1	2	3	4
145	6.7	3.0	5.2	2.3	Iris-virginica
146	6.3	2.5	5.0	1.9	Iris-virginica
147	6.5	3.0	5.2	2.0	Iris-virginica
148	6.2	3.4	5.4	2.3	Iris-virginica
149	5.9	3.0	5.1	1.8	Iris-virginica

You can find a copy of the Iris dataset (and all other datasets used in this book) in the code bundle of this book, which you can use if you are working offline or the UCI server at `https://archive.ics.uci.edu/ml/machine-learning-databases/iris/iris.data` is temporarily unavailable. For instance, to load the Iris dataset from a local directory, you can replace this line:

```
df = pd.read_csv('https://archive.ics.uci.edu/ml/'
                 'machine-learning-databases/iris/iris.data',
                 header=None)
```

Replace it with this:

```
df = pd.read_csv('your/local/path/to/iris.data',
                 header=None)
```

Next, we extract the first 100 class labels that correspond to the 50 `Iris-setosa` and 50 `Iris-versicolor` flowers, and convert the class labels into the two integer class labels 1 (`versicolor`) and -1 (`setosa`) that we assign to a vector `y`, where the values method of a pandas `DataFrame` yields the corresponding NumPy representation.

Similarly, we extract the first feature column (sepal length) and the third feature column (petal length) of those 100 training samples and assign them to a feature matrix x, which we can visualize via a two-dimensional scatter plot:

```
>>> import matplotlib.pyplot as plt
>>> import numpy as np

>>> # select setosa and versicolor
>>> y = df.iloc[0:100, 4].values
>>> y = np.where(y == 'Iris-setosa', -1, 1)

>>> # extract sepal length and petal length
>>> X = df.iloc[0:100, [0, 2]].values

>>> # plot data
>>> plt.scatter(X[:50, 0], X[:50, 1],
...             color='red', marker='o', label='setosa')
>>> plt.scatter(X[50:100, 0], X[50:100, 1],
...             color='blue', marker='x', label='versicolor')
>>> plt.xlabel('sepal length [cm]')
>>> plt.ylabel('petal length [cm]')
>>> plt.legend(loc='upper left')
>>> plt.show()
```

After executing the preceding code example, we should now see the following scatterplot:

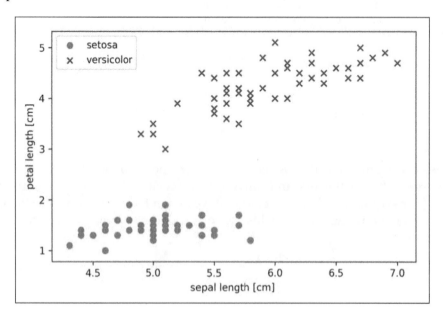

The preceding scatterplot shows the distribution of flower samples in the Iris dataset along the two feature axes, petal length and sepal length. In this two-dimensional feature subspace, we can see that a linear decision boundary should be sufficient to separate Setosa from Versicolor flowers. Thus, a linear classifier such as the perceptron should be able to classify the flowers in this dataset perfectly.

Now, it's time to train our perceptron algorithm on the Iris data subset that we just extracted. Also, we will plot the misclassification error for each epoch to check whether the algorithm converged and found a decision boundary that separates the two Iris flower classes:

```
>>> ppn = Perceptron(eta=0.1, n_iter=10)
>>> ppn.fit(X, y)
>>> plt.plot(range(1, len(ppn.errors_) + 1),
...             ppn.errors_, marker='o')
>>> plt.xlabel('Epochs')
>>> plt.ylabel('Number of updates')
>>> plt.show()
```

After executing the preceding code, we should see the plot of the misclassification errors versus the number of epochs, as shown here:

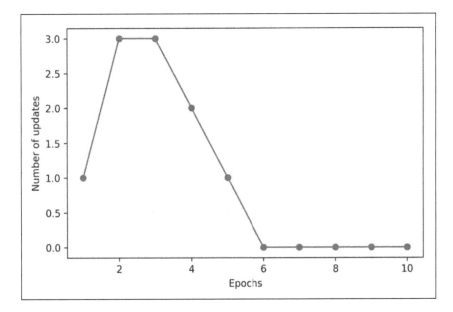

As we can see in the preceding plot, our perceptron converged after the sixth epoch and should now be able to classify the training samples perfectly. Let us implement a small convenience function to visualize the decision boundaries for two-dimensional datasets:

```python
from matplotlib.colors import ListedColormap

def plot_decision_regions(X, y, classifier, resolution=0.02):

    # setup marker generator and color map
    markers = ('s', 'x', 'o', '^', 'v')
    colors = ('red', 'blue', 'lightgreen', 'gray', 'cyan')
    cmap = ListedColormap(colors[:len(np.unique(y))])

    # plot the decision surface
    x1_min, x1_max = X[:, 0].min() - 1, X[:, 0].max() + 1
    x2_min, x2_max = X[:, 1].min() - 1, X[:, 1].max() + 1
    xx1, xx2 = np.meshgrid(np.arange(x1_min, x1_max, resolution),
                           np.arange(x2_min, x2_max, resolution))
    Z = classifier.predict(np.array([xx1.ravel(), xx2.ravel()]).T)
    Z = Z.reshape(xx1.shape)
    plt.contourf(xx1, xx2, Z, alpha=0.3, cmap=cmap)
    plt.xlim(xx1.min(), xx1.max())
    plt.ylim(xx2.min(), xx2.max())

    # plot class samples
    for idx, cl in enumerate(np.unique(y)):
        plt.scatter(x=X[y == cl, 0],
                    y=X[y == cl, 1],
                    alpha=0.8,
                    c=colors[idx],
                    marker=markers[idx],
                    label=cl,
                    edgecolor='black')
```

First, we define a number of `colors` and `markers` and create a colormap from the list of colors via `ListedColormap`. Then, we determine the minimum and maximum values for the two features and use those feature vectors to create a pair of grid arrays xx1 and xx2 via the NumPy `meshgrid` function. Since we trained our perceptron classifier on two feature dimensions, we need to flatten the grid arrays and create a matrix that has the same number of columns as the Iris training subset so that we can use the `predict` method to predict the class labels z of the corresponding grid points.

After reshaping the predicted class labels z into a grid with the same dimensions as xx1 and xx2, we can now draw a contour plot via Matplotlib's `contourf` function, which maps the different decision regions to different colors for each predicted class in the grid array:

```
>>> plot_decision_regions(X, y, classifier=ppn)
>>> plt.xlabel('sepal length [cm]')
>>> plt.ylabel('petal length [cm]')
>>> plt.legend(loc='upper left')
>>> plt.show()
```

After executing the preceding code example, we should now see a plot of the decision regions, as shown in the following figure:

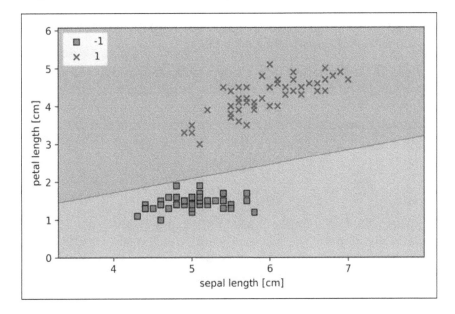

As we can see in the plot, the perceptron learned a decision boundary that is able to classify all flower samples in the Iris training subset perfectly.

 Although the perceptron classified the two Iris flower classes perfectly, convergence is one of the biggest problems of the perceptron. Frank Rosenblatt proved mathematically that the perceptron learning rule converges if the two classes can be separated by a linear hyperplane. However, if classes cannot be separated perfectly by such a linear decision boundary, the weights will never stop updating unless we set a maximum number of epochs.

Adaptive linear neurons and the convergence of learning

In this section, we will take a look at another type of single-layer neural network: **ADAptive LInear NEuron (Adaline)**. Adaline was published by Bernard Widrow and his doctoral student Tedd Hoff, only a few years after Frank Rosenblatt's perceptron algorithm, and can be considered as an improvement on the latter. (Refer to *An Adaptive "Adaline" Neuron Using Chemical "Memistors"*, *Technical Report Number 1553-2, B. Widrow and others, Stanford Electron Labs*, Stanford, CA, October 1960).

The Adaline algorithm is particularly interesting because it illustrates the key concepts of defining and minimizing continuous cost functions. This lays the groundwork for understanding more advanced machine learning algorithms for classification, such as logistic regression, support vector machines, and regression models, which we will discuss in future chapters.

The key difference between the Adaline rule (also known as the *Widrow-Hoff rule*) and Rosenblatt's perceptron is that the weights are updated based on a linear activation function rather than a unit step function like in the perceptron. In Adaline, this linear activation function $\phi(z)$ is simply the identity function of the net input, so that:

$$\phi\left(w^T x\right) = w^T x$$

While the linear activation function is used for learning the weights, we still use a threshold function to make the final prediction, which is similar to the unit step function that we have seen earlier. The main differences between the perceptron and Adaline algorithm are highlighted in the following figure:

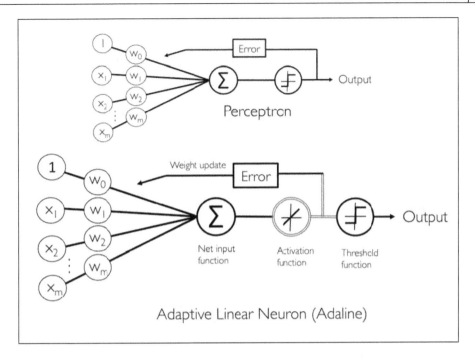

The illustration shows that the Adaline algorithm compares the true class labels with the linear activation function's continuous valued output to compute the model error and update the weights. In contrast, the perceptron compares the true class labels to the predicted class labels.

Minimizing cost functions with gradient descent

One of the key ingredients of supervised machine learning algorithms is a defined **objective function** that is to be optimized during the learning process. This objective function is often a cost function that we want to minimize. In the case of Adaline, we can define the cost function J to learn the weights as the **Sum of Squared Errors (SSE)** between the calculated outcome and the true class label:

$$J(w) = \frac{1}{2}\sum_i \left(y^{(i)} - \phi\left(z^{(i)}\right)\right)^2$$

The term $\frac{1}{2}$ is just added for our convenience, which will make it easier to derive the gradient, as we will see in the following paragraphs. The main advantage of this continuous linear activation function, in contrast to the unit step function, is that the cost function becomes differentiable. Another nice property of this cost function is that it is convex; thus, we can use a simple yet powerful optimization algorithm called **gradient descent** to find the weights that minimize our cost function to classify the samples in the Iris dataset.

As illustrated in the following figure, we can describe the main idea behind gradient descent as *climbing down a hill* until a local or global cost minimum is reached. In each iteration, we take a step in the opposite direction of the gradient where the step size is determined by the value of the learning rate, as well as the slope of the gradient:

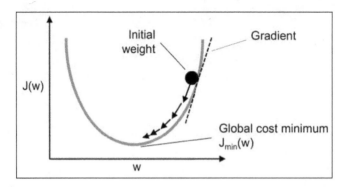

Using gradient descent, we can now update the weights by taking a step in the opposite direction of the gradient $\nabla J(w)$ of our cost function $J(w)$:

$$w := w + \Delta w$$

Where the weight change Δw is defined as the negative gradient multiplied by the learning rate η:

$$\Delta w = -\eta \nabla J(w)$$

To compute the gradient of the cost function, we need to compute the partial derivative of the cost function with respect to each weight w_j:

$$\frac{\partial J}{\partial w_j} = -\sum_i \left(y^{(i)} - \phi\left(z^{(i)}\right) \right) x_j^{(i)}$$

So that we can write the update of weight w_j as:

$$\Delta w_j = -\eta \frac{\partial J}{\partial w_j} = \eta \sum_i \left(y^{(i)} - \phi\left(z^{(i)}\right)\right) x_j^{(i)}$$

Since we update all weights simultaneously, our Adaline learning rule becomes:

$$w := w + \Delta w$$

For those who are familiar with calculus, the partial derivative of the SSE cost function with respect to the *j*th weight can be obtained as follows:

$$\frac{\partial J}{\partial w_j} = \frac{\partial}{\partial w_j} \frac{1}{2} \sum_i \left(y^{(i)} - \phi\left(z^{(i)}\right)\right)^2$$

$$= \frac{1}{2} \frac{\partial}{\partial w_j} \sum_i \left(y^{(i)} - \phi\left(z^{(i)}\right)\right)^2$$

$$= \frac{1}{2} \sum_i 2\left(y^{(i)} - \phi\left(z^{(i)}\right)\right) \frac{\partial}{\partial w_j} \left(y^{(i)} - \phi\left(z^{(i)}\right)\right)$$

$$= \sum_i \left(y^{(i)} - \phi\left(z^{(i)}\right)\right) \frac{\partial}{\partial w_j} \left(y^{(i)} - \sum_k \left(w_k x_k^{(i)}\right)\right)$$

$$= \sum_i \left(y^{(i)} - \phi\left(z^{(i)}\right)\right)\left(-x_j^{(i)}\right)$$

$$= -\sum_i \left(y^{(i)} - \phi\left(z^{(i)}\right)\right) x_j^{(i)}$$

Although the Adaline learning rule looks identical to the perceptron rule, we should note that the $\phi\left(z^{(i)}\right)$ with $z^{(i)} = w^T x^{(i)}$ is a real number and not an integer class label. Furthermore, the weight update is calculated based on all samples in the training set (instead of updating the weights incrementally after each sample), which is why this approach is also referred to as **batch gradient descent**.

Implementing Adaline in Python

Since the perceptron rule and Adaline are very similar, we will take the perceptron implementation that we defined earlier and change the `fit` method so that the weights are updated by minimizing the cost function via gradient descent:

```python
class AdalineGD(object):
    """ADAptive LInear NEuron classifier.

    Parameters
    ------------
    eta : float
      Learning rate (between 0.0 and 1.0)
    n_iter : int
      Passes over the training dataset.
    random_state : int
      Random number generator seed for random weight
      initialization.


    Attributes
    -----------
    w_ : 1d-array
      Weights after fitting.
    cost_ : list
      Sum-of-squares cost function value in each epoch.

    """
    def __init__(self, eta=0.01, n_iter=50, random_state=1):
        self.eta = eta
        self.n_iter = n_iter
        self.random_state = random_state

    def fit(self, X, y):
        """ Fit training data.

        Parameters
        ----------
        X : {array-like}, shape = [n_samples, n_features]
          Training vectors, where n_samples is the number of
          samples and
          n_features is the number of features.
        y : array-like, shape = [n_samples]
```

```
        Target values.

        Returns
        -------
        self : object

        """
        rgen = np.random.RandomState(self.random_state)
        self.w_ = rgen.normal(loc=0.0, scale=0.01,
                              size=1 + X.shape[1])
        self.cost_ = []

        for i in range(self.n_iter):
            net_input = self.net_input(X)
            output = self.activation(net_input)
            errors = (y - output)
            self.w_[1:] += self.eta * X.T.dot(errors)
            self.w_[0] += self.eta * errors.sum()
            cost = (errors**2).sum() / 2.0
            self.cost_.append(cost)
        return self

    def net_input(self, X):
        """Calculate net input"""
        return np.dot(X, self.w_[1:]) + self.w_[0]

    def activation(self, X):
        """Compute linear activation"""
        return X

    def predict(self, X):
        """Return class label after unit step"""
        return np.where(self.activation(self.net_input(X))
                        >= 0.0, 1, -1)
```

Instead of updating the weights after evaluating each individual training sample, as in the perceptron, we calculate the gradient based on the whole training dataset via `self.eta * errors.sum()` for the bias unit (zero-weight) and via `self.eta * X.T.dot(errors)` for the weights 1 to *m* where `X.T.dot(errors)` is a matrix-vector multiplication between our feature matrix and the error vector.

Please note that the `activation` method has no effect in the code since it is simply an identity function. Here, we added the activation function (computed via the `activation` method) to illustrate how information flows through a single layer neural network: features from the input data, net input, activation, and output. In the next chapter, we will learn about a logistic regression classifier that uses a non-identity, nonlinear activation function. We will see that a logistic regression model is closely related to Adaline with the only difference being its activation and cost function.

Now, similar to the previous perceptron implementation, we collect the cost values in a `self.cost_` list to check whether the algorithm converged after training.

Performing a matrix-vector multiplication is similar to calculating a vector dot-product where each row in the matrix is treated as a single row vector. This vectorized approach represents a more compact notation and results in a more efficient computation using NumPy. For example:

$$\begin{bmatrix} 1 & 2 & 3 \\ 4 & 5 & 6 \end{bmatrix} \times \begin{bmatrix} 7 \\ 8 \\ 9 \end{bmatrix} = \begin{bmatrix} 1 \times 7 + 2 \times 8 + 3 \times 9 \\ 4 \times 7 + 5 \times 8 + 6 \times 9 \end{bmatrix} = \begin{bmatrix} 50 \\ 122 \end{bmatrix}$$

In practice, it often requires some experimentation to find a good learning rate η for optimal convergence. So, let's choose two different learning rates, $\eta = 0.1$ and $\eta = 0.0001$, to start with and plot the cost functions versus the number of epochs to see how well the Adaline implementation learns from the training data.

The learning rate η (`eta`), as well as the number of epochs (`n_iter`), are the so-called hyperparameters of the perceptron and Adaline learning algorithms. In *Chapter 6, Learning Best Practices for Model Evaluation and Hyperparameter Tuning*, we will take a look at different techniques to automatically find the values of different hyperparameters that yield optimal performance of the classification model.

Let us now plot the cost against the number of epochs for the two different learning rates:

```
>>> fig, ax = plt.subplots(nrows=1, ncols=2, figsize=(10, 4))

>>> ada1 = AdalineGD(n_iter=10, eta=0.01).fit(X, y)
>>> ax[0].plot(range(1, len(ada1.cost_) + 1),
...            np.log10(ada1.cost_), marker='o')
>>> ax[0].set_xlabel('Epochs')
>>> ax[0].set_ylabel('log(Sum-squared-error)')
```

```
>>> ax[0].set_title('Adaline - Learning rate 0.01')

>>> ada2 = AdalineGD(n_iter=10, eta=0.0001).fit(X, y)
>>> ax[1].plot(range(1, len(ada2.cost_) + 1),
...            ada2.cost_, marker='o')
>>> ax[1].set_xlabel('Epochs')
>>> ax[1].set_ylabel('Sum-squared-error')
>>> ax[1].set_title('Adaline - Learning rate 0.0001')
>>> plt.show()
```

As we can see in the resulting cost-function plots, we encountered two different types of problem. The left chart shows what could happen if we choose a learning rate that is too large. Instead of minimizing the cost function, the error becomes larger in every epoch, because we *overshoot* the global minimum. On the other hand, we can see that the cost decreases on the right plot, but the chosen learning rate $\eta = 0.0001$ is so small that the algorithm would require a very large number of epochs to converge to the global cost minimum:

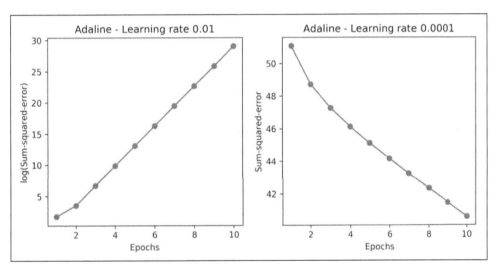

The following figure illustrates what might happen if we change the value of a particular weight parameter to minimize the cost function J. The left subfigure illustrates the case of a well-chosen learning rate, where the cost decreases gradually, moving in the direction of the global minimum. The subfigure on the right, however, illustrates what happens if we choose a learning rate that is too large — we overshoot the global minimum:

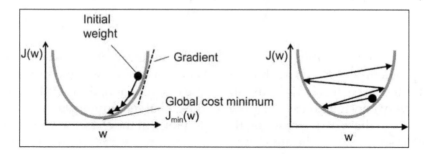

Improving gradient descent through feature scaling

Many machine learning algorithms that we will encounter throughout this book require some sort of feature scaling for optimal performance, which we will discuss in more detail in *Chapter 3, A Tour of Machine Learning Classifiers Using scikit-learn* and *Chapter 4, Building Good Training Sets – Data Preprocessing.*

Gradient descent is one of the many algorithms that benefit from feature scaling. In this section, we will use a feature scaling method called **standardization**, which gives our data the property of a standard normal distribution, which helps gradient descent learning to converge more quickly. Standardization shifts the mean of each feature so that it is centered at zero and each feature has a standard deviation of 1. For instance, to standardize the jth feature, we can simply subtract the sample mean μ_j from every training sample and divide it by its standard deviation σ_j:

$$x'_j = \frac{x_j - \mu_j}{\sigma_j}$$

Here, x_j is a vector consisting of the jth feature values of all training samples n, and this standardization technique is applied to each feature j in our dataset.

One of the reasons why standardization helps with gradient descent learning is that the optimizer has to go through fewer steps to find a good or optimal solution (the global cost minimum), as illustrated in the following figure, where the subfigures represent the cost surface as a function of two model weights in a two-dimensional classification problem:

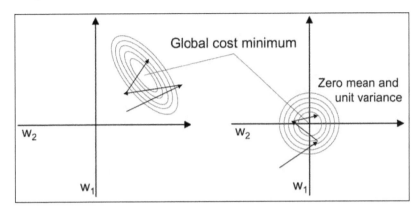

Standardization can easily be achieved using the built-in NumPy methods mean and std:

```
>>> X_std = np.copy(X)
>>> X_std[:,0] = (X[:,0] - X[:,0].mean()) / X[:,0].std()
>>> X_std[:,1] = (X[:,1] - X[:,1].mean()) / X[:,1].std()
```

After standardization, we will train Adaline again and see that it now converges after a small number of epochs using a learning rate $\eta = 0.01$:

```
>>> ada = AdalineGD(n_iter=15, eta=0.01)
>>> ada.fit(X_std, y)

>>> plot_decision_regions(X_std, y, classifier=ada)
>>> plt.title('Adaline - Gradient Descent')
>>> plt.xlabel('sepal length [standardized]')
>>> plt.ylabel('petal length [standardized]')
>>> plt.legend(loc='upper left')
>>> plt.tight_layout()
>>> plt.show()

>>> plt.plot(range(1, len(ada.cost_) + 1), ada.cost_, marker='o')
>>> plt.xlabel('Epochs')
>>> plt.ylabel('Sum-squared-error')
>>> plt.show()
```

After executing this code, we should see a figure of the decision regions as well as a plot of the declining cost, as shown in the following figure:

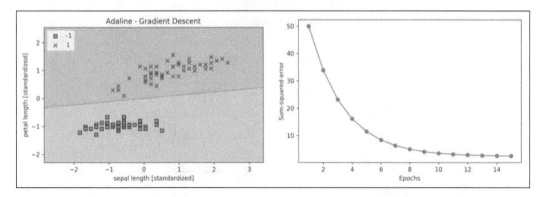

As we can see in the plots, Adaline has now converged after training on the standardized features using a learning rate $\eta = 0.01$. However, note that the SSE remains non-zero even though all samples were classified correctly.

Large-scale machine learning and stochastic gradient descent

In the previous section, we learned how to minimize a cost function by taking a step in the opposite direction of a cost gradient that is calculated from the whole training set; this is why this approach is sometimes also referred to as **batch gradient descent**. Now imagine we have a very large dataset with millions of data points, which is not uncommon in many machine learning applications. Running batch gradient descent can be computationally quite costly in such scenarios since we need to reevaluate the whole training dataset each time we take one step towards the global minimum.

A popular alternative to the batch gradient descent algorithm is **stochastic gradient descent**, sometimes also called iterative or online gradient descent. Instead of updating the weights based on the sum of the accumulated errors over all samples $x^{(i)}$:

$$\Delta w = \eta \sum_i \left(y^{(i)} - \phi\left(z^{(i)}\right)\right) x^{(i)}$$

We update the weights incrementally for each training sample:

$$\eta \left(y^{(i)} - \phi\left(z^{(i)} \right) \right) x^{(i)}$$

Although stochastic gradient descent can be considered as an approximation of gradient descent, it typically reaches convergence much faster because of the more frequent weight updates. Since each gradient is calculated based on a single training example, the error surface is noisier than in gradient descent, which can also have the advantage that stochastic gradient descent can escape shallow local minima more readily if we are working with nonlinear cost functions, as we will see later in *Chapter 12, Implementing a Multilayer Artificial Neural Network from Scratch*. To obtain satisfying results via stochastic gradient descent, it is important to present it training data in a random order; also, we want to shuffle the training set for every epoch to prevent cycles.

In stochastic gradient descent implementations, the fixed learning rate η is often replaced by an adaptive learning rate that decreases over time, for example:

$$\frac{c_1}{\left[number\ of\ iterations \right] + c_2}$$

Where c_1 and c_2 are constants. We shall note that stochastic gradient descent does not reach the global minimum, but an area very close to it. And using an adaptive learning rate, we can achieve further annealing to the cost minimum.

Another advantage of stochastic gradient descent is that we can use it for **online learning**. In online learning, our model is trained on the fly as new training data arrives. This is especially useful if we are accumulating large amounts of data, for example, customer data in web applications. Using online learning, the system can immediately adapt to changes and the training data can be discarded after updating the model if storage space is an issue.

A compromise between batch gradient descent and stochastic gradient descent is so-called **mini-batch learning**. Mini-batch learning can be understood as applying batch gradient descent to smaller subsets of the training data, for example, 32 samples at a time. The advantage over batch gradient descent is that convergence is reached faster via mini-batches because of the more frequent weight updates. Furthermore, mini-batch learning allows us to replace the `for` loop over the training samples in stochastic gradient descent with vectorized operations, which can further improve the computational efficiency of our learning algorithm.

Since we already implemented the Adaline learning rule using gradient descent, we only need to make a few adjustments to modify the learning algorithm to update the weights via stochastic gradient descent. Inside the `fit` method, we will now update the weights after each training sample. Furthermore, we will implement an additional `partial_fit` method, which does not reinitialize the weights, for online learning. In order to check whether our algorithm converged after training, we will calculate the cost as the average cost of the training samples in each epoch. Furthermore, we will add an option to shuffle the training data before each epoch to avoid repetitive cycles when we are optimizing the cost function; via the `random_state` parameter, we allow the specification of a random seed for reproducibility:

```
class AdalineSGD(object):
    """ADAptive LInear NEuron classifier.

    Parameters
    ------------
    eta : float
      Learning rate (between 0.0 and 1.0)
    n_iter : int
      Passes over the training dataset.
    shuffle : bool (default: True)
      Shuffles training data every epoch if True
      to prevent cycles.
    random_state : int
      Random number generator seed for random weight
      initialization.


    Attributes
    -----------
    w_ : 1d-array
      Weights after fitting.
    cost_ : list
```

```
        Sum-of-squares cost function value averaged over all
        training samples in each epoch.


    """
    def __init__(self, eta=0.01, n_iter=10,
                 shuffle=True, random_state=None):
        self.eta = eta
        self.n_iter = n_iter
        self.w_initialized = False
        self.shuffle = shuffle
        self.random_state = random_state

    def fit(self, X, y):
        """ Fit training data.

        Parameters
        ----------
        X : {array-like}, shape = [n_samples, n_features]
          Training vectors, where n_samples is the number
          of samples and
          n_features is the number of features.
        y : array-like, shape = [n_samples]
          Target values.

        Returns
        -------
        self : object

        """
        self._initialize_weights(X.shape[1])
        self.cost_ = []
        for i in range(self.n_iter):
            if self.shuffle:
                X, y = self._shuffle(X, y)
            cost = []
            for xi, target in zip(X, y):
                cost.append(self._update_weights(xi, target))
            avg_cost = sum(cost) / len(y)
            self.cost_.append(avg_cost)
        return self

    def partial_fit(self, X, y):
        """Fit training data without reinitializing the weights"""
```

```
            if not self.w_initialized:
                self._initialize_weights(X.shape[1])
            if y.ravel().shape[0] > 1:
                for xi, target in zip(X, y):
                    self._update_weights(xi, target)
            else:
                self._update_weights(X, y)
            return self

    def _shuffle(self, X, y):
        """Shuffle training data"""
        r = self.rgen.permutation(len(y))
        return X[r], y[r]

    def _initialize_weights(self, m):
        """Initialize weights to small random numbers"""
        self.rgen = np.random.RandomState(self.random_state)
        self.w_ = self.rgen.normal(loc=0.0, scale=0.01,
                                    size=1 + m)
        self.w_initialized = True

    def _update_weights(self, xi, target):
        """Apply Adaline learning rule to update the weights"""
        output = self.activation(self.net_input(xi))
        error = (target - output)
        self.w_[1:] += self.eta * xi.dot(error)
        self.w_[0] += self.eta * error
        cost = 0.5 * error**2
        return cost

    def net_input(self, X):
        """Calculate net input"""
        return np.dot(X, self.w_[1:]) + self.w_[0]

    def activation(self, X):
        """Compute linear activation"""
        return X

    def predict(self, X):
        """Return class label after unit step"""
        return np.where(self.activation(self.net_input(X))
                        >= 0.0, 1, -1)
```

The `_shuffle` method that we are now using in the `AdalineSGD` classifier works as follows: via the `permutation` function in `np.random`, we generate a random sequence of unique numbers in the range 0 to 100. Those numbers can then be used as indices to shuffle our feature matrix and class label vector.

We can then use the `fit` method to train the `AdalineSGD` classifier and use our `plot_decision_regions` to plot our training results:

```
>>> ada = AdalineSGD(n_iter=15, eta=0.01, random_state=1)
>>> ada.fit(X_std, y)

>>> plot_decision_regions(X_std, y, classifier=ada)
>>> plt.title('Adaline - Stochastic Gradient Descent')
>>> plt.xlabel('sepal length [standardized]')
>>> plt.ylabel('petal length [standardized]')
>>> plt.legend(loc='upper left')
>>> plt.show()
>>> plt.plot(range(1, len(ada.cost_) + 1), ada.cost_, marker='o')
>>> plt.xlabel('Epochs')
>>> plt.ylabel('Average Cost')
>>> plt.show()
```

The two plots that we obtain from executing the preceding code example are shown in the following figure:

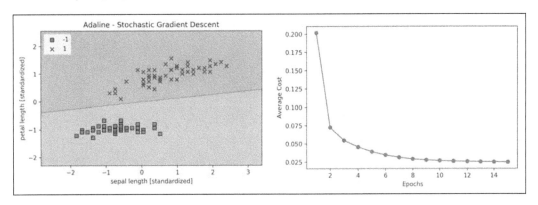

As we can see, the average cost goes down pretty quickly, and the final decision boundary after 15 epochs looks similar to the batch gradient descent Adaline. If we want to update our model, for example, in an online learning scenario with streaming data, we could simply call the `partial_fit` method on individual samples — for instance `ada.partial_fit(X_std[0, :], y[0])`.

Summary

In this chapter, we gained a good understanding of the basic concepts of linear classifiers for supervised learning. After we implemented a perceptron, we saw how we can train adaptive linear neurons efficiently via a vectorized implementation of gradient descent and online learning via stochastic gradient descent.

Now that we have seen how to implement simple classifiers in Python, we are ready to move on to the next chapter, where we will use the Python scikit-learn machine learning library to get access to more advanced and powerful machine learning classifiers that are commonly used in academia as well as in industry. The object-oriented approach that we used to implement the perceptron and Adaline algorithms will help with understanding the scikit-learn API, which is implemented based on the same core concepts that we used in this chapter: the `fit` and `predict` methods. Based on these core concepts, we will learn about logistic regression for modeling class probabilities and support vector machines for working with nonlinear decision boundaries. In addition, we will introduce a different class of supervised learning algorithms, tree-based algorithms, which are commonly combined into robust ensemble classifiers.

3

A Tour of Machine Learning Classifiers Using scikit-learn

In this chapter, we will take a tour through a selection of popular and powerful machine learning algorithms that are commonly used in academia as well as in industry. While learning about the differences between several supervised learning algorithms for classification, we will also develop an intuitive appreciation of their individual strengths and weaknesses. In addition, we will take our first step with the scikit-learn library, which offers a user-friendly interface for using those algorithms efficiently and productively.

The topics that we will learn about throughout this chapter are as follows:

- Introduction to robust and popular algorithms for classification, such as logistic regression, support vector machines, and decision trees

- Examples and explanations using the scikit-learn machine learning library, which provides a wide variety of machine learning algorithms via a user-friendly Python API

- Discussions about the strengths and weaknesses of classifiers with linear and non-linear decision boundaries

Choosing a classification algorithm

Choosing an appropriate classification algorithm for a particular problem task requires practice; each algorithm has its own quirks and is based on certain assumptions. To restate the No Free Lunch theorem by David H. Wolpert, no single classifier works best across all possible scenarios (*The Lack of A Priori Distinctions Between Learning Algorithms*, Wolpert and *David H, Neural Computation 8.7* (1996): 1341-1390). In practice, it is always recommended that you compare the performance of at least a handful of different learning algorithms to select the best model for the particular problem; these may differ in the number of features or samples, the amount of noise in a dataset, and whether the classes are linearly separable or not.

Eventually, the performance of a classifier — computational performance as well as predictive power — depends heavily on the underlying data that is available for learning. The five main steps that are involved in training a machine learning algorithm can be summarized as follows:

1. Selecting features and collecting training samples.
2. Choosing a performance metric.
3. Choosing a classifier and optimization algorithm.
4. Evaluating the performance of the model.
5. Tuning the algorithm.

Since the approach of this book is to build machine learning knowledge step by step, we will mainly focus on the main concepts of the different algorithms in this chapter and revisit topics such as feature selection and preprocessing, performance metrics, and hyperparameter tuning for more detailed discussions later in this book.

First steps with scikit-learn – training a perceptron

In *Chapter 2, Training Simple Machine Learning Algorithms for Classification*, you learned about two related learning algorithms for classification, the **perceptron** rule and **Adaline**, which we implemented in Python by ourselves. Now we will take a look at the scikit-learn API, which combines a user-friendly interface with a highly optimized implementation of several classification algorithms. The scikit-learn library offers not only a large variety of learning algorithms, but also many convenient functions to preprocess data and to fine-tune and evaluate our models. We will discuss this in more detail, together with the underlying concepts, in *Chapter 4, Building Good Training Sets – Data Preprocessing*, and *Chapter 5, Compressing Data via Dimensionality Reduction*.

To get started with the scikit-learn library, we will train a perceptron model similar to the one that we implemented in *Chapter 2, Training Simple Machine Learning Algorithms for Classification*. For simplicity, we will use the already familiar **Iris** dataset throughout the following sections. Conveniently, the Iris dataset is already available via scikit-learn, since it is a simple yet popular dataset that is frequently used for testing and experimenting with algorithms. We will only use two features from the Iris dataset for visualization purposes.

We will assign the petal length and petal width of the 150 flower samples to the feature matrix X and the corresponding class labels of the flower species to the vector y:

```
>>> from sklearn import datasets
>>> import numpy as np

>>> iris = datasets.load_iris()
>>> X = iris.data[:, [2, 3]]
>>> y = iris.target
>>> print('Class labels:', np.unique(y))
Class labels: [0 1 2]
```

The np.unique(y) function returned the three unique class labels stored in iris.target, and as we see, the Iris flower class names Iris-setosa, Iris-versicolor, and Iris-virginica are already stored as integers (here: 0, 1, 2). Although many scikit-learn functions and class methods also work with class labels in string format, using integer labels is a recommended approach to avoid technical glitches and improve computational performance due to a smaller memory footprint; furthermore, encoding class labels as integers is a common convention among most machine learning libraries.

To evaluate how well a trained model performs on unseen data, we will further split the dataset into separate training and test datasets. Later in *Chapter 6, Learning Best Practices for Model Evaluation and Hyperparameter Tuning*, we will discuss the best practices around model evaluation in more detail:

```
>>> from sklearn.model_selection import train_test_split
>>> X_train, X_test, y_train, y_test = train_test_split(
...      X, y, test_size=0.3, random_state=1, stratify=y)
```

Using the train_test_split function from scikit-learn's model_selection module, we randomly split the X and y arrays into 30 percent test data (45 samples) and 70 percent training data (105 samples).

Note that the `train_test_split` function already shuffles the training sets internally before splitting; otherwise, all class 0 and class 1 samples would have ended up in the training set, and the test set would consist of 45 samples from class 2. Via the `random_state` parameter, we provided a fixed random seed (`random_state=1`) for the internal pseudo-random number generator that is used for shuffling the datasets prior to splitting. Using such a fixed `random_state` ensures that our results are reproducible.

Lastly, we took advantage of the built-in support for stratification via `stratify=y`. In this context, stratification means that the `train_test_split` method returns training and test subsets that have the same proportions of class labels as the input dataset. We can use NumPy's `bincount` function, which counts the number of occurrences of each value in an array, to verify that this is indeed the case:

```
>>> print('Labels counts in y:', np.bincount(y))
Labels counts in y: [50 50 50]
>>> print('Labels counts in y_train:', np.bincount(y_train))
Labels counts in y_train: [35 35 35]
>>> print('Labels counts in y_test:', np.bincount(y_test))
Labels counts in y_test: [15 15 15]
```

Many machine learning and optimization algorithms also require feature scaling for optimal performance, as we remember from the **gradient descent** example in *Chapter 2, Training Simple Machine Learning Algorithms for Classification*. Here, we will standardize the features using the `StandardScaler` class from scikit-learn's `preprocessing` module:

```
>>> from sklearn.preprocessing import StandardScaler
>>> sc = StandardScaler()
>>> sc.fit(X_train)
>>> X_train_std = sc.transform(X_train)
>>> X_test_std = sc.transform(X_test)
```

Using the preceding code, we loaded the `StandardScaler` class from the `preprocessing` module and initialized a new `StandardScaler` object that we assigned to the `sc` variable. Using the `fit` method, `StandardScaler` estimated the parameters μ (sample mean) and σ (standard deviation) for each feature dimension from the training data. By calling the `transform` method, we then standardized the training data using those estimated parameters μ and σ. Note that we used the same scaling parameters to standardize the test set so that both the values in the training and test dataset are comparable to each other.

Having standardized the training data, we can now train a perceptron model. Most algorithms in scikit-learn already support multiclass classification by default via the **One-versus-Rest (OvR)** method, which allows us to feed the three flower classes to the perceptron all at once. The code is as follows:

```
>>> from sklearn.linear_model import Perceptron

>>> ppn = Perceptron(n_iter=40, eta0=0.1, random_state=1)
>>> ppn.fit(X_train_std, y_train)
```

The scikit-learn interface reminds us of our perceptron implementation in *Chapter 2, Training Simple Machine Learning Algorithms for Classification*: after loading the `Perceptron` class from the `linear_model` module, we initialized a new `Perceptron` object and trained the model via the `fit` method. Here, the model parameter `eta0` is equivalent to the learning rate `eta` that we used in our own perceptron implementation, and the `n_iter` parameter defines the number of epochs (passes over the training set).

As we remember from *Chapter 2, Training Simple Machine Learning Algorithms for Classification*, finding an appropriate learning rate requires some experimentation. If the learning rate is too large, the algorithm will overshoot the global cost minimum. If the learning rate is too small, the algorithm requires more epochs until convergence, which can make the learning slow — especially for large datasets. Also, we used the `random_state` parameter to ensure the reproducibility of the initial shuffling of the training dataset after each epoch.

Having trained a model in scikit-learn, we can make predictions via the `predict` method, just like in our own perceptron implementation in *Chapter 2, Training Simple Machine Learning Algorithms for Classification*. The code is as follows:

```
>>> y_pred = ppn.predict(X_test_std)
>>> print('Misclassified samples: %d' % (y_test != y_pred).sum())
Misclassified samples: 3
```

Executing the code, we see that the perceptron misclassifies three out of the 45 flower samples. Thus, the misclassification error on the test dataset is approximately 0.067 or 6.7 percent $(3/45 \approx 0.067)$.

Instead of the misclassification *error*, many machine learning practitioners report the classification *accuracy* of a model, which is simply calculated as follows:

1-error = 0.933 or 93.3 percent.

The scikit-learn library also implements a large variety of different performance metrics that are available via the `metrics` module. For example, we can calculate the classification accuracy of the perceptron on the test set as follows:

```
>>> from sklearn.metrics import accuracy_score
>>> print('Accuracy: %.2f' % accuracy_score(y_test, y_pred))
Accuracy: 0.93
```

Here, `y_test` are the true class labels and `y_pred` are the class labels that we predicted previously. Alternatively, each classifier in scikit-learn has a `score` method, which computes a classifier's prediction accuracy by combining the `predict` call with `accuracy_score` as shown here:

```
>>> print('Accuracy: %.2f' % ppn.score(X_test_std, y_test))
Accuracy: 0.93
```

Note that we evaluate the performance of our models based on the test set in this chapter. In *Chapter 6, Learning Best Practices for Model Evaluation and Hyperparameter Tuning*, you will learn about useful techniques, including graphical analysis such as learning curves, to detect and prevent **overfitting**. Overfitting means that the model captures the patterns in the training data well, but fails to generalize well to unseen data.

Finally, we can use our `plot_decision_regions` function from *Chapter 2, Training Simple Machine Learning Algorithms for Classification,* to plot the **decision regions** of our newly trained perceptron model and visualize how well it separates the different flower samples. However, let's add a small modification to highlight the samples from the test dataset via small circles:

```
from matplotlib.colors import ListedColormap
import matplotlib.pyplot as plt


def plot_decision_regions(X, y, classifier, test_idx=None,
                          resolution=0.02):

    # setup marker generator and color map
    markers = ('s', 'x', 'o', '^', 'v')
    colors = ('red', 'blue', 'lightgreen', 'gray', 'cyan')
    cmap = ListedColormap(colors[:len(np.unique(y))])

    # plot the decision surface
    x1_min, x1_max = X[:, 0].min() - 1, X[:, 0].max() + 1
    x2_min, x2_max = X[:, 1].min() - 1, X[:, 1].max() + 1
```

```
xx1, xx2 = np.meshgrid(np.arange(x1_min, x1_max, resolution),
                       np.arange(x2_min, x2_max, resolution))
Z = classifier.predict(np.array([xx1.ravel(), xx2.ravel()]).T)
Z = Z.reshape(xx1.shape)
plt.contourf(xx1, xx2, Z, alpha=0.3, cmap=cmap)
plt.xlim(xx1.min(), xx1.max())
plt.ylim(xx2.min(), xx2.max())

for idx, cl in enumerate(np.unique(y)):
    plt.scatter(x=X[y == cl, 0], y=X[y == cl, 1],
                alpha=0.8, c=colors[idx],
                marker=markers[idx], label=cl,
                edgecolor='black')

# highlight test samples
if test_idx:
    # plot all samples
    X_test, y_test = X[test_idx, :], y[test_idx]

    plt.scatter(X_test[:, 0], X_test[:, 1],
                c='', edgecolor='black', alpha=1.0,
                linewidth=1, marker='o',
                s=100, label='test set')
```

With the slight modification that we made to the plot_decision_regions function, we can now specify the indices of the samples that we want to mark on the resulting plots. The code is as follows:

```
>>> X_combined_std = np.vstack((X_train_std, X_test_std))
>>> y_combined = np.hstack((y_train, y_test))
>>> plot_decision_regions(X=X_combined_std,
...                       y=y_combined,
...                       classifier=ppn,
...                       test_idx=range(105, 150))
>>> plt.xlabel('petal length [standardized]')
>>> plt.ylabel('petal width [standardized]')
>>> plt.legend(loc='upper left')
>>> plt.show()
```

As we can see in the resulting plot, the three flower classes cannot be perfectly separated by a linear decision boundary:

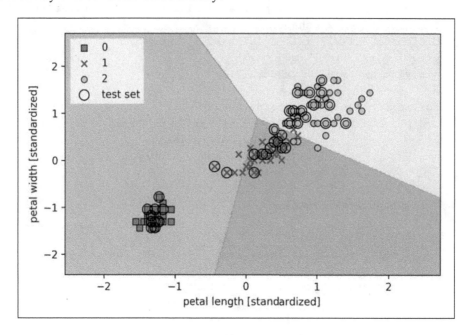

Remember from our discussion in *Chapter 2, Training Simple Machine Learning Algorithms for Classification*, that the perceptron algorithm never converges on datasets that aren't perfectly linearly separable, which is why the use of the perceptron algorithm is typically not recommended in practice. In the following sections, we will look at more powerful linear classifiers that converge to a cost minimum even if the classes are not perfectly linearly separable.

The Perceptron, as well as other scikit-learn functions and classes, often have additional parameters that we omit for clarity. You can read more about those parameters using the help function in Python (for instance, help(Perceptron)) or by going through the excellent scikit-learn online documentation at http://scikit-learn.org/stable/.

Modeling class probabilities via logistic regression

Although the perceptron rule offers a nice and easygoing introduction to machine learning algorithms for classification, its biggest disadvantage is that it never converges if the classes are not perfectly linearly separable. The classification task in the previous section would be an example of such a scenario. Intuitively, we can think of the reason as the weights are continuously being updated since there is always at least one misclassified sample present in each epoch. Of course, you can change the learning rate and increase the number of epochs, but be warned that the perceptron will never converge on this dataset. To make better use of our time, we will now take a look at another simple yet more powerful algorithm for linear and binary classification problems: **logistic regression**. Note that, in spite of its name, logistic regression is a model for classification, not regression.

Logistic regression intuition and conditional probabilities

Logistic regression is a classification model that is very easy to implement but performs very well on linearly separable classes. It is one of the most widely used algorithms for classification in industry. Similar to the perceptron and Adaline, the logistic regression model in this chapter is also a linear model for binary classification that can be extended to multiclass classification, for example, via the OvR technique.

To explain the idea behind logistic regression as a probabilistic model, let's first introduce the **odds ratio**: the odds in favor of a particular event. The odds ratio can be written as $\frac{p}{(1-p)}$ where p stands for the probability of the positive event. The term *positive event* does not necessarily mean *good*, but refers to the event that we want to predict, for example, the probability that a patient has a certain disease; we can think of the positive event as class label $y = 1$. We can then further define the **logit** function, which is simply the logarithm of the odds ratio (log-odds):

$$logit(p) = log \frac{p}{(1-p)}$$

Note that *log* refers to the natural logarithm, as it is the common convention in computer science. The *logit* function takes as input values in the range 0 to 1 and transforms them to values over the entire real-number range, which we can use to express a linear relationship between feature values and the log-odds:

$$logit\left(p\left(y=1\mid \boldsymbol{x}\right)\right)= w_0 x_0 + w_1 x_1 + \cdots + w_m x_m = \sum_{i=0}^{m} w_i x_i = \boldsymbol{w}^T \boldsymbol{x}$$

Here, $p(y=1\mid x)$ is the conditional probability that a particular sample belongs to class 1 given its features **x**.

Now, we are actually interested in predicting the probability that a certain sample belongs to a particular class, which is the inverse form of the `logit` function. It is also called **logistic sigmoid function**, sometimes simply abbreviated to **sigmoid function** due to its characteristic S-shape:

$$\phi(z)=\frac{1}{1+e^{-z}}$$

Here z is the net input, the linear combination of weights and sample features, $z = \boldsymbol{w}^T \boldsymbol{x} = w_0 x_0 + w_1 x_1 + \cdots + w_m x_m$.

> Note that similar to the convention we used in *Chapter 2, Training Simple Machine Learning Algorithms for Classification*, w_0 refers to the bias unit, and is an additional input value that we provide x_0, which is set equal to 1.

Now let us simply plot the sigmoid function for some values in the range -7 to 7 to see how it looks:

```
>>> import matplotlib.pyplot as plt
>>> import numpy as np
>>> def sigmoid(z):
...     return 1.0 / (1.0 + np.exp(-z))
>>> z = np.arange(-7, 7, 0.1)
>>> phi_z = sigmoid(z)
>>> plt.plot(z, phi_z)
>>> plt.axvline(0.0, color='k')
>>> plt.ylim(-0.1, 1.1)
>>> plt.xlabel('z')
```

```
>>> plt.ylabel('$\phi (z)$')
>>> # y axis ticks and gridline
>>> plt.yticks([0.0, 0.5, 1.0])
>>> ax = plt.gca()
>>> ax.yaxis.grid(True)
>>> plt.show()
```

As a result of executing the previous code example, we should now see the S-shaped (sigmoidal) curve:

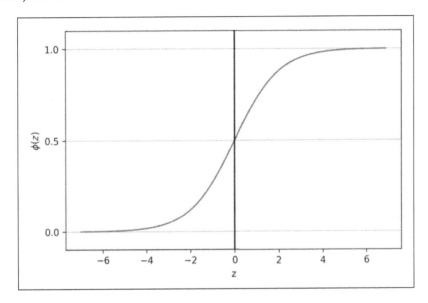

We can see that $\phi(z)$ approaches 1 if z goes towards infinity ($z \rightarrow \infty$) since e^{-z} becomes very small for large values of z. Similarly, $\phi(z)$ goes towards 0 for $z \rightarrow -\infty$ as a result of an increasingly large denominator. Thus, we conclude that this sigmoid function takes real number values as input and transforms them into values in the range [0, 1] with an intercept at $\phi(0) = 0.5$.

To build some intuition for the logistic regression model, we can relate it to *Chapter 2, Training Simple Machine Learning Algorithms for Classification*. In Adaline, we used the identity function $\phi(z) = z$ as the activation function. In logistic regression, this activation function simply becomes the sigmoid function that we defined earlier. The difference between Adaline and logistic regression is illustrated in the following figure:

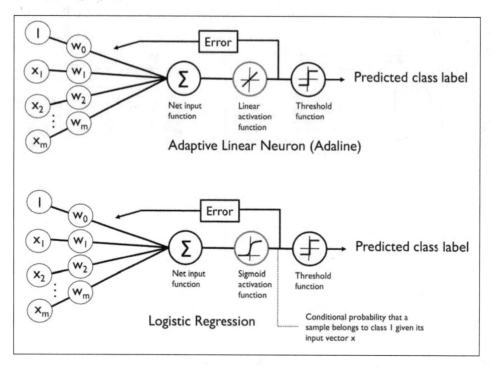

The output of the sigmoid function is then interpreted as the probability of a particular sample belonging to class 1, $\phi(z) = P(y = 1 \mid x; w)$, given its features x parameterized by the weights w. For example, if we compute $\phi(z) = 0.8$ for a particular flower sample, it means that the chance that this sample is an Iris-versicolor flower is 80 percent. Therefore, the probability that this flower is an Iris-setosa flower can be calculated as $P(y = 0 \mid x; w) = 1 - P(y = 1 \mid x; w) = 0.2$ or 20 percent. The predicted probability can then simply be converted into a binary outcome via a threshold function:

$$\hat{y} = \begin{cases} 1 & if\ \phi(z) \geq 0.5 \\ 0 & otherwise \end{cases}$$

If we look at the preceding plot of the sigmoid function, this is equivalent to the following:

$$\hat{y} = \begin{cases} 1 & if \ z \ge 0.0 \\ 0 & otherwise \end{cases}$$

In fact, there are many applications where we are not only interested in the predicted class labels, but where the estimation of the class-membership probability is particularly useful (the output of the sigmoid function prior to applying the threshold function). Logistic regression is used in weather forecasting, for example, not only to predict if it will rain on a particular day but also to report the chance of rain. Similarly, logistic regression can be used to predict the chance that a patient has a particular disease given certain symptoms, which is why logistic regression enjoys great popularity in the field of medicine.

Learning the weights of the logistic cost function

You learned how we could use the logistic regression model to predict probabilities and class labels; now, let us briefly talk about how we fit the parameters of the model, for instance the weights **w**. In the previous chapter, we defined the sum-squared-error cost function as follows:

$$J(w) = \sum_i \frac{1}{2}\left(\phi\left(z^{(i)}\right) - y^{(i)}\right)^2$$

We minimized this function in order to learn the weights **w** for our Adaline classification model. To explain how we can derive the cost function for logistic regression, let's first define the likelihood L that we want to maximize when we build a logistic regression model, assuming that the individual samples in our dataset are independent of one another. The formula is as follows:

$$L(w) = P(y \mid x; w) = \prod_{i=1}^{n} P\left(y^{(i)} \mid x^{(i)}; w\right) = \prod_{i=1}^{n} \left(\phi\left(z^{(i)}\right)\right)^{y^{(i)}} \left(1 - \phi\left(z^{(i)}\right)\right)^{1-y^{(i)}}$$

In practice, it is easier to maximize the (natural) log of this equation, which is called the log-likelihood function:

$$l(w) = \log L(w) = \sum_{i=1}^{n} \left[y^{(i)} \log\left(\phi\left(z^{(i)}\right)\right) + \left(1 - y^{(i)}\right) \log\left(1 - \phi\left(z^{(i)}\right)\right) \right]$$

Firstly, applying the log function reduces the potential for numerical underflow, which can occur if the likelihoods are very small. Secondly, we can convert the product of factors into a summation of factors, which makes it easier to obtain the derivative of this function via the addition trick, as you may remember from calculus.

Now we could use an optimization algorithm such as gradient ascent to maximize this log-likelihood function. Alternatively, let's rewrite the log-likelihood as a cost function J that can be minimized using gradient descent as in *Chapter 2, Training Simple Machine Learning Algorithms for Classification*:

$$J(w) = \sum_{i=1}^{n} \left[-y^{(i)} \log\left(\phi\left(z^{(i)}\right)\right) - \left(1 - y^{(i)}\right) \log\left(1 - \phi\left(z^{(i)}\right)\right) \right]$$

To get a better grasp of this cost function, let us take a look at the cost that we calculate for one single-sample training instance:

$$J(\phi(z), y; w) = -y \log(\phi(z)) - (1 - y) \log(1 - \phi(z))$$

Looking at the equation, we can see that the first term becomes zero if $y = 0$, and the second term becomes zero if $y = 1$:

$$J(\phi(z), y; w) = \begin{cases} -\log(\phi(z)) & \text{if } y = 1 \\ -\log(1 - \phi(z)) & \text{if } y = 0 \end{cases}$$

Let's write a short code snippet to create a plot that illustrates the cost of classifying a single-sample instance for different values of $\phi(z)$:

```
>>> def cost_1(z):
...         return - np.log(sigmoid(z))
>>> def cost_0(z):
...         return - np.log(1 - sigmoid(z))
>>> z = np.arange(-10, 10, 0.1)
>>> phi_z = sigmoid(z)
```

```
>>> c1 = [cost_1(x) for x in z]
>>> plt.plot(phi_z, c1, label='J(w) if y=1')
>>> c0 = [cost_0(x) for x in z]
>>> plt.plot(phi_z, c0, linestyle='--', label='J(w) if y=0')
>>> plt.ylim(0.0, 5.1)
>>> plt.xlim([0, 1])
>>> plt.xlabel('$\phi$(z)')
>>> plt.ylabel('J(w)')
>>> plt.legend(loc='best')
>>> plt.show()
```

The resulting plot shows the sigmoid activation on the x axis, in the range 0 to 1 (the inputs to the sigmoid function were z values in the range -10 to 10) and the associated logistic cost on the y-axis:

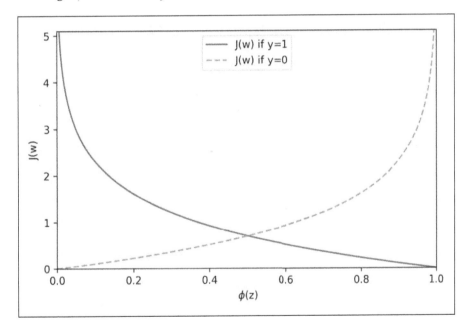

We can see that the cost approaches 0 (continuous line) if we correctly predict that a sample belongs to class 1. Similarly, we can see on the *y*-axis that the cost also approaches 0 if we correctly predict $y = 0$ (dashed line). However, if the prediction is wrong, the cost goes towards infinity. The main point is that we penalize wrong predictions with an increasingly larger cost.

Converting an Adaline implementation into an algorithm for logistic regression

If we were to implement logistic regression ourselves, we could simply substitute the cost function *J* in our Adaline implementation from *Chapter 2, Training Simple Machine Learning Algorithms for Classification* with the new cost function:

$$J(w) = -\sum_i \left[y^{(i)} \log\left(\phi\left(z^{(i)}\right)\right) + \left(1 - y^{(i)}\right) \log\left(1 - \phi\left(z^{(i)}\right)\right) \right]$$

We use this to compute the cost of classifying all training samples per epoch. Also, we need to swap the linear activation function with the sigmoid activation and change the threshold function to return class labels 0 and 1 instead of -1 and 1. If we make those three changes to the Adaline code, we would end up with a working logistic regression implementation, as shown here:

```
class LogisticRegressionGD(object):
    """Logistic Regression Classifier using gradient descent.

    Parameters
    ------------
    eta : float
      Learning rate (between 0.0 and 1.0)
    n_iter : int
      Passes over the training dataset.
    random_state : int
      Random number generator seed for random weight
      initialization.


    Attributes
    -----------
    w_ : 1d-array
      Weights after fitting.
    cost_ : list
```

```
        Logistic cost function value in each epoch.

    """
    def __init__(self, eta=0.05, n_iter=100, random_state=1):
        self.eta = eta
        self.n_iter = n_iter
        self.random_state = random_state

    def fit(self, X, y):
        """ Fit training data.

        Parameters
        ----------
        X : {array-like}, shape = [n_samples, n_features]
          Training vectors, where n_samples is the number of
          samples and
          n_features is the number of features.
        y : array-like, shape = [n_samples]
          Target values.

        Returns
        -------
        self : object

        """
        rgen = np.random.RandomState(self.random_state)
        self.w_ = rgen.normal(loc=0.0, scale=0.01,
                              size=1 + X.shape[1])
        self.cost_ = []

        for i in range(self.n_iter):
            net_input = self.net_input(X)
            output = self.activation(net_input)
            errors = (y - output)
            self.w_[1:] += self.eta * X.T.dot(errors)
            self.w_[0] += self.eta * errors.sum()

            # note that we compute the logistic `cost` now
            # instead of the sum of squared errors cost
            cost = (-y.dot(np.log(output)) -
                    ((1 - y).dot(np.log(1 - output))))
            self.cost_.append(cost)
```

```
                  return self

          def net_input(self, X):
              """Calculate net input"""
              return np.dot(X, self.w_[1:]) + self.w_[0]

          def activation(self, z):
              """Compute logistic sigmoid activation"""
              return 1. / (1. + np.exp(-np.clip(z, -250, 250)))

          def predict(self, X):
              """Return class label after unit step"""
              return np.where(self.net_input(X) >= 0.0, 1, 0)
              # equivalent to:
              # return np.where(self.activation(self.net_input(X))
              #                           >= 0.5, 1, 0)
```

When we fit a logistic regression model, we have to keep in mind that it only works for binary classification tasks. So, let us consider only Iris-setosa and Iris-versicolor flowers (classes 0 and 1) and check that our implementation of logistic regression works:

```
>>> X_train_01_subset = X_train[(y_train == 0) | (y_train == 1)]
>>> y_train_01_subset = y_train[(y_train == 0) | (y_train == 1)]
>>> lrgd = LogisticRegressionGD(eta=0.05,
...                             n_iter=1000,
...                             random_state=1)
>>> lrgd.fit(X_train_01_subset,
...          y_train_01_subset)
>>> plot_decision_regions(X=X_train_01_subset,
...                       y=y_train_01_subset,
...                       classifier=lrgd)
>>> plt.xlabel('petal length [standardized]')
>>> plt.ylabel('petal width [standardized]')
>>> plt.legend(loc='upper left')
>>> plt.show()
```

The resulting decision region plot looks as follows:

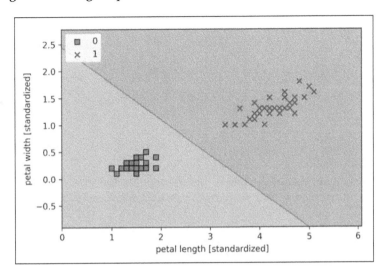

The gradient descent learning algorithm for logistic regression

Using calculus, we can show that the weight update in logistic regression via gradient descent is equal to the equation that we used in Adaline in *Chapter 2, Training Simple Machine Learning Algorithms for Classification*. However, please note that the following derivation of the gradient descent learning rule is intended for readers who are interested in the mathematical concepts behind the gradient descent learning rule for logistic regression. It is not essential for following the rest of this chapter.

Let's start by calculating the partial derivative of the log-likelihood function with respect to the *j*th weight:

$$\frac{\partial}{\partial w_j} l(\mathbf{w}) = \left(y \frac{1}{\phi(z)} - (1-y) \frac{1}{1-\phi(z)} \right) \frac{\partial}{\partial w_j} \phi(z)$$

Before we continue, let's also calculate the partial derivative of the sigmoid function:

$$\frac{\partial}{\partial z} \phi(z) = \frac{\partial}{\partial z} \frac{1}{1+e^{-z}} = \frac{1}{\left(1+e^{-z}\right)^2} e^{-z} = \frac{1}{1+e^{-z}} \left(1 - \frac{1}{1+e^{-z}} \right)$$

$$= \phi(z)(1-\phi(z))$$

Now, we can re-substitute $\frac{\partial}{\partial z}\phi(z) = \phi(z)(1-\phi(z))$ in our first equation to obtain the following:

$$\left(y\frac{1}{\phi(z)} - (1-y)\frac{1}{1-\phi(z)} \right)\frac{\partial}{\partial w_j}\phi(z)$$

$$= \left(y\frac{1}{\phi(z)} - (1-y)\frac{1}{1-\phi(z)} \right)\phi(z)(1-\phi(z))\frac{\partial}{\partial w_j}z$$

$$= \left(y(1-\phi(z)) - (1-y)\phi(z) \right)x_j$$

$$= (y - \phi(z))x_j$$

Remember that the goal is to find the weights that maximize the log-likelihood so that we perform the update for each weight as follows:

$$w_j := w_j + \eta\sum_{i=1}^{n}\left(y^{(i)} - \phi\left(z^{(i)}\right) \right)x_j^{(i)}$$

Since we update all weights simultaneously, we can write the general update rule as follows:

$$w := w + \Delta w$$

We define Δw as follows:

$$\Delta w = \eta\nabla l(w)$$

Since maximizing the log-likelihood is equal to minimizing the cost function J that we defined earlier, we can write the gradient descent update rule as follows:

$$\Delta w_j = -\eta\frac{\partial J}{\partial w_j} = \eta\sum_{i=1}^{n}\left(y^{(i)} - \phi\left(z^{(i)}\right) \right)x_j^{(i)}$$

$$w := w + \Delta w, \ \Delta w = -\eta\nabla J(w)$$

This is equal to the gradient descent rule for Adaline in *Chapter 2, Training Simple Machine Learning Algorithms for Classification*.

Training a logistic regression model with scikit-learn

We just went through useful coding and math exercises in the previous subsection, which helped illustrate the conceptual differences between Adaline and logistic regression. Now, let's learn how to use scikit-learn's more optimized implementation of logistic regression that also supports multi-class settings off the shelf (OvR by default). In the following code example, we will use the `sklearn.linear_model.LogisticRegression` class as well as the familiar `fit` method to train the model on all three classes in the standardized flower training dataset:

```
>>> from sklearn.linear_model import LogisticRegression
>>> lr = LogisticRegression(C=100.0, random_state=1)
>>> lr.fit(X_train_std, y_train)
>>> plot_decision_regions(X_combined_std,
...                       y_combined,
...                       classifier=lr,
...                       test_idx=range(105, 150))
>>> plt.xlabel('petal length [standardized]')
>>> plt.ylabel('petal width [standardized]')
>>> plt.legend(loc='upper left')
>>> plt.show()
```

After fitting the model on the training data, we plotted the decision regions, training samples, and test samples, as shown in the following figure:

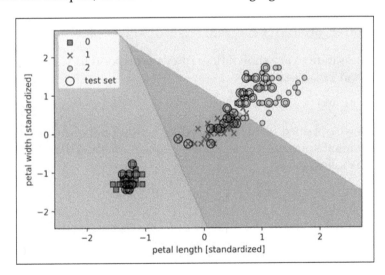

Looking at the preceding code that we used to train the `LogisticRegression` model, you might now be wondering, "What is this mysterious parameter C?" We will discuss this parameter in the next subsection, where we first introduce the concepts of overfitting and regularization. However, before we are moving on to those topics, let's finish our discussion of class-membership probabilities.

The probability that training examples belong to a certain class can be computed using the `predict_proba` method. For example, we can predict the probabilities of the first three samples in the test set as follows:

```
>>> lr.predict_proba(X_test_std[:3, :])
```

This code snippet returns the following array:

```
array([[  3.20136878e-08,   1.46953648e-01,   8.53046320e-01],
       [  8.34428069e-01,   1.65571931e-01,   4.57896429e-12],
       [  8.49182775e-01,   1.50817225e-01,   4.65678779e-13]])
```

The first row corresponds to the class-membership probabilities of the first flower, the second row corresponds to the class-membership probabilities of the second flower, and so forth. Notice that the columns sum all up to one, as expected (you can confirm this by executing `lr.predict_proba(X_test_std[:3, :]).sum(axis=1)`). The highest value in the first row is approximately 0.853, which means that the first sample belongs to class three (`Iris-virginica`) with a predicted probability of 85.7 percent. So, as you may have already noticed, we can get the predicted class labels by identifying the largest column in each row, for example, using NumPy's `argmax` function:

```
>>> lr.predict_proba(X_test_std[:3, :]).argmax(axis=1)
```

The returned class indices are shown here (they correspond to `Iris-virginica`, `Iris-setosa`, and `Iris-setosa`):

```
array([2, 0, 0])
```

The class labels we obtained from the preceding conditional probabilities is, of course, just a manual approach to calling the `predict` method directly, which we can quickly verify as follows:

```
>>> lr.predict(X_test_std[:3, :])
array([2, 0, 0])
```

Lastly, a word of caution if you want to predict the class label of a single flower sample: scikit-learn expects a two-dimensional array as data input; thus, we have to convert a single row slice into such a format first. One way to convert a single row entry into a two-dimensional data array is to use NumPy's `reshape` method to add a new dimension, as demonstrated here:

```
>>> lr.predict(X_test_std[0, :].reshape(1, -1))
array([2])
```

Tackling overfitting via regularization

Overfitting is a common problem in machine learning, where a model performs well on training data but does not generalize well to unseen data (test data). If a model suffers from overfitting, we also say that the model has a high variance, which can be caused by having too many parameters that lead to a model that is too complex given the underlying data. Similarly, our model can also suffer from **underfitting** (high bias), which means that our model is not complex enough to capture the pattern in the training data well and therefore also suffers from low performance on unseen data.

Although we have only encountered linear models for classification so far, the problem of overfitting and underfitting can be best illustrated by comparing a linear decision boundary to more complex, nonlinear decision boundaries as shown in the following figure:

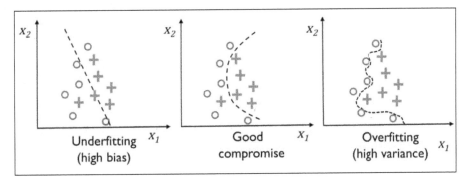

Variance measures the consistency (or variability) of the model prediction for a particular sample instance if we were to retrain the model multiple times, for example, on different subsets of the training dataset. We can say that the model is sensitive to the randomness in the training data. In contrast, bias measures how far off the predictions are from the correct values in general if we rebuild the model multiple times on different training datasets; bias is the measure of the systematic error that is not due to randomness.

One way of finding a good bias-variance tradeoff is to tune the complexity of the model via regularization. Regularization is a very useful method to handle collinearity (high correlation among features), filter out noise from data, and eventually prevent overfitting. The concept behind regularization is to introduce additional information (bias) to penalize extreme parameter (weight) values. The most common form of regularization is so-called L2 regularization (sometimes also called L2 shrinkage or weight decay), which can be written as follows:

$$\frac{\lambda}{2}\|\boldsymbol{w}\|^2 = \frac{\lambda}{2}\sum_{j=1}^{m} w_j^2$$

Here, λ is the so-called **regularization parameter**.

Regularization is another reason why feature scaling such as standardization is important. For regularization to work properly, we need to ensure that all our features are on comparable scales.

The cost function for logistic regression can be regularized by adding a simple regularization term, which will shrink the weights during model training:

$$J(\boldsymbol{w}) = \sum_{i=1}^{n}\left[-y^{(i)}\log\left(\phi\left(z^{(i)}\right)\right)-\left(1-y^{(i)}\right)\log\left(1-\phi\left(z^{(i)}\right)\right)\right]+\frac{\lambda}{2}\|w\|^2$$

Via the regularization parameter λ, we can then control how well we fit the training data while keeping the weights small. By increasing the value of λ, we increase the regularization strength.

The parameter C that is implemented for the LogisticRegression class in scikit-learn comes from a convention in support vector machines, which will be the topic of the next section. The term C is directly related to the regularization parameter λ, which is its inverse. Consequently, decreasing the value of the inverse regularization parameter C means that we are increasing the regularization strength, which we can visualize by plotting the L2-regularization path for the two weight coefficients:

```
>>> weights, params = [], []
>>> for c in np.arange(-5, 5):
...         lr = LogisticRegression(C=10.**c, random_state=1)
...         lr.fit(X_train_std, y_train)
...         weights.append(lr.coef_[1])
...         params.append(10.**c)
>>> weights = np.array(weights)
>>> plt.plot(params, weights[:, 0],
...             label='petal length')
>>> plt.plot(params, weights[:, 1], linestyle='--',
...             label='petal width')
>>> plt.ylabel('weight coefficient')
>>> plt.xlabel('C')
>>> plt.legend(loc='upper left')
>>> plt.xscale('log')
>>> plt.show()
```

By executing the preceding code, we fitted ten logistic regression models with different values for the inverse-regularization parameter C. For the purposes of illustration, we only collected the weight coefficients of class 1 (here, the second class in the dataset, Iris-versicolor) versus all classifiers—remember that we are using the OvR technique for multiclass classification.

As we can see in the resulting plot, the weight coefficients shrink if we decrease parameter C, that is, if we increase the regularization strength:

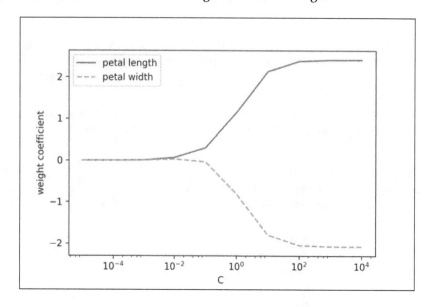

 Since an in-depth coverage of the individual classification algorithms exceeds the scope of this book, I strongly recommend *Logistic Regression: From Introductory to Advanced Concepts and Applications, Dr. Scott Menard's, Sage Publications, 2009,* to readers who want to learn more about logistic regression.

Maximum margin classification with support vector machines

Another powerful and widely used learning algorithm is the **Support Vector Machine (SVM)**, which can be considered an extension of the perceptron. Using the perceptron algorithm, we minimized misclassification errors. However, in SVMs our optimization objective is to maximize the margin. The margin is defined as the distance between the separating hyperplane (decision boundary) and the training samples that are closest to this hyperplane, which are the so-called **support vectors**. This is illustrated in the following figure:

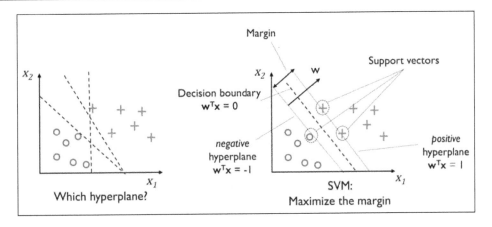

Maximum margin intuition

The rationale behind having decision boundaries with large margins is that they tend to have a lower generalization error whereas models with small margins are more prone to overfitting. To get an idea of the margin maximization, let's take a closer look at those *positive* and *negative* hyperplanes that are parallel to the decision boundary, which can be expressed as follows:

$$w_0 + \boldsymbol{w}^T \boldsymbol{x}_{pos} = 1 \quad (1)$$

$$w_0 + \boldsymbol{w}^T \boldsymbol{x}_{neg} = -1 \quad (2)$$

If we subtract those two linear equations (1) and (2) from each other, we get:

$$\Rightarrow \boldsymbol{w}^T \left(\boldsymbol{x}_{pos} - \boldsymbol{x}_{neg} \right) = 2$$

We can normalize this equation by the length of the vector **w**, which is defined as follows:

$$\|\boldsymbol{w}\| = \sqrt{\sum_{j=1}^{m} w_j^2}$$

So we arrive at the following equation:

$$\frac{w^T\left(x_{pos} - x_{neg}\right)}{\|w\|} = \frac{2}{\|w\|}$$

The left side of the preceding equation can then be interpreted as the distance between the positive and negative hyperplane, which is the so-called **margin** that we want to maximize.

Now, the objective function of the SVM becomes the maximization of this margin by maximizing $\frac{2}{\|w\|}$ under the constraint that the samples are classified correctly, which can be written as:

$$w_0 + w^T x^{(i)} \geq 1 \; if \; y^{(i)} = 1$$

$$w_0 + w^T x^{(i)} \leq -1 \; if \; y^{(i)} = -1$$

$$for \; i = 1 \ldots N$$

Here, N is the number of samples in our dataset.

These two equations basically say that all negative samples should fall on one side of the negative hyperplane, whereas all the positive samples should fall behind the positive hyperplane, which can also be written more compactly as follows:

$$y^{(i)}\left(w_0 + w^T x^{(i)}\right) \geq 1 \; \forall_i$$

In practice though, it is easier to minimize the reciprocal term $\frac{1}{2}\|w\|^2$, which can be solved by quadratic programming. However, a detailed discussion about quadratic programming is beyond the scope of this book. You can learn more about support vector machines in *The Nature of Statistical Learning Theory, Springer Science+Business Media*, Vladimir Vapnik, 2000 or Chris J.C. Burges' excellent explanation in *A Tutorial on Support Vector Machines for Pattern Recognition* (*Data Mining and Knowledge Discovery*, 2(2): 121-167, 1998).

Dealing with a nonlinearly separable case using slack variables

Although we don't want to dive much deeper into the more involved mathematical concepts behind the maximum-margin classification, let us briefly mention the slack variable ξ, which was introduced by Vladimir Vapnik in 1995 and led to the so-called **soft-margin classification**. The motivation for introducing the slack variable ξ was that the linear constraints need to be relaxed for nonlinearly separable data to allow the convergence of the optimization in the presence of misclassifications, under appropriate cost penalization.

The positive-values slack variable is simply added to the linear constraints:

$$w_0 + \boldsymbol{w}^T \boldsymbol{x}^{(i)} \geq 1 - \xi^{(i)} \ \ if \ y^{(i)} = 1$$

$$w_0 + \boldsymbol{w}^T \boldsymbol{x}^{(i)} \leq -1 + \xi^{(i)} \ \ if \ y^{(i)} = -1$$

$$for \ i = 1 \dots N$$

Here, N is the number of samples in our dataset. So the new objective to be minimized (subject to the constraints) becomes:

$$\frac{1}{2} \|\boldsymbol{w}\|^2 + C \left(\sum_i \xi^{(i)} \right)$$

Via the variable C, we can then control the penalty for misclassification. Large values of C correspond to large error penalties, whereas we are less strict about misclassification errors if we choose smaller values for C. We can then use the C parameter to control the width of the margin and therefore tune the bias-variance trade-off, as illustrated in the following figure:

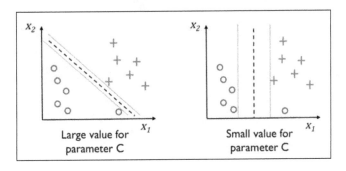

Large value for parameter C   Small value for parameter C

This concept is related to regularization, which we discussed in the previous section in the context of regularized regression where decreasing the value of c increases the bias and lowers the variance of the model.

Now that we have learned the basic concepts behind a linear SVM, let us train an SVM model to classify the different flowers in our Iris dataset:

```
>>> from sklearn.svm import SVC
>>> svm = SVC(kernel='linear', C=1.0, random_state=1)
>>> svm.fit(X_train_std, y_train)
>>> plot_decision_regions(X_combined_std,
...                       y_combined,
...                       classifier=svm,
...                       test_idx=range(105, 150))
>>> plt.xlabel('petal length [standardized]')
>>> plt.ylabel('petal width [standardized]')
>>> plt.legend(loc='upper left')
>>> plt.show()
```

The three decision regions of the SVM, visualized after training the classifier on the Iris dataset by executing the preceding code example, are shown in the following plot:

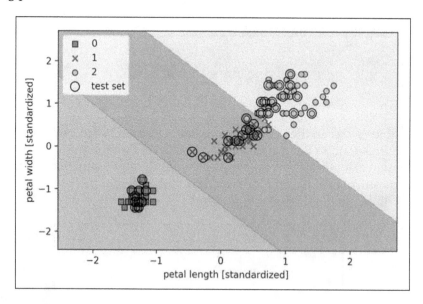

Logistic regression versus support vector machines

In practical classification tasks, linear logistic regression and linear SVMs often yield very similar results. Logistic regression tries to maximize the conditional likelihoods of the training data, which makes it more prone to outliers than SVMs, which mostly care about the points that are closest to the decision boundary (support vectors). On the other hand, logistic regression has the advantage that it is a simpler model and can be implemented more easily. Furthermore, logistic regression models can be easily updated, which is attractive when working with streaming data.

Alternative implementations in scikit-learn

The scikit-learn library's Perceptron and LogisticRegression classes, which we used in the previous sections, make use of the LIBLINEAR library, which is a highly optimized C/C++ library developed at the National Taiwan University (http://www.csie.ntu.edu.tw/~cjlin/liblinear/). Similarly, the SVC class that we used to train an SVM makes use of LIBSVM, which is an equivalent C/C++ library specialized for SVMs (http://www.csie.ntu.edu.tw/~cjlin/libsvm/).

The advantage of using LIBLINEAR and LIBSVM over native Python implementations is that they allow the extremely quick training of large amounts of linear classifiers. However, sometimes our datasets are too large to fit into computer memory. Thus, scikit-learn also offers alternative implementations via the SGDClassifier class, which also supports online learning via the partial_fit method. The concept behind the SGDClassifier class is similar to the stochastic gradient algorithm that we implemented in *Chapter 2, Training Simple Machine Learning Algorithms for Classification*, for Adaline. We could initialize the stochastic gradient descent version of the perceptron, logistic regression, and a support vector machine with default parameters as follows:

```
>>> from sklearn.linear_model import SGDClassifier
>>> ppn = SGDClassifier(loss='perceptron')
>>> lr = SGDClassifier(loss='log')
>>> svm = SGDClassifier(loss='hinge')
```

Solving nonlinear problems using a kernel SVM

Another reason why SVMs enjoy high popularity among machine learning practitioners is that it can be easily **kernelized** to solve nonlinear classification problems. Before we discuss the main concept behind a **kernel SVM**, let's first create a sample dataset to see what such a nonlinear classification problem may look like.

Kernel methods for linearly inseparable data

Using the following code, we will create a simple dataset that has the form of an XOR gate using the `logical_or` function from NumPy, where 100 samples will be assigned the class label 1, and 100 samples will be assigned the class label -1:

```
>>> import matplotlib.pyplot as plt
>>> import numpy as np
>>> np.random.seed(1)
>>> X_xor = np.random.randn(200, 2)
>>> y_xor = np.logical_xor(X_xor[:, 0] > 0,
...                         X_xor[:, 1] > 0)
>>> y_xor = np.where(y_xor, 1, -1)
>>> plt.scatter(X_xor[y_xor == 1, 0],
...             X_xor[y_xor == 1, 1],
...             c='b', marker='x',
...             label='1')
>>> plt.scatter(X_xor[y_xor == -1, 0],
...             X_xor[y_xor == -1, 1],
...             c='r',
...             marker='s',
...             label='-1')
>>> plt.xlim([-3, 3])
>>> plt.ylim([-3, 3])
>>> plt.legend(loc='best')
>>> plt.show()
```

After executing the code, we will have an XOR dataset with random noise, as shown in the following figure:

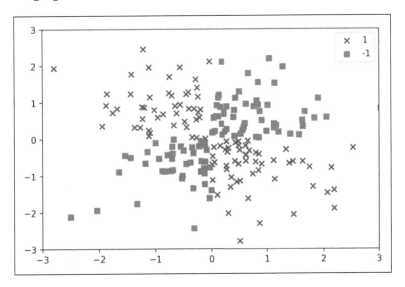

Obviously, we would not be able to separate samples from the positive and negative class very well using a linear hyperplane as a decision boundary via the linear logistic regression or linear SVM model that we discussed in earlier sections.

The basic idea behind **kernel methods** to deal with such linearly inseparable data is to create nonlinear combinations of the original features to project them onto a higher-dimensional space via a mapping function ϕ where it becomes linearly separable. As shown in the following figure, we can transform a two-dimensional dataset onto a new three-dimensional feature space where the classes become separable via the following projection:

$$\phi(x_1, x_2) = (z_1, z_2, z_3) = \left(x_1, x_2, x_1^2 + x_2^2\right)$$

This allows us to separate the two classes shown in the plot via a linear hyperplane that becomes a nonlinear decision boundary if we project it back onto the original feature space:

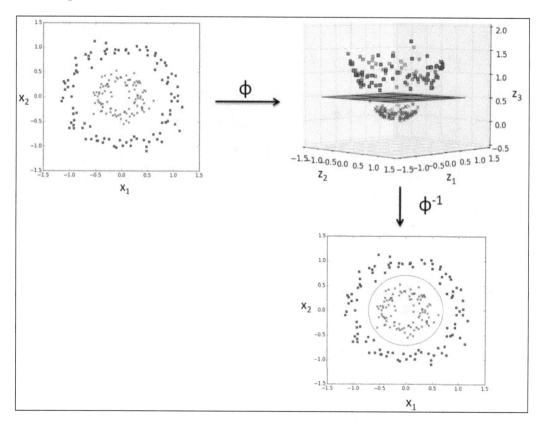

Using the kernel trick to find separating hyperplanes in high-dimensional space

To solve a nonlinear problem using an SVM, we would transform the training data onto a higher-dimensional feature space via a mapping function ϕ and train a linear SVM model to classify the data in this new feature space. Then, we can use the same mapping function ϕ to transform new, unseen data to classify it using the linear SVM model.

However, one problem with this mapping approach is that the construction of the new features is computationally very expensive, especially if we are dealing with high-dimensional data. This is where the so-called kernel trick comes into play. Although we didn't go into much detail about how to solve the quadratic programming task to train an SVM, in practice all we need is to replace the dot product $\boldsymbol{x}^{(i)T}\boldsymbol{x}^{(j)}$ by $\phi\left(\boldsymbol{x}^{(i)}\right)^{T}\phi\left(\boldsymbol{x}^{(j)}\right)$. In order to save the expensive step of calculating this dot product between two points explicitly, we define a so-called **kernel function**: $\mathcal{K}\left(\boldsymbol{x}^{(i)},\boldsymbol{x}^{(j)}\right)=\phi\left(\boldsymbol{x}^{(i)}\right)^{T}\phi\left(\boldsymbol{x}^{(j)}\right)$.

One of the most widely used kernels is the **Radial Basis Function (RBF)** kernel or simply called the **Gaussian kernel**:

$$\mathcal{K}\left(\boldsymbol{x}^{(i)},\boldsymbol{x}^{(j)}\right)=\exp\left(-\frac{\left\|\boldsymbol{x}^{(i)}-\boldsymbol{x}^{(j)}\right\|^{2}}{2\sigma^{2}}\right)$$

This is often simplified to:

$$\mathcal{K}\left(\boldsymbol{x}^{(i)},\boldsymbol{x}^{(j)}\right)=\exp\left(-\gamma\left\|\boldsymbol{x}^{(i)}-\boldsymbol{x}^{(j)}\right\|^{2}\right)$$

Here, $\gamma=\frac{1}{2\sigma^{2}}$ is a free parameter that is to be optimized.

Roughly speaking, the term **kernel** can be interpreted as a **similarity function** between a pair of samples. The minus sign inverts the distance measure into a similarity score, and, due to the exponential term, the resulting similarity score will fall into a range between 1 (for exactly similar samples) and 0 (for very dissimilar samples).

Now that we defined the big picture behind the kernel trick, let us see if we can train a kernel SVM that is able to draw a nonlinear decision boundary that separates the XOR data well. Here, we simply use the svc class from scikit-learn that we imported earlier and replace the kernel='linear' parameter with kernel='rbf':

```
>>> svm = SVC(kernel='rbf', random_state=1, gamma=0.10, C=10.0)
>>> svm.fit(X_xor, y_xor)
>>> plot_decision_regions(X_xor, y_xor, classifier=svm)
>>> plt.legend(loc='upper left')
>>> plt.show()
```

As we can see in the resulting plot, the kernel SVM separates the XOR data relatively well:

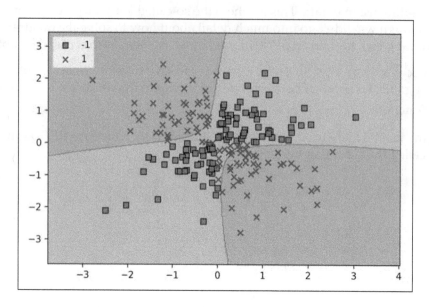

The γ parameter, which we set to `gamma=0.1`, can be understood as a **cut-off** parameter for the Gaussian sphere. If we increase the value for γ, we increase the influence or reach of the training samples, which leads to a tighter and bumpier decision boundary. To get a better intuition for γ, let us apply an RBF kernel SVM to our Iris flower dataset:

```
>>> svm = SVC(kernel='rbf', random_state=1, gamma=0.2, C=1.0)
>>> svm.fit(X_train_std, y_train)
>>> plot_decision_regions(X_combined_std,
...                       y_combined, classifier=svm,
...                       test_idx=range(105,150))
>>> plt.xlabel('petal length [standardized]')
>>> plt.ylabel('petal width [standardized]')
>>> plt.legend(loc='upper left')
>>> plt.show()
```

Since we chose a relatively small value for γ, the resulting decision boundary of the RBF kernel SVM model will be relatively soft, as shown in the following figure:

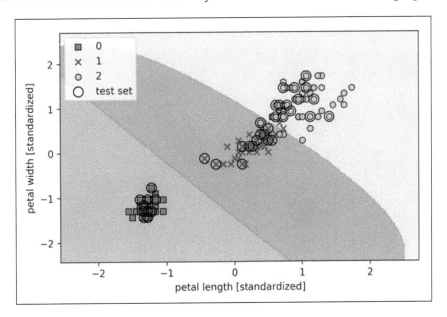

Now, let us increase the value of γ and observe the effect on the decision boundary:

```
>>> svm = SVC(kernel='rbf', random_state=1, gamma=100.0, C=1.0)
>>> svm.fit(X_train_std, y_train)
>>> plot_decision_regions(X_combined_std,
...                       y_combined, classifier=svm,
...                       test_idx=range(105,150))
>>> plt.xlabel('petal length [standardized]')
>>> plt.ylabel('petal width [standardized]')
>>> plt.legend(loc='upper left')
>>> plt.show()
```

In the resulting plot, we can now see that the decision boundary around the classes 0 and 1 is much tighter using a relatively large value of γ:

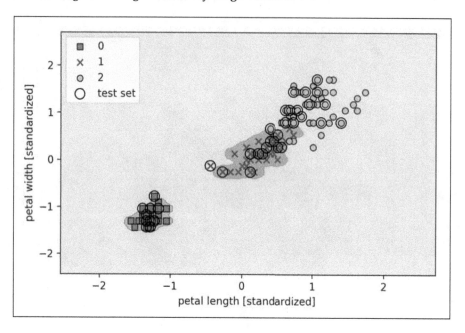

Although the model fits the training dataset very well, such a classifier will likely have a high generalization error on unseen data. This illustrates that the γ parameter also plays an important role in controlling overfitting.

Decision tree learning

Decision tree classifiers are attractive models if we care about interpretability. As the name decision tree suggests, we can think of this model as breaking down our data by making a decision based on asking a series of questions.

Let's consider the following example in which we use a decision tree to decide upon an activity on a particular day:

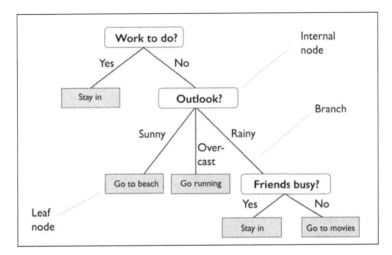

Based on the features in our training set, the decision tree model learns a series of questions to infer the class labels of the samples. Although the preceding figure illustrates the concept of a decision tree based on categorical variables, the same concept applies if our features are real numbers, like in the Iris dataset. For example, we could simply define a cut-off value along the **sepal width** feature axis and ask a binary question "Is sepal width ≥ 2.8 cm?."

Using the decision algorithm, we start at the tree root and split the data on the feature that results in the largest **Information Gain (IG)**, which will be explained in more detail in the following section. In an iterative process, we can then repeat this splitting procedure at each child node until the leaves are pure. This means that the samples at each node all belong to the same class. In practice, this can result in a very deep tree with many nodes, which can easily lead to overfitting. Thus, we typically want to **prune** the tree by setting a limit for the maximal depth of the tree.

Maximizing information gain – getting the most bang for your buck

In order to split the nodes at the most informative features, we need to define an objective function that we want to optimize via the tree learning algorithm. Here, our objective function is to maximize the information gain at each split, which we define as follows:

$$IG\left(D_p, f\right) = I\left(D_p\right) - \sum_{j=1}^{m} \frac{N_j}{N_p} I\left(D_j\right)$$

Here, f is the feature to perform the split, D_p and D_j are the dataset of the parent and jth child node, I is our **impurity** measure, N_p is the total number of samples at the parent node, and N_j is the number of samples in the jth child node. As we can see, the information gain is simply the difference between the impurity of the parent node and the sum of the child node impurities — the lower the impurity of the child nodes, the larger the information gain. However, for simplicity and to reduce the combinatorial search space, most libraries (including scikit-learn) implement binary decision trees. This means that each parent node is split into two child nodes, D_{left} and D_{right}:

$$IG\left(D_p, f\right) = I\left(D_p\right) - \frac{N_{left}}{N_p} I\left(D_{left}\right) - \frac{N_{right}}{N_p} I\left(D_{right}\right)$$

Now, the three impurity measures or splitting criteria that are commonly used in binary decision trees are **Gini impurity** (I_G), **entropy** (I_H), and the **classification error** (I_E). Let us start with the definition of entropy for all **non-empty** classes ($p(i|t) \neq 0$):

$$I_H\left(t\right) = -\sum_{i=1}^{c} p\left(i|t\right) \log_2 p\left(i|t\right)$$

Here, $p(i|t)$ is the proportion of the samples that belong to class i for a particular node t. The entropy is therefore 0 if all samples at a node belong to the same class, and the entropy is maximal if we have a uniform class distribution. For example, in a binary class setting, the entropy is 0 if $p(i=1|t)=1$ or $p(i=0|t)=0$. If the classes are distributed uniformly with $p(i=1|t)=0.5$ and $p(i=0|t)=0.5$, the entropy is 1. Therefore, we can say that the entropy criterion attempts to maximize the mutual information in the tree.

Intuitively, the Gini impurity can be understood as a criterion to minimize the probability of misclassification:

$$I_G(t) = \sum_{i=1}^{c} p(i|t)\big(1-p(i|t)\big) = 1 - \sum_{i=1}^{c} p(i|t)^2$$

Similar to entropy, the Gini impurity is maximal if the classes are perfectly mixed, for example, in a binary class setting ($c=2$):

$$I_G(t) = 1 - \sum_{i=1}^{c} 0.5^2 = 0.5$$

However, in practice both Gini impurity and entropy typically yield very similar results, and it is often not worth spending much time on evaluating trees using different impurity criteria rather than experimenting with different pruning cut-offs.

Another impurity measure is the classification error:

$$I_E = 1 - \max\{p(i|t)\}$$

This is a useful criterion for pruning but not recommended for growing a decision tree, since it is less sensitive to changes in the class probabilities of the nodes. We can illustrate this by looking at the two possible splitting scenarios shown in the following figure:

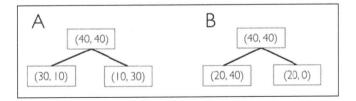

We start with a dataset D_p at the parent node D_p, which consists 40 samples from class 1 and 40 samples from class 2 that we split into two datasets, D_{left} and D_{right}. The information gain using the classification error as a splitting criterion would be the same ($IG_E = 0.25$) in both scenarios, A and B:

$$I_E\left(D_p\right) = 1 - 0.5 = 0.5$$

$$A : I_E\left(D_{left}\right) = 1 - \frac{3}{4} = 0.25$$

$$A : I_E\left(D_{right}\right) = 1 - \frac{3}{4} = 0.25$$

$$A : IG_E = 0.5 - \frac{4}{8} 0.25 - \frac{4}{8} 0.25 = 0.25$$

$$B : I_E\left(D_{left}\right) = 1 - \frac{4}{6} = \frac{1}{3}$$

$$B : I_E\left(D_{right}\right) = 1 - 1 = 0$$

$$B : IG_E = 0.5 - \frac{6}{8} \times \frac{1}{3} - 0 = 0.25$$

However, the Gini impurity would favor the split in scenario B ($IG_G = 0.1\overline{6}$) over scenario A ($IG_G = 0.125$), which is indeed more pure:

$$I_G\left(D_p\right) = 1 - \left(0.5^2 + 0.5^2\right) = 0.5$$

$$A : I_G\left(D_{left}\right) = 1 - \left(\left(\frac{3}{4}\right)^2 + \left(\frac{1}{4}\right)^2\right) = \frac{3}{8} = 0.375$$

$$A: I_G\left(D_{right}\right) = 1 - \left(\left(\frac{1}{4}\right)^2 + \left(\frac{3}{4}\right)^2\right) = \frac{3}{8} = 0.375$$

$$A: IG_G = 0.5 - \frac{4}{8}0.375 - \frac{4}{8}0.375 = 0.125$$

$$B: I_G\left(D_{left}\right) = 1 - \left(\left(\frac{2}{6}\right)^2 + \left(\frac{4}{6}\right)^2\right) = \frac{4}{9} = 0.\overline{4}$$

$$B: I_G\left(D_{right}\right) = 1 - \left(1^2 + 0^2\right) = 0$$

$$B: IG_G = 0.5 - \frac{6}{8}0.\overline{4} - 0 = 0.1\overline{\overline{6}}$$

Similarly, the entropy criterion would also favor scenario B ($IG_H = 0.31$) over scenario A ($IG_H = 0.19$):

$$I_H\left(D_p\right) = -\left(0.5\ \log_2\left(0.5\right) + 0.5\ \log_2\left(0.5\right)\right) = 1$$

$$A: I_H\left(D_{left}\right) = -\left(\frac{3}{4}\log_2\left(\frac{3}{4}\right) + \frac{1}{4}\log_2\left(\frac{1}{4}\right)\right) = 0.81$$

$$A: I_H\left(D_{right}\right) = -\left(\frac{1}{4}\log_2\left(\frac{1}{4}\right) + \frac{3}{4}\log_2\left(\frac{3}{4}\right)\right) = 0.81$$

$$A: IG_H = 1 - \frac{4}{8}0.81 - \frac{4}{8}0.81 = 0.19$$

$$B: I_H\left(D_{left}\right) = -\left(\frac{2}{6}\log_2\left(\frac{2}{6}\right) + \frac{4}{6}\log_2\left(\frac{4}{6}\right)\right) = 0.92$$

$$B : I_H \left(D_{right} \right) = 0$$

$$B : IG_H = 1 - \frac{6}{8} 0.92 - 0 = 0.31$$

For a more visual comparison of the three different impurity criteria that we discussed previously, let us plot the impurity indices for the probability range [0, 1] for class 1. Note that we will also add a scaled version of the entropy (entropy / 2) to observe that the Gini impurity is an intermediate measure between entropy and the classification error. The code is as follows:

```
>>> import matplotlib.pyplot as plt
>>> import numpy as np
>>> def gini(p):
...       return (p)*(1 - (p)) + (1 - p)*(1 - (1-p))
>>> def entropy(p):
...       return - p*np.log2(p) - (1 - p)*np.log2((1 - p))
>>> def error(p):
...       return 1 - np.max([p, 1 - p])
>>> x = np.arange(0.0, 1.0, 0.01)
>>> ent = [entropy(p) if p != 0 else None for p in x]
>>> sc_ent = [e*0.5 if e else None for e in ent]
>>> err = [error(i) for i in x]
>>> fig = plt.figure()
>>> ax = plt.subplot(111)
>>> for i, lab, ls, c, in zip([ent, sc_ent, gini(x), err],
...                     ['Entropy', 'Entropy (scaled)',
...                         'Gini Impurity',
...                         'Misclassification Error'],
...                     ['-', '-', '--', '-.'],
...                     ['black', 'lightgray',
...                         'red', 'green', 'cyan']):
...       line = ax.plot(x, i, label=lab,
...                   linestyle=ls, lw=2, color=c)
>>> ax.legend(loc='upper center', bbox_to_anchor=(0.5, 1.15),
...             ncol=5, fancybox=True, shadow=False)
>>> ax.axhline(y=0.5, linewidth=1, color='k', linestyle='--')
>>> ax.axhline(y=1.0, linewidth=1, color='k', linestyle='--')
>>> plt.ylim([0, 1.1])
>>> plt.xlabel('p(i=1)')
>>> plt.ylabel('Impurity Index')
>>> plt.show()
```

The plot produced by the preceding code example is as follows:

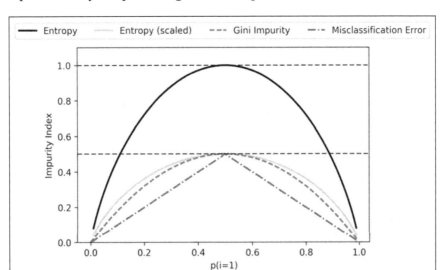

Building a decision tree

Decision trees can build complex decision boundaries by dividing the feature space into rectangles. However, we have to be careful since the deeper the decision tree, the more complex the decision boundary becomes, which can easily result in overfitting. Using scikit-learn, we will now train a decision tree with a maximum depth of 4, using Gini Impurity as a criterion for impurity. Although feature scaling may be desired for visualization purposes, note that feature scaling is not a requirement for decision tree algorithms. The code is as follows:

```
>>> from sklearn.tree import DecisionTreeClassifier
>>> tree = DecisionTreeClassifier(criterion='gini',
...                               max_depth=4,
...                               random_state=1)
>>> tree.fit(X_train, y_train)
>>> X_combined = np.vstack((X_train, X_test))
>>> y_combined = np.hstack((y_train, y_test))
>>> plot_decision_regions(X_combined,
...                       y_combined,
...                       classifier=tree,
...                       test_idx=range(105, 150))
>>> plt.xlabel('petal length [cm]')
>>> plt.ylabel('petal width [cm]')
>>> plt.legend(loc='upper left')
>>> plt.show()
```

After executing the code example, we get the typical axis-parallel decision boundaries of the decision tree:

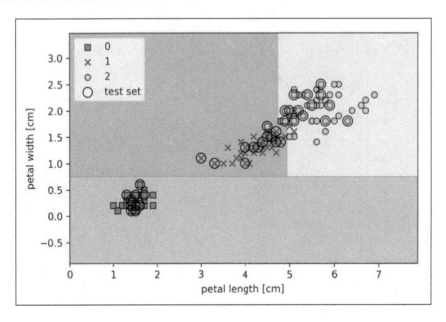

A nice feature in scikit-learn is that it allows us to export the decision tree as a `.dot` file after training, which we can visualize using the GraphViz program, for example.

This program is freely available from `http://www.graphviz.org` and supported by Linux, Windows, and macOS. In addition to GraphViz, we will use a Python library called `pydotplus`, which has capabilities similar to GraphViz and allows us to convert `.dot` data files into a decision tree image file. After you installed GraphViz (by following the instructions on `http://www.graphviz.org/Download.php`), you can install `pydotplus` directly via the pip installer, for example, by executing the following command in your Terminal:

```
> pip3 install pydotplus
```

Note that on some systems, you may have to install the `pydotplus` prerequisites manually by executing the following commands:

```
pip3 install graphviz
pip3 install pyparsing
```

The following code will create an image of our decision tree in PNG format in our local directory:

```
>>> from pydotplus import graph_from_dot_data
>>> from sklearn.tree import export_graphviz
>>> dot_data = export_graphviz(tree,
...                            filled=True,
...                            rounded=True,
...                            class_names=['Setosa',
...                                         'Versicolor',
...                                         'Virginica'],
...                            feature_names=['petal length',
...                                           'petal width'],
...                            out_file=None)
>>> graph = graph_from_dot_data(dot_data)
>>> graph.write_png('tree.png')
```

By using the `out_file=None` setting, we directly assigned the dot data to a `dot_data` variable, instead of writing an intermediate `tree.dot` file to disk. The arguments for `filled`, `rounded`, `class_names`, and `feature_names` are optional but make the resulting image file visually more appealing by adding color, rounding the box edges, showing the name of the majority class label at each node, and displaying the feature names in the splitting criterion. These settings resulted in the following decision tree image:

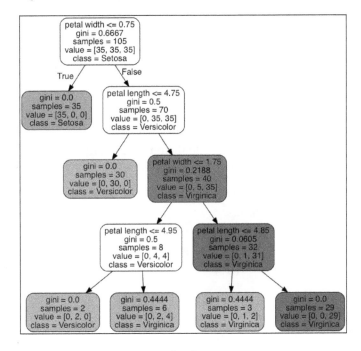

Looking at the decision tree figure, we can now nicely trace back the splits that the decision tree determined from our training dataset. We started with 105 samples at the root and split them into two child nodes with 35 and 70 samples, using the **petal width** cut-off ≤ 0.75 cm. After the first split, we can see that the left child node is already pure and only contains samples from the Iris-setosa class (Gini Impurity = 0). The further splits on the right are then used to separate the samples from the Iris-versicolor and Iris-virginica class.

Looking at this tree, and the decision region plot of the tree, we see that the decision tree does a very good job of separating the flower classes. Unfortunately, scikit-learn currently does not implement functionality to manually post-prune a decision tree. However, we could go back to our previous code example, change the max_depth of our decision tree to 3, and compare it to our current model, but we leave this as an exercise for the interested reader.

Combining multiple decision trees via random forests

Random forests have gained huge popularity in applications of machine learning during the last decade due to their good classification performance, scalability, and ease of use. Intuitively, a random forest can be considered as an **ensemble** of decision trees. The idea behind a random forest is to average multiple (deep) decision trees that individually suffer from high variance, to build a more robust model that has a better generalization performance and is less susceptible to overfitting. The random forest algorithm can be summarized in four simple steps:

1. Draw a random **bootstrap** sample of size n (randomly choose n samples from the training set with replacement).
2. Grow a decision tree from the bootstrap sample. At each node:
   a. Randomly select d features without replacement.
   b. Split the node using the feature that provides the best split according to the objective function, for instance, maximizing the information gain.
3. Repeat the steps 1-2 k times.
4. Aggregate the prediction by each tree to assign the class label by **majority vote**. Majority voting will be discussed in more detail in *Chapter 7, Combining Different Models for Ensemble Learning*.

We should note one slight modification in step 2 when we are training the individual decision trees: instead of evaluating all features to determine the best split at each node, we only consider a random subset of those.

> In case you are not familiar with the terms sampling *with* and *without* replacement, let's walk through a simple thought experiment. Let's assume we are playing a lottery game where we randomly draw numbers from an urn. We start with an urn that holds five unique numbers, 0, 1, 2, 3, and 4, and we draw exactly one number each turn. In the first round, the chance of drawing a particular number from the urn would be 1/5. Now, in sampling without replacement, we do not put the number back into the urn after each turn. Consequently, the probability of drawing a particular number from the set of remaining numbers in the next round depends on the previous round. For example, if we have a remaining set of numbers 0, 1, 2, and 4, the chance of drawing number 0 would become 1/4 in the next turn.
>
> However, in random sampling with replacement, we always return the drawn number to the urn so that the probabilities of drawing a particular number at each turn does not change; we can draw the same number more than once. In other words, in sampling *with* replacement, the samples (numbers) are independent and have a covariance of zero. For example, the results from five rounds of drawing random numbers could look like this:
>
> - Random sampling without replacement: 2, 1, 3, 4, 0
> - Random sampling with replacement: 1, 3, 3, 4, 1

Although random forests don't offer the same level of interpretability as decision trees, a big advantage of random forests is that we don't have to worry so much about choosing good hyperparameter values. We typically don't need to prune the random forest since the ensemble model is quite robust to noise from the individual decision trees. The only parameter that we really need to care about in practice is the number of trees k (step 3) that we choose for the random forest. Typically, the larger the number of trees, the better the performance of the random forest classifier at the expense of an increased computational cost.

Although it is less common in practice, other hyperparameters of the random forest classifier that can be optimized — using techniques we will discuss in *Chapter 5, Compressing Data via Dimensionality Reduction* — are the size n of the bootstrap sample (step 1) and the number of features d that is randomly chosen for each split (step 2.1), respectively. Via the sample size n of the bootstrap sample, we control the bias-variance tradeoff of the random forest.

Decreasing the size of the bootstrap sample increases the diversity among the individual trees, since the probability that a particular training sample is included in the bootstrap sample is lower. Thus, shrinking the size of the bootstrap samples may increase the *randomness* of the random forest, and it can help to reduce the effect of overfitting. However, smaller bootstrap samples typically result in a lower overall performance of the random forest, a small gap between training and test performance, but a low test performance overall. Conversely, increasing the size of the bootstrap sample may increase the degree of overfitting. Because the bootstrap samples, and consequently the individual decision trees, become more similar to each other, they learn to fit the original training dataset more closely.

In most implementations, including the `RandomForestClassifier` implementation in scikit-learn, the size of the bootstrap sample is chosen to be equal to the number of samples in the original training set, which usually provides a good bias-variance tradeoff. For the number of features d at each split, we want to choose a value that is smaller than the total number of features in the training set. A reasonable default that is used in scikit-learn and other implementations is $d = \sqrt{m}$, where m is the number of features in the training set.

Conveniently, we don't have to construct the random forest classifier from individual decision trees by ourselves because there is already an implementation in scikit-learn that we can use:

```
>>> from sklearn.ensemble import RandomForestClassifier
>>> forest = RandomForestClassifier(criterion='gini',
...                                  n_estimators=25,
...                                  random_state=1,
...                                  n_jobs=2)
>>> forest.fit(X_train, y_train)
>>> plot_decision_regions(X_combined, y_combined,
...                 classifier=forest, test_idx=range(105,150))
>>> plt.xlabel('petal length')
>>> plt.ylabel('petal width')
>>> plt.legend(loc='upper left')
>>> plt.show()
```

After executing the preceding code, we should see the decision regions formed by the ensemble of trees in the random forest, as shown in the following figure:

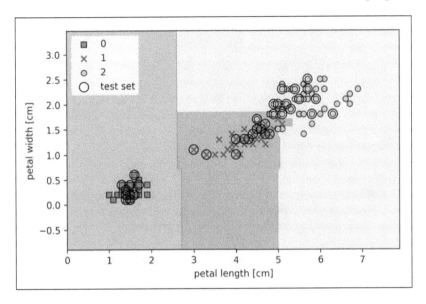

Using the preceding code, we trained a random forest from 25 decision trees via the `n_estimators` parameter and used the entropy criterion as an impurity measure to split the nodes. Although we are growing a very small random forest from a very small training dataset, we used the `n_jobs` parameter for demonstration purposes, which allows us to parallelize the model training using multiple cores of our computer (here two cores).

K-nearest neighbors – a lazy learning algorithm

The last supervised learning algorithm that we want to discuss in this chapter is the **k-nearest neighbor (KNN)** classifier, which is particularly interesting because it is fundamentally different from the learning algorithms that we have discussed so far.

KNN is a typical example of a **lazy learner**. It is called *lazy* not because of its apparent simplicity, but because it doesn't learn a discriminative function from the training data, but memorizes the training dataset instead.

Parametric versus nonparametric models

Machine learning algorithms can be grouped into **parametric** and **nonparametric** models. Using parametric models, we estimate parameters from the training dataset to learn a function that can classify new data points without requiring the original training dataset anymore. Typical examples of parametric models are the perceptron, logistic regression, and the linear SVM. In contrast, nonparametric models can't be characterized by a fixed set of parameters, and the number of parameters grows with the training data. Two examples of non-parametric models that we have seen so far are the decision tree classifier/random forest and the kernel SVM.

KNN belongs to a subcategory of nonparametric models that is described as **instance-based learning**. Models based on instance-based learning are characterized by memorizing the training dataset, and lazy learning is a special case of instance-based learning that is associated with no (zero) cost during the learning process.

The KNN algorithm itself is fairly straightforward and can be summarized by the following steps:

1. Choose the number of k and a distance metric.
2. Find the k-nearest neighbors of the sample that we want to classify.
3. Assign the class label by majority vote.

The following figure illustrates how a new data point (?) is assigned the triangle class label based on majority voting among its five nearest neighbors.

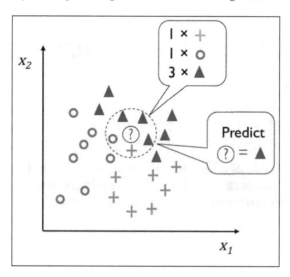

Based on the chosen distance metric, the KNN algorithm finds the k samples in the training dataset that are closest (most similar) to the point that we want to classify. The class label of the new data point is then determined by a majority vote among its k nearest neighbors.

The main advantage of such a memory-based approach is that the classifier immediately adapts as we collect new training data. However, the downside is that the computational complexity for classifying new samples grows linearly with the number of samples in the training dataset in the worst-case scenario—unless the dataset has very few dimensions (features) and the algorithm has been implemented using efficient data structures such as KD-trees. *An Algorithm for Finding Best Matches in Logarithmic Expected Time, J. H. Friedman, J. L. Bentley,* and *R.A. Finkel, ACM transactions on mathematical software (TOMS), 3(3): 209–226, 1977.* Furthermore, we can't discard training samples since no *training* step is involved. Thus, storage space can become a challenge if we are working with large datasets.

By executing the following code, we will now implement a KNN model in scikit-learn using a Euclidean distance metric:

```
>>> from sklearn.neighbors import KNeighborsClassifier
>>> knn = KNeighborsClassifier(n_neighbors=5, p=2,
...                            metric='minkowski')
>>> knn.fit(X_train_std, y_train)
>>> plot_decision_regions(X_combined_std, y_combined,
...                       classifier=knn, test_idx=range(105,150))
>>> plt.xlabel('petal length [standardized]')
>>> plt.ylabel('petal width [standardized]')
>>> plt.legend(loc='upper left')
>>> plt.show()
```

By specifying five neighbors in the KNN model for this dataset, we obtain a relatively smooth decision boundary, as shown in the following figure:

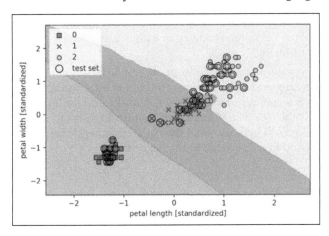

In the case of a tie, the scikit-learn implementation of the KNN algorithm will prefer the neighbors with a closer distance to the sample. If the neighbors have similar distances, the algorithm will choose the class label that comes first in the training dataset.

The *right* choice of k is crucial to find a good balance between overfitting and underfitting. We also have to make sure that we choose a distance metric that is appropriate for the features in the dataset. Often, a simple Euclidean distance measure is used for real-value samples, for example, the flowers in our Iris dataset, which have features measured in centimeters. However, if we are using a Euclidean distance measure, it is also important to standardize the data so that each feature contributes equally to the distance. The `minkowski` distance that we used in the previous code is just a generalization of the Euclidean and Manhattan distance, which can be written as follows:

$$d\left(\boldsymbol{x}^{(i)}, \boldsymbol{x}^{(j)}\right) = \sqrt[p]{\sum_k \left|x_k^{(i)} - x_k^{(j)}\right|^p}$$

It becomes the Euclidean distance if we set the parameter p=2 or the Manhattan distance at p=1. Many other distance metrics are available in scikit-learn and can be provided to the metric parameter. They are listed at http://scikit-learn.org/stable/modules/generated/sklearn.neighbors.DistanceMetric.html.

The curse of dimensionality

It is important to mention that KNN is very susceptible to overfitting due to the **curse of dimensionality**. The curse of dimensionality describes the phenomenon where the feature space becomes increasingly sparse for an increasing number of dimensions of a fixed-size training dataset. Intuitively, we can think of even the closest neighbors being too far away in a high-dimensional space to give a good estimate.

We have discussed the concept of regularization in the section about logistic regression as one way to avoid overfitting. However, in models where regularization is not applicable, such as decision trees and KNN, we can use feature selection and dimensionality reduction techniques to help us avoid the curse of dimensionality. This will be discussed in more detail in the next chapter.

Summary

In this chapter, you learned about many different machine learning algorithms that are used to tackle linear and nonlinear problems. We have seen that decision trees are particularly attractive if we care about interpretability. Logistic regression is not only a useful model for online learning via stochastic gradient descent, but also allows us to predict the probability of a particular event. Although support vector machines are powerful linear models that can be extended to nonlinear problems via the kernel trick, they have many parameters that have to be tuned in order to make good predictions. In contrast, ensemble methods such as random forests don't require much parameter tuning and don't overfit as easily as decision trees, which makes them attractive models for many practical problem domains. The KNN classifier offers an alternative approach to classification via lazy learning that allows us to make predictions without any model training, but with a more computationally expensive prediction step.

However, even more important than the choice of an appropriate learning algorithm is the available data in our training dataset. No algorithm will be able to make good predictions without informative and discriminatory features.

In the next chapter, we will discuss important topics regarding the preprocessing of data, feature selection, and dimensionality reduction, which we will need to build powerful machine learning models. Later in *Chapter 6, Learning Best Practices for Model Evaluation and Hyperparameter Tuning*, we will see how we can evaluate and compare the performance of our models and learn useful tricks to fine-tune the different algorithms.

4
Building Good Training Sets – Data Preprocessing

The quality of the data and the amount of useful information that it contains are key factors that determine how well a machine learning algorithm can learn. Therefore, it is absolutely critical that we make sure to examine and preprocess a dataset before we feed it to a learning algorithm. In this chapter, we will discuss the essential data preprocessing techniques that will help us build good machine learning models.

The topics that we will cover in this chapter are as follows:

- Removing and imputing missing values from the dataset
- Getting categorical data into shape for machine learning algorithms
- Selecting relevant features for the model construction

Dealing with missing data

It is not uncommon in real-world applications for our samples to be missing one or more values for various reasons. There could have been an error in the data collection process, certain measurements are not applicable, or particular fields could have been simply left blank in a survey, for example. We typically see missing values as the blank spaces in our data table or as placeholder strings such as NaN, which stands for not a number, or NULL (a commonly used indicator of unknown values in relational databases).

Unfortunately, most computational tools are unable to handle such missing values, or produce unpredictable results if we simply ignore them. Therefore, it is crucial that we take care of those missing values before we proceed with further analyses. In this section, we will work through several practical techniques for dealing with missing values by removing entries from our dataset or imputing missing values from other samples and features.

Identifying missing values in tabular data

But before we discuss several techniques for dealing with missing values, let's create a simple example data frame from a **Comma-separated Values (CSV)** file to get a better grasp of the problem:

```
>>> import pandas as pd
>>> from io import StringIO

>>> csv_data = \
... '''A,B,C,D
... 1.0,2.0,3.0,4.0
... 5.0,6.0,,8.0
... 10.0,11.0,12.0,'''
>>> # If you are using Python 2.7, you need
>>> # to convert the string to unicode:
>>> # csv_data = unicode(csv_data)
>>> df = pd.read_csv(StringIO(csv_data))
>>> df
     A     B     C    D
0  1.0   2.0   3.0  4.0
1  5.0   6.0   NaN  8.0
2 10.0  11.0  12.0  NaN
```

Using the preceding code, we read CSV-formatted data into a pandas `DataFrame` via the `read_csv` function and noticed that the two missing cells were replaced by NaN. The `StringIO` function in the preceding code example was simply used for the purposes of illustration. It allows us to read the string assigned to `csv_data` into a pandas `DataFrame` as if it was a regular CSV file on our hard drive.

For a larger `DataFrame`, it can be tedious to look for missing values manually; in this case, we can use the `isnull` method to return a `DataFrame` with Boolean values that indicate whether a cell contains a numeric value (`False`) or if data is missing (`True`). Using the `sum` method, we can then return the number of missing values per column as follows:

```
>>> df.isnull().sum()
A    0
B    0
C    1
D    1
dtype: int64
```

This way, we can count the number of missing values per column; in the following subsections, we will take a look at different strategies for how to deal with this missing data.

 Although scikit-learn was developed for working with NumPy arrays, it can sometimes be more convenient to preprocess data using pandas' `DataFrame`. We can always access the underlying NumPy array of a `DataFrame` via the `values` attribute before we feed it into a scikit-learn estimator:

```
>>> df.values
array([[  1.,    2.,    3.,    4.],
       [  5.,    6.,   nan,    8.],
       [ 10.,   11.,   12.,   nan]])
```

Eliminating samples or features with missing values

One of the easiest ways to deal with missing data is to simply remove the corresponding features (columns) or samples (rows) from the dataset entirely; rows with missing values can be easily dropped via the `dropna` method:

```
>>> df.dropna(axis=0)
     A    B    C    D
0  1.0  2.0  3.0  4.0
```

Similarly, we can drop columns that have at least one NaN in any row by setting the axis argument to 1:

```
>>> df.dropna(axis=1)
      A     B
0   1.0   2.0
1   5.0   6.0
2  10.0  11.0
```

The `dropna` method supports several additional parameters that can come in handy:

```
# only drop rows where all columns are NaN
# (returns the whole array here since we don't
# have a row with where all values are NaN
>>> df.dropna(how='all')
     A    B    C    D
0  1.0  2.0  3.0  4.0
```

```
1   5.0   6.0   NaN   8.0
2  10.0  11.0  12.0   NaN


# drop rows that have less than 4 real values
>>> df.dropna(thresh=4)
     A    B    C    D
0  1.0  2.0  3.0  4.0


# only drop rows where NaN appear in specific columns (here: 'C')
>>> df.dropna(subset=['C'])
     A    B    C    D
0  1.0  2.0  3.0  4.0
2 10.0 11.0 12.0 NaN
```

Although the removal of missing data seems to be a convenient approach, it also comes with certain disadvantages; for example, we may end up removing too many samples, which will make a reliable analysis impossible. Or, if we remove too many feature columns, we will run the risk of losing valuable information that our classifier needs to discriminate between classes. In the next section, we will thus look at one of the most commonly used alternatives for dealing with missing values: interpolation techniques.

Imputing missing values

Often, the removal of samples or dropping of entire feature columns is simply not feasible, because we might lose too much valuable data. In this case, we can use different interpolation techniques to estimate the missing values from the other training samples in our dataset. One of the most common interpolation techniques is **mean imputation**, where we simply replace the missing value with the mean value of the entire feature column. A convenient way to achieve this is by using the Imputer class from scikit-learn, as shown in the following code:

```
>>> from sklearn.preprocessing import Imputer
>>> imr = Imputer(missing_values='NaN', strategy='mean', axis=0)
>>> imr = imr.fit(df.values)
>>> imputed_data = imr.transform(df.values)
>>> imputed_data
array([[  1.,    2.,    3.,    4.],
       [  5.,    6.,    7.5,   8.],
       [ 10.,   11.,   12.,    6.]])
```

Here, we replaced each NaN value with the corresponding mean, which is separately calculated for each feature column. If we changed the axis=0 setting to axis=1, we'd calculate the row means. Other options for the strategy parameter are median or most_frequent, where the latter replaces the missing values with the most frequent values. This is useful for imputing categorical feature values, for example, a feature column that stores an encoding of color names, such as red, green, and blue, and we will encounter examples of such data later in this chapter.

Understanding the scikit-learn estimator API

In the previous section, we used the Imputer class from scikit-learn to impute missing values in our dataset. The Imputer class belongs to the so-called **transformer** classes in scikit-learn, which are used for data transformation. The two essential methods of those estimators are fit and transform. The fit method is used to learn the parameters from the training data, and the transform method uses those parameters to transform the data. Any data array that is to be transformed needs to have the same number of features as the data array that was used to fit the model. The following figure illustrates how a transformer, fitted on the training data, is used to transform a training dataset as well as a new test dataset:

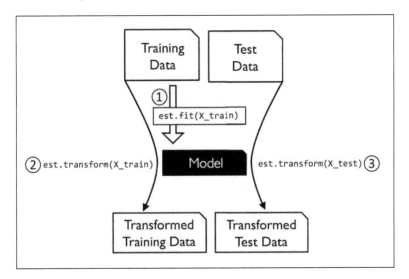

The classifiers that we used in *Chapter 3, A Tour of Machine Learning Classifiers Using scikit-learn*, belong to the so-called **estimators** in scikit-learn with an API that is conceptually very similar to the transformer class. Estimators have a predict method but can also have a transform method, as we will see later in this chapter. As you may recall, we also used the fit method to learn the parameters of a model when we trained those estimators for classification. However, in supervised learning tasks, we additionally provide the class labels for fitting the model, which can then be used to make predictions about new data samples via the predict method, as illustrated in the following figure:

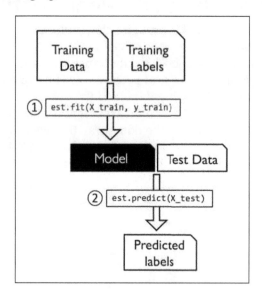

Handling categorical data

So far, we have only been working with numerical values. However, it is not uncommon that real-world datasets contain one or more categorical feature columns. In this section, we will make use of simple yet effective examples to see how we deal with this type of data in numerical computing libraries.

Nominal and ordinal features

When we are talking about categorical data, we have to further distinguish between **nominal** and **ordinal** features. Ordinal features can be understood as categorical values that can be sorted or ordered. For example, t-shirt size would be an ordinal feature, because we can define an order $XL > L > M$. In contrast, nominal features don't imply any order and, to continue with the previous example, we could think of t-shirt color as a nominal feature since it typically doesn't make sense to say that, for example, red is larger than blue.

Creating an example dataset

Before we explore different techniques to handle such categorical data, let's create a new `DataFrame` to illustrate the problem:

```
>>> import pandas as pd
>>> df = pd.DataFrame([
...             ['green', 'M', 10.1, 'class1'],
...             ['red', 'L', 13.5, 'class2'],
...             ['blue', 'XL', 15.3, 'class1']])
>>> df.columns = ['color', 'size', 'price', 'classlabel']
>>> df
   color size  price classlabel
0  green    M   10.1     class1
1    red    L   13.5     class2
2   blue   XL   15.3     class1
```

As we can see in the preceding output, the newly created `DataFrame` contains a nominal feature (`color`), an ordinal feature (`size`), and a numerical feature (`price`) column. The class labels (assuming that we created a dataset for a supervised learning task) are stored in the last column. The learning algorithms for classification that we discuss in this book do not use ordinal information in class labels.

Mapping ordinal features

To make sure that the learning algorithm interprets the ordinal features correctly, we need to convert the categorical string values into integers. Unfortunately, there is no convenient function that can automatically derive the correct order of the labels of our `size` feature, so we have to define the mapping manually. In the following simple example, let's assume that we know the numerical difference between features, for example, $XL = L + 1 = M + 2$:

```
>>> size_mapping = {
...                  'XL': 3,
...                  'L': 2,
```

```
...                     'M': 1}
>>> df['size'] = df['size'].map(size_mapping)
>>> df
   color  size  price classlabel
0  green     1   10.1     class1
1    red     2   13.5     class2
2   blue     3   15.3     class1
```

If we want to transform the integer values back to the original string representation at a later stage, we can simply define a reverse-mapping dictionary inv_size_mapping = {v: k for k, v in size_mapping.items()} that can then be used via the pandas map method on the transformed feature column, similar to the size_mapping dictionary that we used previously. We can use it as follows:

```
>>> inv_size_mapping = {v: k for k, v in size_mapping.items()}
>>> df['size'].map(inv_size_mapping)
0     M
1     L
2    XL
Name: size, dtype: object
```

Encoding class labels

Many machine learning libraries require that class labels are encoded as integer values. Although most estimators for classification in scikit-learn convert class labels to integers internally, it is considered good practice to provide class labels as integer arrays to avoid technical glitches. To encode the class labels, we can use an approach similar to the mapping of ordinal features discussed previously. We need to remember that class labels are *not* ordinal, and it doesn't matter which integer number we assign to a particular string label. Thus, we can simply enumerate the class labels, starting at 0:

```
>>> import numpy as np
>>> class_mapping = {label:idx for idx,label in
...                   enumerate(np.unique(df['classlabel']))}
>>> class_mapping
{'class1': 0, 'class2': 1}
```

Next, we can use the mapping dictionary to transform the class labels into integers:

```
>>> df['classlabel'] = df['classlabel'].map(class_mapping)
>>> df
   color  size  price  classlabel
0  green     1   10.1           0
1    red     2   13.5           1
2   blue     3   15.3           0
```

We can reverse the key-value pairs in the mapping dictionary as follows to map the converted class labels back to the original string representation:

```
>>> inv_class_mapping = {v: k for k, v in class_mapping.items()}
>>> df['classlabel'] = df['classlabel'].map(inv_class_mapping)
>>> df
   color  size  price classlabel
0  green     1   10.1     class1
1    red     2   13.5     class2
2   blue     3   15.3     class1
```

Alternatively, there is a convenient LabelEncoder class directly implemented in scikit-learn to achieve this:

```
>>> from sklearn.preprocessing import LabelEncoder
>>> class_le = LabelEncoder()
>>> y = class_le.fit_transform(df['classlabel'].values)
>>> y
array([0, 1, 0])
```

Note that the fit_transform method is just a shortcut for calling fit and transform separately, and we can use the inverse_transform method to transform the integer class labels back into their original string representation:

```
>>> class_le.inverse_transform(y)
array(['class1', 'class2', 'class1'], dtype=object)
```

> The class_le.inverse_transform(y) call may raise a DeprecationWarning due to an implementation detail in scikit-learn. It was already addressed in a pull request (https://github.com/scikit-learn/scikit-learn/pull/9816), and the patch will be released with the next version of scikit-learn (i.e., v. 0.20.0).

Performing one-hot encoding on nominal features

In the previous section, we used a simple dictionary-mapping approach to convert the ordinal `size` feature into integers. Since scikit-learn's estimators for classification treat class labels as categorical data that does not imply any order (nominal), we used the convenient `LabelEncoder` to encode the string labels into integers. It may appear that we could use a similar approach to transform the nominal `color` column of our dataset, as follows:

```
>>> X = df[['color', 'size', 'price']].values
>>> color_le = LabelEncoder()
>>> X[:, 0] = color_le.fit_transform(X[:, 0])
>>> X
array([[1, 1, 10.1],
       [2, 2, 13.5],
       [0, 3, 15.3]], dtype=object)
```

After executing the preceding code, the first column of the NumPy array X now holds the new `color` values, which are encoded as follows:

- blue = 0
- green = 1
- red = 2

If we stop at this point and feed the array to our classifier, we will make one of the most common mistakes in dealing with categorical data. Can you spot the problem? Although the color values don't come in any particular order, a learning algorithm will now assume that `green` is larger than `blue`, and `red` is larger than `green`. Although this assumption is incorrect, the algorithm could still produce useful results. However, those results would not be optimal.

A common workaround for this problem is to use a technique called **one-hot encoding**. The idea behind this approach is to create a new dummy feature for each unique value in the nominal feature column. Here, we would convert the `color` feature into three new features: `blue`, `green`, and `red`. Binary values can then be used to indicate the particular `color` of a sample; for example, a `blue` sample can be encoded as `blue=1`, `green=0`, `red=0`. To perform this transformation, we can use the `OneHotEncoder` that is implemented in scikit-learn's `preprocessing` module:

```
>>> from sklearn.preprocessing import OneHotEncoder

>>> ohe = OneHotEncoder(categorical_features=[0])
>>> ohe.fit_transform(X).toarray()
```

```
array([[  0. ,    1. ,    0. ,    1. ,   10.1],
       [  0. ,    0. ,    1. ,    2. ,   13.5],
       [  1. ,    0. ,    0. ,    3. ,   15.3]])
```

When we initialized the `OneHotEncoder`, we defined the column position of the variable that we want to transform via the `categorical_features` parameter (note that `color` is the first column in the feature matrix x). By default, the `OneHotEncoder` returns a sparse matrix when we use the `transform` method, and we converted the sparse matrix representation into a regular (*dense*) NumPy array for the purpose of visualization via the `toarray` method. Sparse matrices are a more efficient way of storing large datasets and one that is supported by many scikit-learn functions, which is especially useful if an array contains a lot of zeros. To omit the `toarray` step, we could alternatively initialize the encoder as `OneHotEncoder(...,` `sparse=False)` to return a regular NumPy array.

An even more convenient way to create those dummy features via one-hot encoding is to use the `get_dummies` method implemented in pandas. Applied to a `DataFrame`, the `get_dummies` method will only convert string columns and leave all other columns unchanged:

```
>>> pd.get_dummies(df[['price', 'color', 'size']])
   price  size  color_blue  color_green  color_red
0   10.1    1            0            1          0
1   13.5    2            0            0          1
2   15.3    3            1            0          0
```

When we are using one-hot encoding datasets, we have to keep in mind that it introduces multicollinearity, which can be an issue for certain methods (for instance, methods that require matrix inversion). If features are highly correlated, matrices are computationally difficult to invert, which can lead to numerically unstable estimates. To reduce the correlation among variables, we can simply remove one feature column from the one-hot encoded array. Note that we do not lose any important information by removing a feature column, though; for example, if we remove the column `color_blue`, the feature information is still preserved since if we observe `color_green=0` and `color_red=0`, it implies that the observation must be `blue`.

If we use the `get_dummies` function, we can drop the first column by passing a `True` argument to the `drop_first` parameter, as shown in the following code example:

```
>>> pd.get_dummies(df[['price', 'color', 'size']],
...                 drop_first=True)
   price  size  color_green  color_red
0   10.1    1             1          0
1   13.5    2             0          1
2   15.3    3             0          0
```

The OneHotEncoder does not have a parameter for column removal, but we can simply slice the one-hot encoded NumPy array as shown in the following code snippet:

```
ohe = OneHotEncoder(categorical_features=[0])
ohe.fit_transform(X).toarray()[:, 1:]
array([[  1. ,    0. ,    1. ,   10.1],
       [  0. ,    1. ,    2. ,   13.5],
       [  0. ,    0. ,    3. ,   15.3]])
```

Partitioning a dataset into separate training and test sets

We briefly introduced the concept of partitioning a dataset into separate datasets for training and testing in *Chapter 1, Giving Computers the Ability to Learn from Data*, and *Chapter 3, A Tour of Machine Learning Classifiers Using scikit-learn*. Remember that comparing predictions to true labels in the test set can be understood as the unbiased performance evaluation of our model before we let it loose on the real world. In this section, we will prepare a new dataset, the **Wine** dataset. After we have preprocessed the dataset, we will explore different techniques for feature selection to reduce the dimensionality of a dataset.

The Wine dataset is another open-source dataset that is available from the UCI machine learning repository (https://archive.ics.uci.edu/ml/datasets/Wine); it consists of 178 wine samples with 13 features describing their different chemical properties.

You can find a copy of the Wine dataset (and all other datasets used in this book) in the code bundle of this book, which you can use if you are working offline or the dataset at https://archive.ics.uci.edu/ml/machine-learning-databases/wine/wine.data is temporarily unavailable on the UCI server. For instance, to load the Wine dataset from a local directory, you can replace this line:

```
df = pd.read_csv('https://archive.ics.uci.edu/ml/'
                 'machine-learning-databases/wine/wine.data',
                 header=None)
```

Replace it with this:

```
df = pd.read_csv('your/local/path/to/wine.data',
                 header=None)
```

Using the `pandas` library, we will directly read in the open source Wine dataset from the UCI machine learning repository:

```
>>> df_wine = pd.read_csv('https://archive.ics.uci.edu/'
                          'ml/machine-learning-databases/'
                          'wine/wine.data', header=None)
>>> df_wine.columns = ['Class label', 'Alcohol',
...                    'Malic acid', 'Ash',
...                    'Alcalinity of ash', 'Magnesium',
...                    'Total phenols', 'Flavanoids',
...                    'Nonflavanoid phenols',
...                    'Proanthocyanins',
...                    'Color intensity', 'Hue',
...                    'OD280/OD315 of diluted wines',
...                    'Proline']
>>> print('Class labels', np.unique(df_wine['Class label']))
Class labels [1 2 3]
>>> df_wine.head()
```

The 13 different features in the Wine dataset, describing the chemical properties of the 178 wine samples, are listed in the following table:

	Class label	Alcohol	Malic acid	Ash	Alcalinity of ash	Magnesium	Total phenols	Flavanoids	Nonflavanoid phenols	Proanthocyanins	Color intensity	Hue	OD280/OD315 of diluted wines	Proline
0	1	14.23	1.71	2.43	15.6	127	2.80	3.06	0.28	2.29	5.64	1.04	3.92	1065
1	1	13.20	1.78	2.14	11.2	100	2.65	2.76	0.26	1.28	4.38	1.05	3.40	1050
2	1	13.16	2.36	2.67	18.6	101	2.80	3.24	0.30	2.81	5.68	1.03	3.17	1185
3	1	14.37	1.95	2.50	16.8	113	3.85	3.49	0.24	2.18	7.80	0.86	3.45	1480
4	1	13.24	2.59	2.87	21.0	118	2.80	2.69	0.39	1.82	4.32	1.04	2.93	735

The samples belong to one of three different classes, 1, 2, and 3, which refer to the three different types of grape grown in the same region in Italy but derived from different wine cultivars, as described in the dataset summary (https://archive. ics.uci.edu/ml/machine-learning-databases/wine/wine.names).

A convenient way to randomly partition this dataset into separate test and training datasets is to use the `train_test_split` function from scikit-learn's `model_selection` submodule:

```
>>> from sklearn.model_selection import train_test_split
>>> X, y = df_wine.iloc[:, 1:].values, df_wine.iloc[:, 0].values
>>> X_train, X_test, y_train, y_test =\
...     train_test_split(X, y,
...                      test_size=0.3,
...                      random_state=0,
...                      stratify=y)
```

First, we assigned the NumPy array representation of the feature columns 1-13 to the variable x; we assigned the class labels from the first column to the variable y. Then, we used the `train_test_split` function to randomly split x and y into separate training and test datasets. By setting `test_size=0.3`, we assigned 30 percent of the wine samples to `X_test` and `y_test`, and the remaining 70 percent of the samples were assigned to `X_train` and `y_train`, respectively. Providing the class label array y as an argument to `stratify` ensures that both training and test datasets have the same class proportions as the original dataset.

If we are dividing a dataset into training and test datasets, we have to keep in mind that we are withholding valuable information that the learning algorithm could benefit from. Thus, we don't want to allocate too much information to the test set. However, the smaller the test set, the more inaccurate the estimation of the generalization error. Dividing a dataset into training and test sets is all about balancing this trade-off. In practice, the most commonly used splits are 60:40, 70:30, or 80:20, depending on the size of the initial dataset. However, for large datasets, 90:10 or 99:1 splits into training and test subsets are also common and appropriate. Instead of discarding the allocated test data after model training and evaluation, it is a common practice to retrain a classifier on the entire dataset as it can improve the predictive performance of the model. While this approach is generally recommended, it could lead to worse generalization performance if the dataset is small and the test set contains outliers, for example. Also, after refitting the model on the whole dataset, we don't have any independent data left to evaluate its performance.

Bringing features onto the same scale

Feature scaling is a crucial step in our preprocessing pipeline that can easily be forgotten. Decision trees and random forests are two of the very few machine learning algorithms where we don't need to worry about feature scaling. Those algorithms are scale invariant. However, the majority of machine learning and optimization algorithms behave much better if features are on the same scale, as we have seen in *Chapter 2, Training Simple Machine Learning Algorithms for Classification,* when we implemented the **gradient descent** optimization algorithm.

The importance of feature scaling can be illustrated by a simple example. Let's assume that we have two features where one feature is measured on a scale from 1 to 10 and the second feature is measured on a scale from 1 to 100,000, respectively. When we think of the squared error function in Adaline in *Chapter 2, Training Simple Machine Learning Algorithms for Classification*, it is intuitive to say that the algorithm will mostly be busy optimizing the weights according to the larger errors in the second feature. Another example is the **k-nearest neighbors (KNN)** algorithm with a Euclidean distance measure; the computed distances between samples will be dominated by the second feature axis.

Now, there are two common approaches to bring different features onto the same scale: **normalization** and **standardization**. Those terms are often used quite loosely in different fields, and the meaning has to be derived from the context. Most often, normalization refers to the rescaling of the features to a range of [0, 1], which is a special case of **min-max scaling**. To normalize our data, we can simply apply the min-max scaling to each feature column, where the new value $x_{norm}^{(i)}$ of a sample $x^{(i)}$ can be calculated as follows:

$$x_{norm}^{(i)} = \frac{x^{(i)} - x_{min}}{x_{max} - x_{min}}$$

Here, $x^{(i)}$ is a particular sample, x_{min} is the smallest value in a feature column, and x_{max} the largest value.

The min-max scaling procedure is implemented in scikit-learn and can be used as follows:

```
>>> from sklearn.preprocessing import MinMaxScaler
>>> mms = MinMaxScaler()
>>> X_train_norm = mms.fit_transform(X_train)
>>> X_test_norm = mms.transform(X_test)
```

Although normalization via min-max scaling is a commonly used technique that is useful when we need values in a bounded interval, standardization can be more practical for many machine learning algorithms, especially for optimization algorithms such as gradient descent. The reason is that many linear models, such as the logistic regression and SVM that we remember from *Chapter 3, A Tour of Machine Learning Classifiers Using scikit-learn*, initialize the weights to 0 or small random values close to 0. Using standardization, we center the feature columns at mean 0 with standard deviation 1 so that the feature columns have the same parameters as a standard normal distribution (zero mean and unit variance), which makes it easier to learn the weights. Furthermore, standardization maintains useful information about outliers and makes the algorithm less sensitive to them in contrast to min-max scaling, which scales the data to a limited range of values.

The procedure for standardization can be expressed by the following equation:

$$x_{std}^{(i)} = \frac{x^{(i)} - \mu_x}{\sigma_x}$$

Here, μ_x is the sample mean of a particular feature column and σ_x is the corresponding standard deviation.

The following table illustrates the difference between the two commonly used feature scaling techniques, standardization and normalization, on a simple sample dataset consisting of numbers 0 to 5:

Input	Standardized	Min-max normalized
0.0	-1.46385	0.0
1.0	-0.87831	0.2
2.0	-0.29277	0.4
3.0	0.29277	0.6
4.0	0.87831	0.8
5.0	1.46385	1.0

You can perform the standardization and normalization shown in the table manually by executing the following code examples:

```
>>> ex = np.array([0, 1, 2, 3, 4, 5])
>>> print('standardized:', (ex - ex.mean()) / ex.std())
standardized: [-1.46385011 -0.87831007 -0.29277002  0.29277002
0.87831007  1.46385011]
>>> print('normalized:', (ex - ex.min()) / (ex.max() - ex.min()))
normalized: [ 0.   0.2  0.4  0.6  0.8  1. ]
```

Similar to the `MinMaxScaler` class, scikit-learn also implements a class for standardization:

```
>>> from sklearn.preprocessing import StandardScaler
>>> stdsc = StandardScaler()
>>> X_train_std = stdsc.fit_transform(X_train)
>>> X_test_std = stdsc.transform(X_test)
```

Again, it is also important to highlight that we fit the `StandardScaler` class only once — on the training data — and use those parameters to transform the test set or any new data point.

Selecting meaningful features

If we notice that a model performs much better on a training dataset than on the test dataset, this observation is a strong indicator of **overfitting**. As we discussed in *Chapter 3, A Tour of Machine Learning Classifiers Using scikit-learn*, overfitting means the model fits the parameters too closely with regard to the particular observations in the training dataset, but does not generalize well to new data, and we say the model has a *high variance*. The reason for the overfitting is that our model is too complex for the given training data. Common solutions to reduce the generalization error are listed as follows:

- Collect more training data
- Introduce a penalty for complexity via regularization
- Choose a simpler model with fewer parameters
- Reduce the dimensionality of the data

Collecting more training data is often not applicable. In *Chapter 6, Learning Best Practices for Model Evaluation and Hyperparameter Tuning*, we will learn about a useful technique to check whether more training data is helpful at all. In the following sections, we will look at common ways to reduce overfitting by regularization and dimensionality reduction via feature selection, which leads to simpler models by requiring fewer parameters to be fitted to the data.

L1 and L2 regularization as penalties against model complexity

We recall from *Chapter 3, A Tour of Machine Learning Classifiers Using scikit-learn,* that **L2 regularization** is one approach to reduce the complexity of a model by penalizing large individual weights, where we defined the L2 norm of our weight vector **w** as follows:

$$L2 : \|\boldsymbol{w}\|_2^2 = \sum_{j=1}^{m} w_j^2$$

Another approach to reduce the model complexity is the related **L1 regularization**:

$$L1 : \|\boldsymbol{w}\|_1 = \sum_{j=1}^{m} |w_j|$$

Here, we simply replaced the square of the weights by the sum of the absolute values of the weights. In contrast to L2 regularization, L1 regularization usually yields sparse feature vectors; most feature weights will be zero. Sparsity can be useful in practice if we have a high-dimensional dataset with many features that are irrelevant, especially cases where we have more irrelevant dimensions than samples. In this sense, L1 regularization can be understood as a technique for feature selection.

A geometric interpretation of L2 regularization

As mentioned in the previous section, L2 regularization adds a penalty term to the cost function that effectively results in less extreme weight values compared to a model trained with an unregularized cost function. To better understand how L1 regularization encourages sparsity, let's take a step back and take a look at a geometric interpretation of regularization. Let us plot the contours of a convex cost function for two weight coefficients w_1 and w_2. Here, we will consider the **Sum of Squared Errors (SSE)** cost function that we used for Adaline in *Chapter 2, Training Simple Machine Learning Algorithms for Classification,* since it is spherical and easier to draw than the cost function of logistic regression; however, the same concepts apply to the latter. Remember that our goal is to find the combination of weight coefficients that minimize the cost function for the training data, as shown in the following figure (the point in the center of the ellipses):

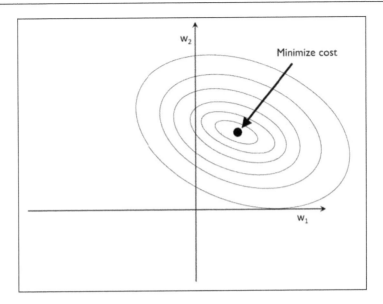

Now, we can think of regularization as adding a penalty term to the cost function to encourage smaller weights; or in other words, we penalize large weights.

Thus, by increasing the regularization strength via the regularization parameter λ, we shrink the weights towards zero and decrease the dependence of our model on the training data. Let us illustrate this concept in the following figure for the L2 penalty term:

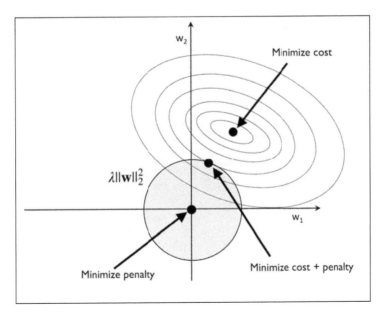

The quadratic L2 regularization term is represented by the shaded ball. Here, our weight coefficients cannot exceed our regularization budget—the combination of the weight coefficients cannot fall outside the shaded area. On the other hand, we still want to minimize the cost function. Under the penalty constraint, our best effort is to choose the point where the L2 ball intersects with the contours of the unpenalized cost function. The larger the value of the regularization parameter λ gets, the faster the penalized cost grows, which leads to a narrower L2 ball. For example, if we increase the regularization parameter towards infinity, the weight coefficients will become effectively zero, denoted by the center of the L2 ball. To summarize the main message of the example, our goal is to minimize the sum of the unpenalized cost plus the penalty term, which can be understood as adding bias and preferring a simpler model to reduce the variance in the absence of sufficient training data to fit the model.

Sparse solutions with L1 regularization

Now, let us discuss L1 regularization and sparsity. The main concept behind L1 regularization is similar to what we have discussed in the previous section. However, since the L1 penalty is the sum of the absolute weight coefficients (remember that the L2 term is quadratic), we can represent it as a diamond-shape budget, as shown in the following figure:

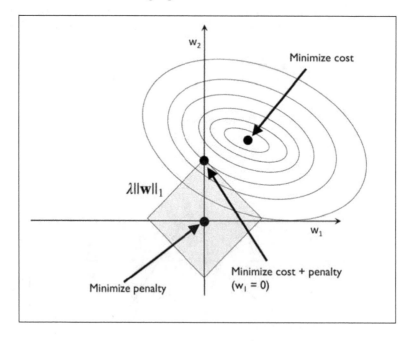

In the preceding figure, we can see that the contour of the cost function touches the L1 diamond at $w_1 = 0$. Since the contours of an L1 regularized system are sharp, it is more likely that the optimum — that is, the intersection between the ellipses of the cost function and the boundary of the L1 diamond — is located on the axes, which encourages sparsity.

 The mathematical details of why L1 regularization can lead to sparse solutions are beyond the scope of this book. If you are interested, an excellent explanation of L2 versus L1 regularization can be found in *Section 3.4, The Elements of Statistical Learning, Trevor Hastie, Robert Tibshirani, and Jerome Friedman, Springer Science+Business Media, 2009)*.

For regularized models in scikit-learn that support L1 regularization, we can simply set the penalty parameter to `'l1'` to obtain a sparse solution:

```
>>> from sklearn.linear_model import LogisticRegression
>>> LogisticRegression(penalty='l1')
```

Applied to the standardized Wine data, the L1 regularized logistic regression would yield the following sparse solution:

```
>>> lr = LogisticRegression(penalty='l1', C=1.0)
# Note that C=1.0 is the default. You can increase
# or decrease it to make the regularization effect
# stronger or weaker, respectively.
>>> lr.fit(X_train_std, y_train)
>>> print('Training accuracy:', lr.score(X_train_std, y_train))
Training accuracy: 1.0
>>> print('Test accuracy:', lr.score(X_test_std, y_test))
Test accuracy: 1.0
```

Both training and test accuracies (both 100 percent) indicate that our model does a perfect job on both datasets. When we access the intercept terms via the `lr.intercept_` attribute, we can see that the array returns three values:

```
>>> lr.intercept_
array([-1.26335036, -1.21602349, -2.37099041])
```

Since we fit the `LogisticRegression` object on a multiclass dataset, it uses the **One-versus-Rest (OvR)** approach by default, where the first intercept belongs to the model that fits class 1 versus class 2 and 3, the second value is the intercept of the model that fits class 2 versus class 1 and 3, and the third value is the intercept of the model that fits class 3 versus class 1 and 2:

```
>>> lr.coef_
array([[ 1.24559337, 0.18041967, 0.74328894, -1.16046277, 0. ,
```

```
      0., 1.1678711, 0., 0., 0., 0., 0.54941931, 2.51017406],
   [-1.53720749, -0.38727002, -0.99539203, 0.3651479,
    -0.0596352 , 0., 0.66833149, 0., 0., -1.9346134,
    1.23297955, 0., -2.23135027],
   [ 0.13579227, 0.16837686, 0.35723831, 0., 0., 0.,
    -2.43809275, 0., 0., 1.56391408, -0.81933286,
    -0.49187817, 0.]])
```

The weight array that we accessed via the `lr.coef_` attribute contains three rows of weight coefficients, one weight vector for each class. Each row consists of 13 weights where each weight is multiplied by the respective feature in the 13-dimensional Wine dataset to calculate the net input:

$$z = w_0 x_0 + \cdots + w_m x_m = \sum_{j=0}^{m} x_j w_j = \boldsymbol{w}^T \boldsymbol{x}$$

 In scikit-learn, w_0 corresponds to the `intercept_` and w_j with $j > 0$ correspond to the values in `coef_`.

As a result of L1 regularization, which serves as a method for feature selection, we just trained a model that is robust to the potentially irrelevant features in this dataset.

Strictly speaking, the weight vectors from the previous example are not necessarily sparse, though, because they contain more non-zero than zero entries. However, we could enforce sparsity (more zero entries) by further increasing the regularization strength—that is, choosing lower values for the C parameter.

In the last example on regularization in this chapter, we will vary the regularization strength and plot the regularization path—the weight coefficients of the different features for different regularization strengths:

```
>>> import matplotlib.pyplot as plt

>>> fig = plt.figure()
>>> ax = plt.subplot(111)

>>> colors = ['blue', 'green', 'red', 'cyan',
...           'magenta', 'yellow', 'black',
...           'pink', 'lightgreen', 'lightblue',
...           'gray', 'indigo', 'orange']
>>> weights, params = [], []
>>> for c in np.arange(-4., 6.):
...     lr = LogisticRegression(penalty='l1',
                                C=10.**c,
```

```
...                              random_state=0)
...          lr.fit(X_train_std, y_train)
...          weights.append(lr.coef_[1])
...          params.append(10**c)

>>> weights = np.array(weights)

>>> for column, color in zip(range(weights.shape[1]), colors):
...          plt.plot(params, weights[:, column],
...                   label=df_wine.columns[column + 1],
...                   color=color)
>>> plt.axhline(0, color='black', linestyle='--', linewidth=3)
>>> plt.xlim([10**(-5), 10**5])
>>> plt.ylabel('weight coefficient')
>>> plt.xlabel('C')
>>> plt.xscale('log')
>>> plt.legend(loc='upper left')
>>> ax.legend(loc='upper center',
...           bbox_to_anchor=(1.38, 1.03),
...           ncol=1, fancybox=True)
>>> plt.show()
```

The resulting plot provides us with further insights into the behavior of L1 regularization. As we can see, all feature weights will be zero if we penalize the model with a strong regularization parameter ($C < 0.1$); C is the inverse of the regularization parameter λ:

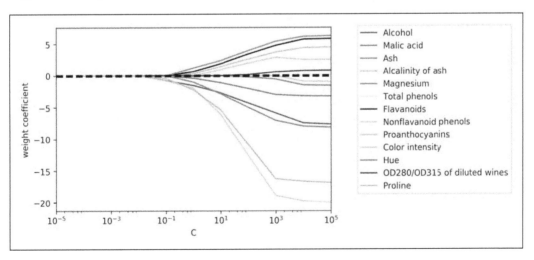

Sequential feature selection algorithms

An alternative way to reduce the complexity of the model and avoid overfitting is **dimensionality reduction** via feature selection, which is especially useful for unregularized models. There are two main categories of dimensionality reduction techniques: **feature selection** and **feature extraction**. Via feature selection, we select a subset of the original features, whereas in feature extraction, we derive information from the feature set to construct a new feature subspace.

In this section, we will take a look at a classic family of feature selection algorithms. In the next chapter, *Chapter 5, Compressing Data via Dimensionality Reduction,* we will learn about different feature extraction techniques to compress a dataset onto a lower-dimensional feature subspace.

Sequential feature selection algorithms are a family of greedy search algorithms that are used to reduce an initial d-dimensional feature space to a k-dimensional feature subspace where $k<d$. The motivation behind feature selection algorithms is to automatically select a subset of features that are most relevant to the problem, to improve computational efficiency or reduce the generalization error of the model by removing irrelevant features or noise, which can be useful for algorithms that don't support regularization.

A classic sequential feature selection algorithm is **Sequential Backward Selection** (**SBS**), which aims to reduce the dimensionality of the initial feature subspace with a minimum decay in performance of the classifier to improve upon computational efficiency. In certain cases, SBS can even improve the predictive power of the model if a model suffers from overfitting.

Greedy algorithms make locally optimal choices at each stage of a combinatorial search problem and generally yield a suboptimal solution to the problem, in contrast to **exhaustive search algorithms**, which evaluate all possible combinations and are guaranteed to find the optimal solution. However, in practice, an exhaustive search is often computationally not feasible, whereas greedy algorithms allow for a less complex, computationally more efficient solution.

The idea behind the SBS algorithm is quite simple: SBS sequentially removes features from the full feature subset until the new feature subspace contains the desired number of features. In order to determine which feature is to be removed at each stage, we need to define the criterion function J that we want to minimize. The criterion calculated by the criterion function can simply be the difference in performance of the classifier before and after the removal of a particular feature. Then, the feature to be removed at each stage can simply be defined as the feature that maximizes this criterion; or in more intuitive terms, at each stage we eliminate the feature that causes the least performance loss after removal. Based on the preceding definition of SBS, we can outline the algorithm in four simple steps:

1. Initialize the algorithm with $k=d$, where d is the dimensionality of the full feature space $\mathbf{X}_d$.

2. Determine the feature x^- that maximizes the criterion: $x^- = \operatorname{argmax} J(\mathbf{X}_k - x))$, where $x \in \mathbf{X}_k$.

3. Remove the feature x^- from the feature set: $\mathbf{X}_{k-1} = \mathbf{X}_k - x^-$; $k = k - 1$.

4. Terminate if k equals the number of desired features; otherwise, go to step 2.

> You can find a detailed evaluation of several sequential feature algorithms in *Comparative Study of Techniques for Large-Scale Feature Selection*, F. Ferri, P. Pudil, M. Hatef, and J. Kittler, pages 403-413, 1994.

Unfortunately, the SBS algorithm has not been implemented in scikit-learn yet. But since it is so simple, let us go ahead and implement it in Python from scratch:

```
from sklearn.base import clone
from itertools import combinations
import numpy as np
from sklearn.metrics import accuracy_score
from sklearn.model_selection import train_test_split


class SBS():
    def __init__(self, estimator, k_features,
                 scoring=accuracy_score,
                 test_size=0.25, random_state=1):
        self.scoring = scoring
        self.estimator = clone(estimator)
        self.k_features = k_features
        self.test_size = test_size
```

```
        self.random_state = random_state

    def fit(self, X, y):

        X_train, X_test, y_train, y_test = \
            train_test_split(X, y, test_size=self.test_size,
                                random_state=self.random_state)

        dim = X_train.shape[1]
        self.indices_ = tuple(range(dim))
        self.subsets_ = [self.indices_]
        score = self._calc_score(X_train, y_train,
                                    X_test, y_test, self.indices_)
        self.scores_ = [score]

        while dim > self.k_features:
            scores = []
            subsets = []

            for p in combinations(self.indices_, r=dim - 1):
                score = self._calc_score(X_train, y_train,
                                            X_test, y_test, p)
                scores.append(score)
                subsets.append(p)

            best = np.argmax(scores)
            self.indices_ = subsets[best]
            self.subsets_.append(self.indices_)
            dim -= 1

            self.scores_.append(scores[best])
        self.k_score_ = self.scores_[-1]

        return self

    def transform(self, X):
        return X[:, self.indices_]

    def _calc_score(self, X_train, y_train, X_test, y_test,
                    indices):
        self.estimator.fit(X_train[:, indices], y_train)
        y_pred = self.estimator.predict(X_test[:, indices])
        score = self.scoring(y_test, y_pred)
        return score
```

In the preceding implementation, we defined the `k_features` parameter to specify the desired number of features we want to return. By default, we use the `accuracy_score` from scikit-learn to evaluate the performance of a model (an estimator for classification) on the feature subsets. Inside the `while` loop of the `fit` method, the feature subsets created by the `itertools.combination` function are evaluated and reduced until the feature subset has the desired dimensionality. In each iteration, the accuracy score of the best subset is collected in a list, `self.scores_`, based on the internally created test dataset `X_test`. We will use those scores later to evaluate the results. The column indices of the final feature subset are assigned to `self.indices_`, which we can use via the `transform` method to return a new data array with the selected feature columns. Note that, instead of calculating the criterion explicitly inside the `fit` method, we simply removed the feature that is not contained in the best performing feature subset.

Now, let us see our SBS implementation in action using the KNN classifier from scikit-learn:

```
>>> import matplotlib.pyplot as plt
>>> from sklearn.neighbors import KNeighborsClassifier

>>> knn = KNeighborsClassifier(n_neighbors=5)

>>> sbs = SBS(knn, k_features=1)
>>> sbs.fit(X_train_std, y_train)
```

Although our SBS implementation already splits the dataset into a test and training dataset inside the `fit` function, we still fed the training dataset `X_train` to the algorithm. The SBS `fit` method will then create new training subsets for testing (validation) and training, which is why this test set is also called the **validation dataset**. This approach is necessary to prevent our *original* test set from becoming part of the training data.

Remember that our SBS algorithm collects the scores of the best feature subset at each stage, so let us move on to the more exciting part of our implementation and plot the classification accuracy of the KNN classifier that was calculated on the validation dataset. The code is as follows:

```
>>> k_feat = [len(k) for k in sbs.subsets_]

>>> plt.plot(k_feat, sbs.scores_, marker='o')
>>> plt.ylim([0.7, 1.02])
>>> plt.ylabel('Accuracy')
>>> plt.xlabel('Number of features')
>>> plt.grid()
>>> plt.show()
```

As we can see in the following figure, the accuracy of the KNN classifier improved on the validation dataset as we reduced the number of features, which is likely due to a decrease in the **curse of dimensionality** that we discussed in the context of the KNN algorithm in *Chapter 3, A Tour of Machine Learning Classifiers Using scikit-learn*. Also, we can see in the following plot that the classifier achieved 100 percent accuracy for *k={3, 7, 8, 9, 10, 11, 12}*:

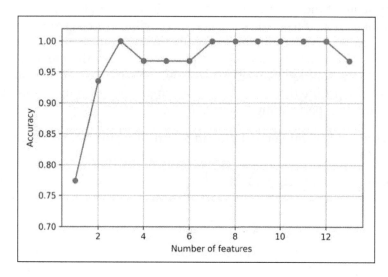

To satisfy our own curiosity, let's see what the smallest feature subset (*k=3*) that yielded such a good performance on the validation dataset looks like:

```
>>> k3 = list(sbs.subsets_[10])
>>> print(df_wine.columns[1:][k3])
Index(['Alcohol', 'Malic acid', 'OD280/OD315 of diluted wines'],
dtype='object')
```

Using the preceding code, we obtained the column indices of the three-feature subset from the 10th position in the `sbs.subsets_` attribute and returned the corresponding feature names from the column-index of the pandas Wine `DataFrame`.

Next let's evaluate the performance of the KNN classifier on the original test set:

```
>>> knn.fit(X_train_std, y_train)
>>> print('Training accuracy:', knn.score(X_train_std, y_train))
Training accuracy: 0.967741935484
>>> print('Test accuracy:', knn.score(X_test_std, y_test))
Test accuracy: 0.962962962963
```

In the preceding code section, we used the complete feature set and obtained approximately 97 percent accuracy on the training dataset and approximately 96 percent accuracy on the test, which indicates that our model already generalizes well to new data. Now, let us use the selected three-feature subset and see how well KNN performs:

```
>>> knn.fit(X_train_std[:, k3], y_train)
>>> print('Training accuracy:',
...           knn.score(X_train_std[:, k3], y_train))
Training accuracy: 0.951612903226
>>> print('Test accuracy:',
...           knn.score(X_test_std[:, k3], y_test))
Test accuracy: 0.925925925926
```

Using less than a quarter of the original features in the Wine dataset, the prediction accuracy on the test set declined slightly. This may indicate that those three features do not provide less discriminatory information than the original dataset. However, we also have to keep in mind that the Wine dataset is a small dataset, which is very susceptible to randomness — that is, the way we split the dataset into training and test subsets, and how we split the training dataset further into a training and validation subset.

While we did not increase the performance of the KNN model by reducing the number of features, we shrank the size of the dataset, which can be useful in real-world applications that may involve expensive data collection steps. Also, by substantially reducing the number of features, we obtain simpler models, which are easier to interpret.

> **Feature selection algorithms in scikit-learn**
>
> There are many more feature selection algorithms available via scikit-learn. Those include **recursive backward elimination** based on feature weights, tree-based methods to select features by importance, and univariate statistical tests. A comprehensive discussion of the different feature selection methods is beyond the scope of this book, but a good summary with illustrative examples can be found at http://scikit-learn.org/stable/modules/feature_selection.html. Furthermore, I implemented several different flavors of sequential feature selection, related to the simple SBS that we implemented previously. You can find these implementations in the Python package mlxtend at http://rasbt.github.io/mlxtend/user_guide/feature_selection/SequentialFeatureSelector/.

Assessing feature importance with random forests

In previous sections, you learned how to use L1 regularization to zero out irrelevant features via logistic regression, and use the SBS algorithm for feature selection and apply it to a KNN algorithm. Another useful approach to select relevant features from a dataset is to use a **random forest**, an ensemble technique that we introduced in *Chapter 3, A Tour of Machine Learning Classifiers Using scikit-learn*. Using a random forest, we can measure the feature importance as the averaged impurity decrease computed from all decision trees in the forest, without making any assumptions about whether our data is linearly separable or not. Conveniently, the random forest implementation in scikit-learn already collects the feature importance values for us so that we can access them via the `feature_importances_` attribute after fitting a `RandomForestClassifier`. By executing the following code, we will now train a forest of 500 trees on the Wine dataset and rank the 13 features by their respective importance measures — remember from our discussion in *Chapter 3, A Tour of Machine Learning Classifiers Using scikit-learn* that we don't need to use standardized or normalized features in tree-based models:

```
>>> from sklearn.ensemble import RandomForestClassifier

>>> feat_labels = df_wine.columns[1:]

>>> forest = RandomForestClassifier(n_estimators=500,
...                                 random_state=1)
>>> forest.fit(X_train, y_train)
>>> importances = forest.feature_importances_

>>> indices = np.argsort(importances)[::-1]

>>> for f in range(X_train.shape[1]):
...     print("%2d) %-*s %f" % (f + 1, 30,
...                             feat_labels[indices[f]],
...                             importances[indices[f]]))
>>> plt.title('Feature Importance')
>>> plt.bar(range(X_train.shape[1]),
...         importances[indices],
...         align='center')

>>> plt.xticks(range(X_train.shape[1]),
...            feat_labels[indices] rotation=90)
>>> plt.xlim([-1, X_train.shape[1]])
```

```
>>> plt.tight_layout()
>>> plt.show()
```

```
 1) Proline                       0.185453
 2) Flavanoids                    0.174751
 3) Color intensity               0.143920
 4) OD280/OD315 of diluted wines  0.136162
 5) Alcohol                       0.118529
 6) Hue                           0.058739
 7) Total phenols                 0.050872
 8) Magnesium                     0.031357
 9) Malic acid                    0.025648
10) Proanthocyanins               0.025570
11) Alcalinity of ash             0.022366
12) Nonflavanoid phenols          0.013354
13) Ash                           0.013279
```

After executing the code, we created a plot that ranks the different features in the Wine dataset by their relative importance; note that the feature importance values are normalized so that they sum up to 1.0:

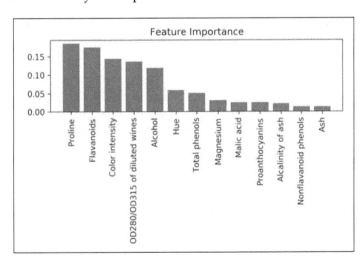

We can conclude that the proline and flavonoid levels, the color intensity, the OD280/OD315 diffraction, and the alcohol concentration of wine are the most discriminative features in the dataset based on the average impurity decrease in the 500 decision trees. Interestingly, two of the top-ranked features in the plot are also in the three-feature subset selection from the SBS algorithm that we implemented in the previous section (alcohol concentration and OD280/OD315 of diluted wines). However, as far as interpretability is concerned, the random forest technique comes with an important *gotcha* that is worth mentioning. If two or more features are highly correlated, one feature may be ranked very highly while the information of the other feature(s) may not be fully captured. On the other hand, we don't need to be concerned about this problem if we are merely interested in the predictive performance of a model rather than the interpretation of feature importance values.

To conclude this section about feature importance values and random forests, it is worth mentioning that scikit-learn also implements a `SelectFromModel` object that selects features based on a user-specified threshold after model fitting, which is useful if we want to use the `RandomForestClassifier` as a feature selector and intermediate step in a scikit-learn `Pipeline` object, which allows us to connect different preprocessing steps with an estimator, as we will see in *Chapter 6, Learning Best Practices for Model Evaluation and Hyperparameter Tuning*. For example, we could set the `threshold` to `0.1` to reduce the dataset to the five most important features using the following code:

```
>>> from sklearn.feature_selection import SelectFromModel

>>> sfm = SelectFromModel(forest, threshold=0.1, prefit=True)
>>> X_selected = sfm.transform(X_train)
>>> print('Number of features that meet this threshold criterion:',
...         X_selected.shape[1])

Number of features that meet this threshold criterion: 5

>>> for f in range(X_selected.shape[1]):
...     print("%2d) %-*s %f" % (f + 1, 30,
...                              feat_labels[indices[f]],
...                              importances[indices[f]]))
 1) Proline                        0.185453
 2) Flavanoids                     0.174751
 3) Color intensity                0.143920
 4) OD280/OD315 of diluted wines   0.136162
 5) Alcohol                        0.118529
```

Summary

We started this chapter by looking at useful techniques to make sure that we handle missing data correctly. Before we feed data to a machine learning algorithm, we also have to make sure that we encode categorical variables correctly, and we have seen how we can map ordinal and nominal feature values to integer representations.

Moreover, we briefly discussed L1 regularization, which can help us to avoid overfitting by reducing the complexity of a model. As an alternative approach to removing irrelevant features, we used a sequential feature selection algorithm to select meaningful features from a dataset.

In the next chapter, you will learn about yet another useful approach to dimensionality reduction: feature extraction. It allows us to compress features onto a lower-dimensional subspace, rather than removing features entirely as in feature selection.

5

Compressing Data via Dimensionality Reduction

In *Chapter 4, Building Good Training Sets – Data Preprocessing*, you learned about the different approaches for reducing the dimensionality of a dataset using different feature selection techniques. An alternative approach to feature selection for dimensionality reduction is **feature extraction**. In this chapter, you will learn about three fundamental techniques that will help us to summarize the information content of a dataset by transforming it onto a new feature subspace of lower dimensionality than the original one. Data compression is an important topic in machine learning, and it helps us to store and analyze the increasing amounts of data that are produced and collected in the modern age of technology.

In this chapter, we will cover the following topics:

- **Principal Component Analysis (PCA)** for unsupervised data compression
- **Linear Discriminant Analysis (LDA)** as a supervised dimensionality reduction technique for maximizing class separability
- Nonlinear dimensionality reduction via **Kernel Principal Component Analysis (KPCA)**

Unsupervised dimensionality reduction via principal component analysis

Similar to feature selection, we can use different feature extraction techniques to reduce the number of features in a dataset. The difference between feature selection and feature extraction is that while we maintain the original features when we used feature selection algorithms, such as *sequential backward selection*, we use feature extraction to transform or project the data onto a new feature space. In the context of dimensionality reduction, feature extraction can be understood as an approach to data compression with the goal of maintaining most of the relevant information. In practice, feature extraction is not only used to improve storage space or the computational efficiency of the learning algorithm, but can also improve the predictive performance by reducing the *curse of dimensionality*—especially if we are working with non-regularized models.

The main steps behind principal component analysis

In this section, we will discuss PCA, an unsupervised linear transformation technique that is widely used across different fields, most prominently for feature extraction and dimensionality reduction. Other popular applications of PCA include exploratory data analyses and de-noising of signals in stock market trading, and the analysis of genome data and gene expression levels in the field of bioinformatics.

PCA helps us to identify patterns in data based on the correlation between features. In a nutshell, PCA aims to find the directions of maximum variance in high-dimensional data and projects it onto a new subspace with equal or fewer dimensions than the original one. The orthogonal axes (principal components) of the new subspace can be interpreted as the directions of maximum variance given the constraint that the new feature axes are orthogonal to each other, as illustrated in the following figure:

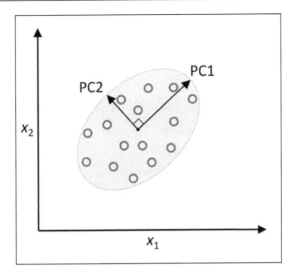

In the preceding figure, x_1 and x_2 are the original feature axes, and **PC1** and **PC2** are the principal components.

If we use PCA for dimensionality reduction, we construct a $d \times k$ –dimensional transformation matrix **W** that allows us to map a sample vector **x** onto a new k-dimensional feature subspace that has fewer dimensions than the original d– dimensional feature space:

$$x = [x_1, x_2, \ldots, x_d], \quad x \in \mathbb{R}^d$$

$$\downarrow xW, \quad W \in \mathbb{R}^{d \times k}$$

$$z = [z_1, z_2, \ldots, z_k], \quad z \in \mathbb{R}^k$$

As a result of transforming the original d-dimensional data onto this new k-dimensional subspace (typically $k \ll d$), the first principal component will have the largest possible variance, and all consequent principal components will have the largest variance given the constraint that these components are uncorrelated (orthogonal) to the other principal components—even if the input features are correlated, the resulting principal components will be mutually orthogonal (uncorrelated). Note that the PCA directions are highly sensitive to data scaling, and we need to standardize the features **prior** to PCA if the features were measured on different scales and we want to assign equal importance to all features.

Before looking at the PCA algorithm for dimensionality reduction in more detail, let's summarize the approach in a few simple steps:

1. Standardize the d-dimensional dataset.
2. Construct the covariance matrix.
3. Decompose the covariance matrix into its eigenvectors and eigenvalues.
4. Sort the eigenvalues by decreasing order to rank the corresponding eigenvectors.
5. Select k eigenvectors which correspond to the k largest eigenvalues, where k is the dimensionality of the new feature subspace ($k \leq d$).
6. Construct a projection matrix $\mathbf{W}$ from the "top" k eigenvectors.
7. Transform the d-dimensional input dataset $\mathbf{X}$ using the projection matrix $\mathbf{W}$ to obtain the new k-dimensional feature subspace.

In the following sections, we will perform a PCA step by step, using Python as a learning exercise. Then, we will see how to perform a PCA more conveniently using scikit-learn.

Extracting the principal components step by step

In this subsection, we will tackle the first four steps of a PCA:

1. Standardizing the data.
2. Constructing the covariance matrix.
3. Obtaining the eigenvalues and eigenvectors of the covariance matrix.
4. Sorting the eigenvalues by decreasing order to rank the eigenvectors.

First, we will start by loading the Wine dataset that we have been working with in *Chapter 4, Building Good Training Sets – Data Preprocessing*:

```
>>> import pandas as pd
df_wine = pd.read_csv('https://archive.ics.uci.edu/ml/'
                      'machine-learning-databases/wine/wine.data',
                      header=None)
```

You can find a copy of the Wine dataset (and all other datasets used in this book) in the code bundle of this book, which you can use if you are working offline or the UCI server at `https://archive.ics.uci.edu/ml/machine-learning-databases/wine/wine.data` is temporarily unavailable. For instance, to load the Wine dataset from a local directory, you can replace the following line:

```
df = pd.read_csv('https://archive.ics.uci.edu/ml/'
                 'machine-learning-databases/wine/wine.data',
                 header=None)
```

Replace it with this:

```
df = pd.read_csv('your/local/path/to/wine.data',
                 header=None)
```

Next, we will process the Wine data into separate training and test sets — using 70 percent and 30 percent of the data, respectively — and standardize it to unit variance:

```
>>> from sklearn.model_selection import train_test_split
>>> X, y = df_wine.iloc[:, 1:].values, df_wine.iloc[:, 0].values
>>> X_train, X_test, y_train, y_test = \
>>>     train_test_split(X, y, test_size=0.3,
...                      stratify=y,
...                      random_state=0)
>>> # standardize the features
>>> from sklearn.preprocessing import StandardScaler
>>> sc = StandardScaler()
>>> X_train_std = sc.fit_transform(X_train)
>>> X_test_std = sc.transform(X_test)
```

After completing the mandatory preprocessing by executing the preceding code, let's advance to the second step: constructing the covariance matrix. The symmetric $d \times d$-dimensional covariance matrix, where d is the number of dimensions in the dataset, stores the pairwise covariances between the different features. For example, the covariance between two features x_j and x_k on the population level can be calculated via the following equation:

$$\sigma_{jk} = \frac{1}{n} \sum_{i=1}^{n} \left(x_j^{(i)} - \mu_j \right) \left(x_k^{(i)} - \mu_k \right)$$

Here, μ_j and μ_k are the sample means of features j and k, respectively. Note that the sample means are zero if we standardized the dataset. A positive covariance between two features indicates that the features increase or decrease together, whereas a negative covariance indicates that the features vary in opposite directions. For example, the covariance matrix of three features can then be written as follows (note that Σ stands for the Greek uppercase letter **sigma**, which is not to be confused with the **sum** symbol):

$$\Sigma = \begin{bmatrix} \sigma_1^2 & \sigma_{12} & \sigma_{13} \\ \sigma_{21} & \sigma_2^2 & \sigma_{23} \\ \sigma_{31} & \sigma_{32} & \sigma_3^2 \end{bmatrix}$$

The eigenvectors of the covariance matrix represent the principal components (the directions of maximum variance), whereas the corresponding eigenvalues will define their magnitude. In the case of the Wine dataset, we would obtain 13 eigenvectors and eigenvalues from the 13 x 13-dimensional covariance matrix.

Now, for our third step, let's obtain the eigenpairs of the covariance matrix. As we remember from our introductory linear algebra classes, an eigenvector $\mathbf{v}$ satisfies the following condition:

$$\Sigma \mathbf{v} = \lambda \mathbf{v}$$

Here, λ is a scalar: the eigenvalue. Since the manual computation of eigenvectors and eigenvalues is a somewhat tedious and elaborate task, we will use the `linalg.eig` function from NumPy to obtain the eigenpairs of the Wine covariance matrix:

```
>>> import numpy as np
>>> cov_mat = np.cov(X_train_std.T)
>>> eigen_vals, eigen_vecs = np.linalg.eig(cov_mat)
>>> print('\nEigenvalues \n%s' % eigen_vals)
Eigenvalues
[ 4.84274532  2.41602459  1.54845825  0.96120438  0.84166161
  0.6620634   0.51828472  0.34650377  0.3131368   0.10754642
  0.21357215  0.15362835  0.1808613 ]
```

Using the `numpy.cov` function, we computed the covariance matrix of the standardized training dataset. Using the `linalg.eig` function, we performed the eigendecomposition, which yielded a vector (`eigen_vals`) consisting of 13 eigenvalues and the corresponding eigenvectors stored as columns in a 13 x 13-dimensional matrix (`eigen_vecs`).

The `numpy.linalg.eig` function was designed to operate on both symmetric and non-symmetric square matrices. However, you may find that it returns complex eigenvalues in certain cases.

A related function, `numpy.linalg.eigh`, has been implemented to decompose Hermetian matrices, which is a numerically more stable approach to work with symmetric matrices such as the covariance matrix; `numpy.linalg.eigh` always returns real eigenvalues.

Total and explained variance

Since we want to reduce the dimensionality of our dataset by compressing it onto a new feature subspace, we only select the subset of the eigenvectors (principal components) that contains most of the information (variance). The eigenvalues define the magnitude of the eigenvectors, so we have to sort the eigenvalues by decreasing magnitude; we are interested in the top k eigenvectors based on the values of their corresponding eigenvalues. But before we collect those k most informative eigenvectors, let us plot the *variance explained ratios* of the eigenvalues. The variance explained ratio of an eigenvalue λ_j is simply the fraction of an eigenvalue λ_j and the total sum of the eigenvalues:

$$\frac{\lambda_j}{\sum_{j=1}^{d} \lambda_j}$$

Using the NumPy `cumsum` function, we can then calculate the cumulative sum of explained variances, which we will then plot via Matplotlib's `step` function:

```
>>> tot = sum(eigen_vals)
>>> var_exp = [(i / tot) for i in
...             sorted(eigen_vals, reverse=True)]
>>> cum_var_exp = np.cumsum(var_exp)
>>> import matplotlib.pyplot as plt
>>> plt.bar(range(1,14), var_exp, alpha=0.5, align='center',
...          label='individual explained variance')
>>> plt.step(range(1,14), cum_var_exp, where='mid',
...          label='cumulative explained variance')
>>> plt.ylabel('Explained variance ratio')
>>> plt.xlabel('Principal component index')
>>> plt.legend(loc='best')
>>> plt.show()
```

The resulting plot indicates that the first principal component alone accounts for approximately 40 percent of the variance. Also, we can see that the first two principal components combined explain almost 60 percent of the variance in the dataset:

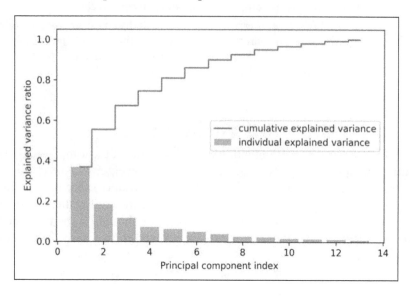

Although the explained variance plot reminds us of the feature importance values that we computed in *Chapter 4, Building Good Training Sets – Data Preprocessing,* via random forests, we should remind ourselves that PCA is an unsupervised method, which means that information about the class labels is ignored. Whereas a random forest uses the class membership information to compute the node impurities, variance measures the spread of values along a feature axis.

Feature transformation

After we have successfully decomposed the covariance matrix into eigenpairs, let's now proceed with the last three steps to transform the Wine dataset onto the new principal component axes. The remaining steps we are going to tackle in this section are the following ones:

- Select k eigenvectors, which correspond to the k largest eigenvalues, where k is the dimensionality of the new feature subspace ($k \leq d$).

- Construct a projection matrix W from the "top" k eigenvectors.

- Transform the d-dimensional input dataset X using the projection matrix W to obtain the new k-dimensional feature subspace.

Or, in less technical terms, we will sort the eigenpairs by descending order of the eigenvalues, construct a projection matrix from the selected eigenvectors, and use the projection matrix to transform the data onto the lower-dimensional subspace.

We start by sorting the eigenpairs by decreasing order of the eigenvalues:

```
>>> # Make a list of (eigenvalue, eigenvector) tuples
>>> eigen_pairs = [(np.abs(eigen_vals[i]), eigen_vecs[:, i])
...                for i in range(len(eigen_vals))]
>>> # Sort the (eigenvalue, eigenvector) tuples from high to low
>>> eigen_pairs.sort(key=lambda k: k[0], reverse=True)
```

Next, we collect the two eigenvectors that correspond to the two largest eigenvalues, to capture about 60 percent of the variance in this dataset. Note that we only chose two eigenvectors for the purpose of illustration, since we are going to plot the data via a two-dimensional scatter plot later in this subsection. In practice, the number of principal components has to be determined by a trade-off between computational efficiency and the performance of the classifier:

```
>>> w = np.hstack((eigen_pairs[0][1][:, np.newaxis],
...                eigen_pairs[1][1][:, np.newaxis]))
>>> print('Matrix W:\n', w)
Matrix W:
 [[-0.13724218   0.50303478]
 [ 0.24724326   0.16487119]
 [-0.02545159   0.24456476]
 [ 0.20694508  -0.11352904]
 [-0.15436582   0.28974518]
 [-0.39376952   0.05080104]
 [-0.41735106  -0.02287338]
 [ 0.30572896   0.09048885]
 [-0.30668347   0.00835233]
 [ 0.07554066   0.54977581]
 [-0.32613263  -0.20716433]
 [-0.36861022  -0.24902536]
 [-0.29669651   0.38022942]]
```

By executing the preceding code, we have created a 13 x 2-dimensional projection matrix **W** from the top two eigenvectors.

Depending on which version of NumPy and LAPACK you are using, you may obtain the matrix W with its signs flipped. Please note that this is not an issue; if **v** is an eigenvector of a matrix Σ, we have:

$$\Sigma v = \lambda v$$

Here, **v** is the eigenvector, and **-v** is also an eigenvector, which we can show as follows. Using basic algebra, we can multiply both sides of the equation by a scalar α:

$$\alpha \sum \mathbf{v} = \alpha \lambda \mathbf{v}$$

Since matrix multiplication is associative for scalar multiplication, we can then rearrange this to the following:

$$\sum (\alpha \mathbf{v}) = \lambda (\alpha \mathbf{v})$$

Now, we can see that α**v** is an eigenvector with the same eigenvalue λ for both $\alpha = 1$ and $\alpha = -1$. Hence, both **v** and **-v** are eigenvectors.

Using the projection matrix, we can now transform a sample **x** (represented as a 1 x 13-dimensional row vector) onto the PCA subspace (the principal components one and two) obtaining $\boldsymbol{x'}$, now a two-dimensional sample vector consisting of two new features:

$$\boldsymbol{x'} = \boldsymbol{xW}$$

```
>>> X_train_std[0].dot(w)
array([ 2.38299011,  0.45458499])
```

Similarly, we can transform the entire 124 x 13-dimensional training dataset onto the two principal components by calculating the matrix dot product:

$$\boldsymbol{X'} = \boldsymbol{XW}$$

```
>>> X_train_pca = X_train_std.dot(w)
```

Lastly, let us visualize the transformed Wine training set, now stored as an 124 x 2-dimensional matrix, in a two-dimensional scatterplot:

```
>>> colors = ['r', 'b', 'g']
>>> markers = ['s', 'x', 'o']
>>> for l, c, m in zip(np.unique(y_train), colors, markers):
...     plt.scatter(X_train_pca[y_train==l, 0],
...             X_train_pca[y_train==l, 1],
```

```
...                          c=c, label=l, marker=m)
>>> plt.xlabel('PC 1')
>>> plt.ylabel('PC 2')
>>> plt.legend(loc='lower left')
>>> plt.show()
```

As we can see in the resulting plot, the data is more spread along the *x*-axis—the first principal component—than the second principal component (*y*-axis), which is consistent with the explained variance ratio plot that we created in the previous subsection. However, we can intuitively see that a linear classifier will likely be able to separate the classes well:

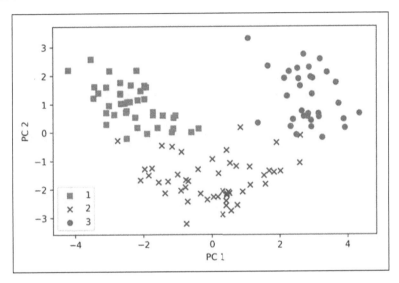

Although we encoded the class label information for the purpose of illustration in the preceding scatter plot, we have to keep in mind that PCA is an unsupervised technique that doesn't use any class label information.

Principal component analysis in scikit-learn

Although the verbose approach in the previous subsection helped us to follow the inner workings of PCA, we will now discuss how to use the PCA class implemented in scikit-learn. The PCA class is another one of scikit-learn's transformer classes, where we first fit the model using the training data before we transform both the training data and the test dataset using the same model parameters. Now, let's use the PCA class from scikit-learn on the Wine training dataset, classify the transformed samples via logistic regression, and visualize the decision regions via the plot_decision_regions function that we defined in *Chapter 2, Training Simple Machine Learning Algorithms for Classification*:

```
from matplotlib.colors import ListedColormap

def plot_decision_regions(X, y, classifier, resolution=0.02):

    # setup marker generator and color map
    markers = ('s', 'x', 'o', '^', 'v')
    colors = ('red', 'blue', 'lightgreen', 'gray', 'cyan')
    cmap = ListedColormap(colors[:len(np.unique(y))])

    # plot the decision surface
    x1_min, x1_max = X[:, 0].min() - 1, X[:, 0].max() + 1
    x2_min, x2_max = X[:, 1].min() - 1, X[:, 1].max() + 1
    xx1, xx2 = np.meshgrid(np.arange(x1_min, x1_max, resolution),
                           np.arange(x2_min, x2_max, resolution))
    Z = classifier.predict(np.array([xx1.ravel(), xx2.ravel()]).T)
    Z = Z.reshape(xx1.shape)
    plt.contourf(xx1, xx2, Z, alpha=0.4, cmap=cmap)
    plt.xlim(xx1.min(), xx1.max())
    plt.ylim(xx2.min(), xx2.max())

    # plot class samples
    for idx, cl in enumerate(np.unique(y)):
        plt.scatter(x=X[y == cl, 0],
                    y=X[y == cl, 1],
                    alpha=0.6,
                    c=cmap(idx),
                    edgecolor='black',
                    marker=markers[idx],
                    label=cl)

>>> from sklearn.linear_model import LogisticRegression
>>> from sklearn.decomposition import PCA
>>> pca = PCA(n_components=2)
>>> lr = LogisticRegression()
>>> X_train_pca = pca.fit_transform(X_train_std)
>>> X_test_pca = pca.transform(X_test_std)
>>> lr.fit(X_train_pca, y_train)
>>> plot_decision_regions(X_train_pca, y_train, classifier=lr)
>>> plt.xlabel('PC 1')
>>> plt.ylabel('PC 2')
>>> plt.legend(loc='lower left')
>>> plt.show()
```

By executing the preceding code, we should now see the decision regions for the training data reduced to two principal component axes:

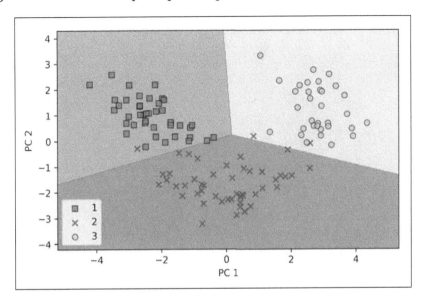

When we compare PCA projections via scikit-learn with our own PCA implementation, it can happen that the resulting plots are mirror images of each other. Note that this is not due to an error in either of those two implementations, but the reason for this difference is that, depending on the eigensolver, eigenvectors can have either negative or positive signs. Not that it matters, but we could simply revert the mirror image by multiplying the data by -1 if we wanted to; note that eigenvectors are typically scaled to unit length 1. For the sake of completeness, let's plot the decision regions of the logistic regression on the transformed test dataset to see if it can separate the classes well:

```
>>> plot_decision_regions(X_test_pca, y_test, classifier=lr)
>>> plt.xlabel('PC1')
>>> plt.ylabel('PC2')
>>> plt.legend(loc='lower left')
>>> plt.show()
```

After we plotted the decision regions for the test set by executing the preceding code, we can see that logistic regression performs quite well on this small two-dimensional feature subspace and only misclassifies very few samples in the test dataset:

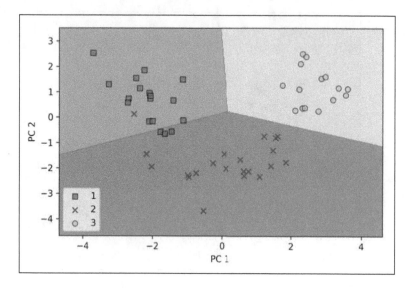

If we are interested in the explained variance ratios of the different principal components, we can simply initialize the PCA class with the n_components parameter set to None, so all principal components are kept and the explained variance ratio can then be accessed via the explained_variance_ratio_ attribute:

```
>>> pca = PCA(n_components=None)
>>> X_train_pca = pca.fit_transform(X_train_std)
>>> pca.explained_variance_ratio_
array([ 0.36951469,  0.18434927,  0.11815159,  0.07334252,
0.06422108, 0.05051724,  0.03954654,  0.02643918,  0.02389319,
0.01629614, 0.01380021,  0.01172226,  0.00820609])
```

Note that we set n_components=None when we initialized the PCA class so that it will return all principal components in a sorted order instead of performing a dimensionality reduction.

Supervised data compression via linear discriminant analysis

Linear Discriminant Analysis (LDA) can be used as a technique for feature extraction to increase the computational efficiency and reduce the degree of overfitting due to the curse of dimensionality in non-regularized models.

The general concept behind LDA is very similar to PCA. Whereas PCA attempts to find the orthogonal component axes of maximum variance in a dataset, the goal in LDA is to find the feature subspace that optimizes class separability. In the following sections, we will discuss the similarities between LDA and PCA in more detail and walk through the LDA approach step by step.

Principal component analysis versus linear discriminant analysis

Both PCA and LDA are linear transformation techniques that can be used to reduce the number of dimensions in a dataset; the former is an unsupervised algorithm, whereas the latter is supervised. Thus, we might intuitively think that LDA is a superior feature extraction technique for classification tasks compared to PCA. However, A.M. Martinez reported that preprocessing via PCA tends to result in better classification results in an image recognition task in certain cases, for instance if each class consists of only a small number of samples (*PCA Versus LDA, A. M. Martinez* and *A. C. Kak, IEEE Transactions on Pattern Analysis and Machine Intelligence, 23(2): 228-233, 2001*).

LDA is sometimes also called Fisher's LDA. Ronald A. Fisher initially formulated *Fisher's Linear Discriminant* for two-class classification problems in 1936 (*The Use of Multiple Measurements in Taxonomic Problems, R. A. Fisher, Annals of Eugenics, 7(2): 179-188, 1936*). Fisher's linear discriminant was later generalized for multi-class problems by C. Radhakrishna Rao under the assumption of equal class covariances and normally distributed classes in 1948, which we now call LDA (*The Utilization of Multiple Measurements in Problems of Biological Classification, C. R. Rao, Journal of the Royal Statistical Society. Series B (Methodological), 10(2): 159-203, 1948*).

The following figure summarizes the concept of LDA for a two-class problem. Samples from class 1 are shown as circles, and samples from class 2 are shown as crosses:

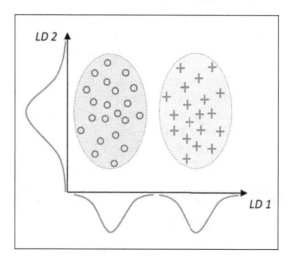

A linear discriminant, as shown on the x-axis (LD 1), would separate the two normal distributed classes well. Although the exemplary linear discriminant shown on the y-axis (LD 2) captures a lot of the variance in the dataset, it would fail as a good linear discriminant since it does not capture any of the class-discriminatory information.

One assumption in LDA is that the data is normally distributed. Also, we assume that the classes have identical covariance matrices and that the samples are statistically independent of each other. However, even if one or more of those assumptions are (slightly) violated, LDA for dimensionality reduction can still work reasonably well (*Pattern Classification 2nd Edition, R. O. Duda, P. E. Hart, and D. G. Stork, New York, 2001*).

The inner workings of linear discriminant analysis

Before we dive into the code implementation, let's briefly summarize the main steps that are required to perform LDA:

1. Standardize the d-dimensional dataset (d is the number of features).
2. For each class, compute the d-dimensional mean vector.
3. Construct the between-class scatter matrix S_B and the within-class scatter matrix S_w.

4. Compute the eigenvectors and corresponding eigenvalues of the matrix $S_w^{-1}S_B$.

5. Sort the eigenvalues by decreasing order to rank the corresponding eigenvectors.

6. Choose the k eigenvectors that correspond to the k largest eigenvalues to construct a $d \times k$-dimensional transformation matrix $\mathbf{W}$; the eigenvectors are the columns of this matrix.

7. Project the samples onto the new feature subspace using the transformation matrix $\mathbf{W}$.

As we can see, LDA is quite similar to PCA in the sense that we are decomposing matrices into eigenvalues and eigenvectors, which will form the new lower-dimensional feature space. However, as mentioned before, LDA takes class label information into account, which is represented in the form of the mean vectors computed in step 2. In the following sections, we will discuss these seven steps in more detail, accompanied by illustrative code implementations.

Computing the scatter matrices

Since we already standardized the features of the Wine dataset in the PCA section at the beginning of this chapter, we can skip the first step and proceed with the calculation of the mean vectors, which we will use to construct the within-class scatter matrix and between-class scatter matrix, respectively. Each mean vector $\mathbf{m}_i$ stores the mean feature value μ_m with respect to the samples of class i:

$$\mathbf{m}_i = \frac{1}{n_i} \sum_{x \in D_i}^{c} \mathbf{x}_m$$

This results in three mean vectors:

$$\mathbf{m}_i = \begin{bmatrix} \mu_{i,alcohol} \\ \mu_{i,malic\ acid} \\ \vdots \\ \mu_{i,proline} \end{bmatrix} \quad i \in \{1,2,3\}$$

```
>>> np.set_printoptions(precision=4)
>>> mean_vecs = []
>>> for label in range(1,4):
```

```
    ...        mean_vecs.append(np.mean(
    ...                   X_train_std[y_train==label], axis=0))
    ...        print('MV %s: %s\n' % (label, mean_vecs[label-1]))
MV 1: [ 0.9066 -0.3497  0.3201 -0.7189  0.5056  0.8807  0.9589 -0.5516
 0.5416  0.2338  0.5897  0.6563  1.2075]

MV 2: [-0.8749 -0.2848 -0.3735  0.3157 -0.3848 -0.0433  0.0635 -0.0946
 0.0703 -0.8286  0.3144  0.3608 -0.7253]

MV 3: [ 0.1992  0.866   0.1682  0.4148 -0.0451 -1.0286 -1.2876  0.8287
-0.7795  0.9649 -1.209  -1.3622 -0.4013]
```

Using the mean vectors, we can now compute the within-class scatter matrix S_W:

$$S_W = \sum_{i=1}^{c} S_i$$

This is calculated by summing up the individual scatter matrices S_i of each individual class i:

$$S_i = \sum_{x \in D_i}^{c} (x - m_i)(x - m_i)^T$$

```
>>> d = 13 # number of features
>>> S_W = np.zeros((d, d))
>>> for label, mv in zip(range(1, 4), mean_vecs):
...        class_scatter = np.zeros((d, d))
>>>        for row in X_train_std[y_train == label]:
...            row, mv = row.reshape(d, 1), mv.reshape(d, 1)
...            class_scatter += (row - mv).dot((row - mv).T)
...        S_W += class_scatter
>>> print('Within-class scatter matrix: %sx%s' % (
...        S_W.shape[0], S_W.shape[1]))
Within-class scatter matrix: 13x13
```

The assumption that we are making when we are computing the scatter matrices is that the class labels in the training set are uniformly distributed. However, if we print the number of class labels, we see that this assumption is violated:

```
>>> print('Class label distribution: %s'
...        % np.bincount(y_train)[1:])
Class label distribution: [41 50 33]
```

Thus, we want to scale the individual scatter matrices S_i before we sum them up as scatter matrix S_W. When we divide the scatter matrices by the number of class-samples n_i, we can see that computing the scatter matrix is in fact the same as computing the covariance matrix Σ_i – the covariance matrix is a normalized version of the scatter matrix:

$$\Sigma_i = \frac{1}{n_i} S_i = \frac{1}{n_i} \sum_{x \in D_i}^{c} \left(x - m_i \right) \left(x - m_i \right)^T$$

```
>>> d = 13 # number of features
>>> S_W = np.zeros((d, d))
>>> for label,mv in zip(range(1, 4), mean_vecs):
...     class_scatter = np.cov(X_train_std[y_train==label].T)
...     S_W += class_scatter
>>> print('Scaled within-class scatter matrix: %sx%s'
...          % (S_W.shape[0], S_W.shape[1]))
Scaled within-class scatter matrix: 13x13
```

After we computed the scaled within-class scatter matrix (or covariance matrix), we can move on to the next step and compute the between-class scatter matrix S_B:

$$S_B = \sum_{i=1}^{c} n_i \left(m_i - m \right) \left(m_i - m \right)^T$$

Here, m is the overall mean that is computed, including samples from all classes:

```
>>> mean_overall = np.mean(X_train_std, axis=0)
>>> d = 13  # number of features
>>> S_B = np.zeros((d, d))
>>> for i, mean_vec in enumerate(mean_vecs):
...     n = X_train[y_train == i + 1, :].shape[0]
...     mean_vec = mean_vec.reshape(d, 1)   # make column vector
...     mean_overall = mean_overall.reshape(d, 1)
...     S_B += n * (mean_vec - mean_overall).dot(
...               (mean_vec - mean_overall).T)
>>> print('Between-class scatter matrix: %sx%s' % (
...               S_B.shape[0], S_B.shape[1]))
Between-class scatter matrix: 13x1
```

Selecting linear discriminants for the new feature subspace

The remaining steps of the LDA are similar to the steps of the PCA. However, instead of performing the eigendecomposition on the covariance matrix, we solve the generalized eigenvalue problem of the matrix $S_w^{-1}S_B$:

```
>>> eigen_vals, eigen_vecs =\
...             np.linalg.eig(np.linalg.inv(S_W).dot(S_B))
```

After we computed the eigenpairs, we can now sort the eigenvalues in descending order:

```
>>> eigen_pairs = [(np.abs(eigen_vals[i]), eigen_vecs[:,i])
...                for i in range(len(eigen_vals))]
>>> eigen_pairs = sorted(eigen_pairs,
...                key=lambda k: k[0], reverse=True)
>>> print('Eigenvalues in descending order:\n')
>>> for eigen_val in eigen_pairs:
...     print(eigen_val[0])


Eigenvalues in descending order:

349.617808906
172.76152219
3.78531345125e-14
2.11739844822e-14
1.51646188942e-14
1.51646188942e-14
1.35795671405e-14
1.35795671405e-14
7.58776037165e-15
5.90603998447e-15
5.90603998447e-15
2.25644197857e-15
0.0
```

In LDA, the number of linear discriminants is at most $c-1$, where c is the number of class labels, since the in-between scatter matrix S_B is the sum of c matrices with rank 1 or less. We can indeed see that we only have two nonzero eigenvalues (the eigenvalues 3-13 are not exactly zero, but this is due to the floating point arithmetic in NumPy).

Note that in the rare case of perfect collinearity (all aligned sample points fall on a straight line), the covariance matrix would have rank one, which would result in only one eigenvector with a nonzero eigenvalue.

To measure how much of the class-discriminatory information is captured by the linear discriminants (eigenvectors), let's plot the linear discriminants by decreasing eigenvalues similar to the explained variance plot that we created in the PCA section. For simplicity, we will call the content of class-discriminatory information **discriminability**:

```
>>> tot = sum(eigen_vals.real)
>>> discr = [(i / tot) for i in sorted(eigen_vals.real, reverse=True)]
>>> cum_discr = np.cumsum(discr)
>>> plt.bar(range(1, 14), discr, alpha=0.5, align='center',
...          label='individual "discriminability"')
>>> plt.step(range(1, 14), cum_discr, where='mid',
...          label='cumulative "discriminability"')
>>> plt.ylabel('"discriminability" ratio')
>>> plt.xlabel('Linear Discriminants')
>>> plt.ylim([-0.1, 1.1])
>>> plt.legend(loc='best')
>>> plt.show()
```

As we can see in the resulting figure, the first two linear discriminants alone capture 100 percent of the useful information in the Wine training dataset:

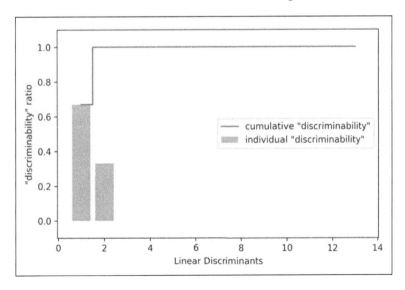

Let's now stack the two most discriminative eigenvector columns to create the transformation matrix **W**:

```
>>> w = np.hstack((eigen_pairs[0][1][:, np.newaxis].real,
...                eigen_pairs[1][1][:, np.newaxis].real))
>>> print('Matrix W:\n', w)
Matrix W:
 [[-0.1481 -0.4092]
 [ 0.0908 -0.1577]
 [-0.0168 -0.3537]
 [ 0.1484  0.3223]
 [-0.0163 -0.0817]
 [ 0.1913  0.0842]
 [-0.7338  0.2823]
 [-0.075  -0.0102]
 [ 0.0018  0.0907]
 [ 0.294  -0.2152]
 [-0.0328  0.2747]
 [-0.3547 -0.0124]
 [-0.3915 -0.5958]]
```

Projecting samples onto the new feature space

Using the transformation matrix **W** that we created in the previous subsection, we can now transform the training dataset by multiplying the matrices:

$$X' = XW$$

```
>>> X_train_lda = X_train_std.dot(w)
>>> colors = ['r', 'b', 'g']
>>> markers = ['s', 'x', 'o']
>>> for l, c, m in zip(np.unique(y_train), colors, markers):
...     plt.scatter(X_train_lda[y_train==l, 0],
...                 X_train_lda[y_train==l, 1] * (-1),
...                 c=c, label=l, marker=m)
>>> plt.xlabel('LD 1')
>>> plt.ylabel('LD 2')
>>> plt.legend(loc='lower right')
>>> plt.show()
```

As we can see in the resulting plot, the three wine classes are now perfectly linearly separable in the new feature subspace:

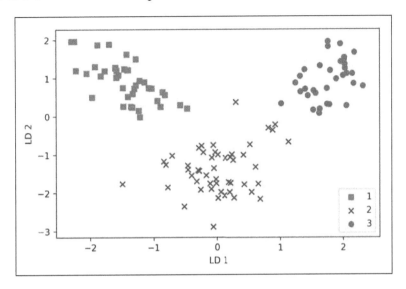

LDA via scikit-learn

The step-by-step implementation was a good exercise to understand the inner workings of an LDA and understand the differences between LDA and PCA. Now, let's look at the LDA class implemented in scikit-learn:

```
>>> from sklearn.discriminant_analysis import
...     LinearDiscriminantAnalysis as LDA
>>> lda = LDA(n_components=2)
>>> X_train_lda = lda.fit_transform(X_train_std, y_train)
```

Next, let's see how the logistic regression classifier handles the lower-dimensional training dataset after the LDA transformation:

```
>>> lr = LogisticRegression()
>>> lr = lr.fit(X_train_lda, y_train)
>>> plot_decision_regions(X_train_lda, y_train, classifier=lr)
>>> plt.xlabel('LD 1')
>>> plt.ylabel('LD 2')
>>> plt.legend(loc='lower left')
>>> plt.show()
```

Looking at the resulting plot, we see that the logistic regression model misclassifies one of the samples from class 2:

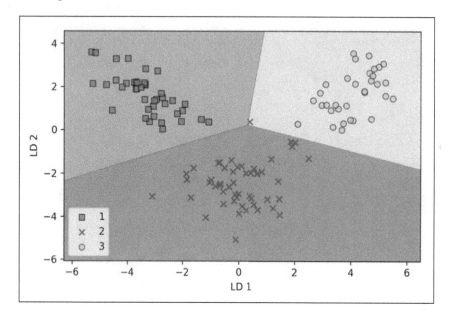

By lowering the regularization strength, we could probably shift the decision boundaries so that the logistic regression model classifies all samples in the training dataset correctly. However, and more importantly, let us take a look at the results on the test set:

```
>>> X_test_lda = lda.transform(X_test_std)
>>> plot_decision_regions(X_test_lda, y_test, classifier=lr)
>>> plt.xlabel('LD 1')
>>> plt.ylabel('LD 2')
>>> plt.legend(loc='lower left')
>>> plt.show()
```

As we can see in the following plot, the logistic regression classifier is able to get a perfect accuracy score for classifying the samples in the test dataset by only using a two-dimensional feature subspace instead of the original 13 Wine features:

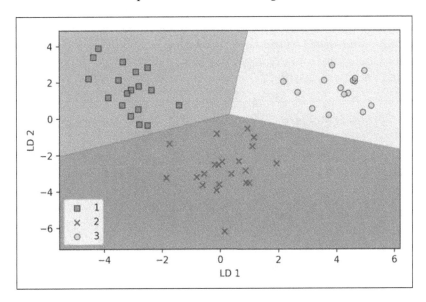

Using kernel principal component analysis for nonlinear mappings

Many machine learning algorithms make assumptions about the linear separability of the input data. You learned that the perceptron even requires perfectly linearly separable training data to converge. Other algorithms that we have covered so far assume that the lack of perfect linear separability is due to noise: Adaline, logistic regression, and the (standard) SVM to just name a few.

However, if we are dealing with nonlinear problems, which we may encounter rather frequently in real-world applications, linear transformation techniques for dimensionality reduction, such as PCA and LDA, may not be the best choice. In this section, we will take a look at a kernelized version of PCA, or KPCA, which relates to the concepts of kernel SVM that we remember from *Chapter 3, A Tour of Machine Learning Classifiers Using scikit-learn*. Using kernel PCA, we will learn how to transform data that is not linearly separable onto a new, lower-dimensional subspace that is suitable for linear classifiers.

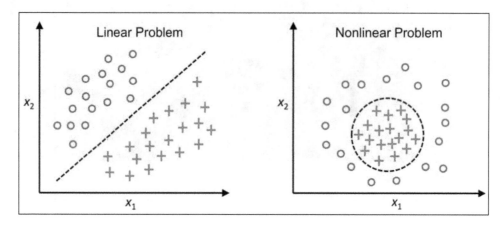

Kernel functions and the kernel trick

As we remember from our discussion about kernel SVMs in *Chapter 3, A Tour of Machine Learning Classifiers Using scikit-learn*, we can tackle nonlinear problems by projecting them onto a new feature space of higher dimensionality where the classes become linearly separable. To transform the samples $x \in \mathbb{R}^d$ onto this higher k-dimensional subspace, we defined a nonlinear mapping function ϕ:

$$\phi : \mathbb{R}^d \to \mathbb{R}^k \quad \left(k \gg d \right)$$

We can think of ϕ as a function that creates nonlinear combinations of the original features to map the original d-dimensional dataset onto a larger, k-dimensional feature space. For example, if we had a feature vector $x \in \mathbb{R}^d$ (x is a column vector consisting of d features) with two dimensions $(d = 2)$, a potential mapping onto a 3D-space could be:

$$x = \left[x_1, \, x_2 \right]^T$$

$$\downarrow \phi$$

$$\mathbf{z} = \left[x_1^2, \sqrt{2 x_1 x_2}, x_2^2 \right]^T$$

In other words, we perform a nonlinear mapping via kernel PCA that transforms the data onto a higher-dimensional space. We then use standard PCA in this higher-dimensional space to project the data back onto a lower-dimensional space where the samples can be separated by a linear classifier (under the condition that the samples can be separated by density in the input space). However, one downside of this approach is that it is computationally very expensive, and this is where we use the **kernel trick**. Using the kernel trick, we can compute the similarity between two high-dimension feature vectors in the original feature space.

Before we proceed with more details about the kernel trick to tackle this computationally expensive problem, let us think back to the standard PCA approach that we implemented at the beginning of this chapter. We computed the covariance between two features k and j as follows:

$$\sigma_{jk} = \frac{1}{n} \sum_{i=1}^{n} \left(x_j^{(i)} - \mu_j \right) \left(x_k^{(i)} - \mu_k \right)$$

Since the standardizing of features centers them at mean zero, for instance, $\mu_j = 0$ and $\mu_k = 0$, we can simplify this equation as follows:

$$\sigma_{jk} = \frac{1}{n}\sum_{i=1}^{n} x_j^{(i)} x_k^{(i)}$$

Note that the preceding equation refers to the covariance between two features; now, let us write the general equation to calculate the covariance matrix Σ:

$$\Sigma = \frac{1}{n}\sum_{i=1}^{n} x^{(i)}\, x^{(i)^T}$$

Bernhard Scholkopf generalized this approach (*Kernel principal component analysis, B. Scholkopf, A. Smola,* and *K.R. Muller,* pages 583-588, 1997) so that we can replace the dot products between samples in the original feature space with the nonlinear feature combinations via ϕ:

$$\Sigma = \frac{1}{n}\sum_{i=1}^{n} \phi\left(x^{(i)}\right)\phi(x^{(i)})^T$$

To obtain the eigenvectors — the principal components — from this covariance matrix, we have to solve the following equation:

$$\Sigma v = \lambda v$$

$$\Rightarrow \frac{1}{n}\sum_{i=1}^{n} \phi\left(x^{(i)}\right)\phi\left(x^{(i)}\right)^T v = \lambda v$$

$$\Rightarrow v = \frac{1}{n\lambda}\sum_{i=1}^{n} \phi\left(x^{(i)}\right)\phi\left(x^{(i)}\right)^T v = \sum_{i=1}^{n} a^{(i)}\phi\left(x^{(i)}\right)$$

Here, λ and **v** are the eigenvalues and eigenvectors of the covariance matrix Σ, and **a** can be obtained by extracting the eigenvectors of the kernel (similarity) matrix **K**, as we will see in the next paragraphs.

The derivation of the kernel matrix can be shown as follows. First, let's write the covariance matrix as in matrix notation, where $\phi(X)$ is an n x k-dimensional matrix:

$$\Sigma = \frac{1}{n}\sum_{i=1}^{n}\phi\left(x^{(i)}\right)\phi\left(x^{(i)}\right)^{T} = \frac{1}{n}\phi(X)^{T}\phi(X)$$

Now, we can write the eigenvector equation as follows:

$$v = \sum_{i=1}^{n}a^{(i)}\phi\left(x^{(i)}\right) = \phi(X)^{T}a$$

Since $\Sigma v = \lambda v$, we get:

$$\frac{1}{n}\phi(X)^{T}\phi(X)\phi(X)^{T}a = \lambda\phi(X)^{T}a$$

Multiplying it by $\phi(X)$ on both sides yields the following result:

$$\frac{1}{n}\phi(X)\phi(X)^{T}\phi(X)\phi(X)^{T}a = \lambda\phi(X)\phi(X)^{T}a$$

$$\Rightarrow \frac{1}{n}\phi(X)\phi(X)^{T}a = \lambda a$$

$$\Rightarrow \frac{1}{n}Ka = \lambda a$$

Here, **K** is the similarity (kernel) matrix:

$$K = \phi(X)\phi(X)^{T}$$

As we recall from the *Solving nonlinear problems using a kernel SVM* section in *Chapter 3, A Tour of Machine Learning Classifiers Using scikit-learn*, we use the kernel trick to avoid calculating the pairwise dot products of the samples **x** under ϕ explicitly by using a kernel function κ so that we don't need to calculate the eigenvectors explicitly:

$$\kappa\left(x^{(i)},x^{(j)}\right)=\phi\left(x^{(i)}\right)^{T}\phi\left(x^{(j)}\right)$$

In other words, what we obtain after kernel PCA are the samples already projected onto the respective components, rather than constructing a transformation matrix as in the standard PCA approach. Basically, the kernel function (or simply **kernel**) can be understood as a function that calculates a dot product between two vectors—a measure of similarity.

The most commonly used kernels are as follows:

- The polynomial kernel:

$$\kappa\left(x^{(i)},x^{(j)}\right)=\left(x^{(i)T}x^{(j)}+\theta\right)^{p}$$

    Here, θ is the threshold and p is the power that has to be specified by the user.

- The hyperbolic tangent (sigmoid) kernel:

$$\kappa\left(x^{(i)},x^{(j)}\right)=\tanh\left(\eta x^{(i)T}x^{(j)}+\theta\right)$$

- The **Radial Basis Function** (**RBF**) or Gaussian kernel, which we will use in the following examples in the next subsection:

$$\kappa\left(x^{(i)},x^{(j)}\right)=\exp\left(-\frac{\left\|x^{(i)}-x^{(j)}\right\|^{2}}{2\sigma^{2}}\right)$$

It is often written in the following form, introducing the variable $\gamma=\dfrac{1}{2\sigma}$:

$$\kappa\left(x^{(i)},x^{(j)}\right)=\exp\left(-\gamma\left\|x^{(i)}-x^{(j)}\right\|^{2}\right)$$

To summarize what we have learned so far, we can define the following three steps to implement an RBF kernel PCA:

1. We compute the kernel (similarity) matrix K, where we need to calculate the following:

$$\kappa\left(x^{(i)}, x^{(j)}\right) = \exp\left(-\gamma \left\|x^{(i)} - x^{(j)}\right\|^2\right)$$

We do this for each pair of samples:

$$K = \begin{bmatrix} \kappa\left(x^{(1)}, x^{(1)}\right) & \kappa\left(x^{(1)}, x^{(2)}\right) & \cdots & \kappa\left(x^{(1)}, x^{(n)}\right) \\ \kappa\left(x^{(2)}, x^{(1)}\right) & \left(x^{(2)}, x^{(2)}\right) & \cdots & \kappa\left(x^{(2)}, x^{(n)}\right) \\ \vdots & \vdots & \ddots & \vdots \\ \kappa\left(x^{(n)}, x^{(1)}\right) & \kappa\left(x^{(n)}, x^{(2)}\right) & \cdots & \kappa\left(x^{(n)}, x^{(n)}\right) \end{bmatrix}$$

For example, if our dataset contains 100 training samples, the symmetric kernel matrix of the pairwise similarities would be 100 x 100-dimensional.

2. We center the kernel matrix K using the following equation:

$$K' = K - 1_n K - K 1_n + 1_n K 1_n$$

Here, 1_n is an $n \times n$-dimensional matrix (the same dimensions as the kernel matrix) where all values are equal to $\frac{1}{n}$.

3. We collect the top k eigenvectors of the centered kernel matrix based on their corresponding eigenvalues, which are ranked by decreasing magnitude. In contrast to standard PCA, the eigenvectors are not the principal component axes, but the samples already projected onto these axes.

At this point, you may be wondering why we need to center the kernel matrix in the second step. We previously assumed that we are working with standardized data, where all features have mean zero when we formulated the covariance matrix and replaced the dot-products with the nonlinear feature combinations via ϕ. Thus, the centering of the kernel matrix in the second step becomes necessary, since we do not compute the new feature space explicitly so that we cannot guarantee that the new feature space is also centered at zero.

In the next section, we will put those three steps into action by implementing a kernel PCA in Python.

Implementing a kernel principal component analysis in Python

In the previous subsection, we discussed the core concepts behind kernel PCA. Now, we are going to implement an RBF kernel PCA in Python following the three steps that summarized the kernel PCA approach. Using some SciPy and NumPy helper functions, we will see that implementing a kernel PCA is actually really simple:

```python
from scipy.spatial.distance import pdist, squareform
from scipy import exp
from scipy.linalg import eigh
import numpy as np

def rbf_kernel_pca(X, gamma, n_components):
    """
    RBF kernel PCA implementation.

    Parameters
    ------------
    X: {NumPy ndarray}, shape = [n_samples, n_features]

    gamma: float
      Tuning parameter of the RBF kernel

    n_components: int
      Number of principal components to return

    Returns
    ------------
     X_pc: {NumPy ndarray}, shape = [n_samples, k_features]
        Projected dataset

    """
    # Calculate pairwise squared Euclidean distances
    # in the MxN dimensional dataset.
    sq_dists = pdist(X, 'sqeuclidean')

    # Convert pairwise distances into a square matrix.
```

```
mat_sq_dists = squareform(sq_dists)

# Compute the symmetric kernel matrix.
K = exp(-gamma * mat_sq_dists)

# Center the kernel matrix.
N = K.shape[0]
one_n = np.ones((N,N)) / N
K = K - one_n.dot(K) - K.dot(one_n) + one_n.dot(K).dot(one_n)

# Obtaining eigenpairs from the centered kernel matrix
# scipy.linalg.eigh returns them in ascending order
eigvals, eigvecs = eigh(K)
eigvals, eigvecs = eigvals[::-1], eigvecs[:, ::-1]

# Collect the top k eigenvectors (projected samples)
X_pc = np.column_stack((eigvecs[:, i]
                        for i in range(n_components)))

return X_pc
```

One downside of using an RBF kernel PCA for dimensionality reduction is that we have to specify the γ parameter a priori. Finding an appropriate value for γ requires experimentation and is best done using algorithms for parameter tuning, for example, performing a grid search, which we will discuss in more detail in *Chapter 6, Learning Best Practices for Model Evaluation and Hyperparameter Tuning.*

Example 1 – separating half-moon shapes

Now, let us apply our `rbf_kernel_pca` on some nonlinear example datasets. We will start by creating a two-dimensional dataset of 100 sample points representing two half-moon shapes:

```
>>> from sklearn.datasets import make_moons
>>> X, y = make_moons(n_samples=100, random_state=123)
>>> plt.scatter(X[y==0, 0], X[y==0, 1],
...             color='red', marker='^', alpha=0.5)
>>> plt.scatter(X[y==1, 0], X[y==1, 1],
...             color='blue', marker='o', alpha=0.5)
>>> plt.show()
```

For the purposes of illustration, the half-moon of triangle symbols shall represent one class, and the half-moon depicted by the circle symbols represent the samples from another class:

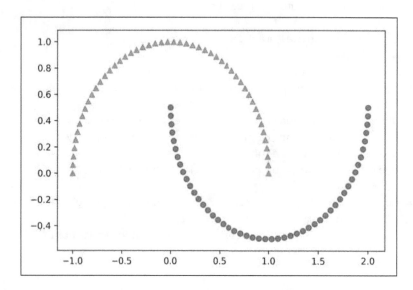

Clearly, these two half-moon shapes are not linearly separable, and our goal is to *unfold* the half-moons via kernel PCA so that the dataset can serve as a suitable input for a linear classifier. But first, let's see how the dataset looks if we project it onto the principal components via standard PCA:

```
>>> from sklearn.decomposition import PCA
>>> scikit_pca = PCA(n_components=2)
>>> X_spca = scikit_pca.fit_transform(X)
>>> fig, ax = plt.subplots(nrows=1,ncols=2, figsize=(7,3))
>>> ax[0].scatter(X_spca[y==0, 0], X_spca[y==0, 1],
...               color='red', marker='^', alpha=0.5)
>>> ax[0].scatter(X_spca[y==1, 0], X_spca[y==1, 1],
...               color='blue', marker='o', alpha=0.5)
>>> ax[1].scatter(X_spca[y==0, 0], np.zeros((50,1))+0.02,
...               color='red', marker='^', alpha=0.5)
>>> ax[1].scatter(X_spca[y==1, 0], np.zeros((50,1))-0.02,
...               color='blue', marker='o', alpha=0.5)
>>> ax[0].set_xlabel('PC1')
>>> ax[0].set_ylabel('PC2')
>>> ax[1].set_ylim([-1, 1])
>>> ax[1].set_yticks([])
>>> ax[1].set_xlabel('PC1')
>>> plt.show()
```

Clearly, we can see in the resulting figure that a linear classifier would be unable to perform well on the dataset transformed via standard PCA:

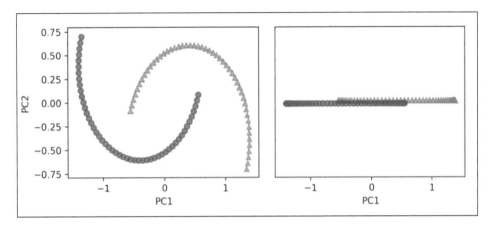

Note that when we plotted the first principal component only (right subplot), we shifted the triangular samples slightly upwards and the circular samples slightly downwards to better visualize the class overlap. As the left subplot shows, the original half-moon shapes are only slightly sheared and flipped across the vertical center — this transformation would not help a linear classifier in discriminating between circles and triangles. Similarly, the circles and triangles corresponding to the two half-moon shapes are not linearly separable if we project the dataset onto a one-dimensional feature axis, as shown in the right subplot.

 Please remember that PCA is an unsupervised method and does not use class label information in order to maximize the variance in contrast to LDA. Here, the triangle and circle symbols were just added for visualization purposes to indicate the degree of separation.

Now, let us try out our kernel PCA function `rbf_kernel_pca`, which we implemented in the previous subsection:

```
>>> X_kpca = rbf_kernel_pca(X, gamma=15, n_components=2)
>>> fig, ax = plt.subplots(nrows=1,ncols=2, figsize=(7,3))
>>> ax[0].scatter(X_kpca[y==0, 0], X_kpca[y==0, 1],
...               color='red', marker='^', alpha=0.5)
>>> ax[0].scatter(X_kpca[y==1, 0], X_kpca[y==1, 1],
...               color='blue', marker='o', alpha=0.5)
>>> ax[1].scatter(X_kpca[y==0, 0], np.zeros((50,1))+0.02,
...               color='red', marker='^', alpha=0.5)
```

```
>>> ax[1].scatter(X_kpca[y==1, 0], np.zeros((50,1))-0.02,
...                color='blue', marker='o', alpha=0.5)
>>> ax[0].set_xlabel('PC1')
>>> ax[0].set_ylabel('PC2')
>>> ax[1].set_ylim([-1, 1])
>>> ax[1].set_yticks([])
>>> ax[1].set_xlabel('PC1')
>>> plt.show()
```

We can now see that the two classes (`circles` and `triangles`) are linearly well separated so that it becomes a suitable training dataset for linear classifiers:

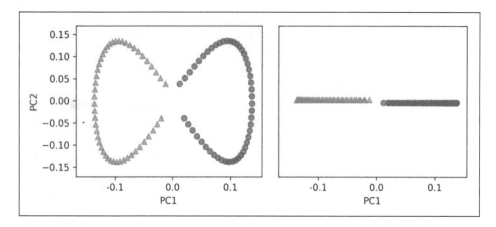

Unfortunately, there is no universal value for the tuning parameter γ that works well for different datasets. Finding a γ value that is appropriate for a given problem requires experimentation. In *Chapter 6, Learning Best Practices for Model Evaluation and Hyperparameter Tuning*, we will discuss techniques that can help us to automate the task of optimizing such tuning parameters. Here, I will use values for γ that I found produce good results.

Example 2 – separating concentric circles

In the previous subsection, we showed how to separate half-moon shapes via kernel PCA. Since we put so much effort into understanding the concepts of kernel PCA, let us take a look at another interesting example of a nonlinear problem, concentric circles:

```
>>> from sklearn.datasets import make_circles
>>> X, y = make_circles(n_samples=1000,
...              random_state=123, noise=0.1, factor=0.2)
>>> plt.scatter(X[y==0, 0], X[y==0, 1],
```

```
...                 color='red', marker='^', alpha=0.5)
>>> plt.scatter(X[y==1, 0], X[y==1, 1],
...                 color='blue', marker='o', alpha=0.5)
>>> plt.show()
```

Again, we assume a two-class problem where the triangle shapes represent one class, and the circle shapes represent another class:

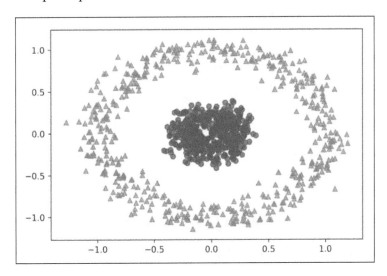

Let's start with the standard PCA approach to compare it to the results of the RBF kernel PCA:

```
>>> scikit_pca = PCA(n_components=2)
>>> X_spca = scikit_pca.fit_transform(X)
>>> fig, ax = plt.subplots(nrows=1,ncols=2, figsize=(7,3))
>>> ax[0].scatter(X_spca[y==0, 0], X_spca[y==0, 1],
...                 color='red', marker='^', alpha=0.5)
>>> ax[0].scatter(X_spca[y==1, 0], X_spca[y==1, 1],
...                 color='blue', marker='o', alpha=0.5)
>>> ax[1].scatter(X_spca[y==0, 0], np.zeros((500,1))+0.02,
...                 color='red', marker='^', alpha=0.5)
>>> ax[1].scatter(X_spca[y==1, 0], np.zeros((500,1))-0.02,
...                 color='blue', marker='o', alpha=0.5)
>>> ax[0].set_xlabel('PC1')
>>> ax[0].set_ylabel('PC2')
>>> ax[1].set_ylim([-1, 1])
>>> ax[1].set_yticks([])
>>> ax[1].set_xlabel('PC1')
>>> plt.show()
```

Again, we can see that standard PCA is not able to produce results suitable for training a linear classifier:

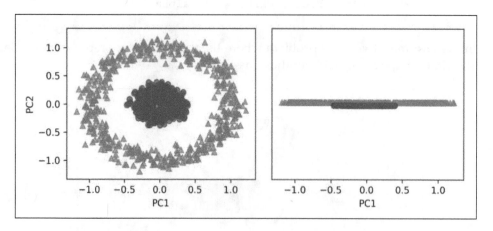

Given an appropriate value for γ, let us see if we are luckier using the RBF kernel PCA implementation:

```
>>> X_kpca = rbf_kernel_pca(X, gamma=15, n_components=2)
>>> fig, ax = plt.subplots(nrows=1,ncols=2, figsize=(7,3))
>>> ax[0].scatter(X_kpca[y==0, 0], X_kpca[y==0, 1],
...                color='red', marker='^', alpha=0.5)
>>> ax[0].scatter(X_kpca[y==1, 0], X_kpca[y==1, 1],
...                color='blue', marker='o', alpha=0.5)
>>> ax[1].scatter(X_kpca[y==0, 0], np.zeros((500,1))+0.02,
...                color='red', marker='^', alpha=0.5)
>>> ax[1].scatter(X_kpca[y==1, 0], np.zeros((500,1))-0.02,
...                color='blue', marker='o', alpha=0.5)
>>> ax[0].set_xlabel('PC1')
>>> ax[0].set_ylabel('PC2')
>>> ax[1].set_ylim([-1, 1])
>>> ax[1].set_yticks([])
>>> ax[1].set_xlabel('PC1')
>>> plt.show()
```

Again, the RBF kernel PCA projected the data onto a new subspace where the two classes become linearly separable:

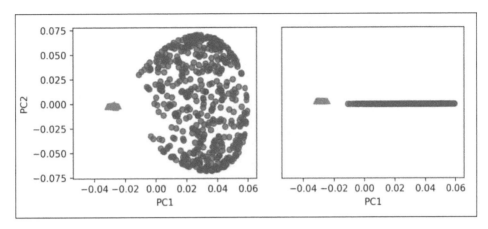

Projecting new data points

In the two previous example applications of kernel PCA, the half-moon shapes and the concentric circles, we projected a single dataset onto a new feature. In real applications, however, we may have more than one dataset that we want to transform, for example, training and test data, and typically also new samples we will collect after the model building and evaluation. In this section, you will learn how to project data points that were not part of the training dataset.

As we remember from the standard PCA approach at the beginning of this chapter, we project data by calculating the dot product between a transformation matrix and the input samples; the columns of the projection matrix are the top **k** eigenvectors (**v**) that we obtained from the covariance matrix.

Now, the question is how we can transfer this concept to kernel PCA. If we think back to the idea behind kernel PCA, we remember that we obtained an eigenvector (**a**) of the centered kernel matrix (not the covariance matrix), which means that those are the samples that are already projected onto the principal component axis **v**. Thus, if we want to project a new sample x' onto this principal component axis, we'd need to compute the following:

$$\phi\left(x'\right)^{T} v$$

Fortunately, we can use the kernel trick so that we don't have to calculate the projection $\phi(x')^T v$ explicitly. However, it is worth noting that kernel PCA, in contrast to standard PCA, is a memory-based method, which means that we have to re-use the original training set each time to project new samples. We have to calculate the pairwise RBF kernel (similarity) between each ith sample in the training dataset and the new sample x':

$$\phi(x')^T v = \sum_i a^{(i)} \phi(x')^T \phi(x^{(i)})$$

$$= \sum_i a^{(i)} \kappa(x', x^{(i)})$$

Here, the eigenvectors **a** and eigenvalues λ of the kernel matrix **K** satisfy the following condition in the equation:

$$Ka = \lambda a$$

After calculating the similarity between the new samples and the samples in the training set, we have to normalize the eigenvector **a** by its eigenvalue. Thus, let us modify the `rbf_kernel_pca` function that we implemented earlier so that it also returns the eigenvalues of the kernel matrix:

```
from scipy.spatial.distance import pdist, squareform
from scipy import exp
from scipy.linalg import eigh
import numpy as np

def rbf_kernel_pca(X, gamma, n_components):
    """
    RBF kernel PCA implementation.

    Parameters
    ------------
    X: {NumPy ndarray}, shape = [n_samples, n_features]

    gamma: float
        Tuning parameter of the RBF kernel

    n_components: int
```

```
    Number of principal components to return

Returns
------------
 alphas {NumPy ndarray}, shape = [n_samples, k_features]
    Projected dataset

 lambdas: list
    Eigenvalues

"""
# Calculate pairwise squared Euclidean distances
# in the MxN dimensional dataset.
sq_dists = pdist(X, 'sqeuclidean')

# Convert pairwise distances into a square matrix.
mat_sq_dists = squareform(sq_dists)

# Compute the symmetric kernel matrix.
K = exp(-gamma * mat_sq_dists)

# Center the kernel matrix.
N = K.shape[0]
one_n = np.ones((N,N)) / N
K = K - one_n.dot(K) - K.dot(one_n) + one_n.dot(K).dot(one_n)

# Obtaining eigenpairs from the centered kernel matrix
# scipy.linalg.eigh returns them in ascending order
eigvals, eigvecs = eigh(K)
eigvals, eigvecs = eigvals[::-1], eigvecs[:, ::-1]

# Collect the top k eigenvectors (projected samples)
alphas = np.column_stack((eigvecs[:, i]
                            for i in range(n_components)))

# Collect the corresponding eigenvalues
lambdas = [eigvals[i] for i in range(n_components)]

return alphas, lambdas
```

Now, let's create a new half-moon dataset and project it onto a one-dimensional subspace using the updated RBF kernel PCA implementation:

```
>>> X, y = make_moons(n_samples=100, random_state=123)
>>> alphas, lambdas = rbf_kernel_pca(X, gamma=15, n_components=1)
```

To make sure that we implemented the code for projecting new samples, let us assume that the 26th point from the half-moon dataset is a new data point x', and our task is to project it onto this new subspace:

```
>>> x_new = X[25]
>>> x_new
array([ 1.8713187 ,   0.00928245])
>>> x_proj = alphas[25] # original projection
>>> x_proj
array([ 0.07877284])
>>> def project_x(x_new, X, gamma, alphas, lambdas):
...      pair_dist = np.array([np.sum(
...                    (x_new-row)**2) for row in X])
...      k = np.exp(-gamma * pair_dist)
...      return k.dot(alphas / lambdas)
```

By executing the following code, we are able to reproduce the original projection. Using the `project_x` function, we will be able to project any new data sample as well. The code is as follows:

```
>>> x_reproj = project_x(x_new, X,
...        gamma=15, alphas=alphas, lambdas=lambdas)
>>> x_reproj
array([ 0.07877284])
```

Lastly, let's visualize the projection on the first principal component:

```
>>> plt.scatter(alphas[y==0, 0], np.zeros((50)),
...              color='red', marker='^',alpha=0.5)
>>> plt.scatter(alphas[y==1, 0], np.zeros((50)),
...              color='blue', marker='o', alpha=0.5)
>>> plt.scatter(x_proj, 0, color='black',
...              label='original projection of point X[25]',
...              marker='^', s=100)
>>> plt.scatter(x_reproj, 0, color='green',
...              label='remapped point X[25]',
...              marker='x', s=500)
>>> plt.legend(scatterpoints=1)
>>> plt.show()
```

As we can now also see in the following scatterplot, we mapped the sample x' onto the first principal component correctly:

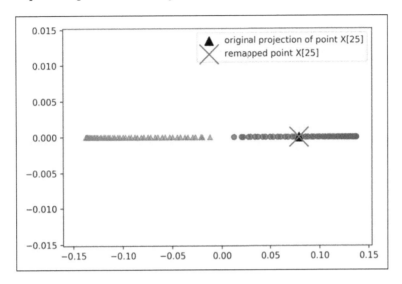

Kernel principal component analysis in scikit-learn

For our convenience, scikit-learn implements a kernel PCA class in the `sklearn.decomposition` submodule. The usage is similar to the standard PCA class, and we can specify the kernel via the `kernel` parameter:

```
>>> from sklearn.decomposition import KernelPCA
>>> X, y = make_moons(n_samples=100, random_state=123)
>>> scikit_kpca = KernelPCA(n_components=2,
...                 kernel='rbf', gamma=15)
>>> X_skernpca = scikit_kpca.fit_transform(X)
```

To check that we get results that are consistent with our own kernel PCA implementation, let's plot the transformed half-moon shape data onto the first two principal components:

```
>>> plt.scatter(X_skernpca[y==0, 0], X_skernpca[y==0, 1],
...                 color='red', marker='^', alpha=0.5)
>>> plt.scatter(X_skernpca[y==1, 0], X_skernpca[y==1, 1],
...                 color='blue', marker='o', alpha=0.5)
>>> plt.xlabel('PC1')
>>> plt.ylabel('PC2')
>>> plt.show()
```

As we can see, the results of scikit-learn's `KernelPCA` are consistent with our own implementation:

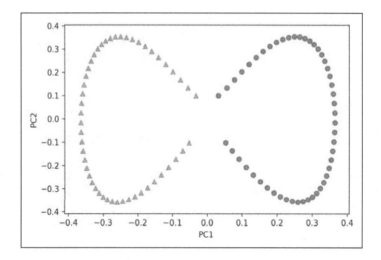

The scikit-learn library also implements advanced techniques for nonlinear dimensionality reduction that are beyond the scope of this book. The interested reader can find a nice overview of the current implementations in scikit-learn, complemented by illustrative examples, at `http://scikit-learn.org/stable/modules/manifold.html`.

Summary

In this chapter, you learned about three different, fundamental dimensionality reduction techniques for feature extraction: standard PCA, LDA, and kernel PCA. Using PCA, we projected data onto a lower-dimensional subspace to maximize the variance along the orthogonal feature axes, while ignoring the class labels. LDA, in contrast to PCA, is a technique for supervised dimensionality reduction, which means that it considers class information in the training dataset to attempt to maximize the class-separability in a linear feature space.

Lastly, you learned about a nonlinear feature extractor, kernel PCA. Using the kernel trick and a temporary projection into a higher-dimensional feature space, you were ultimately able to compress datasets consisting of nonlinear features onto a lower-dimensional subspace where the classes became linearly separable.

Equipped with these essential preprocessing techniques, you are now well prepared to learn about the best practices for efficiently incorporating different preprocessing techniques and evaluating the performance of different models in the next chapter.

6
Learning Best Practices for Model Evaluation and Hyperparameter Tuning

In the previous chapters, you learned about the essential machine learning algorithms for classification and how to get our data into shape before we feed it into those algorithms. Now, it's time to learn about the best practices of building good machine learning models by fine-tuning the algorithms and evaluating the model's performance! In this chapter, we will learn how to do the following:

- Obtain unbiased estimates of a model's performance
- Diagnose the common problems of machine learning algorithms
- Fine-tune machine learning models
- Evaluate predictive models using different performance metrics

Streamlining workflows with pipelines

When we applied different preprocessing techniques in the previous chapters, such as standardization for feature scaling in *Chapter 4, Building Good Training Sets – Data Preprocessing*, or principal component analysis for data compression in *Chapter 5, Compressing Data via Dimensionality Reduction*, you learned that we have to reuse the parameters that were obtained during the fitting of the training data to scale and compress any new data, such as the samples in the separate test dataset. In this section, you will learn about an extremely handy tool, the Pipeline class in scikit-learn. It allows us to fit a model including an arbitrary number of transformation steps and apply it to make predictions about new data.

Loading the Breast Cancer Wisconsin dataset

In this chapter, we will be working with the Breast Cancer Wisconsin dataset, which contains 569 samples of malignant and benign tumor cells. The first two columns in the dataset store the unique ID numbers of the samples and the corresponding diagnoses (M = malignant, B = benign), respectively. Columns 3-32 contain 30 real-valued features that have been computed from digitized images of the cell nuclei, which can be used to build a model to predict whether a tumor is benign or malignant. The Breast Cancer Wisconsin dataset has been deposited in the UCI Machine Learning Repository, and more detailed information about this dataset can be found at https://archive.ics.uci.edu/ml/datasets/Breast+Cancer+Wisconsin+(Diagnostic).

You can find a copy of the breast cancer dataset (and all other datasets used in this book) in the code bundle of this book, which you can use if you are working offline or the UCI server at https://archive.ics.uci.edu/ml/machine-learning-databases/breast-cancer-wisconsin/wdbc.data is temporarily unavailable. For instance, to load the Wine dataset from a local directory, you can take the following lines:

```
df = pd.read_csv('https://archive.ics.uci.edu/ml/'
                 'machine-learning-databases'
                 '/breast-cancer-wisconsin/wdbc.data',
                 header=None)
```

Replace the preceding lines with this:

```
df = pd.read_csv('your/local/path/to/wdbc.data',
                 header=None)
```

In this section, we will read in the dataset and split it into training and test datasets in three simple steps:

1. We will start by reading in the dataset directly from the UCI website using pandas:

```
>>> import pandas as pd
>>> df = pd.read_csv('https://archive.ics.uci.edu/ml/'
...                  'machine-learning-databases'
...                  '/breast-cancer-wisconsin/wdbc.data',
                     header=None)
```

2. Next, we assign the 30 features to a NumPy array x. Using a LabelEncoder object, we transform the class labels from their original string representation ('M' and 'B') into integers:

```
>>> from sklearn.preprocessing import LabelEncoder

>>> X = df.loc[:, 2:].values
>>> y = df.loc[:, 1].values
>>> le = LabelEncoder()
>>> y = le.fit_transform(y)
>>> le.classes_
array(['B', 'M'], dtype=object)
```

After encoding the class labels (diagnosis) in an array y, the malignant tumors are now represented as class 1, and the benign tumors are represented as class 0, respectively. We can double-check this mapping by calling the transform method of the fitted LabelEncoder on two dummy class labels:

```
>>> le.transform(['M', 'B'])
array([1, 0])
```

3. Before we construct our first model pipeline in the following subsection, let us divide the dataset into a separate training dataset (80 percent of the data) and a separate test dataset (20 percent of the data):

```
>>> from sklearn.model_selection import train_test_split

>>> X_train, X_test, y_train, y_test = \
>>>     train_test_split(X, y,
...                      test_size=0.20,
...                      stratify=y,
...                      random_state=1)
```

Combining transformers and estimators in a pipeline

In the previous chapter, you learned that many learning algorithms require input features on the same scale for optimal performance. Thus, we need to standardize the columns in the Breast Cancer Wisconsin dataset before we can feed them to a linear classifier, such as logistic regression. Furthermore, let's assume that we want to compress our data from the initial 30 dimensions onto a lower two-dimensional subspace via **Principal Component Analysis (PCA)**, a feature extraction technique for dimensionality reduction that we introduced in *Chapter 5, Compressing Data via Dimensionality Reduction*.

Instead of going through the fitting and transformation steps for the training and test datasets separately, we can chain the `StandardScaler`, `PCA`, and `LogisticRegression` objects in a pipeline:

```
>>> from sklearn.preprocessing import StandardScaler
>>> from sklearn.decomposition import PCA
>>> from sklearn.linear_model import LogisticRegression
>>> from sklearn.pipeline import make_pipeline
>>> pipe_lr = make_pipeline(StandardScaler(),
...                         PCA(n_components=2),
...                         LogisticRegression(random_state=1))
>>> pipe_lr.fit(X_train, y_train)
>>> y_pred = pipe_lr.predict(X_test)
>> print('Test Accuracy: %.3f' % pipe_lr.score(X_test, y_test))
Test Accuracy: 0.956
```

The `make_pipeline` function takes an arbitrary number of scikit-learn transformers (objects that support the `fit` and `transform` methods as input), followed by a scikit-learn estimator that implements the `fit` and `predict` methods. In our preceding code example, we provided two transformers, `StandardScaler` and `PCA`, and a `LogisticRegression` estimator as inputs to the `make_pipeline` function, which constructs a scikit-learn `Pipeline` object from these objects.

We can think of a scikit-learn `Pipeline` as a meta-estimator or wrapper around those individual transformers and estimators. If we call the `fit` method of `Pipeline`, the data will be passed down a series of transformers via `fit` and `transform` calls on these intermediate steps until it arrives at the estimator object (the final element in a pipeline). The estimator will then be fitted to the transformed training data.

When we executed the `fit` method on the `pipe_lr` pipeline in the preceding code example, `StandardScaler` first performed `fit` and `transform` calls on the training data. Second, the transformed training data was passed on to the next object in the pipeline, `PCA`. Similar to the previous step, `PCA` also executed `fit` and `transform` on the scaled input data and passed it to the final element of the pipeline, the estimator.

Finally, the `LogisticRegression` estimator was fit to the training data after it underwent transformations via `StandardScaler` and `PCA`. Again, we should note that there is no limit to the number of intermediate steps in a pipeline; however, the last pipeline element has to be an estimator.

Similar to calling `fit` on a pipeline, pipelines also implement a `predict` method. If we feed a dataset to the `predict` call of a `Pipeline` object instance, the data will pass through the intermediate steps via `transform` calls. In the final step, the estimator object will then return a prediction on the transformed data.

The pipelines of scikit-learn library are immensely useful wrapper tools, which we will use frequently throughout the rest of this book. To make sure that you've got a good grasp of how `Pipeline` object works, please take a close look at the following illustration, which summarizes our discussion from the previous paragraphs:

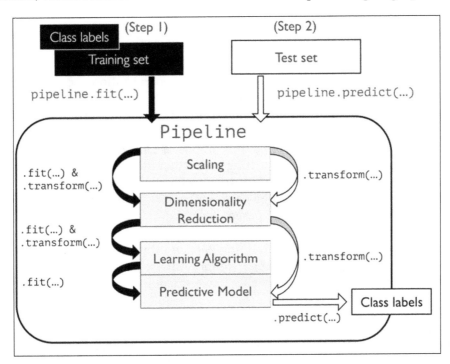

Using k-fold cross-validation to assess model performance

One of the key steps in building a machine learning model is to estimate its performance on data that the model hasn't seen before. Let's assume that we fit our model on a training dataset and use the same data to estimate how well it performs on new data. We remember from the *Tackling overfitting via regularization* section in *Chapter 3, A Tour of Machine Learning Classifiers Using scikit-learn,* that a model can either suffer from underfitting (high bias) if the model is too simple, or it can overfit the training data (high variance) if the model is too complex for the underlying training data.

To find an acceptable bias-variance trade-off, we need to evaluate our model carefully. In this section, you will learn about the common cross-validation techniques **holdout cross-validation** and **k-fold cross-validation**, which can help us obtain reliable estimates of the model's generalization performance, that is, how well the model performs on unseen data.

The holdout method

A classic and popular approach for estimating the generalization performance of machine learning models is holdout cross-validation. Using the holdout method, we split our initial dataset into a separate training and test dataset—the former is used for model training, and the latter is used to estimate its generalization performance. However, in typical machine learning applications, we are also interested in tuning and comparing different parameter settings to further improve the performance for making predictions on unseen data. This process is called **model selection**, where the term model selection refers to a given classification problem for which we want to select the *optimal* values of tuning parameters (also called hyperparameters). However, if we reuse the same test dataset over and over again during model selection, it will become part of our training data and thus the model will be more likely to overfit. Despite this issue, many people still use the test set for model selection, which is not a good machine learning practice.

A better way of using the holdout method for model selection is to separate the data into three parts: a training set, a validation set, and a test set. The training set is used to fit the different models, and the performance on the validation set is then used for the model selection. The advantage of having a test set that the model hasn't seen before during the training and model selection steps is that we can obtain a less biased estimate of its ability to generalize to new data. The following figure illustrates the concept of holdout cross-validation, where we use a validation set to repeatedly evaluate the performance of the model after training using different parameter values. Once we are satisfied with the tuning of hyperparameter values, we estimate the models' generalization performance on the test dataset:

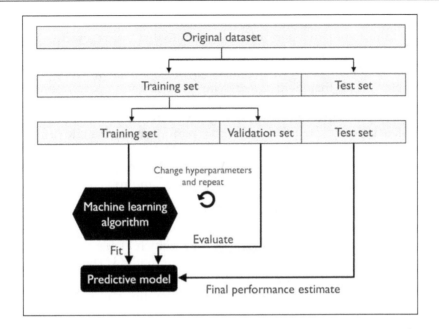

A disadvantage of the holdout method is that the performance estimate may be very sensitive to how we partition the training set into the training and validation subsets; the estimate will vary for different samples of the data. In the next subsection, we will take a look at a more robust technique for performance estimation, k-fold cross-validation, where we repeat the holdout method k times on k subsets of the training data.

K-fold cross-validation

In k-fold cross-validation, we randomly split the training dataset into k folds without replacement, where $k - 1$ folds are used for the model training, and one fold is used for performance evaluation. This procedure is repeated k times so that we obtain k models and performance estimates.

We looked at an example to illustrate sampling *with* and *without* replacement in *Chapter 3, A Tour of Machine Learning Classifiers Using scikit-learn*. If you haven't read that chapter, or want a refresher, refer to the information box in the *Combining multiple decision trees via random forests* section in *Chapter 3, A Tour of Machine Learning Classifiers Using scikit-learn*.

We then calculate the average performance of the models based on the different, independent folds to obtain a performance estimate that is less sensitive to the sub-partitioning of the training data compared to the holdout method. Typically, we use k-fold cross-validation for model tuning, that is, finding the optimal hyperparameter values that yields a satisfying generalization performance.

Once we have found satisfactory hyperparameter values, we can retrain the model on the complete training set and obtain a final performance estimate using the independent test set. The rationale behind fitting a model to the whole training dataset after k-fold cross-validation is that providing more training samples to a learning algorithm usually results in a more accurate and robust model.

Since k-fold cross-validation is a resampling technique without replacement, the advantage of this approach is that each sample point will be used for training and validation (as part of a test fold) exactly once, which yields a lower-variance estimate of the model performance than the holdout method. The following figure summarizes the concept behind k-fold cross-validation with *k = 10*. The training dataset is divided into 10 folds, and during the 10 iterations, nine folds are used for training, and one fold will be used as the test set for the model evaluation. Also, the estimated performances E_i (for example, classification accuracy or error) for each fold are then used to calculate the estimated average performance E of the model:

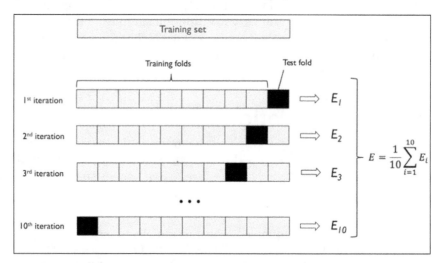

A good standard value for *k* in k-fold cross-validation is 10, as empirical evidence shows. For instance, experiments by Ron Kohavi on various real-world datasets suggest that 10-fold cross-validation offers the best trade-off between bias and variance (*A Study of Cross-Validation and Bootstrap for Accuracy Estimation and Model Selection, Kohavi, Ron, International Joint Conference on Artificial Intelligence (IJCAI)*, 14 (12): 1137-43, *1995*).

However, if we are working with relatively small training sets, it can be useful to increase the number of folds. If we increase the value of *k*, more training data will be used in each iteration, which results in a lower bias towards estimating the generalization performance by averaging the individual model estimates. However, large values of *k* will also increase the runtime of the cross-validation algorithm and yield estimates with higher variance, since the training folds will be more similar to each other. On the other hand, if we are working with large datasets, we can choose a smaller value for *k*, for example, *k* = 5, and still obtain an accurate estimate of the average performance of the model while reducing the computational cost of refitting and evaluating the model on the different folds.

> A special case of k-fold cross-validation is the **Leave-one-out cross-validation (LOOCV)** method. In LOOCV, we set the number of folds equal to the number of training samples (*k* = *n*) so that only one training sample is used for testing during each iteration, which is a recommended approach for working with very small datasets.

A slight improvement over the standard k-fold cross-validation approach is stratified k-fold cross-validation, which can yield better bias and variance estimates, especially in cases of unequal class proportions, as has been shown in a study by Ron Kohavi (*A Study of Cross-Validation and Bootstrap for Accuracy Estimation and Model Selection, International Joint Conference on Artificial Intelligence (IJCAI)*, 14 (12): 1137-43, 1995). In stratified cross-validation, the class proportions are preserved in each fold to ensure that each fold is representative of the class proportions in the training dataset, which we will illustrate by using the StratifiedKFold iterator in scikit-learn:

```
>>> import numpy as np
>>> from sklearn.model_selection import StratifiedKFold

>>> kfold = StratifiedKFold(n_splits=10,
...                         random_state=1).split(X_train,
...                                               y_train)
>>> scores = []
>>> for k, (train, test) in enumerate(kfold):
...     pipe_lr.fit(X_train[train], y_train[train])
...     score = pipe_lr.score(X_train[test], y_train[test])
...     scores.append(score)
...     print('Fold: %2d, Class dist.: %s, Acc: %.3f' % (k+1,
...             np.bincount(y_train[train]), score))
Fold:  1, Class dist.: [256 153], Acc: 0.935
Fold:  2, Class dist.: [256 153], Acc: 0.935
Fold:  3, Class dist.: [256 153], Acc: 0.957
Fold:  4, Class dist.: [256 153], Acc: 0.957
Fold:  5, Class dist.: [256 153], Acc: 0.935
```

```
Fold:  6, Class dist.: [257 153], Acc: 0.956
Fold:  7, Class dist.: [257 153], Acc: 0.978
Fold:  8, Class dist.: [257 153], Acc: 0.933
Fold:  9, Class dist.: [257 153], Acc: 0.956
Fold: 10, Class dist.: [257 153], Acc: 0.956

>>> print('\nCV accuracy: %.3f +/- %.3f' %
...          (np.mean(scores), np.std(scores)))
CV accuracy: 0.950 +/- 0.014
```

First, we initialized the `StratifiedKfold` iterator from the `sklearn.model_selection` module with the `y_train` class labels in the training set, and we specified the number of folds via the `n_splits` parameter. When we used the `kfold` iterator to loop through the `k` folds, we used the returned indices in `train` to fit the logistic regression pipeline that we set up at the beginning of this chapter. Using the `pipe_lr` pipeline, we ensured that the samples were scaled properly (for instance, standardized) in each iteration. We then used the `test` indices to calculate the accuracy score of the model, which we collected in the `scores` list to calculate the average accuracy and the standard deviation of the estimate.

Although the previous code example was useful to illustrate how k-fold cross-validation works, scikit-learn also implements a k-fold cross-validation scorer, which allows us to evaluate our model using stratified k-fold cross-validation less verbosely:

```
>>> from sklearn.model_selection import cross_val_score

>>> scores = cross_val_score(estimator=pipe_lr,
...                          X=X_train,
...                          y=y_train,
...                          cv=10,
...                          n_jobs=1)
>>> print('CV accuracy scores: %s' % scores)
CV accuracy scores: [ 0.93478261  0.93478261  0.95652174
                      0.95652174  0.93478261  0.95555556
                      0.97777778  0.93333333  0.95555556
                      0.95555556]
>>> print('CV accuracy: %.3f +/- %.3f' % (np.mean(scores),
...          np.std(scores)))
CV accuracy: 0.950 +/- 0.014
```

An extremely useful feature of the `cross_val_score` approach is that we can distribute the evaluation of the different folds across multiple CPUs on our machine. If we set the `n_jobs` parameter to 1, only one CPU will be used to evaluate the performances, just like in our `StratifiedKFold` example previously. However, by setting `n_jobs=2`, we could distribute the 10 rounds of cross-validation to two CPUs (if available on our machine), and by setting `n_jobs=-1`, we can use all available CPUs on our machine to do the computation in parallel.

Please note that a detailed discussion of how the variance of the generalization performance is estimated in cross-validation is beyond the scope of this book, but I have written a series of articles about model evaluation and cross-validation that discuss these topics in more depth. These articles are available here:

- `https://sebastianraschka.com/blog/2016/model-evaluation-selection-part1.html`
- `https://sebastianraschka.com/blog/2016/model-evaluation-selection-part2.html`
- `https://sebastianraschka.com/blog/2016/model-evaluation-selection-part3.html`

In addition, you can find a detailed discussion in this excellent article by M. Markatou and others (*Analysis of Variance of Cross-validation Estimators of the Generalization Error, M. Markatou, H. Tian, S. Biswas, and G. M. Hripcsak, Journal of Machine Learning Research, 6: 1127-1168, 2005*).

You can also read about alternative cross-validation techniques, such as the .632 Bootstrap cross-validation method (*Improvements on Cross-validation: The .632+ Bootstrap Method, B. Efron and R. Tibshirani, Journal of the American Statistical Association, 92(438): 548-560, 1997*).

Debugging algorithms with learning and validation curves

In this section, we will take a look at two very simple yet powerful diagnostic tools that can help us improve the performance of a learning algorithm: **learning curves** and **validation curves**. In the next subsections, we will discuss how we can use learning curves to diagnose whether a learning algorithm has a problem with overfitting (high variance) or underfitting (high bias). Furthermore, we will take a look at validation curves that can help us address the common issues of a learning algorithm.

Diagnosing bias and variance problems with learning curves

If a model is too complex for a given training dataset—there are too many degrees of freedom or parameters in this model—the model tends to overfit the training data and does not generalize well to unseen data. Often, it can help to collect more training samples to reduce the degree of overfitting. However, in practice, it can often be very expensive or simply not feasible to collect more data. By plotting the model training and validation accuracies as functions of the training set size, we can easily detect whether the model suffers from high variance or high bias, and whether the collection of more data could help address this problem. But before we discuss how to plot learning curves in scikit-learn, let's discuss those two common model issues by walking through the following illustration:

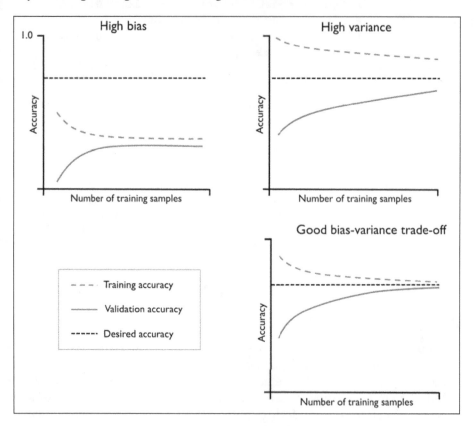

The graph in the upper-left shows a model with high bias. This model has both low training and cross-validation accuracy, which indicates that it underfits the training data. Common ways to address this issue are to increase the number of parameters of the model, for example, by collecting or constructing additional features, or by decreasing the degree of regularization, for example, in SVM or logistic regression classifiers.

The graph in the upper-right shows a model that suffers from high variance, which is indicated by the large gap between the training and cross-validation accuracy. To address this problem of overfitting, we can collect more training data, reduce the complexity of the model, or increase the regularization parameter, for example. For unregularized models, it can also help decrease the number of features via feature selection (*Chapter 4, Building Good Training Sets – Data Preprocessing*) or feature extraction (*Chapter 5, Compressing Data via Dimensionality Reduction*) to decrease the degree of overfitting. While collecting more training data usually tends to decrease the chance of overfitting, it may not always help, for example, if the training data is extremely noisy or the model is already very close to optimal.

In the next subsection, we will see how to address those model issues using validation curves, but let's first see how we can use the learning curve function from scikit-learn to evaluate the model:

```
>>> import matplotlib.pyplot as plt
>>> from sklearn.model_selection import learning_curve

>>> pipe_lr = make_pipeline(StandardScaler(),
...                         LogisticRegression(penalty='l2',
...                                            random_state=1))
>>> train_sizes, train_scores, test_scores =\
...             learning_curve(estimator=pipe_lr,
...                            X=X_train,
...                            y=y_train,
...                            train_sizes=np.linspace(
...                                0.1, 1.0, 10),
...                            cv=10,
...                            n_jobs=1)
>>> train_mean = np.mean(train_scores, axis=1)
>>> train_std = np.std(train_scores, axis=1)
>>> test_mean = np.mean(test_scores, axis=1)
>>> test_std = np.std(test_scores, axis=1)

>>> plt.plot(train_sizes, train_mean,
...          color='blue', marker='o',
```

```
...                 markersize=5, label='training accuracy')

>>> plt.fill_between(train_sizes,
...                     train_mean + train_std,
...                     train_mean - train_std,
...                     alpha=0.15, color='blue')

>>> plt.plot(train_sizes, test_mean,
...          color='green', linestyle='--',
...          marker='s', markersize=5,
...          label='validation accuracy')

>>> plt.fill_between(train_sizes,
...                     test_mean + test_std,
...                     test_mean - test_std,
...                     alpha=0.15, color='green')
>>> plt.grid()
>>> plt.xlabel('Number of training samples')
>>> plt.ylabel('Accuracy')
>>> plt.legend(loc='lower right')
>>> plt.ylim([0.8, 1.0])
>>> plt.show()
```

After we have successfully executed the preceding code, we obtain the following learning curve plot:

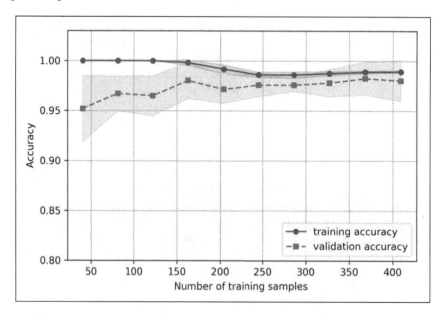

Via the `train_sizes` parameter in the `learning_curve` function, we can control the absolute or relative number of training samples that are used to generate the learning curves. Here, we set `train_sizes=np.linspace(0.1, 1.0, 10)` to use 10 evenly spaced, relative intervals for the training set sizes. By default, the `learning_curve` function uses stratified k-fold cross-validation to calculate the cross-validation accuracy of a classifier, and we set *k=10* via the `cv` parameter for 10-fold stratified cross-validation. Then, we simply calculated the average accuracies from the returned cross-validated training and test scores for the different sizes of the training set, which we plotted using Matplotlib's `plot` function. Furthermore, we added the standard deviation of the average accuracy to the plot using the `fill_between` function to indicate the variance of the estimate.

As we can see in the preceding learning curve plot, our model performs quite well on both the training and validation dataset if it had seen more than 250 samples during training. We can also see that the training accuracy increases for training sets with fewer than 250 samples, and the gap between validation and training accuracy widens—an indicator of an increasing degree of overfitting.

Addressing over- and underfitting with validation curves

Validation curves are a useful tool for improving the performance of a model by addressing issues such as overfitting or underfitting. Validation curves are related to learning curves, but instead of plotting the training and test accuracies as functions of the sample size, we vary the values of the model parameters, for example, the inverse regularization parameter `C` in logistic regression. Let's go ahead and see how we create validation curves via scikit-learn:

```
>>> from sklearn.model_selection import validation_curve
>>> param_range = [0.001, 0.01, 0.1, 1.0, 10.0, 100.0]
>>> train_scores, test_scores = validation_curve(
...                 estimator=pipe_lr,
...                 X=X_train,
...                 y=y_train,
...                 param_name='logisticregression__C',
...                 param_range=param_range,
...                 cv=10)
>>> train_mean = np.mean(train_scores, axis=1)
>>> train_std = np.std(train_scores, axis=1)
>>> test_mean = np.mean(test_scores, axis=1)
>>> test_std = np.std(test_scores, axis=1)
>>> plt.plot(param_range, train_mean,
```

```
...                 color='blue', marker='o',
...                 markersize=5, label='training accuracy')
>>> plt.fill_between(param_range, train_mean + train_std,
...                   train_mean - train_std, alpha=0.15,
...                   color='blue')
>>> plt.plot(param_range, test_mean,
...          color='green', linestyle='--',
...          marker='s', markersize=5,
...          label='validation accuracy')
>>> plt.fill_between(param_range,
...                   test_mean + test_std,
...                   test_mean - test_std,
...                   alpha=0.15, color='green')
>>> plt.grid()
>>> plt.xscale('log')
>>> plt.legend(loc='lower right')
>>> plt.xlabel('Parameter C')
>>> plt.ylabel('Accuracy')
>>> plt.ylim([0.8, 1.03])
>>> plt.show()
```

Using the preceding code, we obtained the validation curve plot for the parameter C:

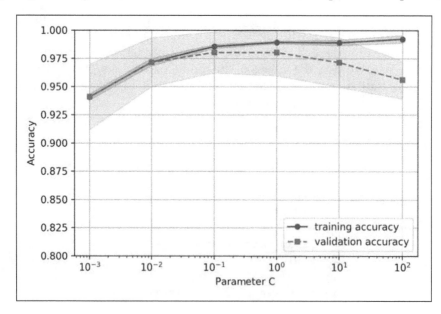

Similar to the `learning_curve` function, the `validation_curve` function uses stratified k-fold cross-validation by default to estimate the performance of the classifier. Inside the `validation_curve` function, we specified the parameter that we wanted to evaluate. In this case, it is `C`, the inverse regularization parameter of the `LogisticRegression` classifier, which we wrote as `'logisticregression__C'` to access the `LogisticRegression` object inside the scikit-learn pipeline for a specified value range that we set via the `param_range` parameter. Similar to the learning curve example in the previous section, we plotted the average training and cross-validation accuracies and the corresponding standard deviations.

Although the differences in the accuracy for varying values of `C` are subtle, we can see that the model slightly underfits the data when we increase the regularization strength (small values of `C`). However, for large values of `C`, it means lowering the strength of regularization, so the model tends to slightly overfit the data. In this case, the sweet spot appears to be between `0.01` and `0.1` of the `C` value.

Fine-tuning machine learning models via grid search

In machine learning, we have two types of parameters: those that are learned from the training data, for example, the weights in logistic regression, and the parameters of a learning algorithm that are optimized separately. The latter are the tuning parameters, also called **hyperparameters**, of a model, for example, the regularization parameter in logistic regression or the depth parameter of a decision tree.

In the previous section, we used validation curves to improve the performance of a model by tuning one of its hyperparameters. In this section, we will take a look at a popular hyperparameter optimization technique called **grid search** that can further help improve the performance of a model by finding the *optimal* combination of hyperparameter values.

Tuning hyperparameters via grid search

The approach of grid search is quite simple; it's a brute-force exhaustive search paradigm where we specify a list of values for different hyperparameters, and the computer evaluates the model performance for each combination of those to obtain the optimal combination of values from this set:

```
>>> from sklearn.model_selection import GridSearchCV
>>> from sklearn.svm import SVC

>>> pipe_svc = make_pipeline(StandardScaler(),
```

```
...                         SVC(random_state=1))
>>> param_range = [0.0001, 0.001, 0.01, 0.1,
...                 1.0, 10.0, 100.0, 1000.0]
>>> param_grid = [{'svc__C': param_range,
...                'svc__kernel': ['linear']},
...               {'svc__C': param_range,
...                'svc__gamma': param_range,
...                'svc__kernel': ['rbf']}]

>>> gs = GridSearchCV(estimator=pipe_svc,
...                   param_grid=param_grid,
...                   scoring='accuracy',
...                   cv=10,
...                   n_jobs=-1)
>>> gs = gs.fit(X_train, y_train)
>>> print(gs.best_score_)
0.9846153846153847
>>> print(gs.best_params_)
{'svc__C': 100.0, 'svc__gamma': 0.001, 'svc__kernel': 'rbf'}
```

Using the preceding code, we initialized a `GridSearchCV` object from the `sklearn.model_selection` module to train and tune a **Support Vector Machine (SVM)** pipeline. We set the `param_grid` parameter of `GridSearchCV` to a list of dictionaries to specify the parameters that we'd want to tune. For the linear SVM, we only evaluated the inverse regularization parameter `C`; for the RBF kernel SVM, we tuned both the `svc__C` and `svc__gamma` parameter. Note that the `svc__gamma` parameter is specific to kernel SVMs.

After we used the training data to perform the grid search, we obtained the score of the best-performing model via the `best_score_` attribute and looked at its parameters that can be accessed via the `best_params_` attribute. In this particular case, the RBF-kernel SVM model with `svc__C = 100.0` yielded the best k-fold cross-validation accuracy: 98.5 percent.

Finally, we will use the independent test dataset to estimate the performance of the best-selected model, which is available via the `best_estimator_` attribute of the `GridSearchCV` object:

```
>>> clf = gs.best_estimator_
>>> clf.fit(X_train, y_train)
>>> print('Test accuracy: %.3f' % clf.score(X_test, y_test))
Test accuracy: 0.974
```

Although grid search is a powerful approach for finding the optimal set of parameters, the evaluation of all possible parameter combinations is also computationally very expensive. An alternative approach to sampling different parameter combinations using scikit-learn is randomized search. Using the `RandomizedSearchCV` class in scikit-learn, we can draw random parameter combinations from sampling distributions with a specified budget. More details and examples of its usage can be found at `http://scikit-learn.org/stable/modules/grid_search.html#randomized-parameter-optimization`.

Algorithm selection with nested cross-validation

Using k-fold cross-validation in combination with grid search is a useful approach for fine-tuning the performance of a machine learning model by varying its hyperparameter values, as we saw in the previous subsection. If we want to select among different machine learning algorithms, though, another recommended approach is nested cross-validation. In a nice study on the bias in error estimation, Varma and Simon concluded that the true error of the estimate is almost unbiased relative to the test set when nested cross-validation is used (*Bias in Error Estimation When Using Cross-validation for Model Selection, BMC Bioinformatics, S. Varma and R. Simon, 7(1): 91, 2006*).

In nested cross-validation, we have an outer k-fold cross-validation loop to split the data into training and test folds, and an inner loop is used to select the model using k-fold cross-validation on the training fold. After model selection, the test fold is then used to evaluate the model performance. The following figure explains the concept of nested cross-validation with only five outer and two inner folds, which can be useful for large datasets where computational performance is important; this particular type of nested cross-validation is also known as **5x2 cross-validation**:

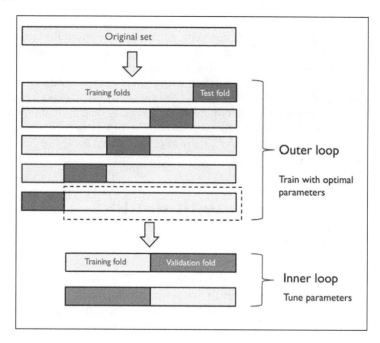

In scikit-learn, we can perform nested cross-validation as follows:

```
>>> gs = GridSearchCV(estimator=pipe_svc,
...                    param_grid=param_grid,
...                    scoring='accuracy',
...                    cv=2)

>>> scores = cross_val_score(gs, X_train, y_train,
...                    scoring='accuracy', cv=5)
>>> print('CV accuracy: %.3f +/- %.3f' % (np.mean(scores),
...                    np.std(scores)))
CV accuracy: 0.974 +/- 0.015
```

The returned average cross-validation accuracy gives us a good estimate of what to expect if we tune the hyperparameters of a model and use it on unseen data. For example, we can use the nested cross-validation approach to compare an SVM model to a simple decision tree classifier; for simplicity, we will only tune its depth parameter:

```
>>> from sklearn.tree import DecisionTreeClassifier

>>> gs = GridSearchCV(estimator=DecisionTreeClassifier(
                              random_state=0),
...                   param_grid=[{'max_depth': [1, 2, 3,
                                                 4, 5, 6, 7, None]}],
...                   scoring='accuracy',
...                   cv=2)

>>> scores = cross_val_score(gs, X_train, y_train,
...                          scoring='accuracy', cv=5)
>>> print('CV accuracy: %.3f +/- %.3f' % (np.mean(scores),
...                                        np.std(scores)))
CV accuracy: 0.934 +/- 0.016
```

As we can see, the nested cross-validation performance of the SVM model (97.4 percent) is notably better than the performance of the decision tree (93.4 percent), and thus, we'd expect that it might be the better choice to classify new data that comes from the same population as this particular dataset.

Looking at different performance evaluation metrics

In the previous sections and chapters, we evaluated our models using model accuracy, which is a useful metric with which to quantify the performance of a model in general. However, there are several other performance metrics that can be used to measure a model's relevance, such as precision, recall, and the F1-score.

Reading a confusion matrix

Before we get into the details of different scoring metrics, let's take a look at a **confusion matrix**, a matrix that lays out the performance of a learning algorithm. The confusion matrix is simply a square matrix that reports the counts of the **True positive (TP)**, **True negative (TN)**, **False positive (FP)**, and **False negative (FN)** predictions of a classifier, as shown in the following figure:

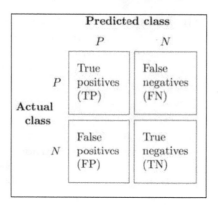

Although these metrics can be easily computed manually by comparing the true and predicted class labels, scikit-learn provides a convenient `confusion_matrix` function that we can use, as follows:

```
>>> from sklearn.metrics import confusion_matrix

>>> pipe_svc.fit(X_train, y_train)
>>> y_pred = pipe_svc.predict(X_test)
>>> confmat = confusion_matrix(y_true=y_test, y_pred=y_pred)
>>> print(confmat)
[[71   1]
 [ 2 40]]
```

The array that was returned after executing the code provides us with information about the different types of error the classifier made on the test dataset. We can map this information onto the confusion matrix illustration in the previous figure using Matplotlib's `matshow` function:

```
>>> fig, ax = plt.subplots(figsize=(2.5, 2.5))
>>> ax.matshow(confmat, cmap=plt.cm.Blues, alpha=0.3)
>>> for i in range(confmat.shape[0]):
...     for j in range(confmat.shape[1]):
...         ax.text(x=j, y=i,
...                 s=confmat[i, j],
```

```
...                    va='center', ha='center')
>>> plt.xlabel('predicted label')
>>> plt.ylabel('true label')
>>> plt.show()
```

Now, the following confusion matrix plot, with the added labels, should make the results a little bit easier to interpret:

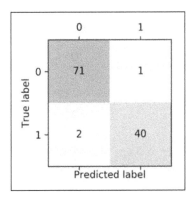

Assuming that class `1` (malignant) is the positive class in this example, our model correctly classified 71 of the samples that belong to class `0` (TNs) and 40 samples that belong to class `1` (TPs), respectively. However, our model also incorrectly misclassified two samples from class `1` as class `0` (FN), and it predicted that one sample is malignant although it is a benign tumor (FP). In the next section, we will learn how we can use this information to calculate various error metrics.

Optimizing the precision and recall of a classification model

Both the prediction **error (ERR)** and **accuracy (ACC)** provide general information about how many samples are misclassified. The error can be understood as the sum of all false predictions divided by the number of total predications, and the accuracy is calculated as the sum of correct predictions divided by the total number of predictions, respectively:

$$ERR = \frac{FP + FN}{FP + FN + TP + TN}$$

The prediction accuracy can then be calculated directly from the error:

$$ACC = \frac{TP + TN}{FP + FN + TP + TN} = 1 - ERR$$

The **True positive rate (TPR)** and **False positive rate (FPR)** are performance metrics that are especially useful for imbalanced class problems:

$$FPR = \frac{FP}{N} = \frac{FP}{FP + TN}$$

$$TPR = \frac{TP}{P} = \frac{TP}{FN + TP}$$

In tumor diagnosis, for example, we are more concerned about the detection of malignant tumors in order to help a patient with the appropriate treatment. However, it is also important to decrease the number of benign tumors that were incorrectly classified as malignant (FPs) to not unnecessarily concern a patient. In contrast to the FPR, the TPR provides useful information about the fraction of positive (or relevant) samples that were correctly identified out of the total pool of positives (P).

The performance metrics **precision (PRE)** and **recall (REC)** are related to those true positive and negative rates, and in fact, REC is synonymous with TPR:

$$PRE = \frac{TP}{TP + FP}$$

$$REC = TPR = \frac{TP}{P} = \frac{TP}{FN + TP}$$

In practice, often a combination of PRE and REC is used, the so-called **F1-score**:

$$F1 = 2 \frac{PRE \times REC}{PRE + REC}$$

Those scoring metrics are all implemented in scikit-learn and can be imported from the `sklearn.metrics` module as shown in the following snippet:

```
>>> from sklearn.metrics import precision_score
>>> from sklearn.metrics import recall_score, f1_score

>>> print('Precision: %.3f' % precision_score(
...                    y_true=y_test, y_pred=y_pred))
Precision: 0.976
>>> print('Recall: %.3f' % recall_score(
...                    y_true=y_test, y_pred=y_pred))
Recall: 0.952
>>> print('F1: %.3f' % f1_score(
...                    y_true=y_test, y_pred=y_pred))
F1: 0.964
```

Furthermore, we can use a different scoring metric than accuracy in the `GridSearchCV` via the scoring parameter. A complete list of the different values that are accepted by the scoring parameter can be found at http://scikit-learn.org/stable/modules/model_evaluation.html.

Remember that the positive class in scikit-learn is the class that is labeled as class 1. If we want to specify a different *positive label*, we can construct our own scorer via the `make_scorer` function, which we can then directly provide as an argument to the scoring parameter in `GridSearchCV` (in this example, using the `f1_score` as a metric):

```
>>> from sklearn.metrics import make_scorer, f1_score
>>> scorer = make_scorer(f1_score, pos_label=0)
>>> gs = GridSearchCV(estimator=pipe_svc,
...                    param_grid=param_grid,
...                    scoring=scorer,
...                    cv=10)
>>> gs = gs.fit(X_train, y_train)
>>> print(gs.best_score_)
0.986202145696
>>> print(gs.best_params_)
{'svc__C': 10.0, 'svc__gamma': 0.01, 'svc__kernel': 'rbf'}
```

Plotting a receiver operating characteristic

Receiver Operating Characteristic (ROC) graphs are useful tools to select models for classification based on their performance with respect to the FPR and TPR, which are computed by shifting the decision threshold of the classifier. The diagonal of an ROC graph can be interpreted as *random guessing*, and classification models that fall below the diagonal are considered as worse than random guessing. A perfect classifier would fall into the top left corner of the graph with a TPR of 1 and an FPR of 0. Based on the ROC curve, we can then compute the so-called **ROC Area Under the Curve (ROC AUC)** to characterize the performance of a classification model.

Similar to ROC curves, we can compute **precision-recall curves** for different probability thresholds of a classifier. A function for plotting those precision-recall curves is also implemented in scikit-learn and is documented at http://scikit-learn.org/stable/modules/generated/sklearn.metrics.precision_recall_curve.html.

Executing the following code example, we will plot an ROC curve of a classifier that only uses two features from the Breast Cancer Wisconsin dataset to predict whether a tumor is benign or malignant. Although we are going to use the same logistic regression pipeline that we defined previously, we are making the classification task more challenging for the classifier so that the resulting ROC curve becomes visually more interesting. For similar reasons, we are also reducing the number of folds in the StratifiedKFold validator to three. The code is as follows:

```
>>> from sklearn.metrics import roc_curve, auc
>>> from scipy import interp

>>> pipe_lr = make_pipeline(StandardScaler(),
...                         PCA(n_components=2),
...                         LogisticRegression(penalty='l2',
...                                            random_state=1,
...                                            C=100.0))

>>> X_train2 = X_train[:, [4, 14]]

>>> cv = list(StratifiedKFold(n_splits=3,
...                           random_state=1).split(X_train,
...                                                 y_train))
>>> fig = plt.figure(figsize=(7, 5))

>>> mean_tpr = 0.0
```

```
>>> mean_fpr = np.linspace(0, 1, 100)
>>> all_tpr = []

>>> for i, (train, test) in enumerate(cv):
...     probas = pipe_lr.fit(X_train2[train],
...                 y_train[train]).predict_proba(X_train2[test])
...     fpr, tpr, thresholds = roc_curve(y_train[test],
...                                 probas[:, 1],
...                                 pos_label=1)
>>>     mean_tpr += interp(mean_fpr, fpr, tpr)
>>>     mean_tpr[0] = 0.0
>>>     roc_auc = auc(fpr, tpr)
>>>     plt.plot(fpr,
...             tpr,
...             label='ROC fold %d (area = %0.2f)'
...                 % (i+1, roc_auc))
>>> plt.plot([0, 1],
...         [0, 1],
...         linestyle='--',
...         color=(0.6, 0.6, 0.6),
...         label='random guessing')

>>> mean_tpr /= len(cv)
>>> mean_tpr[-1] = 1.0
>>> mean_auc = auc(mean_fpr, mean_tpr)
>>> plt.plot(mean_fpr, mean_tpr, 'k--',
...         label='mean ROC (area = %0.2f)' % mean_auc, lw=2)
>>> plt.plot([0, 0, 1],
...         [0, 1, 1],
...         linestyle=':',
...         color='black',
...         label='perfect performance')
>>> plt.xlim([-0.05, 1.05])
>>> plt.ylim([-0.05, 1.05])
>>> plt.xlabel('false positive rate')
>>> plt.ylabel('true positive rate')
>>> plt.legend(loc="lower right")
>>> plt.show()
```

In the preceding code example, we used the already familiar `StratifiedKFold` class from scikit-learn and calculated the ROC performance of the `LogisticRegression` classifier in our `pipe_lr` pipeline using the `roc_curve` function from the `sklearn.metrics` module separately for each iteration. Furthermore, we interpolated the average ROC curve from the three folds via the `interp` function that we imported from SciPy and calculated the area under the curve via the `auc` function. The resulting ROC curve indicates that there is a certain degree of variance between the different folds, and the average ROC AUC (0.76) falls between a perfect score (1.0) and random guessing (0.5):

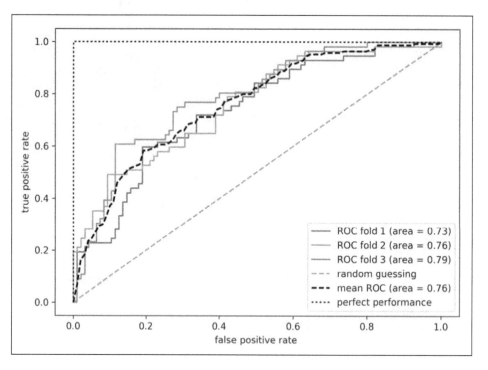

Note if we are just interested in the ROC AUC score, we could also directly import the `roc_auc_score` function from the `sklearn.metrics` submodule.

Reporting the performance of a classifier as the ROC AUC can yield further insights in a classifier's performance with respect to imbalanced samples. However, while the accuracy score can be interpreted as a single cut-off point on an ROC curve, A. P. Bradley showed that the ROC AUC and accuracy metrics mostly agree with each other: *The use of the area under the roc curve in the evaluation of machine learning algorithms, A. P. Bradley, Pattern Recognition, 30(7): 1145-1159, 1997.*

Scoring metrics for multiclass classification

The scoring metrics that we discussed in this section are specific to binary classification systems. However, scikit-learn also implements macro and micro averaging methods to extend those scoring metrics to multiclass problems via **One-versus-All (OvA)** classification. The micro-average is calculated from the individual TPs, TNs, FPs, and FNs of the system. For example, the micro-average of the precision score in a k-class system can be calculated as follows:

$$PRE_{micro} = \frac{TP_1 + \cdots + TP_k}{TP_1 + \cdots + TP_k + FP_1 + \cdots + FP_k}$$

The macro-average is simply calculated as the average scores of the different systems:

$$PRE_{macro} = \frac{PRE_1 + \cdots + PRE_k}{k}$$

Micro-averaging is useful if we want to weight each instance or prediction equally, whereas macro-averaging weights all classes equally to evaluate the overall performance of a classifier with regard to the most frequent class labels.

If we are using binary performance metrics to evaluate multiclass classification models in scikit-learn, a normalized or weighted variant of the macro-average is used by default. The weighted macro-average is calculated by weighting the score of each class label by the number of true instances when calculating the average. The weighted macro-average is useful if we are dealing with class imbalances, that is, different numbers of instances for each label.

While the weighted macro-average is the default for multiclass problems in scikit-learn, we can specify the averaging method via the `average` parameter inside the different scoring functions that we import from the `sklearn.metrics` module, for example, the `precision_score` or `make_scorer` functions:

```
>>> pre_scorer = make_scorer(score_func=precision_score,
...                          pos_label=1,
...                          greater_is_better=True,
...                          average='micro')
```

Dealing with class imbalance

We've mentioned class imbalances several times throughout this chapter, and yet we haven't actually discussed how to deal with such scenarios appropriately if they occur. Class imbalance is a quite common problem when working with real-world data — samples from one class or multiple classes are over-represented in a dataset. Intuitively, we can think of several domains where this may occur, such as spam filtering, fraud detection, or screening for diseases.

Imagine the breast cancer dataset that we've been working with in this chapter consisted of 90 percent healthy patients. In this case, we could achieve 90 percent accuracy on the test dataset by just predicting the majority class (benign tumor) for all samples, without the help of a supervised machine learning algorithm. Thus, training a model on such a dataset that achieves approximately 90 percent test accuracy would mean our model hasn't learned anything useful from the features provided in this dataset.

In this section, we will briefly go over some of the techniques that could help with imbalanced datasets. But before we discuss different methods to approach this problem, let's create an imbalanced dataset from our breast cancer dataset, which originally consisted of 357 benign tumors (class 0) and 212 malignant tumors (class 1):

```
>>> X_imb = np.vstack((X[y == 0], X[y == 1][:40]))
>>> y_imb = np.hstack((y[y == 0], y[y == 1][:40]))
```

In the previous code snippet, we took all 357 benign tumor samples and stacked them with the first 40 malignant samples to create a stark class imbalance. If we were to compute the accuracy of a model that always predicts the majority class (benign, class 0), we would achieve a prediction accuracy of approximately 90 percent:

```
>>> y_pred = np.zeros(y_imb.shape[0])
>>> np.mean(y_pred == y_imb) * 100
89.92443324937027
```

Thus, when we fit classifiers on such datasets, it would make sense to focus on other metrics than accuracy when comparing different models, such as precision, recall, the ROC curve — whatever we care most about in our application. For instance, our priority might be to identify the majority of patients with malignant cancer patients to recommend an additional screening, then recall should be our metric of choice. In spam filtering, where we don't want to label emails as spam if the system is not very certain, precision might be a more appropriate metric.

Aside from evaluating machine learning models, class imbalance influences a learning algorithm during model fitting itself. Since machine learning algorithms typically optimize a reward or cost function that is computed as a sum over the training examples that it sees during fitting, the decision rule is likely going to be biased towards the majority class. In other words, the algorithm implicitly learns a model that optimizes the predictions based on the most abundant class in the dataset, in order to minimize the cost or maximize the reward during training.

One way to deal with imbalanced class proportions during model fitting is to assign a larger penalty to wrong predictions on the minority class. Via scikit-learn, adjusting such a penalty is as convenient as setting the `class_weight` parameter to `class_weight='balanced'`, which is implemented for most classifiers.

Other popular strategies for dealing with class imbalance include upsampling the minority class, downsampling the majority class, and the generation of synthetic training samples. Unfortunately, there's no universally best solution, no technique that works best across different problem domains. Thus, in practice, it is recommended to try out different strategies on a given problem, evaluate the results, and choose the technique that seems most appropriate.

The scikit-learn library implements a simple `resample` function that can help with the upsampling of the minority class by drawing new samples from the dataset with replacement. The following code will take the minority class from our imbalanced breast cancer dataset (here, class `1`) and repeatedly draw new samples from it until it contains the same number of samples as class label `0`:

```
>>> from sklearn.utils import resample

>>> print('Number of class 1 samples before:',
...       X_imb[y_imb == 1].shape[0])
Number of class 1 samples before: 40


>>> X_upsampled, y_upsampled = resample(X_imb[y_imb == 1],
...                          y_imb[y_imb == 1],
...                          replace=True,
...                          n_samples=X_imb[y_imb == 0].shape[0],
...                          random_state=123)
>>> print('Number of class 1 samples after:',
...       X_upsampled.shape[0])
Number of class 1 samples after: 357
```

After resampling, we can then stack the original class 0 samples with the upsampled class 1 subset to obtain a balanced dataset as follows:

```
>>> X_bal = np.vstack((X[y == 0], X_upsampled))
>>> y_bal = np.hstack((y[y == 0], y_upsampled))
```

Consequently, a majority vote prediction rule would only achieve 50 percent accuracy:

```
>>> y_pred = np.zeros(y_bal.shape[0])
>>> np.mean(y_pred == y_bal) * 100
```

Similarly, we could downsample the majority class by removing training examples from the dataset. To perform downsampling using the resample function, we could simply swap the class 1 label with class 0 in the previous code example and vice versa.

Another technique for dealing with class imbalance is the generation of synthetic training samples, which is beyond the scope of this book. The probably most widely used algorithm for synthetic training sample generation is **Synthetic Minority Over-sampling Technique** (**SMOTE**), and you can learn more about this technique in the original research article by Nitesh Chawla and others: *SMOTE: Synthetic Minority Over-sampling Technique, Journal of Artificial Intelligence Research*, 16: 321-357, 2002. It is also highly recommended to check out imbalanced-learn, a Python library that is entirely focused on imbalanced datasets, including an implementation of SMOTE. You can learn more about imbalanced-learn at https://github.com/scikit-learn-contrib/imbalanced-learn.

Summary

At the beginning of this chapter, we discussed how to chain different transformation techniques and classifiers in convenient model pipelines that helped us train and evaluate machine learning models more efficiently. We then used those pipelines to perform k-fold cross-validation, one of the essential techniques for model selection and evaluation. Using k-fold cross-validation, we plotted learning and validation curves to diagnose the common problems of learning algorithms, such as overfitting and underfitting. Using grid search, we further fine-tuned our model. We concluded this chapter by looking at a confusion matrix and various performance metrics that can be useful to further optimize a model's performance for a specific problem task. Now, we should be well-equipped with the essential techniques to build supervised machine learning models for classification successfully.

In the next chapter, we will look at ensemble methods: methods that allow us to combine multiple models and classification algorithms to boost the predictive performance of a machine learning system even further.

7
Combining Different Models for Ensemble Learning

In the previous chapter, we focused on the best practices for tuning and evaluating different models for classification. In this chapter, we will build upon these techniques and explore different methods for constructing a set of classifiers that can often have a better predictive performance than any of its individual members. We will learn how to do the following:

- Make predictions based on majority voting
- Use bagging to reduce overfitting by drawing random combinations of the training set with repetition
- Apply boosting to build powerful models from *weak learners* that learn from their mistakes

Learning with ensembles

The goal of **ensemble methods** is to combine different classifiers into a meta-classifier that has better generalization performance than each individual classifier alone. For example, assuming that we collected predictions from 10 experts, ensemble methods would allow us to strategically combine these predictions by the 10 experts to come up with a prediction that is more accurate and robust than the predictions by each individual expert. As we will see later in this chapter, there are several different approaches for creating an ensemble of classifiers. In this section, we will introduce a basic perception of how ensembles work and why they are typically recognized for yielding a good generalization performance.

In this chapter, we will focus on the most popular ensemble methods that use the **majority voting** principle. Majority voting simply means that we select the class label that has been predicted by the majority of classifiers, that is, received more than 50 percent of the votes. Strictly speaking, the term **majority vote** refers to binary class settings only. However, it is easy to generalize the majority voting principle to multi-class settings, which is called **plurality voting**. Here, we select the class label that received the most votes (mode). The following diagram illustrates the concept of majority and plurality voting for an ensemble of 10 classifiers where each unique symbol (triangle, square, and circle) represents a unique class label:

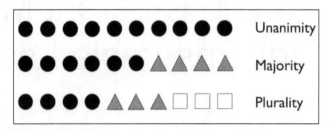

Using the training set, we start by training m different classifiers ($C_1, \ldots, C_m$). Depending on the technique, the ensemble can be built from different classification algorithms, for example, decision trees, support vector machines, logistic regression classifiers, and so on. Alternatively, we can also use the same base classification algorithm, fitting different subsets of the training set. One prominent example of this approach is the random forest algorithm, which combines different decision tree classifiers. The following figure illustrates the concept of a general ensemble approach using majority voting:

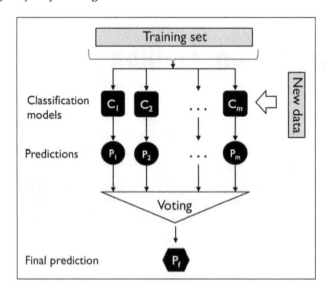

To predict a class label via simple majority or plurality voting, we combine the predicted class labels of each individual classifier, C_j, and select the class label, $\hat{y}$, that received the most votes:

$$\hat{y} = mode\{C_1(x), C_2(x), \ldots, C_m(x)\}$$

For example, in a binary classification task where $class1 = -1$ and $class2 = +1$, we can write the majority vote prediction as follows:

$$C(x) = sign\left[\sum_j^m C_j(x)\right] = \begin{cases} 1 & if \sum_i C_j(x) \geq 0 \\ -1 & otherwise \end{cases}$$

To illustrate why ensemble methods can work better than individual classifiers alone, let's apply the simple concepts of combinatorics. For the following example, we make the assumption that all n-base classifiers for a binary classification task have an equal error rate, ε. Furthermore, we assume that the classifiers are independent and the error rates are not correlated. Under those assumptions, we can simply express the error probability of an ensemble of base classifiers as a probability mass function of a binomial distribution:

$$P(y \geq k) = \sum_k^n \binom{n}{k} \varepsilon^k (1-\varepsilon)^{n-k} = \varepsilon_{ensemble}$$

Here, $\binom{n}{k}$ is the binomial coefficient **n choose k**. In other words, we compute the probability that the prediction of the ensemble is wrong. Now let's take a look at a more concrete example of 11 base classifiers ($n = 11$), where each classifier has an error rate of 0.25 ($\varepsilon = 0.25$):

$$P(y \geq k) = \sum_{k=6}^{11} \binom{11}{k} 0.25^k (1-0.25)^{11-k} = 0.034$$

The binomial coefficient

The binomial coefficient refers to the number of ways we can choose subsets of k unordered elements from a set of size n; thus, it is often called "n choose k." Since the order does not matter here, the binomial coefficient is also sometimes referred to as *combination* or *combinatorial number*, and in its unabbreviated form, it is written as follows:

$$\frac{n!}{(n-k)!k!}$$

Here, the symbol (!) stands for factorial—for example, $3! = 3 \times 2 \times 1 = 6$.

As we can see, the error rate of the ensemble (0.034) is much lower than the error rate of each individual classifier (0.25) if all the assumptions are met. Note that, in this simplified illustration, a 50-50 split by an even number of classifiers n is treated as an error, whereas this is only true half of the time. To compare such an idealistic ensemble classifier to a base classifier over a range of different base error rates, let's implement the probability mass function in Python:

```
>>> from scipy.special import comb
>>> import math
>>> def ensemble_error(n_classifier, error):
...     k_start = int(math.ceil(n_classifier / 2.))
...     probs = [comb(n_classifier, k) *
...             error**k *
...             (1-error)**(n_classifier - k)
...             for k in range(k_start, n_classifier + 1)]
...     return sum(probs)
>>> ensemble_error(n_classifier=11, error=0.25)
0.03432750701904297
```

After we have implemented the `ensemble_error` function, we can compute the ensemble error rates for a range of different base errors from 0.0 to 1.0 to visualize the relationship between ensemble and base errors in a line graph:

```
>>> import numpy as np
>>> import matplotlib.pyplot as plt
>>> error_range = np.arange(0.0, 1.01, 0.01)
>>> ens_errors = [ensemble_error(n_classifier=11, error=error)
...               for error in error_range]
```

```
>>> plt.plot(error_range, ens_errors,
...          label='Ensemble error',
...          linewidth=2)
>>> plt.plot(error_range, error_range,
...          linestyle='--', label='Base error',
...          linewidth=2)
>>> plt.xlabel('Base error')
>>> plt.ylabel('Base/Ensemble error')
>>> plt.legend(loc='upper left')
>>> plt.grid(alpha=0.5)
>>> plt.show()
```

As we can see in the resulting plot, the error probability of an ensemble is always better than the error of an individual base classifier, as long as the base classifiers perform better than random guessing ($\varepsilon < 0.5$). Note that the y-axis depicts the base error (dotted line) as well as the ensemble error (continuous line):

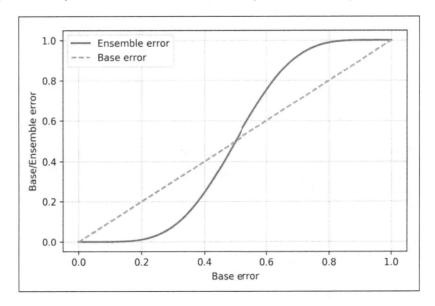

Combining classifiers via majority vote

After the short introduction to ensemble learning in the previous section, let's start with a warm-up exercise and implement a simple ensemble classifier for majority voting in Python.

 Although the majority voting algorithm that we will discuss in this section also generalizes to multi-class settings via plurality voting, we will use the term majority voting for simplicity, as it is also often done in the literature.

Implementing a simple majority vote classifier

The algorithm that we are going to implement in this section will allow us to combine different classification algorithms associated with individual weights for confidence. Our goal is to build a stronger meta-classifier that balances out the individual classifiers' weaknesses on a particular dataset. In more precise mathematical terms, we can write the weighted majority vote as follows:

$$\hat{y} = \arg\max_i \sum_{j=1}^{m} w_j \chi_A \left(C_j(x) = i \right)$$

Here, w_j is a weight associated with a base classifier, C_j, $\hat{y}$ is the predicted class label of the ensemble, χ_A (Greek chi) is the characteristic function $\left[C_j(x) = i \in A \right]$, and A is the set of unique class labels. For equal weights, we can simplify this equation and write it as follows:

$$\hat{y} = mode\{C_1(x), C_2(x), \ldots, C_m(x)\}$$

 In statistics, the *mode* is the most frequent event or result in a set. For example, *mode{1,2,1 1,2,4,5,4} = 1*.

To better understand the concept of *weighting*, we will now take a look at a more concrete example. Let us assume that we have an ensemble of three base classifiers, C_j ($j \in \{0,1\}$), and want to predict the class label of a given sample instance, **x**. Two out of three base classifiers predict the class label 0, and one, C_3, predicts that the sample belongs to class 1. If we weight the predictions of each base classifier equally, the majority vote would predict that the sample belongs to class 0:

$$C_1(x) \rightarrow 0, \ C_2(x) \rightarrow 0, \ C_3(x) \rightarrow 1$$

$$\hat{y} = mode\{0,0,1\} = 0$$

Now, let us assign a weight of 0.6 to C_3 and weight C_1 and C_2 by a coefficient of 0.2:

$$\hat{y} = \arg\max_i \sum_{j=1}^{m} w_j \chi_A \left(C_j(x) = i \right)$$

$$= \arg\max_i \left[0.2 \times i_0 + 0.2 \times i_0 + 0.6 \times i_1 \right] = 1$$

More intuitively, since 3 x 0.2 = 0.6, we can say that the prediction made by C_3 has three times more weight than the predictions by C_1 or C_2, which we can write as follows:

$$\hat{y} = mode\{0,0,1,1,1\} = 1$$

To translate the concept of the weighted majority vote into Python code, we can use NumPy's convenient `argmax` and `bincount` functions:

```
>>> import numpy as np
>>> np.argmax(np.bincount([0, 0, 1],
...            weights=[0.2, 0.2, 0.6]))
1
```

As we remember from the discussion on logistic regression in *Chapter 3, A Tour of Machine Learning Classifiers Using scikit-learn*, certain classifiers in scikit-learn can also return the probability of a predicted class label via the `predict_proba` method. Using the predicted class probabilities instead of the class labels for majority voting can be useful if the classifiers in our ensemble are well calibrated. The modified version of the majority vote for predicting class labels from probabilities can be written as follows:

$$\hat{y} = \arg\max_i \sum_{j=1}^{m} w_j p_{ij}$$

Here, p_{ij} is the predicted probability of the *j*th classifier for class label *i*.

To continue with our previous example, let's assume that we have a binary classification problem with class labels $i \in \{0,1\}$ and an ensemble of three classifiers C_j ($j \in \{1,2,3\}$). Let's assume that the classifiers C_j return the following class membership probabilities for a particular sample **x**:

$$C_1(x) \rightarrow [0.9, 0.1], \ C_2(x) \rightarrow [0.8, 0.2], \ C_3(x) \rightarrow [0.4, 0.6]$$

We can then calculate the individual class probabilities as follows:

$$p(i_0 \mid x) = 0.2 \times 0.9 + 0.2 \times 0.8 + 0.6 \times 0.4 = 0.58$$

$$p(i_1 \mid x) = 0.2 \times 0.1 + 0.2 \times 0.2 + 0.6 \times 0.6 = 0.42$$

$$\hat{y} = \arg\max_i \left[p(i_0 \mid x), p(i_1 \mid x) \right] = 0$$

To implement the weighted majority vote based on class probabilities, we can again make use of NumPy using `numpy.average` and `np.argmax`:

```
>>> ex = np.array([[0.9, 0.1],
...                [0.8, 0.2],
...                [0.4, 0.6]])
>>> p = np.average(ex, axis=0, weights=[0.2, 0.2, 0.6])
>>> p
array([ 0.58,  0.42])
>>> np.argmax(p)
0
```

Putting everything together, let's now implement `MajorityVoteClassifier` in Python:

```
from sklearn.base import BaseEstimator
from sklearn.base import ClassifierMixin
from sklearn.preprocessing import LabelEncoder
from sklearn.externals import six
from sklearn.base import clone
from sklearn.pipeline import _name_estimators
import numpy as np
import operator


class MajorityVoteClassifier(BaseEstimator,
                             ClassifierMixin):
    """ A majority vote ensemble classifier

    Parameters
    ----------
    classifiers : array-like, shape = [n_classifiers]
      Different classifiers for the ensemble

    vote : str, {'classlabel', 'probability'}
      Default: 'classlabel'
      If 'classlabel' the prediction is based on
      the argmax of class labels. Else if
      'probability', the argmax of the sum of
      probabilities is used to predict the class label
      (recommended for calibrated classifiers).

    weights : array-like, shape = [n_classifiers]
      Optional, default: None
      If a list of `int` or `float` values are
      provided, the classifiers are weighted by
      importance; Uses uniform weights if `weights=None`.

    """
    def __init__(self, classifiers,
                 vote='classlabel', weights=None):

        self.classifiers = classifiers
        self.named_classifiers = {key: value for
                                  key, value in
                                  _name_estimators(classifiers)}
        self.vote = vote
```

```
            self.weights = weights

    def fit(self, X, y):
        """ Fit classifiers.

        Parameters
        ----------
        X : {array-like, sparse matrix},
            shape = [n_samples, n_features]
            Matrix of training samples.

        y : array-like, shape = [n_samples]
            Vector of target class labels.

        Returns
        -------
        self : object

        """
        # Use LabelEncoder to ensure class labels start
        # with 0, which is important for np.argmax
        # call in self.predict
        self.lablenc_ = LabelEncoder()
        self.lablenc_.fit(y)
        self.classes_ = self.lablenc_.classes_
        self.classifiers_ = []
        for clf in self.classifiers:
            fitted_clf = clone(clf).fit(X,
                              self.lablenc_.transform(y))
            self.classifiers_.append(fitted_clf)
        return self
```

I've added a lot of comments to the code to explain the individual parts. However, before we implement the remaining methods, let's take a quick break and discuss some of the code that may look confusing at first. We used the `BaseEstimator` and `ClassifierMixin` parent classes to get some base functionality *for free*, including the `get_params` and `set_params` methods to set and return the classifier's parameters, as well as the `score` method to calculate the prediction accuracy. Also note that we imported `six` to make `MajorityVoteClassifier` compatible with Python 2.6.

Next, we will add the `predict` method to predict the class label via a majority vote based on the class labels if we initialize a new `MajorityVoteClassifier` object with `vote='classlabel'`. Alternatively, we will be able to initialize the ensemble classifier with `vote='probability'` to predict the class label based on the class membership probabilities. Furthermore, we will also add a `predict_proba` method to return the averaged probabilities, which is useful when computing the ROC AUC:

```
def predict(self, X):
    """ Predict class labels for X.

    Parameters
    ----------
    X : {array-like, sparse matrix},
        Shape = [n_samples, n_features]
        Matrix of training samples.

    Returns
    ----------
    maj_vote : array-like, shape = [n_samples]
        Predicted class labels.

    """
    if self.vote == 'probability':
        maj_vote = np.argmax(self.predict_proba(X),
                             axis=1)
    else:  # 'classlabel' vote

        #  Collect results from clf.predict calls
        predictions = np.asarray([clf.predict(X)
                                  for clf in
                                  self.classifiers_]).T

        maj_vote = np.apply_along_axis(
                    lambda x:
                    np.argmax(np.bincount(x,
                            weights=self.weights)),
                    axis=1,
                    arr=predictions)
    maj_vote = self.lablenc_.inverse_transform(maj_vote)
    return maj_vote

def predict_proba(self, X):
```

```
    """ Predict class probabilities for X.

    Parameters
    ----------
    X : {array-like, sparse matrix},
        shape = [n_samples, n_features]
        Training vectors, where n_samples is
        the number of samples and
        n_features is the number of features.

    Returns
    ----------
    avg_proba : array-like,
        shape = [n_samples, n_classes]
        Weighted average probability for
        each class per sample.

    """
    probas = np.asarray([clf.predict_proba(X)
                    for clf in self.classifiers_])
    avg_proba = np.average(probas,
                    axis=0, weights=self.weights)
    return avg_proba

def get_params(self, deep=True):
    """ Get classifier parameter names for GridSearch"""
    if not deep:
        return super(MajorityVoteClassifier,
                    self).get_params(deep=False)
    else:
        out = self.named_classifiers.copy()
        for name, step in\
                six.iteritems(self.named_classifiers):
            for key, value in six.iteritems(
                    step.get_params(deep=True)):
                out['%s__%s' % (name, key)] = value
        return out
```

Also, note that we defined our own modified version of the `get_params` method to use the `_name_estimators` function to access the parameters of individual classifiers in the ensemble; this may look a little bit complicated at first, but it will make perfect sense when we use grid search for hyperparameter tuning in later sections.

Although the `MajorityVoteClassifier` implementation is very useful for demonstration purposes, we implemented a more sophisticated version of this majority vote classifier in scikit-learn based on the implementation in the first edition of this book. The ensemble classifier is available as `sklearn.ensemble.VotingClassifier` in scikit-learn version 0.17 and newer.

Using the majority voting principle to make predictions

Now it is about time to put the `MajorityVoteClassifier` that we implemented in the previous section into action. But first, let's prepare a dataset that we can test it on. Since we are already familiar with techniques to load datasets from CSV files, we will take a shortcut and load the Iris dataset from scikit-learn's dataset module. Furthermore, we will only select two features, **sepal width** and **petal length**, to make the classification task more challenging for illustration purposes. Although our `MajorityVoteClassifier` generalizes to multiclass problems, we will only classify flower samples from the `Iris-versicolor` and `Iris-virginica` classes, with which we will compute the ROC AUC later. The code is as follows:

```
>>> from sklearn import datasets
>>> from sklearn.model_selection import train_test_split
>>> from sklearn.preprocessing import StandardScaler
>>> from sklearn.preprocessing import LabelEncoder
>>> iris = datasets.load_iris()
>>> X, y = iris.data[50:, [1, 2]], iris.target[50:]
>>> le = LabelEncoder()
>>> y = le.fit_transform(y)
```

Note that scikit-learn uses the `predict_proba` method (if applicable) to compute the ROC AUC score. In *Chapter 3, A Tour of Machine Learning Classifiers Using scikit-learn*, we saw how the class probabilities are computed in logistic regression models. In decision trees, the probabilities are calculated from a frequency vector that is created for each node at training time. The vector collects the frequency values of each class label computed from the class label distribution at that node. Then, the frequencies are normalized so that they sum up to 1. Similarly, the class labels of the k-nearest neighbors are aggregated to return the normalized class label frequencies in the k-nearest neighbors algorithm. Although the normalized probabilities returned by both the decision tree and k-nearest neighbors classifier may look similar to the probabilities obtained from a logistic regression model, we have to be aware that these are actually not derived from probability mass functions.

Next, we split the Iris samples into 50 percent training and 50 percent test data:

```
>>> X_train, X_test, y_train, y_test =\
...         train_test_split(X, y,
...                          test_size=0.5,
...                          random_state=1,
...                          stratify=y)
```

Using the training dataset, we now will train three different classifiers:

- Logistic regression classifier
- Decision tree classifier
- k-nearest neighbors classifier

We then evaluate the model performance of each classifier via 10-fold cross-validation on the training dataset before we combine them into an ensemble classifier:

```
>>> from sklearn.model_selection import cross_val_score
>>> from sklearn.linear_model import LogisticRegression
>>> from sklearn.tree import DecisionTreeClassifier
>>> from sklearn.neighbors import KNeighborsClassifier
>>> from sklearn.pipeline import Pipeline
>>> import numpy as np
>>> clf1 = LogisticRegression(penalty='l2',
...                           C=0.001,
...                           random_state=1)
>>> clf2 = DecisionTreeClassifier(max_depth=1,
...                               criterion='entropy',
...                               random_state=0)
```

```
>>> clf3 = KNeighborsClassifier(n_neighbors=1,
...                             p=2,
...                             metric='minkowski')
>>> pipe1 = Pipeline([['sc', StandardScaler()],
...                   ['clf', clf1]])
>>> pipe3 = Pipeline([['sc', StandardScaler()],
...                   ['clf', clf3]])
>>> clf_labels = ['Logistic regression', 'Decision tree', 'KNN']
>>> print('10-fold cross validation:\n')
>>> for clf, label in zip([pipe1, clf2, pipe3], clf_labels):
...     scores = cross_val_score(estimator=clf,
...                              X=X_train,
...                              y=y_train,
...                              cv=10,
...                              scoring='roc_auc')
...     print("ROC AUC: %0.2f (+/- %0.2f) [%s]"
...           % (scores.mean(), scores.std(), label))
```

The output that we receive, as shown in the following snippet, shows that the predictive performances of the individual classifiers are almost equal:

```
10-fold cross validation:

ROC AUC: 0.87 (+/- 0.17) [Logistic regression]
ROC AUC: 0.89 (+/- 0.16) [Decision tree]
ROC AUC: 0.88 (+/- 0.15) [KNN]
```

You may be wondering why we trained the logistic regression and k-nearest neighbors classifier as part of a pipeline. The reason behind it is that, as discussed in *Chapter 3, A Tour of Machine Learning Classifiers Using scikit-learn*, both the logistic regression and k-nearest neighbors algorithms (using the Euclidean distance metric) are not scale-invariant, in contrast to decision trees. Although the Iris features are all measured on the same scale (cm), it is a good habit to work with standardized features.

Now let's move on to the more exciting part and combine the individual classifiers for majority rule voting in our MajorityVoteClassifier:

```
>>> mv_clf = MajorityVoteClassifier(
...                 classifiers=[pipe1, clf2, pipe3])
>>> clf_labels += ['Majority voting']
>>> all_clf = [pipe1, clf2, pipe3, mv_clf]
>>> for clf, label in zip(all_clf, clf_labels):
...     scores = cross_val_score(estimator=clf,
...                              X=X_train,
...                              y=y_train,
```

```
...                                       cv=10,
...                                       scoring='roc_auc')
...       print("Accuracy: %0.2f (+/- %0.2f) [%s]"
...                 % (scores.mean(), scores.std(), label))
ROC AUC: 0.87 (+/- 0.17) [Logistic regression]
ROC AUC: 0.89 (+/- 0.16) [Decision tree]
ROC AUC: 0.88 (+/- 0.15) [KNN]
ROC AUC: 0.94 (+/- 0.13) [Majority voting]
```

As we can see, the performance of `MajorityVotingClassifier` has improved over the individual classifiers in the 10-fold cross-validation evaluation.

Evaluating and tuning the ensemble classifier

In this section, we are going to compute the ROC curves from the test set to check that `MajorityVoteClassifier` generalizes well with unseen data. We shall remember that the test set is not to be used for model selection; its purpose is merely to report an unbiased estimate of the generalization performance of a classifier system:

```
>>> from sklearn.metrics import roc_curve
>>> from sklearn.metrics import auc
>>> colors = ['black', 'orange', 'blue', 'green']
>>> linestyles = [':', '--', '-.', '-']
>>> for clf, label, clr, ls \
...         in zip(all_clf, clf_labels, colors, linestyles):
...       # assuming the label of the positive class is 1
...       y_pred = clf.fit(X_train,
...                        y_train).predict_proba(X_test)[:, 1]
...       fpr, tpr, thresholds = roc_curve(y_true=y_test,
...                                        y_score=y_pred)
...       roc_auc = auc(x=fpr, y=tpr)
...       plt.plot(fpr, tpr,
...                color=clr,
...                linestyle=ls,
...                label='%s (auc = %0.2f)' % (label, roc_auc))
>>> plt.legend(loc='lower right')
>>> plt.plot([0, 1], [0, 1],
...          linestyle='--',
...          color='gray',
...          linewidth=2)
>>> plt.xlim([-0.1, 1.1])
>>> plt.ylim([-0.1, 1.1])
>>> plt.grid(alpha=0.5)
```

```
>>> plt.xlabel('False positive rate (FPR)')
>>> plt.ylabel('True positive rate (TPR)')
>>> plt.show()
```

As we can see in the resulting ROC, the ensemble classifier also performs well on the test set (ROC AUC = 0.95). However, we can see that the logistic regression classifier performs similarly well on the same dataset, which is probably due to the high variance (in this case, sensitivity of how we split the dataset) given the small size of the dataset:

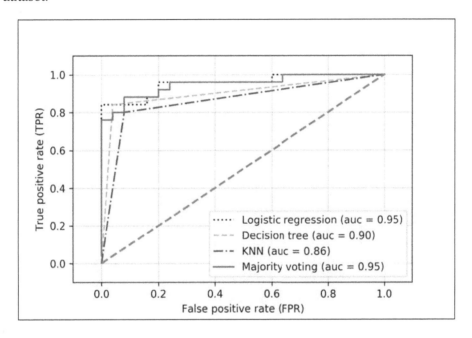

Since we only selected two features for the classification examples, it would be interesting to see what the decision region of the ensemble classifier actually looks like. Although it is not necessary to standardize the training features prior to model fitting, because our logistic regression and k-nearest neighbors pipelines will automatically take care of it, we will standardize the training set so that the decision regions of the decision tree will be on the same scale for visual purposes. The code is as follows:

```
>>> sc = StandardScaler()
>>> X_train_std = sc.fit_transform(X_train)
>>> from itertools import product
>>> x_min = X_train_std[:, 0].min() - 1
>>> x_max = X_train_std[:, 0].max() + 1
>>> y_min = X_train_std[:, 1].min() - 1
```

```
>>> y_max = X_train_std[:, 1].max() + 1
>>> xx, yy = np.meshgrid(np.arange(x_min, x_max, 0.1),
...                      np.arange(y_min, y_max, 0.1))
>>> f, axarr = plt.subplots(nrows=2, ncols=2,
...                         sharex='col',
...                         sharey='row',
...                         figsize=(7, 5))
>>> for idx, clf, tt in zip(product([0, 1], [0, 1]),
...                         all_clf, clf_labels):
...     clf.fit(X_train_std, y_train)
...     Z = clf.predict(np.c_[xx.ravel(), yy.ravel()])
...     Z = Z.reshape(xx.shape)
...     axarr[idx[0], idx[1]].contourf(xx, yy, Z, alpha=0.3)
...     axarr[idx[0], idx[1]].scatter(X_train_std[y_train==0, 0],
...                                   X_train_std[y_train==0, 1],
...                                   c='blue',
...                                   marker='^',
...                                   s=50)
...     axarr[idx[0], idx[1]].scatter(X_train_std[y_train==1, 0],
...                                   X_train_std[y_train==1, 1],
...                                   c='green',
...                                   marker='o',
...                                   s=50)
...     axarr[idx[0], idx[1]].set_title(tt)
>>> plt.text(-3.5, -4.5,
...          s='Sepal width [standardized]',
...          ha='center', va='center', fontsize=12)
>>> plt.text(-10.5, 4.5,
...          s='Petal length [standardized]',
...          ha='center', va='center',
...          fontsize=12, rotation=90)
>>> plt.show()
```

Interestingly, but also as expected, the decision regions of the ensemble classifier seem to be a hybrid of the decision regions from the individual classifiers. At first glance, the majority vote decision boundary looks a lot like the decision of the decision tree stump, which is orthogonal to the y axis for *sepal width* ≥ 1. However, we also notice the non-linearity from the k-nearest neighbor classifier mixed in:

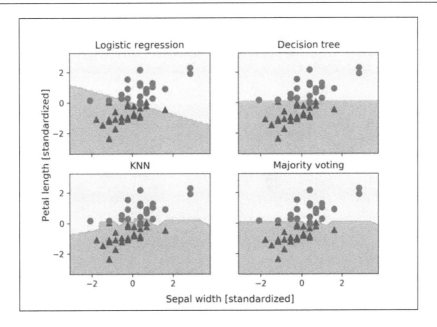

Before we tune the individual classifier's parameters for ensemble classification, let's call the get_params method to get a basic idea of how we can access the individual parameters inside a GridSearch object:

```
>>> mv_clf.get_params()
{'decisiontreeclassifier': DecisionTreeClassifier(class_weight=None,
criterion='entropy', max_depth=1,
            max_features=None,
            max_leaf_nodes=None,
            min_samples_leaf=1,
            min_samples_split=2, min_weight_fraction_leaf=0.0,
            random_state=0, splitter='best'),
 'decisiontreeclassifier__class_weight': None,
 'decisiontreeclassifier__criterion': 'entropy',
 [...]
 'decisiontreeclassifier__random_state': 0,
 'decisiontreeclassifier__splitter': 'best',
 'pipeline-1': Pipeline(steps=[('sc', StandardScaler(copy=True,
with_mean=True, with_std=True)), ('clf', LogisticRegression(C=0.001,
class_weight=None, dual=False, fit_intercept=True,
intercept_scaling=1, max_iter=100, multi_class='ovr',
penalty='l2', random_state=0, solver='liblinear', tol=0.0001,
verbose=0))]),
```

```
 'pipeline-1__clf': LogisticRegression(C=0.001, class_weight=None,
dual=False, fit_intercept=True,
          intercept_scaling=1, max_iter=100, multi_class='ovr',
          penalty='l2', random_state=0, solver='liblinear',
tol=0.0001,
          verbose=0),
 'pipeline-1__clf__C': 0.001,
 'pipeline-1__clf__class_weight': None,
 'pipeline-1__clf__dual': False,
 [...]
 'pipeline-1__sc__with_std': True,
 'pipeline-2': Pipeline(steps=[('sc', StandardScaler(copy=True, with_
mean=True, with_std=True)), ('clf', KNeighborsClassifier(algorithm='au
to', leaf_size=30, metric='minkowski',
          metric_params=None, n_neighbors=1, p=2,
weights='uniform'))]),
 'pipeline-2__clf': KNeighborsClassifier(algorithm='auto', leaf_
size=30, metric='minkowski',
          metric_params=None, n_neighbors=1, p=2,
weights='uniform'),
 'pipeline-2__clf__algorithm': 'auto',
 [...]
 'pipeline-2__sc__with_std': True}
```

Based on the values returned by the `get_params` method, we now know how to access the individual classifier's attributes. Let's now tune the inverse regularization parameter C of the logistic regression classifier and the decision tree depth via a grid search for demonstration purposes:

```
>>> from sklearn.model_selection import GridSearchCV
>>> params = {'decisiontreeclassifier__max_depth': [1, 2],
...           'pipeline-1__clf__C': [0.001, 0.1, 100.0]}
>>> grid = GridSearchCV(estimator=mv_clf,
...                     param_grid=params,
...                     cv=10,
...                     scoring='roc_auc')
>>> grid.fit(X_train, y_train)
```

After the grid search has completed, we can print the different hyperparameter value combinations and the average ROC AUC scores computed via 10-fold cross-validation as follows:

```
>>> for params, mean_score, scores in grid.grid_scores_:
...     print("%0.3f+/-%0.2f %r"
...            % (mean_score, scores.std() / 2, params))
```

```
0.933 +/- 0.07 {'pipeline-1__clf__C': 0.001, 'decisiontreeclassifier__
max_depth': 1}
0.947 +/- 0.07 {'pipeline-1__clf__C': 0.1, 'decisiontreeclassifier__
max_depth': 1}
0.973 +/- 0.04 {'pipeline-1__clf__C': 100.0, 'decisiontreeclassifier__
max_depth': 1}
0.947 +/- 0.07 {'pipeline-1__clf__C': 0.001, 'decisiontreeclassifier__
max_depth': 2}
0.947 +/- 0.07 {'pipeline-1__clf__C': 0.1, 'decisiontreeclassifier__
max_depth': 2}
0.973 +/- 0.04 {'pipeline-1__clf__C': 100.0, 'decisiontreeclassifier__
max_depth': 2}

>>> print('Best parameters: %s' % grid.best_params_)
Best parameters: {'pipeline-1__clf__C': 100.0,
'decisiontreeclassifier__max_depth': 1}

>>> print('Accuracy: %.2f' % grid.best_score_)
Accuracy: 0.97
```

As we can see, we get the best cross-validation results when we choose a lower regularization strength (C=100.0), whereas the tree depth does not seem to affect the performance at all, suggesting that a decision stump is sufficient to separate the data. To remind ourselves that it is a bad practice to use the test dataset more than once for model evaluation, we are not going to estimate the generalization performance of the tuned hyperparameters in this section. We will move on swiftly to an alternative approach for ensemble learning: **bagging**.

The majority vote approach we implemented in this section is not to be confused with **stacking**. The stacking algorithm can be understood as a two-layer ensemble, where the first layer consists of individual classifiers that feed their predictions to the second level, where another classifier (typically logistic regression) is fit to the level-1 classifier predictions to make the final predictions. The stacking algorithm has been described in more detail by David H. Wolpert in *Stacked generalization, Neural Networks*, 5(2):241–259, 1992.

Unfortunately, an implementation of this algorithm has not been implemented in scikit-learn at the time of writing; however, this feature is under way. In the meantime, you can find scikit-learn-compatible implementations of stacking at http://rasbt.github.io/mlxtend/user_guide/classifier/StackingClassifier/ and http://rasbt.github.io/mlxtend/user_guide/classifier/StackingCVClassifier/.

Bagging – building an ensemble of classifiers from bootstrap samples

Bagging is an ensemble learning technique that is closely related to the `MajorityVoteClassifier` that we implemented in the previous section. However, instead of using the same training set to fit the individual classifiers in the ensemble, we draw bootstrap samples (random samples with replacement) from the initial training set, which is why bagging is also known as bootstrap aggregating.

The concept of bagging is summarized in the following diagram:

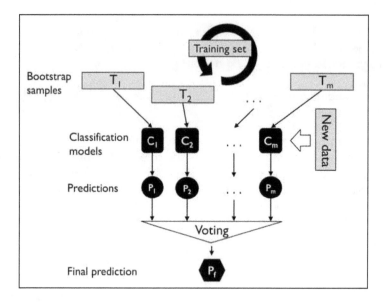

In the following subsections, we will work through a simple example of bagging by hand and use scikit-learn for classifying wine samples.

Bagging in a nutshell

To provide a more concrete example of how the bootstrapping aggregating of a bagging classifier works, let's consider the example shown in the following figure. Here, we have seven different training instances (denoted as indices 1-7) that are sampled randomly with replacement in each round of bagging. Each bootstrap sample is then used to fit a classifier C_j, which is most typically an unpruned decision tree:

Sample indices	Bagging round 1	Bagging round 2	...
1	2	7	...
2	2	3	...
3	1	2	...
4	3	1	...
5	7	1	...
6	2	7	...
7	4	7	...

$$C_1 \qquad C_2 \qquad C_m$$

As we can see from the previous illustration, each classifier receives a random subset of samples from the training set. Each subset contains a certain portion of duplicates and some of the original samples don't appear in a resampled dataset at all due to sampling with replacement. Once the individual classifiers are fit to the bootstrap samples, the predictions are combined using majority voting.

Note that bagging is also related to the random forest classifier that we introduced in *Chapter 3, A Tour of Machine Learning Classifiers Using scikit-learn*. In fact, random forests are a special case of bagging where we also use random feature subsets when fitting the individual decision trees.

 Bagging was first proposed by Leo Breiman in a technical report in 1994; he also showed that bagging can improve the accuracy of unstable models and decrease the degree of overfitting. I highly recommend you read about his research in *Bagging predictors, L. Breiman, Machine Learning*, 24(2):123–140, *1996*, which is freely available online, to learn more details about bagging.

Applying bagging to classify samples in the Wine dataset

To see bagging in action, let's create a more complex classification problem using the Wine dataset that we introduced in *Chapter 4, Building Good Training Sets -- Data Preprocessing*. Here, we will only consider the Wine classes 2 and 3, and we select two features: `Alcohol` and `OD280/OD315 of diluted wines`:

```
>>> import pandas as pd
>>> df_wine = pd.read_csv('https://archive.ics.uci.edu/ml/'
                          'machine-learning-databases/wine/wine.data',
                          header=None)
>>> df_wine.columns = ['Class label', 'Alcohol',
...                        'Malic acid', 'Ash',
...                        'Alcalinity of ash',
...                        'Magnesium', 'Total phenols',
...                        'Flavanoids', 'Nonflavanoid phenols',
...                        'Proanthocyanins',
...                        'Color intensity', 'Hue',
...                        'OD280/OD315 of diluted wines',
...                        'Proline']
>>> # drop 1 class
>>> df_wine = df_wine[df_wine['Class label'] != 1]
>>> y = df_wine['Class label'].values
>>> X = df_wine[['Alcohol',
...              'OD280/OD315 of diluted wines']].values
```

Next, we encode the class labels into binary format and split the dataset into 80 percent training and 20 percent test sets, respectively:

```
>>> from sklearn.preprocessing import LabelEncoder
>>> from sklearn.model_selection import train_test_split
>>> le = LabelEncoder()
>>> y = le.fit_transform(y)
>>> X_train, X_test, y_train, y_test =\
...             train_test_split(X, y,
...                              test_size=0.2,
...                              random_state=1,
...                              stratify=y)
```

You can find a copy of the Wine dataset (and all other datasets used in this book) in the code bundle of this book, which you can use if you are working offline or the UCI server at `https://archive. ics.uci.edu/ml/machine-learning-databases/wine/ wine.data` is temporarily unavailable. For instance, to load the Wine dataset from a local directory, take these lines:

```
df = pd.read_csv('https://archive.ics.uci.edu/ml/'
                 'machine-learning-databases'
                 '/wine/wine.data',
                 header=None)
```

Replace them with this:

```
df = pd.read_csv('your/local/path/to/wine.data',
                 header=None)
```

A `BaggingClassifier` algorithm is already implemented in scikit-learn, which we can import from the `ensemble` submodule. Here, we will use an unpruned decision tree as the base classifier and create an ensemble of 500 decision trees fit on different bootstrap samples of the training dataset:

```
>>> from sklearn.ensemble import BaggingClassifier
>>> tree = DecisionTreeClassifier(criterion='entropy',
...                               random_state=1,
...                               max_depth=None)
>>> bag = BaggingClassifier(base_estimator=tree,
...                         n_estimators=500,
...                         max_samples=1.0,
...                         max_features=1.0,
...                         bootstrap=True,
...                         bootstrap_features=False,
...                         n_jobs=1,
...                         random_state=1)
```

Next, we will calculate the accuracy score of the prediction on the training and test dataset to compare the performance of the bagging classifier to the performance of a single unpruned decision tree:

```
>>> from sklearn.metrics import accuracy_score
>>> tree = tree.fit(X_train, y_train)
>>> y_train_pred = tree.predict(X_train)
>>> y_test_pred = tree.predict(X_test)
>>> tree_train = accuracy_score(y_train, y_train_pred)
>>> tree_test = accuracy_score(y_test, y_test_pred)
>>> print('Decision tree train/test accuracies %.3f/%.3f'
...       % (tree_train, tree_test))
Decision tree train/test accuracies 1.000/0.833
```

Based on the accuracy values that we printed here, the unpruned decision tree predicts all the class labels of the training samples correctly; however, the substantially lower test accuracy indicates high variance (overfitting) of the model:

```
>>> bag = bag.fit(X_train, y_train)
>>> y_train_pred = bag.predict(X_train)
>>> y_test_pred = bag.predict(X_test)
>>> bag_train = accuracy_score(y_train, y_train_pred)
>>> bag_test = accuracy_score(y_test, y_test_pred)
>>> print('Bagging train/test accuracies %.3f/%.3f'
...       % (bag_train, bag_test))
Bagging train/test accuracies 1.000/0.917
```

Although the training accuracies of the decision tree and bagging classifier are similar on the training set (both 100 percent), we can see that the bagging classifier has a slightly better generalization performance, as estimated on the test set. Next, let's compare the decision regions between the decision tree and the bagging classifier:

```
>>> x_min = X_train[:, 0].min() - 1
>>> x_max = X_train[:, 0].max() + 1
>>> y_min = X_train[:, 1].min() - 1
>>> y_max = X_train[:, 1].max() + 1
>>> xx, yy = np.meshgrid(np.arange(x_min, x_max, 0.1),
...                      np.arange(y_min, y_max, 0.1))
>>> f, axarr = plt.subplots(nrows=1, ncols=2,
...                         sharex='col',
...                         sharey='row',
...                         figsize=(8, 3))
>>> for idx, clf, tt in zip([0, 1],
...                         [tree, bag],
...                         ['Decision tree', 'Bagging']):
```

```
...          clf.fit(X_train, y_train)
...
...          Z = clf.predict(np.c_[xx.ravel(), yy.ravel()])
...          Z = Z.reshape(xx.shape)
...          axarr[idx].contourf(xx, yy, Z, alpha=0.3)
...          axarr[idx].scatter(X_train[y_train==0, 0],
...                             X_train[y_train==0, 1],
...                             c='blue', marker='^')
...          axarr[idx].scatter(X_train[y_train==1, 0],
...                             X_train[y_train==1, 1],
...                             c='green', marker='o')
...          axarr[idx].set_title(tt)
>>> axarr[0].set_ylabel('Alcohol', fontsize=12)
>>> plt.text(10.2, -1.2,
...          s='OD280/OD315 of diluted wines',
...          ha='center', va='center', fontsize=12)
>>> plt.show()
```

As we can see in the resulting plot, the piece-wise linear decision boundary of the three-node deep decision tree looks smoother in the bagging ensemble:

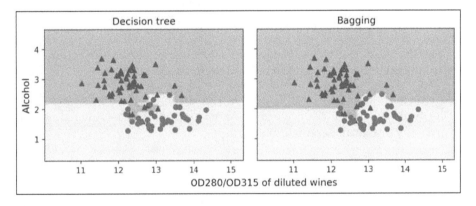

We only looked at a very simple bagging example in this section. In practice, more complex classification tasks and a dataset's high dimensionality can easily lead to overfitting in single decision trees, and this is where the bagging algorithm can really play to its strengths. Finally, we shall note that the bagging algorithm can be an effective approach to reduce the variance of a model. However, bagging is ineffective in reducing model bias, that is, models that are too simple to capture the trend in the data well. This is why we want to perform bagging on an ensemble of classifiers with low bias, for example, unpruned decision trees.

Leveraging weak learners via adaptive boosting

In this last section about ensemble methods, we will discuss **boosting** with a special focus on its most common implementation, **AdaBoost (Adaptive Boosting)**.

> The original idea behind AdaBoost was formulated by Robert E. Schapire in 1990. *The Strength of Weak Learnability, R. E. Schapire, Machine Learning, 5(2): 197-227, 1990.* After Robert Schapire and Yoav Freund presented the AdaBoost algorithm in the *Proceedings of the Thirteenth International Conference* (ICML 1996), AdaBoost became one of the most widely used ensemble methods in the years that followed (*Experiments with a New Boosting Algorithm* by Y. Freund, R. E. Schapire, and others, *ICML, volume 96, 148-156, 1996*). In 2003, Freund and Schapire received the Goedel Prize for their groundbreaking work, which is a prestigious prize for the most outstanding publications in the field of computer science.

In boosting, the ensemble consists of very simple base classifiers, also often referred to as **weak learners**, which often only have a slight performance advantage over random guessing — a typical example of a weak learner is a decision tree stump. The key concept behind boosting is to focus on training samples that are hard to classify, that is, to let the weak learners subsequently learn from misclassified training samples to improve the performance of the ensemble.

The following subsections will introduce the algorithmic procedure behind the general concept boosting and a popular variant called **AdaBoost**. Lastly, we will use scikit-learn for a practical classification example.

How boosting works

In contrast to bagging, the initial formulation of boosting, the algorithm uses random subsets of training samples drawn from the training dataset without replacement; the original boosting procedure is summarized in the following four key steps:

1. Draw a random subset of training samples d_1 without replacement from training set D to train a weak learner C_1.

2. Draw a second random training subset d_2 without replacement from the training set and add 50 percent of the samples that were previously misclassified to train a weak learner C_2.

3. Find the training samples d_3 in training set D, which C_1 and C_2 disagree upon, to train a third weak learner C_3.

4. Combine the weak learners C_1, C_2, and C_3 via majority voting.

As discussed by Leo Breiman (*Bias, variance, and arcing classifiers, L. Breiman, 1996*), boosting can lead to a decrease in bias as well as variance compared to bagging models. In practice, however, boosting algorithms such as AdaBoost are also known for their high variance, that is, the tendency to overfit the training data (*An improvement of AdaBoost to avoid overfitting, G. Raetsch, T. Onoda*, and *K. R. Mueller*. Proceedings of the International Conference on Neural Information Processing, CiteSeer, 1998).

In contrast to the original boosting procedure as described here, AdaBoost uses the complete training set to train the weak learners where the training samples are reweighted in each iteration to build a strong classifier that learns from the mistakes of the previous weak learners in the ensemble. Before we dive deeper into the specific details of the AdaBoost algorithm, let's take a look at the following figure to get a better grasp of the basic concept behind AdaBoost:

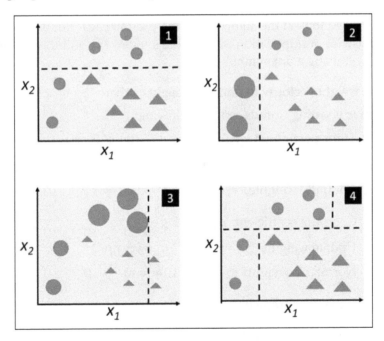

To walk through the AdaBoost illustration step by step, we start with subfigure **1**, which represents a training set for binary classification where all training samples are assigned equal weights. Based on this training set, we train a decision stump (shown as a dashed line) that tries to classify the samples of the two classes (triangles and circles), as well as possibly by minimizing the cost function (or the impurity score in the special case of decision tree ensembles).

For the next round (subfigure **2**), we assign a larger weight to the two previously misclassified samples (circles). Furthermore, we lower the weight of the correctly classified samples. The next decision stump will now be more focused on the training samples that have the largest weights — the training samples that are supposedly hard to classify. The weak learner shown in subfigure **2** misclassifies three different samples from the circle class, which are then assigned a larger weight, as shown in subfigure **3**.

Assuming that our AdaBoost ensemble only consists of three rounds of boosting, we would then combine the three weak learners trained on different reweighted training subsets by a weighted majority vote, as shown in subfigure **4**.

Now that have a better understanding behind the basic concept of AdaBoost, let's take a more detailed look at the algorithm using pseudo code. For clarity, we will denote element-wise multiplication by the cross symbol $(\times)$ and the dot-product between two vectors by a dot symbol $(\cdot)$:

1. Set the weight vector **w** to uniform weights, where $\sum_i w_i = 1$.
2. For j in m boosting rounds, do the following:
   a. Train a weighted weak learner: $C_j = \text{train}(X, y, w)$.
   b. Predict class labels: $\hat{y} = \text{predict}(C_j, X)$.
   c. Compute weighted error rate: $\varepsilon = w \cdot (\hat{y} \neq y)$.
   d. Compute coefficient: $\alpha_j = 0.5 \log \dfrac{1-\varepsilon}{\varepsilon}$.
   e. Update weights: $w := w \times \exp(-\alpha_j \times \hat{y} \times y)$.
   f. Normalize weights to sum to 1: $w := w / \sum_i w_i$.

3. Compute the final prediction: $\hat{y} = \left(\sum_{j=1}^{m} \left(\alpha_j \times \text{predict}(C_j, X) \right) > 0 \right)$.

Note that the expression $(\hat{y} \neq y)$ in step 2c refers to a binary vector consisting of 1s and 0s, where a 1 is assigned if the prediction is incorrect and 0 is assigned otherwise.

Although the AdaBoost algorithm seems to be pretty straightforward, let's walk through a more concrete example using a training set consisting of 10 training samples, as illustrated in the following table:

Sample indices	x	y	Weights	$\hat{y}$(x <= 3.0)?	Correct?	Updated weights
1	1.0	1	0.1	1	Yes	0.072
2	2.0	1	0.1	1	Yes	0.072
3	3.0	1	0.1	1	Yes	0.072
4	4.0	-1	0.1	-1	Yes	0.072
5	5.0	-1	0.1	-1	Yes	0.072
6	6.0	-1	0.1	-1	Yes	0.072
7	7.0	1	0.1	-1	No	0.167
8	8.0	1	0.1	-1	No	0.167
9	9.0	1	0.1	-1	No	0.167
10	10.0	-1	0.1	-1	Yes	0.072

The first column of the table depicts the sample indices of training samples 1 to 10. In the second column, we see the feature values of the individual samples, assuming this is a one-dimensional dataset. The third column shows the true class label, y_i, for each training sample x_i, where $y_i \in \{1, -1\}$. The initial weights are shown in the fourth column; we initialize the weights uniformly (assigning the same constant value) and normalize them to sum to one. In the case of the 10-sample training set, we therefore assign 0.1 to each weight w_i in the weight vector $\mathbf{w}$. The predicted class labels $\hat{y}$ are shown in the fifth column, assuming that our splitting criterion is $x \leq 3.0$. The last column of the table then shows the updated weights based on the update rules that we defined in the pseudo code.

Since the computation of the weight updates may look a little bit complicated at first, we will now follow the calculation step by step. We start by computing the weighted error rate ε as described in step 2c:

$$\varepsilon = 0.1 \times 0 + 0.1 \times 0 + 0.1 \times 0 + 0.1 \times 0 + 0.1 \times 0 + 0.1 \times 0 + 0.1 \times 1 + 0.1 \times 1$$

$$+ 0.1 \times 1 + 0.1 \times 0 = \frac{3}{10} = 0.3$$

Next, we compute the coefficient α_j —shown in step 2d—which is later used in step 2e to update the weights, as well as for the weights in the majority vote prediction (step 4):

$$\alpha_j = 0.5\log\left(\frac{1-\varepsilon}{\varepsilon}\right) \approx 0.424$$

After we have computed the coefficient α_j, we can now update the weight vector using the following equation:

$$w := w \times \exp\left(-\alpha_j \times \hat{y} \times y\right)$$

Here, $\hat{y} \times y$ is an element-wise multiplication between the vectors of the predicted and true class labels, respectively. Thus, if a prediction $\hat{y}_i$ is correct, $\hat{y}_i \times y_i$ will have a positive sign so that we decrease the ith weight, since α_j is a positive number as well:

$$0.1 \times \exp\left(-0.424 \times 1 \times 1\right) \approx 0.065$$

Similarly, we will increase the ith weight if $\hat{y}_i$ predicted the label incorrectly, like this:

$$0.1 \times \exp\left(-0.424 \times 1 \times (-1)\right) \approx 0.153$$

Alternatively, it's like this:

$$0.1 \times \exp\left(-0.424 \times (-1) \times (1)\right) \approx 0.153$$

After we have updated each weight in the weight vector, we normalize the weights so that they sum up to one (step 2f):

$$w := \frac{w}{\sum_i w_i}$$

Here, $\sum_i w_i = 7 \times 0.065 + 3 \times 0.153 = 0.914$.

Thus, each weight that corresponds to a correctly classified sample will be reduced from the initial value of 0.1 to $0.065/0.914 \approx 0.071$ for the next round of boosting. Similarly, the weights of the incorrectly classified samples will increase from 0.1 to $0.153/0.914 \approx 0.167$.

Applying AdaBoost using scikit-learn

The previous subsection introduced AdaBoost in a nutshell. Skipping to the more practical part, let's now train an AdaBoost ensemble classifier via scikit-learn. We will use the same Wine subset that we used in the previous section to train the bagging meta-classifier. Via the `base_estimator` attribute, we will train the `AdaBoostClassifier` on 500 decision tree stumps:

```
>>> from sklearn.ensemble import AdaBoostClassifier
>>> tree = DecisionTreeClassifier(criterion='entropy',
...                               random_state=1,
...                               max_depth=1)
>>> ada = AdaBoostClassifier(base_estimator=tree,
...                          n_estimators=500,
...                          learning_rate=0.1,
...                          random_state=1)
>>> tree = tree.fit(X_train, y_train)
>>> y_train_pred = tree.predict(X_train)
>>> y_test_pred = tree.predict(X_test)
>>> tree_train = accuracy_score(y_train, y_train_pred)
>>> tree_test = accuracy_score(y_test, y_test_pred)
>>> print('Decision tree train/test accuracies %.3f/%.3f'
...        % (tree_train, tree_test))
Decision tree train/test accuracies 0.916/0.875
```

As we can see, the decision tree stump seems to underfit the training data in contrast to the unpruned decision tree that we saw in the previous section:

```
>>> ada = ada.fit(X_train, y_train)
>>> y_train_pred = ada.predict(X_train)
>>> y_test_pred = ada.predict(X_test)
>>> ada_train = accuracy_score(y_train, y_train_pred)
>>> ada_test = accuracy_score(y_test, y_test_pred)
>>> print('AdaBoost train/test accuracies %.3f/%.3f'
...        % (ada_train, ada_test))
AdaBoost train/test accuracies 1.000/0.917
```

As we can see, the AdaBoost model predicts all class labels of the training set correctly and also shows a slightly improved test set performance compared to the decision tree stump. However, we also see that we introduced additional variance by our attempt to reduce the model bias — a higher gap between training and test performance.

Although we used another simple example for demonstration purposes, we can see that the performance of the AdaBoost classifier is slightly improved compared to the decision stump and achieved the very similar accuracy scores as the bagging classifier that we trained in the previous section. However, we shall note that it is considered bad practice to select a model based on the repeated usage of the test set. The estimate of the generalization performance may be over-optimistic, which we discussed in more detail in *Chapter 6, Learning Best Practices for Model Evaluation and Hyperparameter Tuning*.

Lastly, let us check what the decision regions look like:

```
>>> x_min = X_train[:, 0].min() - 1
>>> x_max = X_train[:, 0].max() + 1
>>> y_min = X_train[:, 1].min() - 1
>>> y_max = X_train[:, 1].max() + 1
>>> xx, yy = np.meshgrid(np.arange(x_min, x_max, 0.1),
...                      np.arange(y_min, y_max, 0.1))
>>> f, axarr = plt.subplots(1, 2,
...                         sharex='col',
...                         sharey='row',
...                         figsize=(8, 3))
>>> for idx, clf, tt in zip([0, 1],
...                         [tree, ada],
...                         ['Decision Tree', 'AdaBoost']):
...     clf.fit(X_train, y_train)
...     Z = clf.predict(np.c_[xx.ravel(), yy.ravel()])
...     Z = Z.reshape(xx.shape)
...     axarr[idx].contourf(xx, yy, Z, alpha=0.3)
...     axarr[idx].scatter(X_train[y_train==0, 0],
...                        X_train[y_train==0, 1],
...                        c='blue',
...                        marker='^')
...     axarr[idx].scatter(X_train[y_train==1, 0],
...                        X_train[y_train==1, 1],
...                        c='red',
...                        marker='o')
...     axarr[idx].set_title(tt)
```

```
...         axarr[0].set_ylabel('Alcohol', fontsize=12)
>>> plt.text(10.2, -0.5,
...         s='OD280/OD315 of diluted wines',
...         ha='center',
...         va='center',
...         fontsize=12)
>>> plt.show()
```

By looking at the decision regions, we can see that the decision boundary of the AdaBoost model is substantially more complex than the decision boundary of the decision stump. In addition, we note that the AdaBoost model separates the feature space very similarly to the bagging classifier that we trained in the previous section:

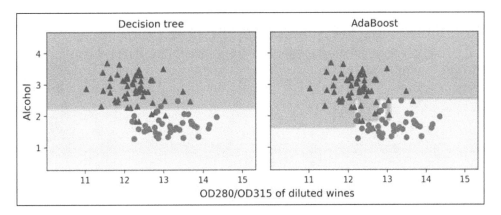

As concluding remarks about ensemble techniques, it is worth noting that ensemble learning increases the computational complexity compared to individual classifiers. In practice, we need to think carefully about whether we want to pay the price of increased computational costs for an often relatively modest improvement in predictive performance.

An often-cited example of this trade-off is the famous $1 million *Netflix Prize*, which was won using ensemble techniques. The details about the algorithm were published in *The BigChaos Solution to the Netflix Grand Prize* by *A. Toescher, M. Jahrer*, and *R. M. Bell*, Netflix prize documentation, *2009*, which is available at http://www.stat.osu.edu/~dmsl/GrandPrize2009_BPC_BigChaos.pdf. The winning team received the $1 million grand prize money; however, Netflix never implemented their model due to its complexity, which made it infeasible for a real-world application:

"We evaluated some of the new methods offline but the additional accuracy gains that we measured did not seem to justify the engineering effort needed to bring them into a production environment." (http://techblog.netflix.com/2012/04/netflix-recommendations-beyond-5-stars.html).

Summary

In this chapter, we looked at some of the most popular and widely used techniques for ensemble learning. Ensemble methods combine different classification models to cancel out their individual weaknesses, which often results in stable and well-performing models that are very attractive for industrial applications as well as machine learning competitions.

At the beginning of this chapter, we implemented `MajorityVoteClassifier` in Python, which allows us to combine different algorithms for classification. We then looked at bagging, a useful technique to reduce the variance of a model by drawing random bootstrap samples from the training set and combining the individually trained classifiers via majority vote. Lastly, we learned about AdaBoost, which is an algorithm that is based on weak learners that subsequently learn from mistakes.

Throughout the previous chapters, we learned a lot about different learning algorithms, tuning, and evaluation techniques. In the next chapter, we will look at a particular application of machine learning, sentiment analysis, which has become an interesting topic in the internet and social media era.

8

Applying Machine Learning to Sentiment Analysis

In this internet and social media age, people's opinions, reviews, and recommendations have become a valuable resource for political science and businesses. Thanks to modern technologies, we are now able to collect and analyze such data most efficiently. In this chapter, we will delve into a subfield of **Natural Language Processing (NLP)** called **sentiment analysis** and learn how to use machine learning algorithms to classify documents based on their polarity: the attitude of the writer. In particular, we are going to work with a dataset of 50,000 movie reviews from the **Internet Movie Database (IMDb)** and build a predictor that can distinguish between positive and negative reviews.

The topics that we will cover in the following sections include the following:

- Cleaning and preparing text data
- Building feature vectors from text documents
- Training a machine learning model to classify positive and negative movie reviews
- Working with large text datasets using out-of-core learning
- Inferring topics from document collections for categorization

Preparing the IMDb movie review data for text processing

Sentiment analysis, sometimes also called **opinion mining**, is a popular subdiscipline of the broader field of NLP; it is concerned with analyzing the polarity of documents. A popular task in sentiment analysis is the classification of documents based on the expressed opinions or emotions of the authors with regard to a particular topic.

In this chapter, we will be working with a large dataset of movie reviews from the IMDb that has been collected by Maas and others (*Learning Word Vectors for Sentiment Analysis, A. L. Maas, R. E. Daly, P. T. Pham, D. Huang, A. Y. Ng,* and *C. Potts, Proceedings of the 49th Annual Meeting of the Association for Computational Linguistics: Human Language Technologies*, pages 142–150, Portland, Oregon, USA, Association for Computational Linguistics, *June 2011*). The movie review dataset consists of 50,000 polar movie reviews that are labeled as either positive or negative; here, positive means that a movie was rated with more than six stars on IMDb, and negative means that a movie was rated with fewer than five stars on IMDb. In the following sections, we will download the dataset, preprocess it into a useable format for machine learning tools, and extract meaningful information from a subset of these movie reviews to build a machine learning model that can predict whether a certain reviewer liked or disliked a movie.

Obtaining the movie review dataset

A compressed archive of the movie review dataset (84.1 MB) can be downloaded from http://ai.stanford.edu/~amaas/data/sentiment/ as a Gzip-compressed tarball archive:

- If you are working with Linux or macOS, you can open a new Terminal window, cd into the download directory, and execute tar -zxf aclImdb_v1.tar.gz to decompress the dataset.

- If you are working with Windows, you can download a free archiver such as 7Zip (http://www.7-zip.org) to extract the files from the download archive.

- Alternatively, you can directly unpack the Gzip-compressed tarball archive directly in Python as follows:

```
>>> import tarfile
>>> with tarfile.open('aclImdb_v1.tar.gz', 'r:gz') as tar:
...     tar.extractall()
```

Preprocessing the movie dataset into more convenient format

Having successfully extracted the dataset, we will now assemble the individual text documents from the decompressed download archive into a single CSV file. In the following code section, we will be reading the movie reviews into a pandas `DataFrame` object, which can take up to 10 minutes on a standard desktop computer. To visualize the progress and estimated time until completion, we will use the **Python Progress Indicator (PyPrind,** `https://pypi.python.org/pypi/PyPrind/`) package that I developed several years ago for such purposes. PyPrind can be installed by executing the `pip install pyprind` command.

```
>>> import pyprind
>>> import pandas as pd
>>> import os

>>> # change the `basepath` to the directory of the
>>> # unzipped movie dataset

>>> basepath = 'aclImdb'
>>>
>>> labels = {'pos': 1, 'neg': 0}
>>> pbar = pyprind.ProgBar(50000)
>>> df = pd.DataFrame()
>>> for s in ('test', 'train'):
...     for l in ('pos', 'neg'):
...         path = os.path.join(basepath, s, l)
...         for file in sorted(os.listdir(path)):
...             with open(os.path.join(path, file),
...                       'r', encoding='utf-8') as infile:
...                 txt = infile.read()
...             df = df.append([[txt, labels[l]]],
...                            ignore_index=True)
...             pbar.update()
>>> df.columns = ['review', 'sentiment']
0%                    100%
[##############################] | ETA: 00:00:00
Total time elapsed: 00:03:37
```

In the preceding code, we first initialized a new progress bar object `pbar` with 50,000 iterations, which is the number of documents we were going to read in. Using the nested `for` loops, we iterated over the `train` and `test` subdirectories in the main `aclImdb` directory and read the individual text files from the `pos` and `neg` subdirectories that we eventually appended to the `df` pandas `DataFrame`, together with an integer class label (`1` = positive and `0` = negative).

Since the class labels in the assembled dataset are sorted, we will now shuffle `DataFrame` using the `permutation` function from the `np.random` submodule — this will be useful to split the dataset into training and test sets in later sections when we will stream the data from our local drive directly. For our own convenience, we will also store the assembled and shuffled movie review dataset as a CSV file:

```
>>> import numpy as np

>>> np.random.seed(0)
>>> df = df.reindex(np.random.permutation(df.index))
>>> df.to_csv('movie_data.csv', index=False, encoding='utf-8')
```

Since we are going to use this dataset later in this chapter, let's quickly confirm that we have successfully saved the data in the right format by reading in the CSV and printing an excerpt of the first three samples:

```
>>> df = pd.read_csv('movie_data.csv', encoding='utf-8')
>>> df.head(3)
```

If you are running the code examples in a Jupyter Notebook, you should now see the first three samples of the dataset, as shown in the following table:

	review	sentiment
0	In 1974, the teenager Martha Moxley (Maggie Gr...	1
1	OK... so... I really like Kris Kristofferson a...	0
2	***SPOILER*** Do not read this, if you think a...	0

As a sanity check, before we proceed to the next section, let us make sure that the DataFrame contains all 50,000 rows:

```
>>> df.shape
(50000, 2)
```

Introducing the bag-of-words model

You may remember from *Chapter 4, Building Good Training Sets – Data Preprocessing*, that we have to convert categorical data, such as text or words, into a numerical form before we can pass it on to a machine learning algorithm. In this section, we will introduce the **bag-of-words**, which allows us to represent text as numerical feature vectors. The idea behind the bag-of-words model is quite simple and can be summarized as follows:

1. We create a vocabulary of unique tokens—for example, words—from the entire set of documents.

2. We construct a feature vector from each document that contains the counts of how often each word occurs in the particular document.

Since the unique words in each document represent only a small subset of all the words in the bag-of-words vocabulary, the feature vectors will mostly consist of zeros, which is why we call them **sparse**. Do not worry if this sounds too abstract; in the following subsections, we will walk through the process of creating a simple bag-of-words model step-by-step.

Transforming words into feature vectors

To construct a bag-of-words model based on the word counts in the respective documents, we can use the CountVectorizer class implemented in scikit-learn. As we will see in the following code section, CountVectorizer takes an array of text data, which can be documents or sentences, and constructs the bag-of-words model for us:

```
>>> import numpy as np
>>> from sklearn.feature_extraction.text import CountVectorizer
>>> count = CountVectorizer()
>>> docs = np.array([
...         'The sun is shining',
...         'The weather is sweet',
...         'The sun is shining, the weather is sweet,'
...         'and one and one is two'])
>>> bag = count.fit_transform(docs)
```

By calling the `fit_transform` method on `CountVectorizer`, we constructed the vocabulary of the bag-of-words model and transformed the following three sentences into sparse feature vectors:

- `'The sun is shining'`
- `'The weather is sweet'`
- `'The sun is shining, the weather is sweet, and one and one is two'`

Now let's print the contents of the vocabulary to get a better understanding of the underlying concepts:

```
>>> print(count.vocabulary_)
{'and': 0,
 'two': 7,
 'shining': 3,
 'one': 2,
 'sun': 4,
 'weather': 8,
 'the': 6,
 'sweet': 5,
 'is': 1}
```

As we can see from executing the preceding command, the vocabulary is stored in a Python dictionary that maps the unique words to integer indices. Next, let's print the feature vectors that we just created:

```
>>> print(bag.toarray())
[[0 1 0 1 1 0 1 0 0]
 [0 1 0 0 0 1 1 0 1]
 [2 3 2 1 1 1 2 1 1]]
```

Each index position in the feature vectors shown here corresponds to the integer values that are stored as dictionary items in the `CountVectorizer` vocabulary. For example, the first feature at index position 0 resembles the count of the word `'and'`, which only occurs in the last document, and the word `'is'`, at index position 1 (the second feature in the document vectors), occurs in all three sentences. These values in the feature vectors are also called the **raw term frequencies**: $\text{tf}(t, d)$ — the number of times a term t occurs in a document d.

The sequence of items in the bag-of-words model that we just created is also called the **1-gram** or **unigram** model—each item or token in the vocabulary represents a single word. More generally, the contiguous sequences of items in NLP—words, letters, or symbols—are also called **n-grams**. The choice of the number *n* in the n-gram model depends on the particular application; for example, a study by Kanaris and others revealed that n-grams of size 3 and 4 yield good performances in anti-spam filtering of email messages (*Words versus character n-grams for anti-spam filtering, Ioannis Kanaris, Konstantinos Kanaris, Ioannis Houvardas,* and *Efstathios Stamatatos, International Journal on Artificial Intelligence Tools, World Scientific Publishing Company,* 16(06): 1047-1067, 2007). To summarize the concept of the n-gram representation, the 1-gram and 2-gram representations of our first document "the sun is shining" would be constructed as follows:

- 1-gram: "the", "sun", "is", "shining"
- 2-gram: "the sun", "sun is", "is shining"

The CountVectorizer class in scikit-learn allows us to use different n-gram models via its ngram_range parameter. While a 1-gram representation is used by default, we could switch to a 2-gram representation by initializing a new CountVectorizer instance with ngram_range=(2,2).

Assessing word relevancy via term frequency-inverse document frequency

When we are analyzing text data, we often encounter words that occur across multiple documents from both classes. These frequently occurring words typically don't contain useful or discriminatory information. In this subsection, we will learn about a useful technique called **term frequency-inverse document frequency (tf-idf)** that can be used to downweight these frequently occurring words in the feature vectors. The tf-idf can be defined as the product of the term frequency and the inverse document frequency:

$$\text{tf-idf}(t,d) = tf(t,d) \times \text{idf}(t,d)$$

Here the *tf(t, d)* is the term frequency that we introduced in the previous section, and *idf(t, d)* is the inverse document frequency and can be calculated as follows:

$$\text{idf}(t,d) = log\frac{n_d}{1+\text{df}(d,t)}$$

Here n_d is the total number of documents, and $df(d, t)$ is the number of documents d that contain the term t. Note that adding the constant *1* to the denominator is optional and serves the purpose of assigning a non-zero value to terms that occur in none of the training samples; the *log* is used to ensure that low document frequencies are not given too much weight.

The scikit-learn library implements yet another transformer, the `TfidfTransformer` class, that takes the raw term frequencies from the `CountVectorizer` class as input and transforms them into tf-idfs:

```
>>> from sklearn.feature_extraction.text import TfidfTransformer
>>> tfidf = TfidfTransformer(use_idf=True,
...                          norm='l2',
...                          smooth_idf=True)
>>> np.set_printoptions(precision=2)
>>> print(tfidf.fit_transform(count.fit_transform(docs))
...       .toarray())
[[ 0.    0.43  0.    0.56  0.56  0.    0.43  0.    0.  ]
 [ 0.    0.43  0.    0.    0.    0.56  0.43  0.    0.56]
 [ 0.5   0.45  0.5   0.19  0.19  0.19  0.3   0.25  0.19]]
```

As we saw in the previous subsection, the word `'is'` had the largest term frequency in the third document, being the most frequently occurring word. However, after transforming the same feature vector into tf-idfs, we see that the word `'is'` is now associated with a relatively small tf-idf (`0.45`) in the third document, since it is also present in the first and second document and thus is unlikely to contain any useful discriminatory information.

However, if we'd manually calculated the tf-idfs of the individual terms in our feature vectors, we'd notice that `TfidfTransformer` calculates the tf-idfs slightly differently compared to the standard textbook equations that we defined previously. The equations for the inverse document frequency implemented in scikit-learn is computed as follows:

$$\text{idf}\left(t,d\right)=log\frac{1+n_d}{1+\text{df}\left(d,t\right)}$$

Similarly, the tf-idf computed in scikit-learn deviates slightly from the default equation we defined earlier:

$$\text{tf-idf}\left(t,d\right)=\text{tf}\left(t,d\right)\times\left(\text{idf}\left(t,d\right)+1\right)$$

While it is also more typical to normalize the raw term frequencies before calculating the tf-idfs, TfidfTransformer class normalizes the tf-idfs directly. By default (norm='l2'), scikit-learn's TfidfTransformer applies the L2-normalization, which returns a vector of length 1 by dividing an un-normalized feature vector **v** by its L2-norm:

$$v_{norm} = \frac{v}{\|v\|_2} = \frac{v}{\sqrt{v_1^2 + v_2^2 + \cdots + v_n^2}} = \frac{v}{\left(\sum_{i=1}^{n} v_i^2\right)^{1/2}}$$

To make sure that we understand how TfidfTransformer works, let's walk through an example and calculate the tf-idf of the word 'is' in the third document.

The word 'is' has a term frequency of 3 (*tf*=3) in the third document, and the document frequency of this term is 3 since the term 'is' occurs in all three documents (*df*=3). Thus, we can calculate the inverse document frequency as follows:

$$idf\left("is",d3\right) = \log\frac{1+3}{1+3} = 0$$

Now, in order to calculate the tf-idf, we simply need to add *1* to the inverse document frequency and multiply it by the term frequency:

$$\text{tf-idf}\left("is",d3\right) = 3 \times (0+1) = 3$$

If we repeated this calculation for all terms in the third document, we'd obtain the following tf-idf vectors: *[3.39, 3.0, 3.39, 1.29, 1.29, 1.29, 2.0, 1.69, 1.29]*. However, notice that the values in this feature vector are different from the values that we obtained from TfidfTransformer that we used previously. The final step that we are missing in this tf-idf calculation is the L2-normalization, which can be applied as follows:

$$\text{tf-idf}\left(d3\right)_{norm} = \frac{[3.39,\ 3.0,\ 3.39,\ 1.29,\ 1.29,\ 1.29,\ 2.0,\ 1.69,\ 1.29]}{\sqrt{3.39^2 + 3.0^2 + 3.39^2 + 1.29^2 + 1.29^2 + 1.29^2 + 2.0^2 + 1.69^2 + 1.29^2}}$$

$$= [0.5,\ 0.45,\ 0.5,\ 0.19,\ 0.19,\ 0.19,\ 0.3,\ 0.25,\ 0.19]$$

$$\text{tf-idf}\left("is",d3\right) = 0.45$$

As we can see, the results now match the results returned by scikit-learn's `TfidfTransformer`, and since we now understand how tf-idfs are calculated, let's proceed to the next section and apply those concepts to the movie review dataset.

Cleaning text data

In the previous subsections, we learned about the bag-of-words model, term bag-of-words model, term frequencies, and tf-idfs. However, the first important step — before we build our bag-of-words model — is to clean the text data by stripping it of all unwanted characters. To illustrate why this is important, let's display the last 50 characters from the first document in the reshuffled movie review dataset:

```
>>> df.loc[0, 'review'][-50:]
'is seven.<br /><br />Title (Brazil): Not Available'
```

As we can see here, the text contains HTML markup as well as punctuation and other non-letter characters. While HTML markup does not contain much useful semantics, punctuation marks can represent useful, additional information in certain NLP contexts. However, for simplicity, we will now remove all punctuation marks except for emoticon characters such as :) since those are certainly useful for sentiment analysis. To accomplish this task, we will use Python's **regular expression (regex)** library, `re`, as shown here:

```
>>> import re
>>> def preprocessor(text):
...     text = re.sub('<[^>]*>', '', text)
...     emoticons = re.findall('(?::|;|=)(?:-)?(?:\)|\(|D|P)',
...                            text)
...     text = (re.sub('[\W]+', ' ', text.lower()) +
...             ' '.join(emoticons).replace('-', ''))
...     return text
```

Via the first regex `<[^>]*>` in the preceding code section, we tried to remove all of the HTML markup from the movie reviews. Although many programmers generally advise against the use of regex to parse HTML, this regex should be sufficient to *clean* this particular dataset. After we removed the HTML markup, we used a slightly more complex regex to find emoticons, which we temporarily stored as `emoticons`. Next, we removed all non-word characters from the text via the regex `[\W]+` and converted the text into lowercase characters.

In the context of this analysis, we assume that the capitalization of a word — for example, whether it appears at the beginning of a sentence — does not contain semantically relevant information. However, note that there are exceptions, for instance, we remove the notation of proper names. But again, in the context of this analysis, it is a simplifying assumption that the letter case does not contain information that is relevant for sentiment analysis.

Eventually, we added the temporarily stored emoticons to the end of the processed document string. Additionally, we removed the *nose* character (-) from the emoticons for consistency.

Although regular expressions offer an efficient and convenient approach to searching for characters in a string, they also come with a steep learning curve. Unfortunately, an in-depth discussion of regular expressions is beyond the scope of this book. However, you can find a great tutorial on the Google Developers portal at https://developers.google.com/edu/python/regular-expressions or check out the official documentation of Python's re module at https://docs.python.org/3.6/library/re.html.

Although the addition of the emoticon characters to the end of the cleaned document strings may not look like the most elegant approach, we shall note that the order of the words doesn't matter in our bag-of-words model if our vocabulary consists of only one-word tokens. But before we talk more about the splitting of documents into individual terms, words, or tokens, let's confirm that our preprocessor works correctly:

```
>>> preprocessor(df.loc[0, 'review'][-50:])
'is seven title brazil not available'
>>> preprocessor("</a>This :) is :( a test :-)!")
'this is a test :) :( :)'
```

Lastly, since we will make use of the *cleaned* text data over and over again during the next sections, let us now apply our preprocessor function to all the movie reviews in our DataFrame:

```
>>> df['review'] = df['review'].apply(preprocessor)
```

Processing documents into tokens

After successfully preparing the movie review dataset, we now need to think about how to split the text corpora into individual elements. One way to *tokenize* documents is to split them into individual words by splitting the cleaned documents at its whitespace characters:

```
>>> def tokenizer(text):
...     return text.split()
>>> tokenizer('runners like running and thus they run')
['runners', 'like', 'running', 'and', 'thus', 'they', 'run']
```

In the context of tokenization, another useful technique is **word stemming**, which is the process of transforming a word into its root form. It allows us to map related words to the same stem. The original stemming algorithm was developed by Martin F. Porter in 1979 and is hence known as the **Porter stemmer** algorithm (*An algorithm for suffix stripping*, Martin F. Porter, Program: *Electronic Library and Information Systems*, 14(3): 130–137, *1980*). The **Natural Language Toolkit** (**NLTK**, http://www.nltk.org) for Python implements the Porter stemming algorithm, which we will use in the following code section. In order to install the NLTK, you can simply execute `conda install nltk` or `pip install nltk`.

> Although the NLTK is not the focus of the chapter, I highly recommend that you visit the NLTK website as well as read the official NLTK book, which is freely available at http://www.nltk.org/book/, if you are interested in more advanced applications in NLP.

The following code shows how to use the Porter stemming algorithm:

```
>>> from nltk.stem.porter import PorterStemmer
>>> porter = PorterStemmer()
>>> def tokenizer_porter(text):
...     return [porter.stem(word) for word in text.split()]
>>> tokenizer_porter('runners like running and thus they run')
['runner', 'like', 'run', 'and', 'thu', 'they', 'run']
```

Using the `PorterStemmer` from the `nltk` package, we modified our `tokenizer` function to reduce words to their root form, which was illustrated by the simple preceding example where the word `'running'` was *stemmed* to its root form `'run'`.

The Porter stemming algorithm is probably the oldest and simplest stemming algorithm. Other popular stemming algorithms include the newer **Snowball stemmer** (Porter2 or English stemmer) and the **Lancaster stemmer** (Paice/Husk stemmer), which is faster but also more aggressive than the Porter stemmer. These alternative stemming algorithms are also available through the NLTK package (http://www.nltk.org/api/nltk.stem.html).

While stemming can create non-real words, such as 'thu' (from 'thus'), as shown in the previous example, a technique called **lemmatization** aims to obtain the canonical (grammatically correct) forms of individual words—the so-called **lemmas**. However, lemmatization is computationally more difficult and expensive compared to stemming and, in practice, it has been observed that stemming and lemmatization have little impact on the performance of text classification (*Influence of Word Normalization on Text Classification, Michal Toman, Roman Tesar*, and *Karel Jezek*, Proceedings of InSciT, pages 354–358, 2006).

Before we jump into the next section, where we will train a machine learning model using the bag-of-words model, let's briefly talk about another useful topic called **stop-word removal**. Stop-words are simply those words that are extremely common in all sorts of texts and probably bear no (or only little) useful information that can be used to distinguish between different classes of documents. Examples of stop-words are *is*, *and*, *has*, and *like*. Removing stop-words can be useful if we are working with raw or normalized term frequencies rather than tf-idfs, which are already downweighting frequently occurring words.

In order to remove stop-words from the movie reviews, we will use the set of 127 English stop-words that is available from the NLTK library, which can be obtained by calling the nltk.download function:

```
>>> import nltk

>>> nltk.download('stopwords')
```

After we download the stop-words set, we can load and apply the English stop-word set as follows:

```
>>> from nltk.corpus import stopwords

>>> stop = stopwords.words('english')
>>> [w for w in tokenizer_porter('a runner likes running and runs a
lot')[-10:] if w not in stop]

['runner', 'like', 'run', 'run', 'lot']
```

Training a logistic regression model for document classification

In this section, we will train a logistic regression model to classify the movie reviews into *positive* and *negative* reviews. First, we will divide the DataFrame of cleaned text documents into 25,000 documents for training and 25,000 documents for testing:

```
>>> X_train = df.loc[:25000, 'review'].values
>>> y_train = df.loc[:25000, 'sentiment'].values
>>> X_test = df.loc[25000:, 'review'].values
>>> y_test = df.loc[25000:, 'sentiment'].values
```

Next, we will use a GridSearchCV object to find the optimal set of parameters for our logistic regression model using 5-fold stratified cross-validation:

```
>>> from sklearn.model_selection import GridSearchCV
>>> from sklearn.pipeline import Pipeline
>>> from sklearn.linear_model import LogisticRegression
>>> from sklearn.feature_extraction.text import TfidfVectorizer

>>> tfidf = TfidfVectorizer(strip_accents=None,
...                         lowercase=False,
...                         preprocessor=None)
>>> param_grid = [{'vect__ngram_range': [(1,1)],
...                'vect__stop_words': [stop, None],
...                'vect__tokenizer': [tokenizer,
...                                    tokenizer_porter],
...                'clf__penalty': ['l1', 'l2'],
...                'clf__C': [1.0, 10.0, 100.0]},
...               {'vect__ngram_range': [(1,1)],
...                'vect__stop_words': [stop, None],
...                'vect__tokenizer': [tokenizer,
...                                    tokenizer_porter],
...                'vect__use_idf':[False],
...                'vect__norm':[None],
...                'clf__penalty': ['l1', 'l2'],
...                'clf__C': [1.0, 10.0, 100.0]}
...               ]
>>> lr_tfidf = Pipeline([('vect', tfidf),
...                      ('clf',
...                       LogisticRegression(random_state=0))])
>>> gs_lr_tfidf = GridSearchCV(lr_tfidf, param_grid,
```

```
...                          scoring='accuracy',
...                          cv=5, verbose=1,
...                          n_jobs=1)
>>> gs_lr_tfidf.fit(X_train, y_train)
```

 Please note that it is highly recommended to set n_jobs=-1 (instead of n_jobs=1) in the previous code example to utilize all available cores on your machine and speed up the grid search. However, some Windows users reported issues when running the previous code with the n_jobs=-1 setting related to pickling the tokenizer and tokenizer_porter functions for multiprocessing on Windows. Another workaround would be to replace those two functions, [tokenizer, tokenizer_porter], with [str.split]. However, note that the replacement by the simple str.split would not support stemming.

When we initialized the GridSearchCV object and its parameter grid using the preceding code, we restricted ourselves to a limited number of parameter combinations, since the number of feature vectors, as well as the large vocabulary, can make the grid search computationally quite expensive. Using a standard desktop computer, our grid search may take up to 40 minutes to complete.

In the previous code example, we replaced CountVectorizer and TfidfTransformer from the previous subsection with TfidfVectorizer, which combines the latter transformer objects. Our param_grid consisted of two parameter dictionaries. In the first dictionary, we used the TfidfVectorizer with its default settings (use_idf=True, smooth_idf=True, and norm='l2') to calculate the tf-idfs; in the second dictionary, we set those parameters to use_idf=False, smooth_idf=False, and norm=None in order to train a model based on raw term frequencies. Furthermore, for the logistic regression classifier itself, we trained models using L2 and L1 regularization via the penalty parameter and compared different regularization strengths by defining a range of values for the inverse-regularization parameter C.

After the grid search has finished, we can print the best parameter set:

```
>>> print('Best parameter set: %s ' % gs_lr_tfidf.best_params_)
Best parameter set: {'clf__C': 10.0, 'vect__stop_words': None,
'clf__penalty': 'l2', 'vect__tokenizer': <function tokenizer at
0x7f6c704948c8>, 'vect__ngram_range': (1, 1)}
```

As we can see in the preceding output, we obtained the best grid search results using the regular `tokenizer` without Porter stemming, no stop-word library, and tf-idfs in combination with a logistic regression classifier that uses L2-regularization with the regularization strength C of `10.0`.

Using the best model from this grid search, let's print the average 5-fold cross-validation accuracy scores on the training set and the classification accuracy on the test dataset:

```
>>> print('CV Accuracy: %.3f'
...         % gs_lr_tfidf.best_score_)
CV Accuracy: 0.892
>>> clf = gs_lr_tfidf.best_estimator_
>>> print('Test Accuracy: %.3f'
...        % clf.score(X_test, y_test))
Test Accuracy: 0.899
```

The results reveal that our machine learning model can predict whether a movie review is positive or negative with 90 percent accuracy.

A still very popular classifier for text classification is the Naïve Bayes classifier, which gained popularity in applications of email spam filtering. Naïve Bayes classifiers are easy to implement, computationally efficient, and tend to perform particularly well on relatively small datasets compared to other algorithms. Although we don't discuss Naïve Bayes classifiers in this book, the interested reader can find my article about Naïve text classification that I made freely available on *arXiv* (*Naive Bayes and Text Classification I – Introduction and Theory*, S. Raschka, *Computing Research Repository (CoRR)*, abs/1410.5329, 2014, `http://arxiv.org/pdf/1410.5329v3.pdf`).

Working with bigger data – online algorithms and out-of-core learning

If you executed the code examples in the previous section, you may have noticed that it could be computationally quite expensive to construct the feature vectors for the 50,000 movie review dataset during grid search. In many real-world applications, it is not uncommon to work with even larger datasets that can exceed our computer's memory. Since not everyone has access to supercomputer facilities, we will now apply a technique called **out-of-core learning**, which allows us to work with such large datasets by fitting the classifier incrementally on smaller batches of the dataset.

Back in *Chapter 2, Training Simple Machine Learning Algorithms for Classification,* we introduced the concept of **stochastic gradient descent**, which is an optimization algorithm that updates the model's weights using one sample at a time. In this section, we will make use of the `partial_fit` function of the `SGDClassifier` in scikit-learn to stream the documents directly from our local drive, and train a logistic regression model using small mini-batches of documents.

First, we define a `tokenizer` function that cleans the unprocessed text data from the `movie_data.csv` file that we constructed at the beginning of this chapter and separate it into word tokens while removing stop words:

```
>>> import numpy as np
>>> import re
>>> from nltk.corpus import stopwords
>>> stop = stopwords.words('english')
>>> def tokenizer(text):
...     text = re.sub('<[^>]*>', '', text)
...     emoticons = re.findall('(?::|;|=)(?:-)?(?:\)|\(|D|P)',
...                            text.lower())
...     text = re.sub('[\W]+', ' ', text.lower()) \
...         + ' '.join(emoticons).replace('-', '')
...     tokenized = [w for w in text.split() if w not in stop]
...     return tokenized
```

Next, we define a generator function `stream_docs` that reads in and returns one document at a time:

```
>>> def stream_docs(path):
...     with open(path, 'r', encoding='utf-8') as csv:
...         next(csv) # skip header
...         for line in csv:
...             text, label = line[:-3], int(line[-2])
...             yield text, label
```

To verify that our `stream_docs` function works correctly, let's read in the first document from the `movie_data.csv` file, which should return a tuple consisting of the review text as well as the corresponding class label:

```
>>> next(stream_docs(path='movie_data.csv'))
('"In 1974, the teenager Martha Moxley ... ',1)
```

We will now define a function, `get_minibatch`, that will take a document stream from the `stream_docs` function and return a particular number of documents specified by the `size` parameter:

```
>>> def get_minibatch(doc_stream, size):
...     docs, y = [], []
...     try:
...         for _ in range(size):
...             text, label = next(doc_stream)
...             docs.append(text)
...             y.append(label)
...     except StopIteration:
...         return None, None
...     return docs, y
```

Unfortunately, we can't use `CountVectorizer` for out-of-core learning since it requires holding the complete vocabulary in memory. Also, `TfidfVectorizer` needs to keep all the feature vectors of the training dataset in memory to calculate the inverse document frequencies. However, another useful vectorizer for text processing implemented in scikit-learn is `HashingVectorizer`. `HashingVectorizer` is data-independent and makes use of the hashing trick via the 32-bit MurmurHash3 function by Austin Appleby (`https://sites.google.com/site/murmurhash/`):

```
>>> from sklearn.feature_extraction.text import HashingVectorizer
>>> from sklearn.linear_model import SGDClassifier
>>> vect = HashingVectorizer(decode_error='ignore',
...                          n_features=2**21,
...                          preprocessor=None,
...                          tokenizer=tokenizer)
>>> clf = SGDClassifier(loss='log', random_state=1, n_iter=1)
>>> doc_stream = stream_docs(path='movie_data.csv')
```

 You can replace `SGDClassifier(..., n_iter=1, ...)` by `SGDClassifier(..., max_iter=1, ...)` in scikit-learn versions greater than 0.18. The n_iter parameter is used here deliberately, because scikit-learn 0.18 is still widely used.

Using the preceding code, we initialized `HashingVectorizer` with our tokenizer function and set the number of features to `2**21`. Furthermore, we reinitialized a logistic regression classifier by setting the `loss` parameter of the `SGDClassifier` to `'log'` — note that by choosing a large number of features in the `HashingVectorizer`, we reduce the chance of causing hash collisions, but we also increase the number of coefficients in our logistic regression model. Now comes the really interesting part. Having set up all the complementary functions, we can now start the out-of-core learning using the following code:

```
>>> import pyprind
>>> pbar = pyprind.ProgBar(45)
>>> classes = np.array([0, 1])
>>> for _ in range(45):
...     X_train, y_train = get_minibatch(doc_stream, size=1000)
...     if not X_train:
...         break
...     X_train = vect.transform(X_train)
...     clf.partial_fit(X_train, y_train, classes=classes)
...     pbar.update()
0%                        100%
[############################] | ETA: 00:00:00
Total time elapsed: 00:00:39
```

Again, we made use of the PyPrind package in order to estimate the progress of our learning algorithm. We initialized the progress bar object with 45 iterations and, in the following `for` loop, we iterated over 45 mini-batches of documents where each mini-batch consists of 1,000 documents. Having completed the incremental learning process, we will use the last 5,000 documents to evaluate the performance of our model:

```
>>> X_test, y_test = get_minibatch(doc_stream, size=5000)
>>> X_test = vect.transform(X_test)
>>> print('Accuracy: %.3f' % clf.score(X_test, y_test))
Accuracy: 0.878
```

As we can see, the accuracy of the model is approximately 88 percent, slightly below the accuracy that we achieved in the previous section using the grid search for hyperparameter tuning. However, out-of-core learning is very memory efficient and took less than a minute to complete. Finally, we can use the last 5,000 documents to update our model:

```
>>> clf = clf.partial_fit(X_test, y_test)
```

If you are planning to continue directly with *Chapter 9, Embedding a Machine Learning Model into a Web Application*, I recommend you keep the current Python session open. In the next chapter, we will use the model that we just trained to learn how to save it to disk for later use and embed it into a web application.

> A more modern alternative to the bag-of-words model is **word2vec**, an algorithm that Google released in 2013 (*Efficient Estimation of Word Representations in Vector Space*, T. Mikolov, K. Chen, G. Corrado, and J. Dean, arXiv preprint arXiv:1301.3781, 2013). The word2vec algorithm is an unsupervised learning algorithm based on neural networks that attempts to automatically learn the relationship between words. The idea behind word2vec is to put words that have similar meanings into similar clusters, and via clever vector-spacing, the model can reproduce certain words using simple vector math, for example, *king – man + woman = queen*.
>
> The original C-implementation with useful links to the relevant papers and alternative implementations can be found at `https://code.google.com/p/word2vec/`.

Topic modeling with Latent Dirichlet Allocation

Topic modeling describes the broad task of assigning topics to unlabelled text documents. For example, a typical application would be the categorization of documents in a large text corpus of newspaper articles where we don't know on which specific page or category they appear in. In applications of topic modeling, we then aim to assign category labels to those articles—for example, sports, finance, world news, politics, local news, and so forth. Thus, in the context of the broad categories of machine learning that we discussed in *Chapter 1, Giving Computers the Ability to Learn from Data*, we can consider topic modeling as a clustering task, a subcategory of unsupervised learning.

In this section, we will introduce a popular technique for topic modeling called **Latent Dirichlet Allocation (LDA)**. However, note that while Latent Dirichlet Allocation is often abbreviated as LDA, it is not to be confused with Linear discriminant analysis, a supervised dimensionality reduction technique that we introduced in *Chapter 5, Compressing Data via Dimensionality Reduction*.

LDA is different from the supervised learning approach that we took in this chapter to classify movie reviews as positive and negative. Thus, if you are interested in embedding scikit-learn models into a web application via the Flask framework using the movie reviewer as an example, please feel free to jump to the next chapter and revisit this standalone section on topic modeling later on.

Decomposing text documents with LDA

Since the mathematics behind LDA is quite involved and requires knowledge about Bayesian inference, we will approach this topic from a practitioner's perspective and interpret LDA using layman's terms. However, the interested reader can read more about LDA in the following research paper: *Latent Dirichlet Allocation, David M. Blei, Andrew Y. Ng*, and *Michael I. Jordan, Journal of Machine Learning Research 3*, pages: 993-1022, Jan 2003.

LDA is a generative probabilistic model that tries to find groups of words that appear frequently together across different documents. These frequently appearing words represent our topics, assuming that each document is a mixture of different words. The input to an LDA is the bag-of-words model we discussed earlier in this chapter. Given a bag-of-words matrix as input, LDA decomposes it into two new matrices:

- A document to topic matrix
- A word to topic matrix

LDA decomposes the bag-of-words matrix in such a way that if we multiply those two matrices together, we would be able to reproduce the input, the bag-of-words matrix, with the lowest possible error. In practice, we are interested in those topics that LDA found in the bag-of-words matrix. The only downside may be that we must define the number of topics beforehand—the number of topics is a hyperparameter of LDA that has to be specified manually.

LDA with scikit-learn

In this subsection, we will use the `LatentDirichletAllocation` class implemented in scikit-learn to decompose the movie review dataset and categorize it into different topics. In the following example, we restrict the analysis to 10 different topics, but readers are encouraged to experiment with the hyperparameters of the algorithm to explore the topics that can be found in this dataset further.

First, we are going to load the dataset into a pandas `DataFrame` using the local `movie_data.csv` file of the movie reviews that we have created at the beginning of this chapter:

```
>>> import pandas as pd
>>> df = pd.read_csv('movie_data.csv', encoding='utf-8')
```

Next, we are going to use the already familiar `CountVectorizer` to create the bag-of-words matrix as input to the LDA. For convenience, we will use scikit-learn's built-in English stop word library via `stop_words='english'`:

```
>>> from sklearn.feature_extraction.text import CountVectorizer
>>> count = CountVectorizer(stop_words='english',
...                         max_df=.1,
...                         max_features=5000)
>>> X = count.fit_transform(df['review'].values)
```

Notice that we set the maximum document frequency of words to be considered to 10 percent (`max_df=.1`) to exclude words that occur too frequently across documents. The rationale behind the removal of frequently occurring words is that these might be common words appearing across all documents and are therefore less likely associated with a specific topic category of a given document. Also, we limited the number of words to be considered to the most frequently occurring 5,000 words (`max_features=5000`), to limit the dimensionality of this dataset so that it improves the inference performed by LDA. However, both `max_df=.1` and `max_features=5000` are hyperparameter values that I chose arbitrarily, and readers are encouraged to tune them while comparing the results.

The following code example demonstrates how to fit a `LatentDirichletAllocation` estimator to the bag-of-words matrix and infer the 10 different topics from the documents (note that the model fitting can take up to five minutes or more on a laptop or standard desktop computer):

```
>>> from sklearn.decomposition import LatentDirichletAllocation
>>> lda = LatentDirichletAllocation(n_topics=10,
...                                 random_state=123,
...                                 learning_method='batch')
>>> X_topics = lda.fit_transform(X)
```

By setting `learning_method='batch'`, we let the `lda` estimator do its estimation based on all available training data (the bag-of-words matrix) in one iteration, which is slower than the alternative `'online'` learning method but can lead to more accurate results (setting `learning_method='online'` is analogous to online or mini-batch learning that we discussed in *Chapter 2, Training Simple Machine Learning Algorithms for Classification,* and in this chapter).

The scikit-learn library's implementation of LDA uses the **Expectation-Maximization (EM)** algorithm to update its parameter estimates iteratively. We haven't discussed the EM algorithm in this chapter, but if you are curious to learn more, please see the excellent overview on Wikipedia (https://en.wikipedia.org/wiki/Expectation-maximization_algorithm) and the detailed tutorial on how it is used in LDA in Colorado Reed's tutorial, *Latent Dirichlet Allocation: Towards a Deeper Understanding*, which is freely available at http://obphio.us/pdfs/lda_tutorial.pdf.

After fitting the LDA, we now have access to the components_ attribute of the lda instance, which stores a matrix containing the word importance (here, 5000) for each of the 10 topics in increasing order:

```
>>> lda.components_.shape
(10, 5000)
```

To analyze the results, let's print the five most important words for each of the 10 topics. Note that the word importance values are ranked in increasing order. Thus, to print the top five words, we need to sort the topic array in reverse order:

```
>>> n_top_words = 5
>>> feature_names = count.get_feature_names()
>>> for topic_idx, topic in enumerate(lda.components_):
...     print("Topic %d:" % (topic_idx + 1))
...     print(" ".join([feature_names[i]
...                     for i in topic.argsort()\
...                         [:-n_top_words - 1:-1]]))

Topic 1:
worst minutes awful script stupid
Topic 2:
family mother father children girl
Topic 3:
american war dvd music tv
Topic 4:
human audience cinema art sense
Topic 5:
police guy car dead murder
Topic 6:
horror house sex girl woman
Topic 7:
role performance comedy actor performances
Topic 8:
series episode war episodes tv
```

```
Topic 9:
book version original read novel
Topic 10:
action fight guy guys cool
```

Based on reading the five most important words for each topic, we may guess that the LDA identified the following topics:

1. Generally bad movies (not really a topic category)
2. Movies about families
3. War movies
4. Art movies
5. Crime movies
6. Horror movies
7. Comedy movies
8. Movies somehow related to TV shows
9. Movies based on books
10. Action movies

To confirm that the categories make sense based on the reviews, let's plot three movies from the horror movie category (horror movies belong to category 6 at index position 5):

```
>>> horror = X_topics[:, 5].argsort()[::-1]
>>> for iter_idx, movie_idx in enumerate(horror[:3]):
...     print('\nHorror movie #%d:' % (iter_idx + 1))
...     print(df['review'][movie_idx][:300], '...')
Horror movie #1:
House of Dracula works from the same basic premise as House of
Frankenstein from the year before; namely that Universal's three most
famous monsters; Dracula, Frankenstein's Monster and The Wolf Man are
appearing in the movie together. Naturally, the film is rather messy
therefore, but the fact that ...

Horror movie #2:
Okay, what the hell kind of TRASH have I been watching now? "The
Witches' Mountain" has got to be one of the most incoherent and insane
Spanish exploitation flicks ever and yet, at the same time, it's also
strangely compelling. There's absolutely nothing that makes sense here
and I even doubt there  ...

Horror movie #3:
```

```
<br /><br />Horror movie time, Japanese style. Uzumaki/Spiral was a
total freakfest from start to finish. A fun freakfest at that, but at
times it was a tad too reliant on kitsch rather than the horror. The
story is difficult to summarize succinctly: a carefree, normal teenage
girl starts coming fac ...
```

Using the preceding code example, we printed the first 300 characters from the top three horror movies, and we can see that the reviews—even though we don't know which exact movie they belong to—sound like reviews of horror movies (however, one might argue that Horror movie #2 could also be a good fit for topic category 1: *Generally bad movies*).

Summary

In this chapter, we learned how to use machine learning algorithms to classify text documents based on their polarity, which is a basic task in sentiment analysis in the field of NLP. Not only did we learn how to encode a document as a feature vector using the bag-of-words model, but we also learned how to weight the term frequency by relevance using tf-idf.

Working with text data can be computationally quite expensive due to the large feature vectors that are created during this process; in the last section, we learned how to utilize out-of-core or incremental learning to train a machine learning algorithm without loading the whole dataset into a computer's memory.

Lastly, we introduced the concept of topic modeling using LDA to categorize the movie reviews into different categories in unsupervised fashion.

In the next chapter, we will use our document classifier and learn how to embed it into a web application.

9
Embedding a Machine Learning Model into a Web Application

In the previous chapters, you learned about the many different machine learning concepts and algorithms that can help us with better and more efficient decision-making. However, machine learning techniques are not limited to offline applications and analysis, and they can be the predictive engine of your web services. For example, popular and useful applications of machine learning models in web applications include spam detection in submission forms, search engines, recommendation systems for media or shopping portals, and many more.

In this chapter, you will learn how to embed a machine learning model into a web application that can not only classify, but also learn from data in real time. The topics that we will cover are as follows:

- Saving the current state of a trained machine learning model
- Using SQLite databases for data storage
- Developing a web application using the popular Flask web framework
- Deploying a machine learning application to a public web server

Serializing fitted scikit-learn estimators

Training a machine learning model can be computationally quite expensive, as we have seen in *Chapter 8, Applying Machine Learning to Sentiment Analysis*. Surely we don't want to train our model every time we close our Python interpreter and want to make a new prediction or reload our web application? One option for model persistence is Python's in-built `pickle` module (https://docs.python.org/3.6/library/pickle.html), which allows us to serialize and deserialize Python object structures to compact bytecode so that we can save our classifier in its current state and reload it if we want to classify new samples, without needing the model to learn from the training data all over again. Before you execute the following code, please make sure that you have trained the out-of-core logistic regression model from the last section of *Chapter 8, Applying Machine Learning to Sentiment Analysis* and have it ready in your current Python session:

```
>>> import pickle
>>> import os
>>> dest = os.path.join('movieclassifier', 'pkl_objects')
>>> if not os.path.exists(dest):
...      os.makedirs(dest)

>>> pickle.dump(stop,
...             open(os.path.join(dest, 'stopwords.pkl'),'wb'),
...             protocol=4)
>>> pickle.dump(clf,
...             open(os.path.join(dest, 'classifier.pkl'), 'wb'),
...             protocol=4)
```

Using the preceding code, we created a `movieclassifier` directory where we will later store the files and data for our web application. Within this `movieclassifier` directory, we created a `pkl_objects` subdirectory to save the serialized Python objects to our local drive. Via the `dump` method of the `pickle` module, we then serialized the trained logistic regression model as well as the stop word set from the **Natural Language Toolkit** (**NLTK**) library, so that we don't have to install the NLTK vocabulary on our server.

The `dump` method takes as its first argument the object that we want to pickle, and for the second argument we provided an open file object that the Python object will be written to. Via the `wb` argument inside the `open` function, we opened the file in binary mode for pickle, and we set `protocol=4` to choose the latest and most efficient pickle protocol that has been added to Python 3.4, which is compatible with Python 3.4 or newer. If you have problems using `protocol=4`, please check whether you are using the latest Python 3 version. Alternatively, you may consider choosing a lower protocol number.

Our logistic regression model contains several NumPy arrays, such as the weight vector, and a more efficient way to serialize NumPy arrays is to use the alternative joblib library. To ensure compatibility with the server environment that we will use in later sections, we will use the standard pickle approach. If you are interested, you can find more information about joblib at http://pythonhosted.org/joblib/.

We don't need to pickle HashingVectorizer, since it does not need to be fitted. Instead, we can create a new Python script file from which we can import the vectorizer into our current Python session. Now, copy the following code and save it as vectorizer.py in the movieclassifier directory:

```python
from sklearn.feature_extraction.text import HashingVectorizer
import re
import os
import pickle

cur_dir = os.path.dirname(__file__)
stop = pickle.load(open(
                os.path.join(cur_dir,
                'pkl_objects',
                'stopwords.pkl'), 'rb'))

def tokenizer(text):
    text = re.sub('<[^>]*>', '', text)
    emoticons = re.findall('(?::|;|=)(?:-)?(?:\)|\(|D|P)',
                           text.lower())
    text = re.sub('[\W]+', ' ', text.lower()) \
                   + ' '.join(emoticons).replace('-', '')
    tokenized = [w for w in text.split() if w not in stop]
    return tokenized

vect = HashingVectorizer(decode_error='ignore',
                        n_features=2**21,
                        preprocessor=None,
                        tokenizer=tokenizer)
```

After we have pickled the Python objects and created the vectorizer.py file, it would now be a good idea to restart our Python interpreter or IPython Notebook kernel to test if we can deserialize the objects without error.

However, please note that unpickling data from an untrusted source can be a potential security risk, since the `pickle` module is not secured against malicious code. Since `pickle` was designed to serialize arbitrary objects, the unpickling process will execute code that has been stored in a pickle file. Thus, if you receive pickle files from an untrusted source (for example, by downloading them from the internet), please proceed with extra care and unpickle the items in a virtual environment and/or on a non-essential machine that does not store important data that no one except you should have access to.

From your Terminal, navigate to the `movieclassifier` directory, start a new Python session and execute the following code to verify that you can import the `vectorizer` and unpickle the classifier:

```
>>> import pickle
>>> import re
>>> import os
>>> from vectorizer import vect
>>> clf = pickle.load(open(
...          os.path.join('pkl_objects',
...                       'classifier.pkl'), 'rb'))
```

After we have successfully loaded the `vectorizer` and unpickled the classifier, we can now use these objects to preprocess document samples and make predictions about their sentiment:

```
>>> import numpy as np
>>> label = {0:'negative', 1:'positive'}

>>> example = ['I love this movie']
>>> X = vect.transform(example)
>>> print('Prediction: %s\nProbability: %.2f%%' %\
...          (label[clf.predict(X)[0]],
...           np.max(clf.predict_proba(X))*100))
Prediction: positive
Probability: 91.56%
```

Since our classifier returns the class labels as integers, we defined a simple Python dictionary to map these integers to their sentiment. We then used `HashingVectorizer` to transform the simple example document into a word vector X. Finally, we used the `predict` method of the logistic regression classifier to predict the class label, as well as the `predict_proba` method to return the corresponding probability of our prediction. Note that the `predict_proba` method call returns an array with a probability value for each unique class label. Since the class label with the largest probability corresponds to the class label that is returned by the `predict` call, we used the `np.max` function to return the probability of the predicted class.

Setting up an SQLite database for data storage

In this section, we will set up a simple SQLite database to collect optional feedback about the predictions from users of the web application. We can use this feedback to update our classification model. SQLite is an open source SQL database engine that doesn't require a separate server to operate, which makes it ideal for smaller projects and simple web applications. Essentially, a SQLite database can be understood as a single, self-contained database file that allows us to directly access storage files.

Furthermore, SQLite doesn't require any system-specific configuration and is supported by all common operating systems. It has gained a reputation for being very reliable as it is used by popular companies such as Google, Mozilla, Adobe, Apple, Microsoft, and many more. If you want to learn more about SQLite, I recommend you visit the official website at http://www.sqlite.org.

Fortunately, following Python's *batteries included* philosophy, there is already an API in the Python standard library, `sqlite3`, which allows us to work with SQLite databases (for more information about `sqlite3`, please visit https://docs.python.org/3.6/library/sqlite3.html).

By executing the following code, we will create a new SQLite database inside the `movieclassifier` directory and store two example movie reviews:

```
>>> import sqlite3
>>> import os

>>> if os.path.exists('reviews.sqlite'):
...     os.remove('reviews.sqlite')
>>> conn = sqlite3.connect('reviews.sqlite')
>>> c = conn.cursor()
>>> c.execute('CREATE TABLE review_db'\
```

```
...                ' (review TEXT, sentiment INTEGER, date TEXT)')

>>> example1 = 'I love this movie'
>>> c.execute("INSERT INTO review_db"\
...           " (review, sentiment, date) VALUES"\
...           " (?, ?, DATETIME('now'))", (example1, 1))

>>> example2 = 'I disliked this movie'
>>> c.execute("INSERT INTO review_db"\
...           " (review, sentiment, date) VALUES"\
...           " (?, ?, DATETIME('now'))", (example2, 0))
>>> conn.commit()
>>> conn.close()
```

Following the preceding code example, we created a connection (conn) to a SQLite database file by calling the connect method of the sqlite3 library, which created the new database file reviews.sqlite in the movieclassifier directory if it didn't already exist. Please note that SQLite doesn't implement a replace function for existing tables; you need to delete the database file manually from your file browser if you want to execute the code a second time.

Next, we created a cursor via the cursor method, which allows us to traverse over the database records using the versatile SQL syntax. Via the first execute call, we then created a new database table, review_db. We used this to store and access database entries. Along with review_db, we also created three columns in this database table: review, sentiment, and date. We used these to store two example movie reviews and respective class labels (sentiments).

Using the DATETIME('now') SQL command, we also added date and timestamps to our entries. In addition to the timestamps, we used the question mark symbols (?) to pass the movie review texts (example1 and example2) and the corresponding class labels (1 and 0) as positional arguments to the execute method, as members of a tuple. Lastly, we called the commit method to save the changes that we made to the database and closed the connection via the close method.

To check if the entries have been stored in the database table correctly, we will now reopen the connection to the database and use the SQL SELECT command to fetch all rows in the database table that have been committed between the beginning of the year 2017 and today:

```
>>> conn = sqlite3.connect('reviews.sqlite')
>>> c = conn.cursor()
>>> c.execute("SELECT * FROM review_db WHERE date"\
...       " BETWEEN '2017-01-01 00:00:00' AND DATETIME('now')")
```

```
>>> results = c.fetchall()

>>> conn.close()
>>> print(results)
[('I love this movie', 1, '2017-04-24 00:14:38'),
 ('I disliked this movie', 0, '2017-04-24 00:14:38')
```

Alternatively, we could also use the free Firefox browser plugin SQLite Manager (available at `https://addons.mozilla.org/en-US/firefox/addon/sqlite-manager/`), which offers a nice GUI interface for working with SQLite databases, as shown in the following figure:

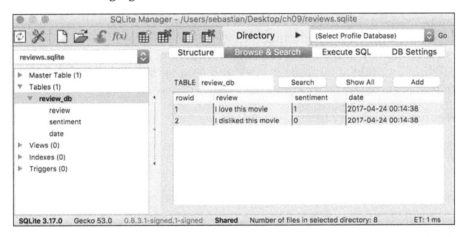

Developing a web application with Flask

Having prepared the code for classifying movie reviews in the previous subsection, let's discuss the basics of the Flask web framework to develop our web application. After Armin Ronacher's initial release of Flask in 2010, the framework has gained huge popularity over the years, and examples of popular applications that make use of Flask include LinkedIn and Pinterest. Since Flask is written in Python, it provides us Python programmers with a convenient interface for embedding existing Python code, such as our movie classifier.

> Flask is also known as a **microframework**, which means that its core is kept lean and simple but can be easily extended with other libraries. Although the learning curve of the lightweight Flask API is not nearly as steep as those of other popular Python web frameworks, such as Django, I encourage you to take a look at the official Flask documentation at `http://flask.pocoo.org/docs/0.12/` to learn more about its functionality.

If the Flask library is not already installed in your current Python environment, you can simply install it via conda or pip from your Terminal (at the time of writing, the latest stable release was version 0.12.1):

```
conda install flask
# or: pip install flask
```

Our first Flask web application

In this subsection, we will develop a very simple web application to become more familiar with the Flask API before we implement our movie classifier. This first application we are going to build consists of a simple web page with a form field that lets us enter a name. After submitting the name to the web application, it will render it on a new page. While this is a very simple example of a web application, it helps with building intuition about how to store and pass variables and values between the different parts of our code within the Flask framework.

First, we create a directory tree:

```
1st_flask_app_1/
    app.py
    templates/
        first_app.html
```

The app.py file will contain the main code that will be executed by the Python interpreter to run the Flask web application. The templates directory is the directory in which Flask will look for static HTML files for rendering in the web browser. Let's now take a look at the contents of app.py:

```python
from flask import Flask, render_template

app = Flask(__name__)
@app.route('/')
def index():
    return render_template('first_app.html')


if __name__ == '__main__':
    app.run()
```

After looking at the previous code example, let's discuss the individual pieces step by step:

1. We ran our application as a single module; thus we initialized a new Flask instance with the argument __name__ to let Flask know that it can find the HTML template folder (templates) in the same directory where it is located.

2. Next, we used the route decorator (@app.route('/')) to specify the URL that should trigger the execution of the index function.

3. Here, our index function simply rendered the first_app.html HTML file, which is located in the templates folder.

4. Lastly, we used the run function to only run the application on the server when this script is directly executed by the Python interpreter, which we ensured using the if statement with __name__ == '__main__'.

Now, let's take a look at the contents of the first_app.html file:

```html
<!doctype html>
<html>
  <head>
    <title>First app</title>
  </head>
  <body>
    <div>Hi, this is my first Flask web app!</div>
  </body>
</html>
```

If you are not familiar with the HTML syntax yet, I recommend you visit https://developer.mozilla.org/en-US/docs/Web/HTML for useful tutorials for learning the basics of HTML.

Here, we have simply filled an empty HTML template file with a <div> element (a block level element) that contains this sentence: Hi, this is my first Flask web app!.

Conveniently, Flask allows us to run our applications locally, which is useful for developing and testing web applications before we deploy them on a public web server. Now, let's start our web application by executing the command from the Terminal inside the 1st_flask_app_1 directory:

python3 app.py

We should see a line such as the following displayed in the Terminal:

```
* Running on http://127.0.0.1:5000/
```

This line contains the address of our local server. We can enter this address in our web browser to see the web application in action. If everything has executed correctly, we should see a simple website with the content `Hi, this is my first Flask web app!` as shown in the following figure:

Form validation and rendering

In this subsection, we will extend our simple Flask web application with HTML form elements to learn how to collect data from a user using the WTForms library (`https://wtforms.readthedocs.org/en/latest/`), which can be installed via conda or pip:

```
conda install wtforms
# or pip install wtforms
```

This web application will prompt a user to type in his or her name into a text field, as shown in the following screenshot:

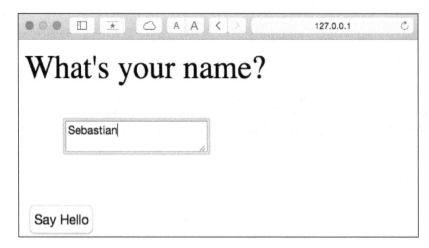

After the submission button (**Say Hello**) has been clicked and the form is validated, a new HTML page will be rendered to display the user's name:

Setting up the directory structure

The new directory structure that we need to set up for this application looks like this:

```
1st_flask_app_2/
      app.py
      static/
          style.css
      templates/
          _formhelpers.html
          first_app.html
          hello.html
```

The following are the contents of our modified `app.py` file:

```python
from flask import Flask, render_template, request
from wtforms import Form, TextAreaField, validators

app = Flask(__name__)

class HelloForm(Form):
    sayhello = TextAreaField('', [validators.DataRequired()])

@app.route('/')
def index():
    form = HelloForm(request.form)
    return render_template('first_app.html', form=form)

@app.route('/hello', methods=['POST'])
def hello():
    form = HelloForm(request.form)
    if request.method == 'POST' and form.validate():
        name = request.form['sayhello']
```

```
        return render_template('hello.html', name=name)
    return render_template('first_app.html', form=form)
if __name__ == '__main__':
    app.run(debug=True)
```

Let's discuss what the previous code does step by step:

1. Using `wtforms`, we extended the `index` function with a text field that we will embed in our start page using the `TextAreaField` class, which automatically checks whether a user has provided valid input text or not.

2. Furthermore, we defined a new function, `hello`, which will render an HTML page `hello.html` after validating the HTML form.

3. Here, we used the `POST` method to transport the form data to the server in the message body. Finally, by setting the `debug=True` argument inside the `app.run` method, we further activated Flask's debugger. This is a useful feature for developing new web applications.

Implementing a macro using the Jinja2 templating engine

Now, we will implement a generic macro in the `_formhelpers.html` file via the Jinja2 templating engine, which we will later import in our `first_app.html` file to render the text field:

```
{% macro render_field(field) %}
  <dt>{{ field.label }}
  <dd>{{ field(**kwargs)|safe }}
  {% if field.errors %}
    <ul class=errors>
    {% for error in field.errors %}
      <li>{{ error }}</li>
    {% endfor %}
    </ul>
  {% endif %}
  </dd>
  </dt>
{% endmacro %}
```

An in-depth discussion about the Jinja2 templating language is beyond the scope of this book. However, you can find a comprehensive documentation of the Jinja2 syntax at http://jinja.pocoo.org.

Adding style via CSS

Next, we set up a simple **Cascading Style Sheet (CSS)** file, `style.css`, to demonstrate how the look and feel of HTML documents can be modified. We have to save the following CSS file, which will simply double the font size of our HTML body elements, in a subdirectory called `static`, which is the default directory where Flask looks for static files such as CSS. The file content is as follows:

```
body {
    font-size: 2em;
}
```

The following are the contents of the modified `first_app.html` file that will now render a text form where a user can enter a name:

```
<!doctype html>
<html>
  <head>
    <title>First app</title>
      <link rel="stylesheet" href="{{ url_for('static',
      filename='style.css') }}">
  </head>
  <body>
    {% from "_formhelpers.html" import render_field %}
    <div>What's your name?</div>
    <form method=post action="/hello">
      <dl>
        {{ render_field(form.sayhello) }}
      </dl>
      <input type=submit value='Say Hello' name='submit_btn'>
    </form>
  </body>
</html>
```

In the header section of `first_app.html`, we loaded the CSS file. It should now alter the size of all text elements in the HTML body. In the HTML body section, we imported the form macro from `_formhelpers.html`, and we rendered the `sayhello` form that we specified in the `app.py` file. Furthermore, we added a button to the same form element so that a user can submit the text field entry.

Creating the result page

Lastly, we will create a `hello.html` file that will be rendered via the `render_template('hello.html', name=name)` line return inside the `hello` function, which we defined in the `app.py` script to display the text that a user submitted via the text field. The file content is as follows:

```
<!doctype html>
<html>
  <head>
    <title>First app</title>
      <link rel="stylesheet" href="{{ url_for('static',
      filename='style.css') }}">
  </head>
  <body>
    <div>Hello {{ name }}</div>
  </body>

</html>
```

Having set up our modified Flask web application, we can run it locally by executing the following command from the application's main directory, and we can view the result in our web browser at `http://127.0.0.1:5000/`:

python3 app.py

> If you are new to web development, some of those concepts may seem very complicated at first sight. In that case, I encourage you to simply set up the preceding files in a directory on your hard drive and examine them closely. You will see that the Flask web framework is relatively straightforward and much simpler than it might initially appear! Also, for more help, don't forget to consult the excellent Flask documentation and examples at `http://flask.pocoo.org/docs/0.12/`.

Turning the movie review classifier into a web application

Now that we are somewhat familiar with the basics of Flask web development, let's advance to the next step and implement our movie classifier into a web application. In this section, we will develop a web application that will first prompt a user to enter a movie review, as shown in the following screenshot:

After the review has been submitted, the user will see a new page that shows the predicted class label and the probability of the prediction. Furthermore, the user will be able to provide feedback about this prediction by clicking on the **Correct** or **Incorrect** button, as shown in the following screenshot:

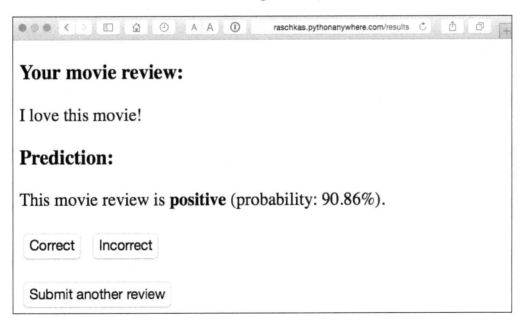

If a user clicked on either the **Correct** or **Incorrect** button, our classification model will be updated with respect to the user's feedback. Furthermore, we will also store the movie review text provided by the user as well as the suggested class label, which can be inferred from the button click, in a SQLite database for future reference. (Alternatively, a user could skip the update step and click the **Submit another review** button to submit another review.)

The third page that the user will see after clicking on one of the feedback buttons is a simple *thank you* screen with a **Submit another review** button that redirects the user back to the start page. This is shown in the following screenshot:

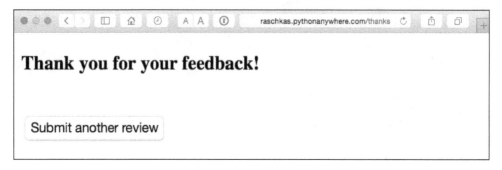

Before we take a closer look at the code implementation of this web application, I encourage you to take a look at the live demo that I uploaded at http://raschkas.pythonanywhere.com to get a better understanding of what we are trying to accomplish in this section.

Files and folders – looking at the directory tree

To start with the big picture, let's take a look at the directory tree that we are going to create for this movie classification application, which is shown here:

In the previous section of this chapter, we already created the vectorizer.py file, the SQLite database reviews.sqlite, and the pkl_objects subdirectory with the pickled Python objects.

The app.py file in the main directory is the Python script that contains our Flask code, and we will use the review.sqlite database file (which we created earlier in this chapter) to store the movie reviews that are being submitted to our web application. The templates subdirectory contains the HTML templates that will be rendered by Flask and displayed in the browser, and the static subdirectory will contain a simple CSS file to adjust the look of the rendered HTML code.

A separate directory containing the movie review classifier application with the code discussed in this section is provided with the code examples for this book, which you can either obtain directly from Packt or download from GitHub at https://github.com/rasbt/python-machine-learning-book-2nd-edition/. The code in this section can be found in the.../code/ch09/movieclassifier subdirectory.

Implementing the main application as app.py

Since the app.py file is rather long, we will conquer it in two steps. The first section of app.py imports the Python modules and objects that we are going to need, as well as the code to unpickle and set up our classification model:

```
from flask import Flask, render_template, request
from wtforms import Form, TextAreaField, validators
import pickle
import sqlite3
import os
import numpy as np

# import HashingVectorizer from local dir
from vectorizer import vect

app = Flask(__name__)

######## Preparing the Classifier
cur_dir = os.path.dirname(__file__)
clf = pickle.load(open(os.path.join(cur_dir,
                  'pkl_objects',
                  'classifier.pkl'), 'rb'))
db = os.path.join(cur_dir, 'reviews.sqlite')

def classify(document):
    label = {0: 'negative', 1: 'positive'}
    X = vect.transform([document])
    y = clf.predict(X)[0]
    proba = np.max(clf.predict_proba(X))
    return label[y], proba

def train(document, y):
    X = vect.transform([document])
    clf.partial_fit(X, [y])

def sqlite_entry(path, document, y):
    conn = sqlite3.connect(path)
    c = conn.cursor()
    c.execute("INSERT INTO review_db (review, sentiment, date)"\
    " VALUES (?, ?, DATETIME('now'))", (document, y))
    conn.commit()
    conn.close()
```

This first part of the `app.py` script should look very familiar to us by now. We simply imported the `HashingVectorizer` and unpickled the logistic regression classifier. Next, we defined a `classify` function to return the predicted class label as well as the corresponding probability prediction of a given text document. The `train` function can be used to update the classifier, given that a document and a class label are provided.

Using the `sqlite_entry` function, we can store a submitted movie review in our SQLite database along with its class label and timestamp for our personal records. Note that the `clf` object will be reset to its original, pickled state if we restart the web application. At the end of this chapter, you will learn how to use the data that we collect in the SQLite database to update the classifier permanently.

The concepts in the second part of the `app.py` script should also look quite familiar to us:

```
######## Flask
class ReviewForm(Form):
    moviereview = TextAreaField('',
                                [validators.DataRequired(),
                                validators.length(min=15)])

@app.route('/')
def index():
    form = ReviewForm(request.form)
    return render_template('reviewform.html', form=form)

@app.route('/results', methods=['POST'])
def results():
    form = ReviewForm(request.form)
    if request.method == 'POST' and form.validate():
        review = request.form['moviereview']
        y, proba = classify(review)
        return render_template('results.html',
                               content=review,
                               prediction=y,
                               probability=round(proba*100, 2))
    return render_template('reviewform.html', form=form)

@app.route('/thanks', methods=['POST'])
def feedback():
    feedback = request.form['feedback_button']
    review = request.form['review']
```

```
    prediction = request.form['prediction']

    inv_label = {'negative': 0, 'positive': 1}
    y = inv_label[prediction]
    if feedback == 'Incorrect':
        y = int(not(y))
    train(review, y)
    sqlite_entry(db, review, y)
    return render_template('thanks.html')

if __name__ == '__main__':
    app.run(debug=True)
```

We defined a `ReviewForm` class that instantiates a `TextAreaField`, which will be rendered in the `reviewform.html` template file (the landing page of our web application). This, in turn, is rendered by the `index` function. With the `validators.length(min=15)` parameter, we require the user to enter a review that contains at least 15 characters. Inside the `results` function, we fetch the contents of the submitted web form and pass it on to our classifier to predict the sentiment of the movie classifier, which will then be displayed in the rendered `results.html` template.

The `feedback` function, which we implemented in `app.py` in the previous subsection, may look a little bit complicated at first glance. It essentially fetches the predicted class label from the `results.html` template if a user clicked on the **Correct** or **Incorrect** feedback button, and transforms the predicted sentiment back into an integer class label that will be used to update the classifier via the `train` function, which we implemented in the first section of the `app.py` script. Also, a new entry to the SQLite database will be made via the `sqlite_entry` function if feedback was provided, and eventually the `thanks.html` template will be rendered to thank the user for the feedback.

Setting up the review form

Next, let's take a look at the `reviewform.html` template, which constitutes the starting page of our application:

```
<!doctype html>
<html>
  <head>
    <title>Movie Classification</title>
      <link rel="stylesheet"
      href="{{ url_for('static', filename='style.css') }}">
  </head>
```

```
<body>

    <h2>Please enter your movie review:</h2>

    {% from "_formhelpers.html" import render_field %}

    <form method=post action="/results">
      <dl>
        {{ render_field(form.moviereview, cols='30', rows='10') }}
      </dl>
      <div>
        <input type=submit value='Submit review'
        name='submit_btn'>
      </div>
    </form>

  </body>
</html>
```

Here, we simply imported the same _formhelpers.html template that we defined in the *Form validation and rendering* section earlier in this chapter. The render_field function of this macro is used to render a TextAreaField where a user can provide a movie review and submit it via the **Submit review** button displayed at the bottom of the page. This TextAreaField is 30 columns wide and 10 rows tall, and would look like this:

Creating a results page template

Our next template, `results.html`, looks a little bit more interesting:

```html
<!doctype html>
<html>
  <head>
    <title>Movie Classification</title>
      <link rel="stylesheet"
      href="{{ url_for('static', filename='style.css') }}">
  </head>
  <body>

    <h3>Your movie review:</h3>
    <div>{{ content }}</div>

    <h3>Prediction:</h3>
    <div>This movie review is <strong>{{ prediction }}</strong>
    (probability: {{ probability }}%).</div>

    <div id='button'>
      <form action="/thanks" method="post">
        <input type=submit value='Correct'
        name='feedback_button'>
        <input type=submit value='Incorrect'
        name='feedback_button'>
        <input type=hidden value='{{ prediction }}'
        name='prediction'>
        <input type=hidden value='{{ content }}' name='review'>
      </form>
    </div>

    <div id='button'>
      <form action="/">
       <input type=submit value='Submit another review'>
      </form>
    </div>

  </body>
</html>
```

First, we inserted the submitted review, as well as the results of the prediction, in the corresponding fields {{ content }}, {{ prediction }}, and {{ probability }}. You may notice that we used the {{ content }} and {{ prediction }} placeholder variables a second time in the form that contains the **Correct** and **Incorrect** buttons. This is a workaround to POST those values back to the server to update the classifier and store the review in case the user clicks on one of those two buttons.

Furthermore, we imported a CSS file (style.css) at the beginning of the results. html file. The setup of this file is quite simple; it limits the width of the contents of this web application to 600 pixels and moves the **Incorrect** and **Correct** buttons labeled with the div ID button down by 20 pixels:

```
body{
  width:600px;
}

.button{
  padding-top: 20px;
}
```

This CSS file is merely a placeholder, so please feel free to adjust it to adjust the look and feel of the web application to your liking.

The last HTML file we will implement for our web application is the thanks.html template. As the name suggests, it simply provides a nice *thank you* message to the user after providing feedback via the **Correct** or **Incorrect** button. Furthermore, we will put a **Submit another review** button at the bottom of this page, which will redirect the user to the starting page. The contents of the thanks.html file are as follows:

```
<!doctype html>
<html>
  <head>
    <title>Movie Classification</title>
      <link rel="stylesheet"
      href="{{ url_for('static', filename='style.css') }}">
  </head>
  <body>

    <h3>Thank you for your feedback!</h3>

    <div id='button'>
      <form action="/">
        <input type=submit value='Submit another review'>
      </form>
```

```
        </div>

      </body>
    </html>
```

Now, it would be a good idea to start the web application locally from our Terminal via the following command before we advance to the next subsection and deploy it on a public web server:

python3 app.py

After we have finished testing our application, we also shouldn't forget to remove the debug=True argument in the app.run() command of our app.py script.

Deploying the web application to a public server

After we have tested the web application locally, we are now ready to deploy our web application onto a public web server. For this tutorial, we will be using the PythonAnywhere web hosting service, which specializes in the hosting of Python web applications and makes it extremely simple and hassle-free. Furthermore, PythonAnywhere offers a beginner account option that lets us run a single web application free of charge.

Creating a PythonAnywhere account

To create a new PythonAnywhere account, we visit the website at https://www.pythonanywhere.com/ and click on the **Pricing & signup** link that is located in the top-right corner. Next, we click on the **Create a Beginner account** button where we need to provide a username, password, and valid email address. After we have read and agreed to the terms and conditions, we should have a new account.

Unfortunately, the free beginner account doesn't allow us to access the remote server via the SSH protocol from our Terminal. Thus, we need to use the PythonAnywhere web interface to manage our web application. But before we can upload our local application files to the server, we need to create a new web application for our PythonAnywhere account. After we click on the **Dashboard** button in the top-right corner, we have access to the control panel shown at the top of the page. Next, we click on the **Web** tab that is now visible at the top of the page. We proceed by clicking on the **+Add a new web app** button on the left, which lets us create a new Python 3.5 Flask web application that we name movieclassifier.

Uploading the movie classifier application

After creating a new application for our PythonAnywhere account, we head over to the **Files** tab, to upload the files from our local `movieclassifier` directory using the PythonAnywhere web interface. After uploading the web application files that we created locally on our computer, we should have a `movieclassifier` directory in our PythonAnywhere account. It contains the same directories and files as our local `movieclassifier` directory has, as shown in the following screenshot:

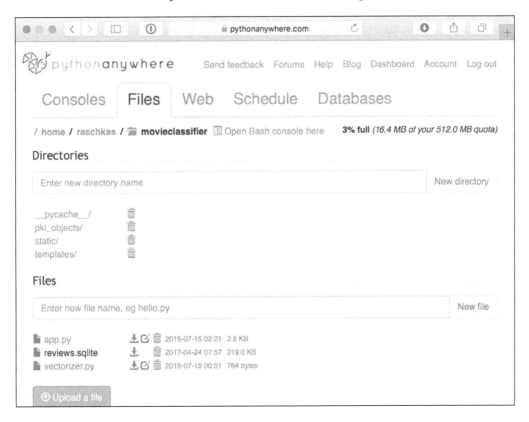

Lastly, we head over to the **Web** tab one more time and click on the **Reload <username>.pythonanywhere.com** button to propagate the changes and refresh our web application. Finally, our web application should now be up and running and publicly available via `<username>.pythonanywhere.com`.

Troubleshooting

Unfortunately, web servers can be quite sensitive to the tiniest problems in our web application. If you are experiencing problems with running the web application on PythonAnywhere and are receiving error messages in your browser, you can check the server and error logs, which can be accessed from the **Web** tab in your PythonAnywhere account, to better diagnose the problem.

Updating the movie classifier

While our predictive model is updated on the fly whenever a user provides feedback about the classification, the updates to the clf object will be reset if the web server crashes or restarts. If we reload the web application, the clf object will be reinitialized from the classifier.pkl pickle file. One option to apply the updates permanently would be to pickle the clf object once again after each update. However, this would become computationally very inefficient with a growing number of users, and could corrupt the pickle file if users provide feedback simultaneously.

An alternative solution is to update the predictive model from the feedback data that is being collected in the SQLite database. One option would be to download the SQLite database from the PythonAnywhere server, update the clf object locally on our computer, and upload the new pickle file to PythonAnywhere. To update the classifier locally on our computer, we create an update.py script file in the movieclassifier directory with the following contents:

```
import pickle
import sqlite3
import numpy as np
import os

# import HashingVectorizer from local dir
from vectorizer import vect

def update_model(db_path, model, batch_size=10000):

    conn = sqlite3.connect(db_path)
    c = conn.cursor()
    c.execute('SELECT * from review_db')

    results = c.fetchmany(batch_size)
```

```
    while results:
        data = np.array(results)
        X = data[:, 0]
        y = data[:, 1].astype(int)

        classes = np.array([0, 1])
        X_train = vect.transform(X)
        model.partial_fit(X_train, y, classes=classes)
        results = c.fetchmany(batch_size)

    conn.close()
    return model


cur_dir = os.path.dirname(__file__)

clf = pickle.load(open(os.path.join(cur_dir,
                  'pkl_objects',
                  'classifier.pkl'), 'rb'))
db = os.path.join(cur_dir, 'reviews.sqlite')

clf = update_model(db_path=db, model=clf, batch_size=10000)

# Uncomment the following lines if you are sure that
# you want to update your classifier.pkl file
# permanently.

# pickle.dump(clf, open(os.path.join(cur_dir,
#             'pkl_objects', 'classifier.pkl'), 'wb')
#             , protocol=4)
```

> A separate directory containing the movie review classifier application
> with the update functionality discussed in this chapter comes with the
> code examples for this book, which you can either obtain directly from
> Packt or download from GitHub at `https://github.com/rasbt/`
> `python-machine-learning-book-2nd-edition/`. The code in
> this section is located in the `.../code/ch09/movieclassifier_`
> `with_update` subdirectory.

The `update_model` function will fetch entries from the SQLite database in batches
of 10,000 entries at a time, unless the database contains fewer entries. Alternatively,
we could also fetch one entry at a time by using `fetchone` instead of `fetchmany`,
which would be computationally very inefficient. However, keep in mind that using
the alternative `fetchall` method could be a problem if we are working with large
datasets that exceed the computer or server's memory capacity.

Now that we have created the `update.py` script, we could also upload it to the `movieclassifier` directory on PythonAnywhere, and import the `update_model` function in the main application script `app.py` to update the classifier from the SQLite database every time we restart the web application. In order to do so, we just need to add a line of code to import the `update_model` function from the `update.py` script at the top of `app.py`:

```
# import update function from local dir
from update import update_model
```

We then need to call the `update_model` function in the main application body:

```
...
if __name__ == '__main__':
    clf = update_model(db_path=db,
                       model=clf,
                       batch_size=10000)
...
```

As discussed, the modification in the previous code snippet will update the pickle file on PythonAnywhere. However, in practice, we do not often have to restart our web application, and it would make sense to validate the user feedback in the SQLite database prior to the update to make sure the feedback is valuable information for the classifier.

Summary

In this chapter, you learned about many useful and practical topics that extend our knowledge of machine learning theory. You learned how to serialize a model after training and how to load it for later use cases. Furthermore, we created a SQLite database for efficient data storage and created a web application that lets us make our movie classifier available to the outside world.

Throughout this book, we have really discussed a lot about machine learning concepts, best practices, and supervised models for classification. In the next chapter, we will take a look at another subcategory of supervised learning, regression analysis, which lets us predict outcome variables on a continuous scale, in contrast to the categorical class labels of the classification models that we have been working with so far.

10

Predicting Continuous Target Variables with Regression Analysis

Throughout the previous chapters, you learned a lot about the main concepts behind **supervised learning** and trained many different models for classification tasks to predict group memberships or categorical variables. In this chapter, we will dive into another subcategory of supervised learning: **regression analysis**.

Regression models are used to predict target variables on a continuous scale, which makes them attractive for addressing many questions in science as well as applications in industry, such as understanding relationships between variables, evaluating trends, or making forecasts. One example would be predicting the sales of a company in future months.

In this chapter, we will discuss the main concepts of regression models and cover the following topics:

- Exploring and visualizing datasets
- Looking at different approaches to implement linear regression models
- Training regression models that are robust to outliers
- Evaluating regression models and diagnosing common problems
- Fitting regression models to nonlinear data

Introducing linear regression

The goal of linear regression is to model the relationship between one or multiple features and a continuous target variable. As discussed in *Chapter 1, Giving Computers the Ability to Learn from Data*, regression analysis is a subcategory of supervised machine learning. In contrast to classification—another subcategory of supervised learning—regression analysis aims to predict outputs on a continuous scale rather than categorical class labels.

In the following subsections, we will introduce the most basic type of linear regression, simple linear regression, and relate it to the more general, multivariate case (linear regression with multiple features).

Simple linear regression

The goal of simple (**univariate**) linear regression is to model the relationship between a single feature (**explanatory variable** x) and a continuous valued **response** (**target variable** y). The equation of a linear model with one explanatory variable is defined as follows:

$$y = w_0 + w_1 x$$

Here, the weight w_0 represents the y-axis intercept and w_1 is the weight coefficient of the explanatory variable. Our goal is to learn the weights of the linear equation to describe the relationship between the explanatory variable and the target variable, which can then be used to predict the responses of new explanatory variables that were not part of the training dataset.

Based on the linear equation that we defined previously, linear regression can be understood as finding the best-fitting straight line through the sample points, as shown in the following figure:

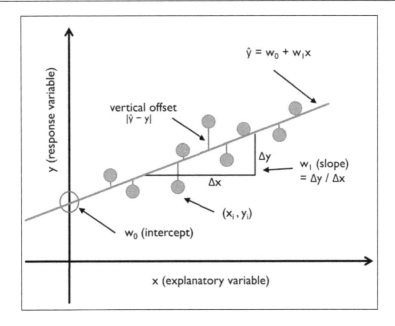

This best-fitting line is also called the **regression line**, and the vertical lines from the regression line to the sample points are the so-called **offsets** or **residuals**— the errors of our prediction.

Multiple linear regression

The special case of linear regression with one explanatory variable that we introduced in the previous subsection is also called **simple linear regression**. Of course, we can also generalize the linear regression model to multiple explanatory variables; this process is called **multiple linear regression**:

$$y = w_0 x_0 + w_1 x_1 + \ldots + w_m x_m = \sum_{i=0}^{m} w_i x_i = w^T x$$

Here, w_0 is the y-axis intercept with $x_0 = 1$.

The following figure shows how the two-dimensional, fitted hyperplane of a multiple linear regression model with two features could look:

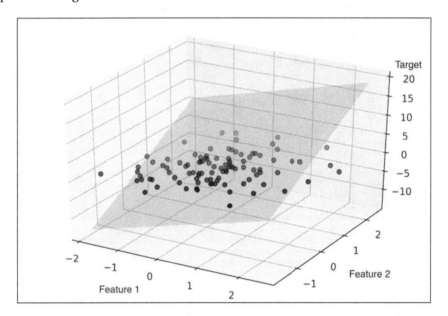

As we can see, visualizing multiple linear regression fits in three-dimensional scatter plot are already challenging to interpret when looking at static figures. Since we have no good means of visualizing hyperplanes with two dimensions in a scatterplot (multiple linear regression models fit to datasets with three or more features), the examples and visualizations in this chapter will mainly focus on the univariate case, using simple linear regression. However, simple and multiple linear regression are based on the same concepts and the same evaluation techniques; the code implementations that we will discuss in this chapter are also compatible with both types of regression model.

Exploring the Housing dataset

Before we implement our first linear regression model, we will introduce a new dataset, the Housing dataset, which contains information about houses in the suburbs of Boston collected by D. Harrison and D.L. Rubinfeld in 1978. The Housing dataset has been made freely available and is included in the code bundle of this book. The dataset has been recently removed from the UCI Machine Learning Repository but is available online at `https://raw.githubusercontent.com/rasbt/python-machine-learning-book-2nd-edition/master/code/ch10/housing.data.txt`. As with each new dataset, it is always helpful to explore the data through a simple visualization, to get a better feeling of what we are working with.

Loading the Housing dataset into a data frame

In this section, we will load the Housing dataset using the pandas `read_csv` function, which is fast and versatile—a recommended tool for working with tabular data stored in a plaintext format.

The features of the 506 samples in the Housing dataset are summarized here, taken from the original source that was previously shared on `https://archive.ics.uci.edu/ml/datasets/Housing`:

- `CRIM`: Per capita crime rate by town

- `ZN`: Proportion of residential land zoned for lots over 25,000 sq. ft.

- `INDUS`: Proportion of non-retail business acres per town

- `CHAS`: Charles River dummy variable (= 1 if tract bounds river; 0 otherwise)

- `NOX`: Nitric oxide concentration (parts per 10 million)

- `RM`: Average number of rooms per dwelling

- `AGE`: Proportion of owner-occupied units built prior to 1940

- `DIS`: Weighted distances to five Boston employment centers

- `RAD`: Index of accessibility to radial highways

- `TAX`: Full-value property tax rate per $10,000

- `PTRATIO`: Pupil-teacher ratio by town

- `B`: 1000(Bk - 0.63)^2, where *Bk* is the proportion of [people of African American descent] by town

- `LSTAT`: Percentage of lower status of the population

- `MEDV`: Median value of owner-occupied homes in $1000s

For the rest of this chapter, we will regard the house prices (`MEDV`) as our target variable—the variable that we want to predict using one or more of the 13 explanatory variables. Before we explore this dataset further, let us copy it from the UCI repository into a pandas DataFrame:

```
>>> import pandas as pd
>>> df = pd.read_csv('https://raw.githubusercontent.com/rasbt/'
...                  'python-machine-learning-book-2nd-edition'
...                  '/master/code/ch10/housing.data.txt',
...                  header=None,
...                  sep='\s+')
>>> df.columns = ['CRIM', 'ZN', 'INDUS', 'CHAS',
...               'NOX', 'RM', 'AGE', 'DIS', 'RAD',
...               'TAX', 'PTRATIO', 'B', 'LSTAT', 'MEDV']
>>> df.head()
```

To confirm that the dataset was loaded successfully, we displayed the first five lines of the dataset, as shown in the following figure:

	CRIM	ZN	INDUS	CHAS	NOX	RM	AGE	DIS	RAD	TAX	PTRATIO	B	LSTAT	MEDV
0	0.00632	18.0	2.31	0	0.538	6.575	65.2	4.0900	1	296.0	15.3	396.90	4.98	24.0
1	0.02731	0.0	7.07	0	0.469	6.421	78.9	4.9671	2	242.0	17.8	396.90	9.14	21.6
2	0.02729	0.0	7.07	0	0.469	7.185	61.1	4.9671	2	242.0	17.8	392.83	4.03	34.7
3	0.03237	0.0	2.18	0	0.458	6.998	45.8	6.0622	3	222.0	18.7	394.63	2.94	33.4
4	0.06905	0.0	2.18	0	0.458	7.147	54.2	6.0622	3	222.0	18.7	396.90	5.33	36.2

You can find a copy of the Housing dataset (and all other datasets used in this book) in the code bundle of this book, which you can use if you are working offline or the web link `https://raw.githubusercontent.com/rasbt/python-machine-learning-book-2nd-edition/master/code/ch10/housing.data.txt` is temporarily unavailable. For instance, to load the Housing dataset from a local directory, you can replace these lines:

```
df = pd.read_csv(
            'https://raw.githubusercontent.com/rasbt/'
            'python-machine-learning-book-2nd-edition'
            '/master/code/ch10/housing.data.txt',
            sep='\s+')
```

Replace them in the following code example with this:

```
df = pd.read_csv('./housing.data.txt'), sep='\s+')
```

Visualizing the important characteristics of a dataset

Exploratory Data Analysis (EDA) is an important and recommended first step prior to the training of a machine learning model. In the rest of this section, we will use some simple yet useful techniques from the graphical EDA toolbox that may help us to visually detect the presence of outliers, the distribution of the data, and the relationships between features.

First, we will create a **scatterplot matrix** that allows us to visualize the pair-wise correlations between the different features in this dataset in one place. To plot the scatterplot matrix, we will use the `pairplot` function from the Seaborn library (`http://stanford.edu/~mwaskom/software/seaborn/`), which is a Python library for drawing statistical plots based on Matplotlib.

You can install the `seaborn` package via `conda install seaborn` or `pip install seaborn`. After the installation is complete, you can import the package and create the scatterplot matrix as follows:

```
>>> import matplotlib.pyplot as plt
>>> import seaborn as sns
>>> cols = ['LSTAT', 'INDUS', 'NOX', 'RM', 'MEDV']
>>> sns.pairplot(df[cols], size=2.5)
>>> plt.tight_layout()
>>> plt.show()
```

As we can see in the following figure, the scatterplot matrix provides us with a useful graphical summary of the relationships in a dataset:

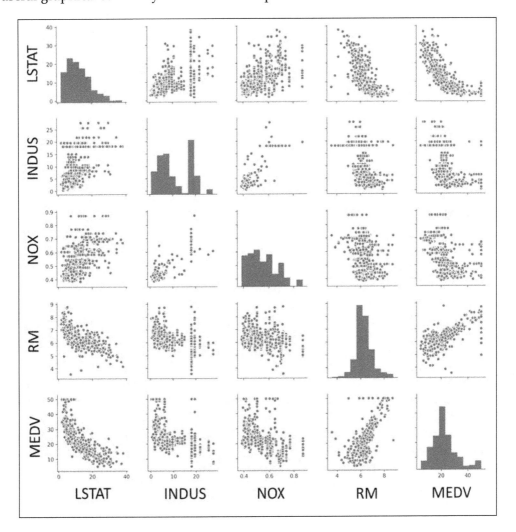

Due to space constraints and in the interest of readability, we only plotted five columns from the dataset: LSTAT, INDUS, NOX, RM, and MEDV. However, you are encouraged to create a scatterplot matrix of the whole DataFrame to explore the dataset further by choosing different column names in the previous sns.pairplot call, or include all variables in the scatterplot matrix by omitting the column selector (sns.pairplot(df)).

Using this scatterplot matrix, we can now quickly eyeball how the data is distributed and whether it contains outliers. For example, we can see that there is a linear relationship between RM and house prices, MEDV (the fifth column of the fourth row). Furthermore, we can see in the histogram — the lower-right subplot in the scatter plot matrix — that the MEDV variable seems to be normally distributed but contains several outliers.

Note that in contrast to common belief, training a linear regression model does not require that the explanatory or target variables are normally distributed. The normality assumption is only a requirement for certain statistics and hypothesis tests that are beyond the scope of this book (*Introduction to Linear Regression Analysis, Montgomery, Douglas C. Montgomery, Elizabeth A. Peck, and G. Geoffrey Vining, Wiley, 2012*, pages: 318-319).

Looking at relationships using a correlation matrix

In the previous section, we visualized the data distributions of the Housing dataset variables in the form of histograms and scatter plots. Next, we will create a correlation matrix to quantify and summarize linear relationships between variables. A correlation matrix is closely related to the covariance matrix that we have seen in the section about **Principal Component Analysis (PCA)** in *Chapter 5, Compressing Data via Dimensionality Reduction*. Intuitively, we can interpret the correlation matrix as a rescaled version of the covariance matrix. In fact, the correlation matrix is identical to a covariance matrix computed from standardized features.

The correlation matrix is a square matrix that contains the **Pearson product-moment correlation coefficient** (often abbreviated as **Pearson's r**), which measure the linear dependence between pairs of features. The correlation coefficients are in the range -1 to 1. Two features have a perfect positive correlation if $r = 1$, no correlation if $r = 0$, and a perfect negative correlation if $r = -1$. As mentioned previously, Pearson's correlation coefficient can simply be calculated as the covariance between two features x and y (numerator) divided by the product of their standard deviations (denominator):

$$r = \frac{\sum_{i=1}^{n}\left[\left(x^{(i)} - \mu_x\right)\left(y^{(i)} - \mu_y\right)\right]}{\sqrt{\sum_{i=1}^{n}\left(x^{(i)} - \mu_x\right)^2}\sqrt{\sum_{i=1}^{n}\left(y^{(i)} - \mu_y\right)^2}} = \frac{\sigma_{xy}}{\sigma_x \sigma_y}$$

Here, μ denotes the sample mean of the corresponding feature, σ_{xy} is the covariance between the features x and y, and σ_x and σ_y are the features' standard deviations.

We can show that the covariance between a pair of standardized features is in fact equal to their linear correlation coefficient. To show this, let us first standardize the features x and y to obtain their z-scores, which we will denote as x' and y', respectively:

$$x' = \frac{x - \mu_x}{\sigma_x}, y' = \frac{y - \mu_y}{\sigma_y}$$

Remember that we compute the (population) covariance between two features as follows:

$$\sigma_{xy} = \frac{1}{n}\sum_{i}^{n}\left(x^{(i)} - \mu_x\right)\left(y^{(i)} - \mu_y\right)$$

Since standardization centers a feature variable at mean zero, we can now calculate the covariance between the scaled features as follows:

$$\sigma'_{xy} = \frac{1}{n}\sum_{i}^{n}(x'-0)(y'-0)$$

Through resubstitution, we then get the following result:

$$\frac{1}{n}\sum_{i}^{n}\left(\frac{x - \mu_x}{\sigma_x}\right)\left(\frac{y - \mu_y}{\sigma_y}\right)$$

$$\frac{1}{n \cdot \sigma_x \sigma_y}\sum_{i}^{n}\left(x^{(i)} - \mu_x\right)\left(y^{(i)} - \mu_y\right)$$

Finally, we can simplify this equation as follows:

$$\sigma'_{xy} = \frac{\sigma_{xy}}{\sigma_x \sigma_y}$$

In the following code example, we will use NumPy's `corrcoef` function on the five feature columns that we previously visualized in the scatterplot matrix, and we will use Seaborn's `heatmap` function to plot the correlation matrix array as a heat map:

```
>>> import numpy as np
>>> cm = np.corrcoef(df[cols].values.T)
>>> sns.set(font_scale=1.5)
>>> hm = sns.heatmap(cm,
...              cbar=True,
...              annot=True,
...              square=True,
...              fmt='.2f',
...              annot_kws={'size': 15},
...              yticklabels=cols,
...              xticklabels=cols)
>>> plt.show()
```

As we can see in the resulting figure, the correlation matrix provides us with another useful summary graphic that can help us to select features based on their respective linear correlations:

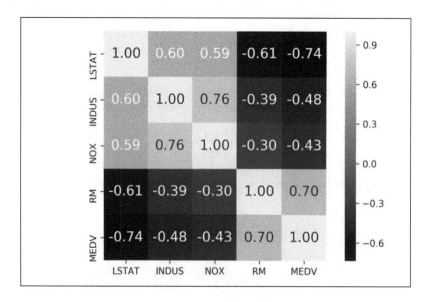

To fit a linear regression model, we are interested in those features that have a high correlation with our target variable MEDV. Looking at the previous correlation matrix, we see that our target variable MEDV shows the largest correlation with the LSTAT variable (-0.74); however, as you might remember from inspecting the scatterplot matrix, there is a clear nonlinear relationship between LSTAT and MEDV. On the other hand, the correlation between RM and MEDV is also relatively high (0.70). Given the linear relationship between these two variables that we observed in the scatterplot, RM seems to be a good choice for an exploratory variable to introduce the concepts of a simple linear regression model in the following section.

Implementing an ordinary least squares linear regression model

At the beginning of this chapter, we mentioned that linear regression can be understood as obtaining the best-fitting straight line through the sample points of our training data. However, we have neither defined the term **best-fitting** nor have we discussed the different techniques of fitting such a model. In the following subsections, we will fill in the missing pieces of this puzzle using the **Ordinary Least Squares (OLS)** method (sometimes also called **linear least squares**) to estimate the parameters of the linear regression line that minimizes the sum of the squared vertical distances (residuals or errors) to the sample points.

Solving regression for regression parameters with gradient descent

Consider our implementation of the **ADAptive LInear NEuron (Adaline)** from *Chapter 2, Training Simple Machine Learning Algorithms for Classification*; we remember that the artificial neuron uses a linear activation function. Also, we defined a cost function $J(\cdot)$, which we minimized to learn the weights via optimization algorithms, such as **Gradient Descent (GD)** and **Stochastic Gradient Descent (SGD)**. This cost function in Adaline is the **Sum of Squared Errors (SSE)**, which is identical to the cost function that we use for OLS:

$$J(w) = \frac{1}{2} \sum_{i=1}^{n} \left(y^{(i)} - \hat{y}^{(i)} \right)^2$$

Here, $\hat{y}$ is the predicted value $\hat{y} = w^T x$ (note that the term $\frac{1}{2}$ is just used for convenience to derive the update rule of GD). Essentially, OLS regression can be understood as Adaline without the unit step function so that we obtain continuous target values instead of the class labels -1 and 1. To demonstrate this, let us take the GD implementation of Adaline from *Chapter 2, Training Simple Machine Learning Algorithms for Classification* and remove the unit step function to implement our first linear regression model:

```python
class LinearRegressionGD(object):

    def __init__(self, eta=0.001, n_iter=20):
        self.eta = eta
        self.n_iter = n_iter

    def fit(self, X, y):
        self.w_ = np.zeros(1 + X.shape[1])
        self.cost_ = []

        for i in range(self.n_iter):
            output = self.net_input(X)
            errors = (y - output)
            self.w_[1:] += self.eta * X.T.dot(errors)
            self.w_[0] += self.eta * errors.sum()
            cost = (errors**2).sum() / 2.0
            self.cost_.append(cost)
        return self

    def net_input(self, X):
        return np.dot(X, self.w_[1:]) + self.w_[0]

    def predict(self, X):
        return self.net_input(X)
```

 If you need a refresher about how the weights are being updated — taking a step into the opposite direction of the gradient — please revisit the *Adaptive linear neurons and the convergence of learning* section in *Chapter 2, Training Simple Machine Learning Algorithms for Classification*.

To see our `LinearRegressionGD` regressor in action, let's use the `RM` (number of rooms) variable from the Housing dataset as the explanatory variable and train a model that can predict `MEDV` (house prices). Furthermore, we will standardize the variables for better convergence of the GD algorithm. The code is as follows:

```
>>> X = df[['RM']].values
>>> y = df['MEDV'].values
>>> from sklearn.preprocessing import StandardScaler
>>> sc_x = StandardScaler()
>>> sc_y = StandardScaler()
>>> X_std = sc_x.fit_transform(X)
>>> y_std = sc_y.fit_transform(y[:, np.newaxis]).flatten()
>>> lr = LinearRegressionGD()
>>> lr.fit(X_std, y_std)
```

Notice the workaround regarding `y_std`, using `np.newaxisx` and `flatten`. Most transformers in scikit-learn expect data to be stored in two-dimensional arrays. In the previous code example, the use of `np.newaxis` in `y[:, np.newaxis]` added a new dimension to the array. Then, after the `StandardScaler` returned the scaled variable, we converted it back to the original one-dimensional array representation using the `flatten()` method for our convenience.

We discussed in *Chapter 2, Training Simple Machine Learning Algorithms for Classification* that it is always a good idea to plot the cost as a function of the number of epochs passes over the training dataset when we are using optimization algorithms, such as gradient descent, to check the algorithm converged to a cost minimum (here, a *global* cost minimum):

```
>>> sns.reset_orig() # resets matplotlib style
>>> plt.plot(range(1, lr.n_iter+1), lr.cost_)
>>> plt.ylabel('SSE')
>>> plt.xlabel('Epoch')
>>> plt.show()
```

As we can see in the following plot, the GD algorithm converged after the fifth epoch:

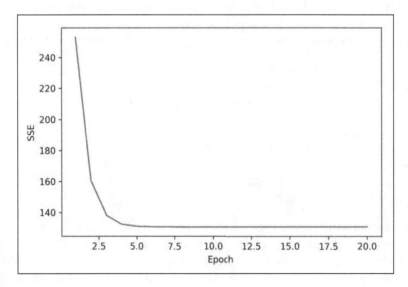

Next, let's visualize how well the linear regression line fits the training data. To do so, we will define a simple helper function that will plot a scatterplot of the training samples and add the regression line:

```
>>> def lin_regplot(X, y, model):
...     plt.scatter(X, y, c='steelblue', edgecolor='white', s=70)
...     plt.plot(X, model.predict(X), color='black', lw=2)
...     return None
```

Now, we will use this lin_regplot function to plot the number of rooms against house price:

```
>>> lin_regplot(X_std, y_std, lr)
>>> plt.xlabel('Average number of rooms [RM] (standardized)')
>>> plt.ylabel('Price in $1000s [MEDV] (standardized)')
>>> plt.show()
```

As we can see in the following plot, the linear regression line reflects the general trend that house prices tend to increase with the number of rooms:

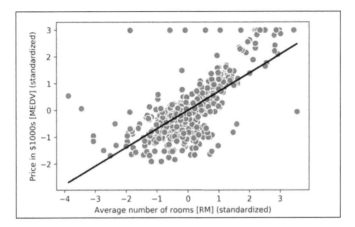

Although this observation makes intuitive sense, the data also tells us that the number of rooms does not explain the house prices very well in many cases. Later in this chapter, we will discuss how to quantify the performance of a regression model. Interestingly, we also observe that several data points lined up at $y = 3$, which suggests that the prices may have been clipped. In certain applications, it may also be important to report the predicted outcome variables on their original scale. To scale the predicted price outcome back onto the `Price in $1000s` axis, we can simply apply the `inverse_transform` method of the `StandardScaler`:

```
>>> num_rooms_std = sc_x.transform([5.0])
>>> price_std = lr.predict(num_rooms_std)
>>> print("Price in $1000s: %.3f" % \
...         sc_y.inverse_transform(price_std))
Price in $1000s: 10.840
```

In this code example, we used the previously trained linear regression model to predict the price of a house with five rooms. According to our model, such a house is worth $10,840.

On a side note, it is also worth mentioning that we technically don't have to update the weights of the intercept if we are working with standardized variables since the y-axis intercept is always 0 in those cases. We can quickly confirm this by printing the weights:

```
>>> print('Slope: %.3f' % lr.w_[1])
Slope: 0.695
>>> print('Intercept: %.3f' % lr.w_[0])
Intercept: -0.000
```

Estimating coefficient of a regression model via scikit-learn

In the previous section, we implemented a working model for regression analysis; however, in a real-world application we may be interested in more efficient implementations. For example many of scikit-learn's estimators for regression make use of the **LIBLINEAR** library, advanced optimization algorithms, and other code optimizations that work better with unstandardized variables, which is sometimes desirable for certain applications:

```
>>> from sklearn.linear_model import LinearRegression
>>> slr = LinearRegression()
>>> slr.fit(X, y)
>>> print('Slope: %.3f' % slr.coef_[0])
Slope: 9.102
>>> print('Intercept: %.3f' % slr.intercept_)
Intercept: -34.671
```

As we can see from executing this code, scikit-learn's LinearRegression model, fitted with the unstandardized RM and MEDV variables, yielded different model coefficients. Let's compare it to our GD implementation by plotting MEDV against RM:

```
>>> lin_regplot(X, y, slr)
>>> plt.xlabel('Average number of rooms [RM]')
>>> plt.ylabel('Price in $1000s [MEDV]')
>>> plt.show()
```

Now, when we plot the training data and our fitted model by executing this code, we can see that the overall result looks identical to our GD implementation:

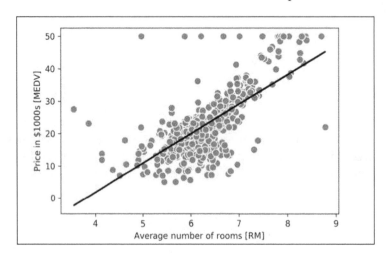

As an alternative to using machine learning libraries, there is also a closed-form solution for solving OLS involving a system of linear equations that can be found in most introductory statistics textbooks:

$$w = \left(X^T X\right)^{-1} X^T y$$

We can implement it in Python as follows:

```
# adding a column vector of "ones"
>>> Xb = np.hstack((np.ones((X.shape[0], 1)), X))
>>> w = np.zeros(X.shape[1])
>>> z = np.linalg.inv(np.dot(Xb.T, Xb))
>>> w = np.dot(z, np.dot(Xb.T, y))
>>> print('Slope: %.3f' % w[1])
Slope: 9.102
>>> print('Intercept: %.3f' % w[0])
Intercept: -34.671
```

The advantage of this method is that it is guaranteed to find the optimal solution analytically. However, if we are working with very large datasets, it can be computationally too expensive to invert the matrix in this formula (sometimes also called the **normal equation**) or the sample matrix may be singular (non-invertible), which is why we may prefer iterative methods in certain cases.

If you are interested in more information on how to obtain normal equations, I recommend you take a look at Dr. Stephen Pollock's chapter *The Classical Linear Regression Model* from his lectures at the University of Leicester, which is available for free at: http://www.le.ac.uk/users/dsgp1/COURSES/MESOMET/ECMETXT/06mesmet.pdf.

Fitting a robust regression model using RANSAC

Linear regression models can be heavily impacted by the presence of outliers. In certain situations, a very small subset of our data can have a big effect on the estimated model coefficients. There are many statistical tests that can be used to detect outliers, which are beyond the scope of the book. However, removing outliers always requires our own judgment as data scientists as well as our domain knowledge.

As an alternative to throwing out outliers, we will look at a robust method of regression using the **RANdom SAmple Consensus (RANSAC)** algorithm, which fits a regression model to a subset of the data, the so-called **inliers**.

We can summarize the iterative RANSAC algorithm as follows:

1. Select a random number of samples to be inliers and fit the model.
2. Test all other data points against the fitted model and add those points that fall within a user-given tolerance to the inliers.
3. Refit the model using all inliers.
4. Estimate the error of the fitted model versus the inliers.
5. Terminate the algorithm if the performance meets a certain user-defined threshold or if a fixed number of iterations were reached; go back to step 1 otherwise.

Let us now wrap our linear model in the RANSAC algorithm using scikit-learn's `RANSACRegressor` class:

```
>>> from sklearn.linear_model import RANSACRegressor
>>> ransac = RANSACRegressor(LinearRegression(),
...                          max_trials=100,
...                          min_samples=50,
...                          loss='absolute_loss',
...                          residual_threshold=5.0,
...                          random_state=0)
>>> ransac.fit(X, y)
```

We set the maximum number of iterations of the `RANSACRegressor` to 100, and using `min_samples=50`, we set the minimum number of the randomly chosen samples to be at least 50. Using the `'absolute_loss'` as an argument for the `residual_metric` parameter, the algorithm computes absolute vertical distances between the fitted line and the sample points. By setting the `residual_threshold` parameter to `5.0`, we only allowed samples to be included in the inlier set if their vertical distance to the fitted line is within 5 distance units, which works well on this particular dataset.

By default, scikit-learn uses the **MAD** estimate to select the inlier threshold, where MAD stands for the **Median Absolute Deviation** of the target values y. However, the choice of an appropriate value for the inlier threshold is problem-specific, which is one disadvantage of RANSAC. Many different approaches have been developed in recent years to select a good inlier threshold automatically. You can find a detailed discussion in: *Automatic Estimation of the Inlier Threshold in Robust Multiple Structures Fitting, R. Toldo, A. Fusiello's, Springer, 2009* (in Image Analysis and Processing–ICIAP 2009, pages: 123-131).

After we fit the RANSAC model, let's obtain the inliers and outliers from the fitted RANSAC-linear regression model and plot them together with the linear fit:

```
>>> inlier_mask = ransac.inlier_mask_
>>> outlier_mask = np.logical_not(inlier_mask)
>>> line_X = np.arange(3, 10, 1)
>>> line_y_ransac = ransac.predict(line_X[:, np.newaxis])
>>> plt.scatter(X[inlier_mask], y[inlier_mask],
...             c='steelblue', edgecolor='white',
...             marker='o', label='Inliers')
>>> plt.scatter(X[outlier_mask], y[outlier_mask],
...             c='limegreen', edgecolor='white',
...             marker='s', label='Outliers')
>>> plt.plot(line_X, line_y_ransac, color='black', lw=2)
>>> plt.xlabel('Average number of rooms [RM]')
>>> plt.ylabel('Price in $1000s [MEDV]')
>>> plt.legend(loc='upper left')
>>> plt.show()
```

As we can see in the following scatterplot, the linear regression model was fitted on the detected set of inliers, shown as circles:

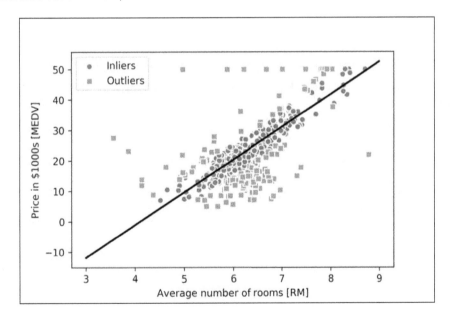

When we print the slope and intercept of the model by executing the following code, we can see that the linear regression line is slightly different from the fit that we obtained in the previous section without using RANSAC:

```
>>> print('Slope: %.3f' % ransac.estimator_.coef_[0])
Slope: 10.735
>>> print('Intercept: %.3f' % ransac.estimator_.intercept_)
Intercept: -44.089
```

Using RANSAC, we reduced the potential effect of the outliers in this dataset, but we don't know if this approach has a positive effect on the predictive performance for unseen data. Thus, in the next section we will look at different approaches to evaluating a regression model, which is a crucial part of building systems for predictive modeling.

Evaluating the performance of linear regression models

In the previous section, we learned how to fit a regression model on training data. However, you learned in previous chapters that it is crucial to test the model on data that it hasn't seen during training to obtain a more unbiased estimate of its performance.

As we remember from *Chapter 6*, *Learning Best Practices for Model Evaluation and Hyperparameter Tuning*, we want to split our dataset into separate training and test datasets where we use the former to fit the model and the latter to evaluate its performance to generalize to unseen data. Instead of proceeding with the simple regression model, we will now use all variables in the dataset and train a multiple regression model:

```
>>> from sklearn.model_selection import train_test_split
>>> X = df.iloc[:, :-1].values
>>> y = df['MEDV'].values
>>> X_train, X_test, y_train, y_test = train_test_split(
...         X, y, test_size=0.3, random_state=0)
>>> slr = LinearRegression()
>>> slr.fit(X_train, y_train)
>>> y_train_pred = slr.predict(X_train)
>>> y_test_pred = slr.predict(X_test)
```

Since our model uses multiple explanatory variables, we can't visualize the linear regression line (or hyperplane to be precise) in a two-dimensional plot, but we can plot the residuals (the differences or vertical distances between the actual and predicted values) versus the predicted values to diagnose our regression model. **Residual plots** are a commonly used graphical tool for diagnosing regression models. They can help detect nonlinearity and outliers, and check whether the errors are randomly distributed.

Using the following code, we will now plot a residual plot where we simply subtract the true target variables from our predicted responses:

```
>>> plt.scatter(y_train_pred,  y_train_pred - y_train,
...             c='steelblue', marker='o', edgecolor='white',
...             label='Training data')
>>> plt.scatter(y_test_pred,  y_test_pred - y_test,
...             c='limegreen', marker='s', edgecolor='white',
...             label='Test data')
>>> plt.xlabel('Predicted values')
>>> plt.ylabel('Residuals')
>>> plt.legend(loc='upper left')
>>> plt.hlines(y=0, xmin=-10, xmax=50, color='black', lw=2)
>>> plt.xlim([-10, 50])
>>> plt.show()
```

After executing the code, we should see a residual plot with a line passing through the *x*-axis origin as shown here:

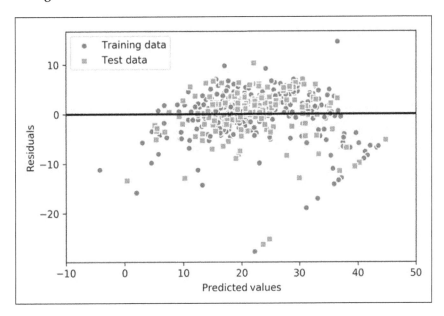

In case of a perfect prediction, the residuals would be exactly zero, which we will probably never encounter in realistic and practical applications. However, for a good regression model, we would expect that the errors are randomly distributed and the residuals should be randomly scattered around the centerline. If we see patterns in a residual plot, it means that our model is unable to capture some explanatory information, which has leaked into the residuals, as we can slightly see in our previous residual plot. Furthermore, we can also use residual plots to detect outliers, which are represented by the points with a large deviation from the centerline.

Another useful quantitative measure of a model's performance is the so-called **Mean Squared Error (MSE)**, which is simply the averaged value of the SSE cost that we minimized to fit the linear regression model. The MSE is useful to compare different regression models or for tuning their parameters via grid search and cross-validation, as it normalizes the SSE by the sample size:

$$MSE = \frac{1}{n} \sum_{i=1}^{n} \left(y^{(i)} - \hat{y}^{(i)} \right)^2$$

Let's compute the MSE of our training and test predictions:

```
>>> from sklearn.metrics import mean_squared_error
>>> print('MSE train: %.3f, test: %.3f' % (
...          mean_squared_error(y_train, y_train_pred),
...          mean_squared_error(y_test, y_test_pred)))
MSE train: 19.958, test: 27.196
```

We see that the MSE on the training set is 19.96, and the MSE of the test set is much larger, with a value of 27.20, which is an indicator that our model is overfitting the training data.

Sometimes it may be more useful to report the **coefficient of determination** (R^2), which can be understood as a standardized version of the MSE, for better interpretability of the model's performance. Or in other words, R^2 is the fraction of response variance that is captured by the model. The R^2 value is defined as:

$$R^2 = 1 - \frac{SSE}{SST}$$

Here, SSE is the sum of squared errors and SST is the total sum of squares:

$$SST = \sum_{i=1}^{n} \left(y^{(i)} - \mu_y \right)^2$$

In other words, SST is simply the variance of the response.

Let us quickly show that R^2 is indeed just a rescaled version of the MSE:

$$R^2 = 1 - \frac{SSE}{SST}$$

$$1 - \frac{\frac{1}{n} \sum_{i=1}^{n} \left(y^{(i)} - \hat{y}^{(i)} \right)^2}{\frac{1}{n} \sum_{i=1}^{n} \left(y^{(i)} - \mu_y \right)^2}$$

$$1 - \frac{MSE}{Var(y)}$$

For the training dataset, the R^2 is bounded between 0 and 1, but it can become negative for the test set. If $R^2 = 1$, the model fits the data perfectly with a corresponding $MSE = 0$.

Evaluated on the training data, the R^2 of our model is 0.765, which doesn't sound too bad. However, the R^2 on the test dataset is only 0.673, which we can compute by executing the following code:

```
>>> from sklearn.metrics import r2_score
>>> print('R^2 train: %.3f, test: %.3f' %
...         (r2_score(y_train, y_train_pred),
...          r2_score(y_test, y_test_pred)))
R^2 train: 0.765, test: 0.673
```

Using regularized methods for regression

As we discussed in *Chapter 3, A Tour of Machine Learning Classifiers Using scikit-learn*, regularization is one approach to tackle the problem of overfitting by adding additional information, and thereby shrinking the parameter values of the model to induce a penalty against complexity. The most popular approaches to regularized linear regression are the so-called **Ridge Regression, Least Absolute Shrinkage and Selection Operator (LASSO)**, and **Elastic Net**.

Ridge regression is an L2 penalized model where we simply add the squared sum of the weights to our least-squares cost function:

$$J(w)_{Ridge} = \sum_{i=1}^{n}\left(y^{(i)} - \hat{y}^{(i)}\right)^2 + \lambda \| w \|_2^2$$

Here:

$$L2: \quad \lambda \| w \|_2^2 = \lambda \sum_{j=1}^{m} w_j^2$$

By increasing the value of hyperparameter λ, we increase the regularization strength and shrink the weights of our model. Please note that we don't regularize the intercept term w_0.

An alternative approach that can lead to sparse models is LASSO. Depending on the regularization strength, certain weights can become zero, which also makes LASSO useful as a supervised feature selection technique:

$$J(w)_{LASSO} = \sum_{i=1}^{n}\left(y^{(i)} - \hat{y}^{(i)}\right)^2 + \lambda \| w \|_1$$

Here:

$$L1: \lambda \| w \|_1 = \lambda \sum_{j=1}^{m} \left| w_j \right|$$

However, a limitation of LASSO is that it selects at most n variables if $m>n$. A compromise between Ridge regression and LASSO is Elastic Net, which has an L1 penalty to generate sparsity and an L2 penalty to overcome some of the limitations of LASSO, such as the number of selected variables:

$$ J\left(w\right)_{ElasticNet} = \sum_{i=1}^{n}\left(y^{(i)} - \hat{y}^{(i)}\right)^{2} + \lambda_{1}\sum_{j=1}^{m}w_{j}^{2} + \lambda_{2}\sum_{j=1}^{m}\left|w_{j}\right| $$

Those regularized regression models are all available via scikit-learn, and the usage is similar to the regular regression model except that we have to specify the regularization strength via the parameter λ, for example, optimized via k-fold cross-validation.

A Ridge regression model can be initialized via:

```
>>> from sklearn.linear_model import Ridge
>>> ridge = Ridge(alpha=1.0)
```

Note that the regularization strength is regulated by the parameter `alpha`, which is similar to the parameter λ. Likewise, we can initialize a LASSO regressor from the `linear_model` submodule:

```
>>> from sklearn.linear_model import Lasso
>>> lasso = Lasso(alpha=1.0)
```

Lastly, the `ElasticNet` implementation allows us to vary the L1 to L2 ratio:

```
>>> from sklearn.linear_model import ElasticNet
>>> elanet = ElasticNet(alpha=1.0, l1_ratio=0.5)
```

For example, if we set the `l1_ratio` to 1.0, the `ElasticNet` regressor would be equal to LASSO regression. For more detailed information about the different implementations of linear regression, please see the documentation at `http://scikit-learn.org/stable/modules/linear_model.html`.

Turning a linear regression model into a curve – polynomial regression

In the previous sections, we assumed a linear relationship between explanatory and response variables. One way to account for the violation of linearity assumption is to use a polynomial regression model by adding polynomial terms:

$$y = w_0 + w_1 x + w_2 x^2 + \ldots + w_d x^d$$

Here, d denotes the degree of the polynomial. Although we can use polynomial regression to model a nonlinear relationship, it is still considered a multiple linear regression model because of the linear regression coefficients w. In the following subsections, we will see how we can add such polynomial terms to an existing dataset conveniently and fit a polynomial regression model.

Adding polynomial terms using scikit-learn

We will now learn how to use the `PolynomialFeatures` transformer class from scikit-learn to add a quadratic term ($d = 2$) to a simple regression problem with one explanatory variable. Then, we compare the polynomial to the linear fit following these steps:

1. Add a second degree polynomial term:

    ```
    from sklearn.preprocessing import PolynomialFeatures
    >>> X = np.array([ 258.0, 270.0, 294.0, 320.0, 342.0,
    ...                368.0, 396.0, 446.0, 480.0, 586.0])\
    ...               [:, np.newaxis]
    >>> y = np.array([ 236.4, 234.4, 252.8, 298.6, 314.2,
    ...                342.2, 360.8, 368.0, 391.2, 390.8])
    >>> lr = LinearRegression()
    >>> pr = LinearRegression()
    >>> quadratic = PolynomialFeatures(degree=2)
    >>> X_quad = quadratic.fit_transform(X)
    ```

2. Fit a simple linear regression model for comparison:

    ```
    >>> lr.fit(X, y)
    >>> X_fit = np.arange(250,600,10)[:, np.newaxis]
    >>> y_lin_fit = lr.predict(X_fit)
    ```

3. Fit a multiple regression model on the transformed features for polynomial regression:

```
>>> pr.fit(X_quad, y)
>>> y_quad_fit = pr.predict(quadratic.fit_transform(X_fit))
```

4. Plot the results:

```
>>> plt.scatter(X, y, label='training points')
>>> plt.plot(X_fit, y_lin_fit,
...          label='linear fit', linestyle='--')
>>> plt.plot(X_fit, y_quad_fit,
...          label='quadratic fit')
>>> plt.legend(loc='upper left')
>>> plt.show()
```

In the resulting plot, we can see that the polynomial fit captures the relationship between the response and explanatory variable much better than the linear fit:

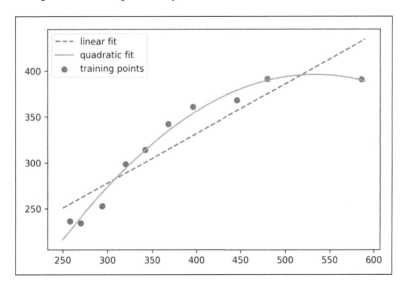

```
>>> y_lin_pred = lr.predict(X)
>>> y_quad_pred = pr.predict(X_quad)
>>> print('Training MSE linear: %.3f, quadratic: %.3f' % (
...       mean_squared_error(y, y_lin_pred),
...       mean_squared_error(y, y_quad_pred)))
Training MSE linear: 569.780, quadratic: 61.330
>>> print('Training  R^2 linear: %.3f, quadratic: %.3f' % (
...       r2_score(y, y_lin_pred),
...       r2_score(y, y_quad_pred)))
Training  R^2 linear: 0.832, quadratic: 0.982
```

As we can see after executing the code, the MSE decreased from 570 (linear fit) to 61 (quadratic fit); also, the coefficient of determination reflects a closer fit of the quadratic model ($R^2 = 0.982$) as opposed to the linear fit ($R^2 = 0.832$) in this particular toy problem.

Modeling nonlinear relationships in the Housing dataset

After we learned how to construct polynomial features to fit nonlinear relationships in a toy problem, let's now take a look at a more concrete example and apply those concepts to the data in the Housing dataset. By executing the following code, we will model the relationship between house prices and LSTAT (percent lower status of the population) as using second degree (quadratic) and third degree (cubic) polynomials and compare it to a linear fit:

```
>>> X = df[['LSTAT']].values
>>> y = df['MEDV'].values

>>> regr = LinearRegression()

# create quadratic features
>>> quadratic = PolynomialFeatures(degree=2)
>>> cubic = PolynomialFeatures(degree=3)
>>> X_quad = quadratic.fit_transform(X)
>>> X_cubic = cubic.fit_transform(X)

# fit features
>>> X_fit = np.arange(X.min(), X.max(), 1)[:, np.newaxis]

>>> regr = regr.fit(X, y)
>>> y_lin_fit = regr.predict(X_fit)
>>> linear_r2 = r2_score(y, regr.predict(X))

>>> regr = regr.fit(X_quad, y)
>>> y_quad_fit = regr.predict(quadratic.fit_transform(X_fit))
>>> quadratic_r2 = r2_score(y, regr.predict(X_quad))

>>> regr = regr.fit(X_cubic, y)
>>> y_cubic_fit = regr.predict(cubic.fit_transform(X_fit))
>>> cubic_r2 = r2_score(y, regr.predict(X_cubic))


# plot results
```

```
>>> plt.scatter(X, y, label='training points', color='lightgray')

>>> plt.plot(X_fit, y_lin_fit,
...          label='linear (d=1), $R^2=%.2f$' % linear_r2,
...          color='blue',
...          lw=2,
...          linestyle=':')

>>> plt.plot(X_fit, y_quad_fit,
...          label='quadratic (d=2), $R^2=%.2f$' % quadratic_r2,
...          color='red',
...          lw=2,
...          linestyle='-')

>>> plt.plot(X_fit, y_cubic_fit,
...          label='cubic (d=3), $R^2=%.2f$' % cubic_r2,
...          color='green',
...          lw=2,
...          linestyle='--')

>>> plt.xlabel('% lower status of the population [LSTAT]')
>>> plt.ylabel('Price in $1000s [MEDV]')
>>> plt.legend(loc='upper right')
>>> plt.show()
```

The resulting plot is as follows:

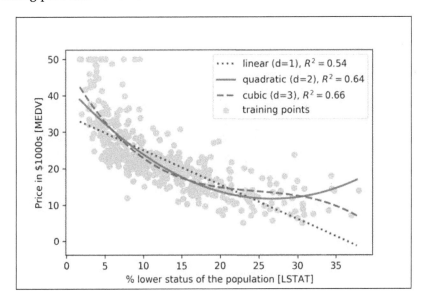

As we can see, the cubic fit captures the relationship between house prices and LSTAT better than the linear and quadratic fit. However, we should be aware that adding more and more polynomial features increases the complexity of a model and therefore increases the chance of overfitting. Thus, in practice it is always recommended to evaluate the performance of the model on a separate test dataset to estimate the generalization performance.

In addition, polynomial features are not always the best choice for modeling nonlinear relationships. For example, with some experience or intuition, just looking at the MEDV-LSTAT scatterplot may lead to the hypothesis that a log-transformation of the LSTAT feature variable and the square root of MEDV may project the data onto a linear feature space suitable for a linear regression fit. For instance, my perception is that this relationship between the two variables looks quite similar to an exponential function:

$$f(x) = 2^{-x}$$

Since the natural logarithm of an exponential function is a straight line, I assume that such a log-transformation can be usefully applied here:

$$\log(f(x)) = -x$$

Let's test this hypothesis by executing the following code:

```
# transform features
>>> X_log = np.log(X)
>>> y_sqrt = np.sqrt(y)


# fit features
>>> X_fit = np.arange(X_log.min()-1,
...                    X_log.max()+1, 1)[:, np.newaxis]
>>> regr = regr.fit(X_log, y_sqrt)
>>> y_lin_fit = regr.predict(X_fit)
>>> linear_r2 = r2_score(y_sqrt, regr.predict(X_log))


# plot results
>>> plt.scatter(X_log, y_sqrt,
...             label='training points',
...             color='lightgray')
>>> plt.plot(X_fit, y_lin_fit,
...          label='linear (d=1), $R^2=%.2f$' % linear_r2,
...          color='blue',
```

```
...             lw=2)
>>> plt.xlabel('log(% lower status of the population [LSTAT])')
>>> plt.ylabel('$\sqrt{Price \; in \; \$1000s \; [MEDV]}$')
>>> plt.legend(loc='lower left')
>>> plt.show()
```

After transforming the explanatory onto the log space and taking the square root of the target variables, we were able to capture the relationship between the two variables with a linear regression line that seems to fit the data better ($R^2 = 0.69$) than any of the polynomial feature transformations previously:

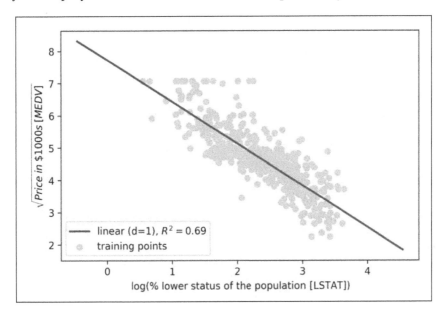

Dealing with nonlinear relationships using random forests

In this section, we are going to take a look at **random forest** regression, which is conceptually different from the previous regression models in this chapter. A random forest, which is an ensemble of multiple **decision trees**, can be understood as the sum of piecewise linear functions in contrast to the global linear and polynomial regression models that we discussed previously. In other words, via the decision tree algorithm, we are subdividing the input space into smaller regions that become more *manageable*.

Decision tree regression

An advantage of the decision tree algorithm is that it does not require any transformation of the features if we are dealing with nonlinear data. We remember from *Chapter 3, A Tour of Machine Learning Classifiers Using scikit-learn*, that we grow a decision tree by iteratively splitting its nodes until the leaves are pure or a stopping criterion is satisfied. When we used decision trees for classification, we defined entropy as a measure of impurity to determine which feature split maximizes the **Information Gain** (**IG**), which can be defined as follows for a binary split:

$$IG\left(D_p,x_i\right) = I\left(D_p\right) - \frac{N_{left}}{N_p}I\left(D_{left}\right) - \frac{N_{right}}{N_p}I\left(D_{right}\right)$$

Here, x_i is the feature to perform the split, N_p is the number of samples in the parent node, I is the impurity function, D_p is the subset of training samples at the parent node, and D_{left} and D_{right} are the subsets of training samples at the left and right child node after the split. Remember that our goal is to find the feature split that maximizes the information gain; or in other words, we want to find the feature split that reduces the impurities in the child nodes most. In *Chapter 3, A Tour of Machine Learning Classifiers Using scikit-learn* we discussed Gini impurity and entropy as measures of impurity, which are both useful criteria for classification. To use a decision tree for regression, however, we need an impurity metric that is suitable for continuous variables, so we define the impurity measure of a node t as the MSE instead:

$$I\left(t\right) = MSE\left(t\right) = \frac{1}{N_t}\sum_{i\in D_t}\left(y^{(i)} - \hat{y}_t\right)^2$$

Here, N_t is the number of training samples at node t, D_t is the training subset at node t, $y^{(i)}$ is the true target value, and $\hat{y}_t$ is the predicted target value (sample mean):

$$\hat{y}_t = \frac{1}{N_t}\sum_{i\in D_t}y^{(i)}$$

In the context of decision tree regression, the MSE is often also referred to as **within-node variance**, which is why the splitting criterion is also better known as **variance reduction**. To see what the line fit of a decision tree looks like, let us use the `DecisionTreeRegressor` implemented in scikit-learn to model the nonlinear relationship between the `MEDV` and `LSTAT` variables:

```
>>> from sklearn.tree import DecisionTreeRegressor
>>> X = df[['LSTAT']].values
>>> y = df['MEDV'].values
>>> tree = DecisionTreeRegressor(max_depth=3)
>>> tree.fit(X, y)
>>> sort_idx = X.flatten().argsort()
>>> lin_regplot(X[sort_idx], y[sort_idx], tree)
>>> plt.xlabel('% lower status of the population [LSTAT]')
>>> plt.ylabel('Price in $1000s [MEDV]')
>>> plt.show()
```

As we can see in the resulting plot, the decision tree captures the general trend in the data. However, a limitation of this model is that it does not capture the continuity and differentiability of the desired prediction. In addition, we need to be careful about choosing an appropriate value for the depth of the tree to not overfit or underfit the data; here, a depth of three seemed to be a good choice:

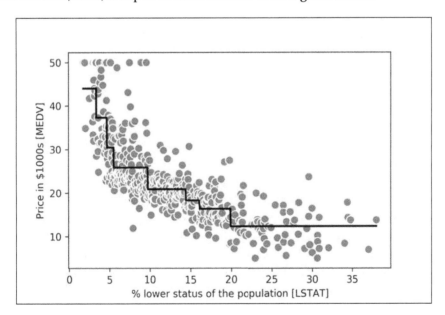

In the next section, we will take a look at a more robust way of fitting regression trees: random forests.

Random forest regression

As we learned in *Chapter 3, A Tour of Machine Learning Classifiers Using scikit-learn*, the random forest algorithm is an ensemble technique that combines multiple decision trees. A random forest usually has a better generalization performance than an individual decision tree due to randomness, which helps to decrease the model's variance. Other advantages of random forests are that they are less sensitive to outliers in the dataset and don't require much parameter tuning. The only parameter in random forests that we typically need to experiment with is the number of trees in the ensemble. The basic random forest algorithm for regression is almost identical to the random forest algorithm for classification that we discussed in *Chapter 3, A Tour of Machine Learning Classifiers Using scikit-learn*, the only difference is that we use the MSE criterion to grow the individual decision trees, and the predicted target variable is calculated as the average prediction over all decision trees.

Now, let's use all features in the Housing dataset to fit a random forest regression model on 60 percent of the samples and evaluate its performance on the remaining 40 percent. The code is as follows:

```
>>> X = df.iloc[:, :-1].values
>>> y = df['MEDV'].values
>>> X_train, X_test, y_train, y_test =\
...        train_test_split(X, y,
...                         test_size=0.4,
...                         random_state=1)

>>> from sklearn.ensemble import RandomForestRegressor
>>> forest = RandomForestRegressor(n_estimators=1000,
...                                criterion='mse',
...                                random_state=1,
...                                n_jobs=-1)
>>> forest.fit(X_train, y_train)
>>> y_train_pred = forest.predict(X_train)
>>> y_test_pred = forest.predict(X_test)
>>> print('MSE train: %.3f, test: %.3f' % (
...        mean_squared_error(y_train, y_train_pred),
...        mean_squared_error(y_test, y_test_pred)))
MSE train: 1.642, test: 11.052
>>> print('R^2 train: %.3f, test: %.3f' % (
...        r2_score(y_train, y_train_pred),
...        r2_score(y_test, y_test_pred)))
R^2 train: 0.979, test: 0.878
```

Unfortunately, we see that the random forest tends to overfit the training data. However, it's still able to explain the relationship between the target and explanatory variables relatively well ($R^2 = 0.871$ on the test dataset).

Lastly, let us also take a look at the residuals of the prediction:

```
>>> plt.scatter(y_train_pred,
...             y_train_pred - y_train,
...             c='steelblue',
...             edgecolor='white',
...             marker='o',
...             s=35,
...             alpha=0.9,
...             label='Training data')
>>> plt.scatter(y_test_pred,
...             y_test_pred - y_test,
...             c='limegreen',
...             edgecolor='white',
...             marker='s',
...             s=35,
...             alpha=0.9,
...             label='Test data')
>>> plt.xlabel('Predicted values')
>>> plt.ylabel('Residuals')
>>> plt.legend(loc='upper left')
>>> plt.hlines(y=0, xmin=-10, xmax=50, lw=2, color='black')
>>> plt.xlim([-10, 50])
>>> plt.show()
```

As it was already summarized by the R^2 coefficient, we can see that the model fits the training data better than the test data, as indicated by the outliers in the *y*-axis direction. Also, the distribution of the residuals does not seem to be completely random around the zero center point, indicating that the model is not able to capture all the exploratory information.

However, the residual plot indicates a large improvement over the residual plot of the linear model that we plotted earlier in this chapter:

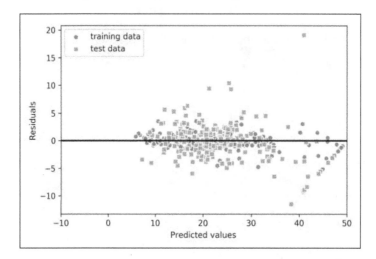

Ideally, our model error should be random or unpredictable. In other words, the error of the predictions should not be related to any of the information contained in the explanatory variables, but should reflect the randomness of the real-world distributions or patterns. If we observe patterns in the prediction errors, for example, by inspecting the residual plot, it means that the residual plots contain predictive information. A common reason for this could be that explanatory information is leaking into those residuals.

Unfortunately, there is not a universal approach for dealing with non-randomness in residual plots, and it requires experimentation. Depending on the data that is available to us, we may be able to improve the model by transforming variables, tuning the hyperparameters of the learning algorithm, choosing simpler or more complex models, removing outliers, or including additional variables.

In *Chapter 3, A Tour of Machine Learning Classifiers Using scikit-learn*, we also learned about the kernel trick, which can be used in combination with a **Support Vector Machine (SVM)** for classification, and is useful if we are dealing with nonlinear problems. Although a discussion is beyond the scope of this book, SVMs can also be used in nonlinear regression tasks. The interested reader can find more information about SVMs for regression in an excellent report: *Support Vector Machines for Classification and Regression, S. R. Gunn and others,* ISIS technical report, 14, 1998. An SVM regressor is also implemented in scikit-learn, and more information about its usage can be found at http://scikit-learn.org/stable/modules/generated/sklearn.svm.SVR.html#sklearn.svm.SVR.

Summary

At the beginning of this chapter, you learned about simple linear regression analysis to model the relationship between a single explanatory variable and a continuous response variable. We then discussed a useful explanatory data analysis technique to look at patterns and anomalies in data, which is an important first step in predictive modeling tasks.

We built our first model by implementing linear regression using a gradient-based optimization approach. We then saw how to utilize scikit-learn's linear models for regression and also implement a robust regression technique (RANSAC) as an approach for dealing with outliers. To assess the predictive performance of regression models, we computed the mean sum of squared errors and the related R^2 metric. Furthermore, we also discussed a useful graphical approach to diagnose problems of regression models: the residual plot.

After we discussed how regularization can be applied to regression models to reduce the model complexity and avoid overfitting, we also introduced several approaches to model nonlinear relationships including polynomial feature transformation and random forest regressors.

We have discussed supervised learning, classification, and regression analysis in great detail throughout the previous chapters. In the next chapter, we are going to learn about another interesting subfield of machine learning, unsupervised learning and also we will learn how to use cluster analysis for finding hidden structures in data in the absence of target variables.

11
Working with Unlabeled Data – Clustering Analysis

In the previous chapters, we used supervised learning techniques to build machine learning models using data where the answer was already known—the class labels were already available in our training data. In this chapter, we will switch gears and explore cluster analysis, a category of **unsupervised learning** techniques that allows us to discover hidden structures in data where we do not know the right answer upfront. The goal of clustering is to find a natural grouping in data so that items in the same cluster are more similar to each other than to those from different clusters.

Given its exploratory nature, clustering is an exciting topic and, in this chapter, we will learn about the following concepts, which can help us to organize data into meaningful structures:

- Finding centers of similarity using the popular k-means algorithm
- Taking a bottom-up approach to building hierarchical clustering trees
- Identifying arbitrary shapes of objects using a density-based clustering approach

Grouping objects by similarity using k-means

In this section, we will learn about one of the most popular **clustering** algorithms, **k-means**, which is widely used in academia as well as in industry. Clustering (or cluster analysis) is a technique that allows us to find groups of similar objects, objects that are more related to each other than to objects in other groups. Examples of business-oriented applications of clustering include the grouping of documents, music, and movies by different topics, or finding customers that share similar interests based on common purchase behaviors as a basis for recommendation engines.

K-means clustering using scikit-learn

As we will see in a moment, the k-means algorithm is extremely easy to implement but is also computationally very efficient compared to other clustering algorithms, which might explain its popularity. The k-means algorithm belongs to the category of **prototype-based clustering**. We will discuss two other categories of clustering, **hierarchical** and **density-based clustering**, later in this chapter.

Prototype-based clustering means that each cluster is represented by a prototype, which can either be the **centroid** (*average*) of similar points with continuous features, or the **medoid** (the most *representative* or most frequently occurring point) in the case of categorical features. While k-means is very good at identifying clusters with a spherical shape, one of the drawbacks of this clustering algorithm is that we have to specify the number of clusters, *k*, *a priori*. An inappropriate choice for *k* can result in poor clustering performance. Later in this chapter, we will discuss the **elbow** method and **silhouette plots**, which are useful techniques to evaluate the quality of a clustering to help us determine the optimal number of clusters *k*.

Although k-means clustering can be applied to data in higher dimensions, we will walk through the following examples using a simple two-dimensional dataset for the purpose of visualization:

```
>>> from sklearn.datasets import make_blobs
>>> X, y = make_blobs(n_samples=150,
...                    n_features=2,
...                    centers=3,
...                    cluster_std=0.5,
...                    shuffle=True,
...                    random_state=0)

>>> import matplotlib.pyplot as plt
>>> plt.scatter(X[:,0],
```

```
...                       X[:,1],
...                       c='white',
...                       marker='o',
...                       edgecolor='black',
...                       s=50)
>>> plt.grid()
>>> plt.show()
```

The dataset that we just created consists of 150 randomly generated points that are roughly grouped into three regions with higher density, which is visualized via a two-dimensional scatterplot:

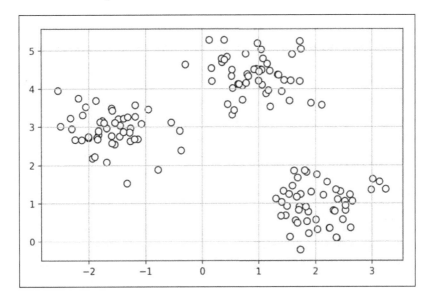

In real-world applications of clustering, we do not have any ground truth category information (information provided as empirical evidence as opposed to inference) about those samples; otherwise, it would fall into the category of supervised learning. Thus, our goal is to group the samples based on their feature similarities, which can be achieved using the k-means algorithm that can be summarized by the following four steps:

1. Randomly pick k centroids from the sample points as initial cluster centers.

2. Assign each sample to the nearest centroid $\mu^{(j)}$, $j \in \{1,...,k\}$.

3. Move the centroids to the center of the samples that were assigned to it.

4. Repeat steps 2 and 3 until the cluster assignments do not change or a user-defined tolerance or maximum number of iterations is reached.

Now, the next question is *how do we measure similarity between objects?* We can define similarity as the opposite of distance, and a commonly used distance for clustering samples with continuous features is the **squared Euclidean distance** between two points **x** and **y** in *m*-dimensional space:

$$d\left(\boldsymbol{x},\boldsymbol{y}\right)^{2} = \sum_{j=1}^{m}\left(x_{j}-y_{j}\right)^{2} = \left\|\boldsymbol{x}-\boldsymbol{y}\right\|_{2}^{2}$$

Note that, in the preceding equation, the index *j* refers to the *j*th dimension (feature column) of the sample points **x** and **y**. In the rest of this section, we will use the superscripts *i* and *j* to refer to the sample index and cluster index, respectively.

Based on this Euclidean distance metric, we can describe the k-means algorithm as a simple optimization problem, an iterative approach for minimizing the within-cluster **Sum of Squared Errors (SSE)**, which is sometimes also called **cluster inertia**:

$$SSE = \sum_{i=1}^{n}\sum_{j=1}^{k} w^{(i,j)}\left\|\boldsymbol{x}^{(i)}-\boldsymbol{\mu}^{(j)}\right\|_{2}^{2}$$

Here $\boldsymbol{\mu}^{(j)}$ is the representative point (centroid) for cluster *j*, and $w^{(i,j)}=1$ if the sample $\boldsymbol{x}^{(i)}$ is in cluster *j*; $w^{(i,j)}=0$ otherwise.

Now that we have learned how the simple k-means algorithm works, let's apply it to our sample dataset using the KMeans class from scikit-learn's `cluster` module:

```
>>> from sklearn.cluster import KMeans
>>> km = KMeans(n_clusters=3,
...             init='random',
...             n_init=10,
...             max_iter=300,
...             tol=1e-04,
...             random_state=0)
>>> y_km = km.fit_predict(X)
```

Using the preceding code, we set the number of desired clusters to 3; specifying the number of clusters *a priori* is one of the limitations of k-means. We set n_init=10 to run the k-means clustering algorithms 10 times independently with different random centroids to choose the final model as the one with the lowest SSE. Via the max_iter parameter, we specify the maximum number of iterations for each single run (here, 300). Note that the k-means implementation in scikit-learn stops early if it converges before the maximum number of iterations is reached. However, it is possible that k-means does not reach convergence for a particular run, which can be problematic (computationally expensive) if we choose relatively large values for max_iter. One way to deal with convergence problems is to choose larger values for tol, which is a parameter that controls the tolerance with regard to the changes in the within-cluster sum-squared-error to declare convergence. In the preceding code, we chose a tolerance of 1e-04 (=0.0001).

A problem with k-means is that one or more clusters can be empty. Note that this problem does not exist for k-medoids or fuzzy C-means, an algorithm that we will discuss later in this section. However, this problem is accounted for in the current k-means implementation in scikit-learn. If a cluster is empty, the algorithm will search for the sample that is farthest away from the centroid of the empty cluster. Then it will reassign the centroid to be this farthest point.

When we are applying k-means to real-world data using a Euclidean distance metric, we want to make sure that the features are measured on the same scale and apply z-score standardization or min-max scaling if necessary.

After we predicted the cluster labels y_km and discussed some of the challenges of the k-means algorithm, let's now visualize the clusters that k-means identified in the dataset together with the cluster centroids. These are stored under the cluster_centers_ attribute of the fitted KMeans object:

```
>>> plt.scatter(X[y_km == 0, 0],
...             X[y_km == 0, 1],
...             s=50, c='lightgreen',
...             marker='s', edgecolor='black',
...             label='cluster 1')
>>> plt.scatter(X[y_km == 1, 0],
...             X[y_km == 1, 1],
...             s=50, c='orange',
...             marker='o', edgecolor='black',
...             label='cluster 2')
>>> plt.scatter(X[y_km == 2, 0],
...             X[y_km == 2, 1],
```

```
...                 s=50, c='lightblue',
...                 marker='v', edgecolor='black',
...                 label='cluster 3')
>>> plt.scatter(km.cluster_centers_[:, 0],
...             km.cluster_centers_[:, 1],
...             s=250, marker='*',
...             c='red', edgecolor='black',
...             label='centroids')
>>> plt.legend(scatterpoints=1)
>>> plt.grid()
>>> plt.show()
```

In the following scatterplot, we can see that k-means placed the three centroids at the center of each sphere, which looks like a reasonable grouping given this dataset:

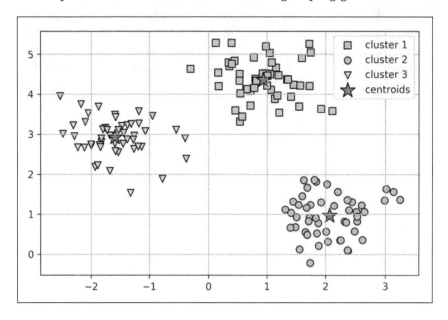

Although k-means worked well on this toy dataset, we shall highlight another drawback of k-means: we have to specify the number of clusters, *k*, *a priori*. The number of clusters to choose may not always be so obvious in real-world applications, especially if we are working with a higher dimensional dataset that cannot be visualized. The other properties of k-means are that clusters do not overlap and are not hierarchical, and we also assume that there is at least one item in each cluster. Later in this chapter, we will encounter different types of clustering algorithms, hierarchical and density-based clustering. Neither type of algorithm requires us to specify the number of clusters upfront or assume spherical structures in our dataset.

In the next subsection, we will introduce a popular variant of the classic k-means algorithm called **k-means++**. While it doesn't address those assumptions and drawbacks of k-means discussed in the previous paragraph, it can greatly improve the clustering results through more clever seeding of the initial cluster centers.

A smarter way of placing the initial cluster centroids using k-means++

So far, we have discussed the classic k-means algorithm that uses a random seed to place the initial centroids, which can sometimes result in bad clusterings or slow convergence if the initial centroids are chosen poorly. One way to address this issue is to run the k-means algorithm multiple times on a dataset and choose the best performing model in terms of the SSE. Another strategy is to place the initial centroids far away from each other via the k-means++ algorithm, which leads to better and more consistent results than the classic k-means (*k-means++: The Advantages of Careful Seeding*, D. Arthur and S. Vassilvitskii in proceedings of the eighteenth annual ACM-SIAM symposium on Discrete algorithms, pages 1027-1035. Society for Industrial and Applied Mathematics, *2007*). The initialization in k-means++ can be summarized as follows:

1. Initialize an empty set **M** to store the k centroids being selected.

2. Randomly choose the first centroid $\mu^{(j)}$ from the input samples and assign it to **M**.

3. For each sample $x^{(i)}$ that is not in **M**, find the minimum squared distance $d\left(x^{(i)}, \mathbf{M}\right)^2$ to any of the centroids in **M**.

4. To randomly select the next centroid $\mu^{(p)}$, use a weighted probability distribution equal to $\dfrac{d\left(\mu^{(p)}, \mathbf{M}\right)^2}{\sum_i d\left(x^{(i)}, \mathbf{M}\right)^2}$.

5. Repeat steps 2 and 3 until k centroids are chosen.

6. Proceed with the classic k-means algorithm.

To use k-means++ with scikit-learn's `KMeans` object, we just need to set the `init` parameter to `'k-means++'`. In fact, `'k-means++'` is the default argument to the `init` parameter, which is strongly recommended in practice. The only reason why we haven't used it in the previous example was to not introduce too many concepts all at once. The rest of this section on k-means will use k-means++, but readers are encouraged to experiment more with the two different approaches (classic k-means via `init='random'` versus k-means++ via `init='k-means++'`) for placing the initial cluster centroids.

Hard versus soft clustering

Hard clustering describes a family of algorithms where each sample in a dataset is assigned to exactly one cluster, as in the k-means algorithm that we discussed in the previous subsection. In contrast, algorithms for **soft clustering** (sometimes also called **fuzzy clustering**) assign a sample to one or more clusters. A popular example of soft clustering is the **fuzzy C-means (FCM)** algorithm (also called **soft k-means** or **fuzzy k-means**). The original idea goes back to the 1970s, when Joseph C. Dunn first proposed an early version of fuzzy clustering to improve k-means (*A Fuzzy Relative of the ISODATA Process and Its Use in Detecting Compact Well-Separated Clusters, J. C. Dunn, 1973*). Almost a decade later, James C. Bedzek published his work on the improvement of the fuzzy clustering algorithm, which is now known as the FCM algorithm (*Pattern Recognition with Fuzzy Objective Function Algorithms, J. C. Bezdek, Springer Science+Business Media, 2013*).

The FCM procedure is very similar to k-means. However, we replace the hard cluster assignment with probabilities for each point belonging to each cluster. In k-means, we could express the cluster membership of a sample x with a sparse vector of binary values:

$$\begin{bmatrix} \mu^{(1)} \to 0 \\ \mu^{(2)} \to 1 \\ \mu^{(3)} \to 0 \end{bmatrix}$$

Here, the index position with value 1 indicates the cluster centroid $\mu^{(j)}$ the sample is assigned to (assuming $k = 3$, $j \in \{1, 2, 3\}$). In contrast, a membership vector in FCM could be represented as follows:

$$\begin{bmatrix} \mu^{(1)} \to 0.10 \\ \mu^{(2)} \to 0.85 \\ \mu^{(3)} \to 0.05 \end{bmatrix}$$

Here, each value falls in the range *[0, 1]* and represents a probability of membership of the respective cluster centroid. The sum of the memberships for a given sample is equal to 1. Similar to the k-means algorithm, we can summarize the FCM algorithm in four key steps:

1. Specify the number of k centroids and randomly assign the cluster memberships for each point.

2. Compute the cluster centroids $\mu^{(j)}$, $j \in \{1,...,k\}$.

3. Update the cluster memberships for each point.

4. Repeat steps 2 and 3 until the membership coefficients do not change, or a user-defined tolerance or maximum number of iterations is reached.

The objective function of FCM — we abbreviate it as J_m — looks very similar to the within cluster sum-squared-error that we minimize in k-means:

$$J_m = \sum_{i=1}^{n} \sum_{j=1}^{k} w^{m\,(i,j)} \left\| x^{(i)} - \mu^{(j)} \right\|_2^2$$

However, note that the membership indicator $w^{(i,j)}$ is not a binary value as in k-means ($w^{(i,j)} \in \{0,1\}$), but a real value that denotes the cluster membership probability ($w^{(i,j)} \in [0,1]$). You also may have noticed that we added an additional exponent to $w^{(i,j)}$; the exponent m, any number greater than or equal to one (typically $m=2$), is the so-called **fuzziness coefficient** (or simply **fuzzifier**) that controls the degree of *fuzziness*. The larger the value of m the smaller the cluster membership $w^{(i,j)}$ becomes, which leads to fuzzier clusters. The cluster membership probability itself is calculated as follows:

$$
w^{(i,j)} = \left[\sum_{p=1}^{k} \left(\frac{\left\| \boldsymbol{x}^{(i)} - \boldsymbol{\mu}^{(j)} \right\|_2}{\left\| \boldsymbol{x}^{(i)} - \boldsymbol{\mu}^{(p)} \right\|_2} \right)^{\frac{2}{m-1}} \right]^{-1}
$$

For example, if we chose three cluster centers as in the previous k-means example, we could calculate the membership of the $\boldsymbol{x}^{(i)}$ sample belonging to the $\boldsymbol{\mu}^{(j)}$ cluster as follows:

$$
w^{(i,j)} = \left[\left(\frac{\left\| \boldsymbol{x}^{(i)} - \boldsymbol{\mu}^{(j)} \right\|_2}{\left\| \boldsymbol{x}^{(i)} - \boldsymbol{\mu}^{(1)} \right\|_2} \right)^{\frac{2}{m-1}} + \left(\frac{\left\| \boldsymbol{x}^{(i)} - \boldsymbol{\mu}^{(j)} \right\|_2}{\left\| \boldsymbol{x}^{(i)} - \boldsymbol{\mu}^{(2)} \right\|_2} \right)^{\frac{2}{m-1}} + \left(\frac{\left\| \boldsymbol{x}^{(i)} - \boldsymbol{\mu}^{(j)} \right\|_2}{\left\| \boldsymbol{x}^{(i)} - \boldsymbol{\mu}^{(3)} \right\|_2} \right)^{\frac{2}{m-1}} \right]^{-1}
$$

The center $\boldsymbol{\mu}^{(j)}$ of a cluster itself is calculated as the mean of all samples weighted by the degree to which each sample belongs to that cluster ($w^{m(i,j)}$):

$$
\boldsymbol{\mu}^{(j)} = \frac{\sum_{i=1}^{n} w^{m(i,j)} \boldsymbol{x}^{(i)}}{\sum_{i=1}^{n} w^{m(i,j)}}
$$

Just by looking at the equation to calculate the cluster memberships, it is intuitive to say that each iteration in FCM is more expensive than an iteration in k-means. However, FCM typically requires fewer iterations overall to reach convergence. Unfortunately, the FCM algorithm is currently not implemented in scikit-learn. However, it has been found in practice that both k-means and FCM produce very similar clustering outputs, as described in a study (*Comparative Analysis of k-means and Fuzzy C-Means Algorithms*, *S. Ghosh*, and *S. K. Dubey*, *IJACSA*, 4: 35–38, 2013).

Using the elbow method to find the optimal number of clusters

One of the main challenges in unsupervised learning is that we do not know the definitive answer. We don't have the ground truth class labels in our dataset that allow us to apply the techniques that we used in *Chapter 6*, *Learning Best Practices for Model Evaluation and Hyperparameter Tuning*, in order to evaluate the performance of a supervised model. Thus, to quantify the quality of clustering, we need to use intrinsic metrics — such as the within-cluster SSE (distortion) that we discussed earlier in this chapter — to compare the performance of different k-means clusterings. Conveniently, we don't need to compute the within-cluster SSE explicitly when we are using scikit-learn, as it is already accessible via the `inertia_` attribute after fitting a `KMeans` model:

```
>>> print('Distortion: %.2f' % km.inertia_)
Distortion: 72.48
```

Based on the within-cluster SSE, we can use a graphical tool, the so-called **elbow method**, to estimate the optimal number of clusters k for a given task. Intuitively, we can say that, if k increases, the distortion will decrease. This is because the samples will be closer to the centroids they are assigned to. The idea behind the elbow method is to identify the value of k where the distortion begins to increase most rapidly, which will become clearer if we plot the distortion for different values of k:

```
>>> distortions = []
>>> for i in range(1, 11):
...     km = KMeans(n_clusters=i,
...                 init='k-means++',
...                 n_init=10,
...                 max_iter=300,
...                 random_state=0)
>>>     km.fit(X)
>>>     distortions.append(km.inertia_)
```

```
>>> plt.plot(range(1,11), distortions, marker='o')
>>> plt.xlabel('Number of clusters')
>>> plt.ylabel('Distortion')
>>> plt.show()
```

As we can see in the following plot, the *elbow* is located at k=3, which is evidence that k=3 is indeed a good choice for this dataset:

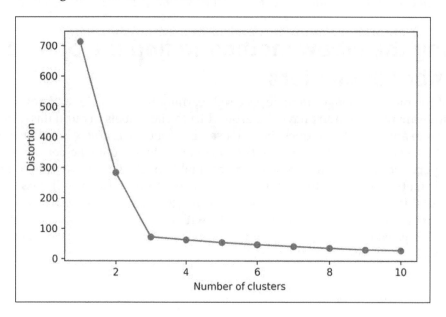

Quantifying the quality of clustering via silhouette plots

Another intrinsic metric to evaluate the quality of a clustering is **silhouette analysis**, which can also be applied to clustering algorithms other than k-means that we will discuss later in this chapter. Silhouette analysis can be used as a graphical tool to plot a measure of how tightly grouped the samples in the clusters are. To calculate the **silhouette coefficient** of a single sample in our dataset, we can apply the following three steps:

1. Calculate the **cluster cohesion** $a^{(i)}$ as the average distance between a sample $x^{(i)}$ and all other points in the same cluster.

2. Calculate the **cluster separation** $b^{(i)}$ from the next closest cluster as the average distance between the sample $x^{(i)}$ and all samples in the nearest cluster.

3. Calculate the silhouette $s^{(i)}$ as the difference between cluster cohesion and separation divided by the greater of the two, as shown here:

$$s^{(i)} = \frac{b^{(i)} - a^{(i)}}{\max\left\{b^{(i)}, a^{(i)}\right\}}$$

The silhouette coefficient is bounded in the range -1 to 1. Based on the preceding equation, we can see that the silhouette coefficient is 0 if the cluster separation and cohesion are equal ($b^{(i)} = a^{(i)}$). Furthermore, we get close to an ideal silhouette coefficient of 1 if $b^{(i)} \gg a^{(i)}$, since $b^{(i)}$ quantifies how dissimilar a sample is to other clusters, and $a^{(i)}$ tells us how similar it is to the other samples in its own cluster.

The silhouette coefficient is available as `silhouette_samples` from scikit-learn's `metric` module, and optionally, the `silhouette_scores` function can be imported for convenience. The `silhouette_scores` function calculates the average silhouette coefficient across all samples, which is equivalent to `numpy.mean(silhouette_samples(...))`. By executing the following code, we will now create a plot of the silhouette coefficients for a k-means clustering with $k = 3$:

```
>>> km = KMeans(n_clusters=3,
...             init='k-means++',
...             n_init=10,
...             max_iter=300,
...             tol=1e-04,
...             random_state=0)
>>> y_km = km.fit_predict(X)

>>> import numpy as np
>>> from matplotlib import cm
>>> from sklearn.metrics import silhouette_samples
>>> cluster_labels = np.unique(y_km)
>>> n_clusters = cluster_labels.shape[0]
>>> silhouette_vals = silhouette_samples(X,
...                                      y_km,
...                                      metric='euclidean')
>>> y_ax_lower, y_ax_upper = 0, 0
>>> yticks = []
>>> for i, c in enumerate(cluster_labels):
...     c_silhouette_vals = silhouette_vals[y_km == c]
...     c_silhouette_vals.sort()
```

```
...        y_ax_upper += len(c_silhouette_vals)
...        color = cm.jet(float(i) / n_clusters)
...        plt.barh(range(y_ax_lower, y_ax_upper),
...                 c_silhouette_vals,
...                 height=1.0,
...                 edgecolor='none',
...                 color=color)
...        yticks.append((y_ax_lower + y_ax_upper) / 2.)
...        y_ax_lower += len(c_silhouette_vals)
>>> silhouette_avg = np.mean(silhouette_vals)
>>> plt.axvline(silhouette_avg,
...             color="red",
...             linestyle="--")
>>> plt.yticks(yticks, cluster_labels + 1)
>>> plt.ylabel('Cluster')
>>> plt.xlabel('Silhouette coefficient')
>>> plt.show()
```

Through a visual inspection of the silhouette plot, we can quickly scrutinize the sizes of the different clusters and identify clusters that contain *outliers*:

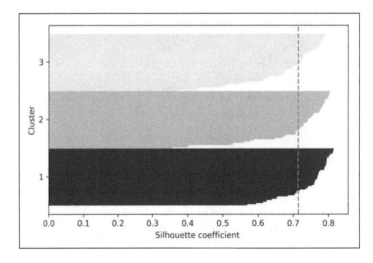

However, as we can see in the preceding silhouette plot, the silhouette coefficients are not even close to **0**, which is in this case an indicator of a *good* clustering. Furthermore, to summarize the goodness of our clustering, we added the average silhouette coefficient to the plot (dotted line).

To see what a silhouette plot looks like for a relatively *bad* clustering, let's seed the k-means algorithm with only two centroids:

```
>>> km = KMeans(n_clusters=2,
...             init='k-means++',
...             n_init=10,
...             max_iter=300,
...             tol=1e-04,
...             random_state=0)
>>> y_km = km.fit_predict(X)

>>> plt.scatter(X[y_km==0,0],
...             X[y_km==0,1],
...             s=50, c='lightgreen',
...             edgecolor='black',
...             marker='s',
...             label='cluster 1')
>>> plt.scatter(X[y_km==1,0],
...             X[y_km==1,1],
...             s=50,
...             c='orange',
...             edgecolor='black',
...             marker='o',
...             label='cluster 2')
>>> plt.scatter(km.cluster_centers_[:,0],
...             km.cluster_centers_[:,1],
...             s=250,
...             marker='*',
...             c='red',
...             label='centroids')
>>> plt.legend()
>>> plt.grid()
>>> plt.show()
```

As we can see in the resulting plot, one of the centroids falls between two of the three spherical groupings of the sample points. Although the clustering does not look completely terrible, it is suboptimal:

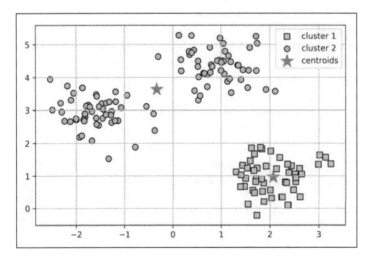

Please keep in mind that we typically do not have the luxury of visualizing datasets in two-dimensional scatterplots in real-world problems, since we typically work with data in higher dimensions. So, next, we create the silhouette plot to evaluate the results:

```
>>> cluster_labels = np.unique(y_km)
>>> n_clusters = cluster_labels.shape[0]
>>> silhouette_vals = silhouette_samples(X,
...                                       y_km,
...                                       metric='euclidean')
>>> y_ax_lower, y_ax_upper = 0, 0
>>> yticks = []
>>> for i, c in enumerate(cluster_labels):
...     c_silhouette_vals = silhouette_vals[y_km == c]
...     c_silhouette_vals.sort()
...     y_ax_upper += len(c_silhouette_vals)
...     color = cm.jet(i / n_clusters)
...     plt.barh(range(y_ax_lower, y_ax_upper),
...              c_silhouette_vals,
...              height=1.0,
...              edgecolor='none',
...              color=color)
...     yticks.append((y_ax_lower + y_ax_upper) / 2)
...     y_ax_lower += len(c_silhouette_vals)
```

```
>>> silhouette_avg = np.mean(silhouette_vals)
>>> plt.axvline(silhouette_avg, color="red", linestyle="--")
>>> plt.yticks(yticks, cluster_labels + 1)
>>> plt.ylabel('Cluster')
>>> plt.xlabel('Silhouette coefficient')
>>> plt.show()
```

As we can see in the resulting plot, the silhouettes now have visibly different lengths and widths, which is evidence for a relatively *bad* or at least *suboptimal* clustering:

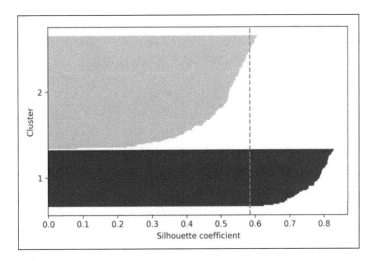

Organizing clusters as a hierarchical tree

In this section, we will take a look at an alternative approach to prototype-based clustering: **hierarchical clustering**. One advantage of hierarchical clustering algorithms is that it allows us to plot **dendrograms** (visualizations of a binary hierarchical clustering), which can help with the interpretation of the results by creating meaningful taxonomies. Another useful advantage of this hierarchical approach is that we do not need to specify the number of clusters up front.

The two main approaches to hierarchical clustering are **agglomerative** and **divisive** hierarchical clustering. In divisive hierarchical clustering, we start with one cluster that encompasses all our samples, and we iteratively split the cluster into smaller clusters until each cluster only contains one sample. In this section, we will focus on agglomerative clustering, which takes the opposite approach. We start with each sample as an individual cluster and merge the closest pairs of clusters until only one cluster remains.

Grouping clusters in bottom-up fashion

The two standard algorithms for agglomerative hierarchical clustering are **single linkage** and **complete linkage**. Using single linkage, we compute the distances between the most similar members for each pair of clusters and merge the two clusters for which the distance between the most similar members is the smallest. The complete linkage approach is similar to single linkage but, instead of comparing the most similar members in each pair of clusters, we compare the most dissimilar members to perform the merge. This is shown in the following diagram:

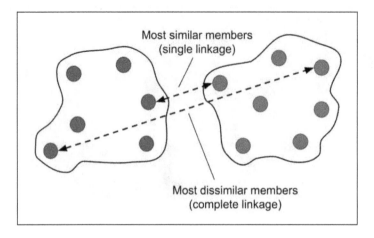

Other commonly used algorithms for agglomerative hierarchical clustering include **average linkage** and **Ward's linkage**. In average linkage, we merge the cluster pairs based on the minimum average distances between all group members in the two clusters. In Ward's linkage, the two clusters that lead to the minimum increase of the total within-cluster SSE are merged.

In this section, we will focus on agglomerative clustering using the complete linkage approach. Hierarchical complete linkage clustering is an iterative procedure that can be summarized by the following steps:

1. Compute the distance matrix of all samples.
2. Represent each data point as a singleton cluster.
3. Merge the two closest clusters based on the distance between the most dissimilar (distant) members.
4. Update the similarity matrix.
5. Repeat steps 2-4 until one single cluster remains.

Next, we will discuss how to compute the distance matrix (step 1). But first, let's generate some random sample data to work with: the rows represent different observations (IDs 0-4), and the columns are the different features (X, Y, Z) of those samples:

```
>>> import pandas as pd
>>> import numpy as np
>>> np.random.seed(123)
>>> variables = ['X', 'Y', 'Z']
>>> labels = ['ID_0','ID_1','ID_2','ID_3','ID_4']
>>> X = np.random.random_sample([5,3])*10
>>> df = pd.DataFrame(X, columns=variables, index=labels)
>>> df
```

After executing the preceding code, we should now see the following data frame containing the randomly generated samples:

	X	Y	Z
ID_0	6.964692	2.861393	2.268515
ID_1	5.513148	7.194690	4.231065
ID_2	9.807642	6.848297	4.809319
ID_3	3.921175	3.431780	7.290497
ID_4	4.385722	0.596779	3.980443

Performing hierarchical clustering on a distance matrix

To calculate the distance matrix as input for the hierarchical clustering algorithm, we will use the pdist function from SciPy's spatial.distance submodule:

```
>>> from scipy.spatial.distance import pdist, squareform
>>> row_dist = pd.DataFrame(squareform(
...              pdist(df, metric='euclidean')),
...              columns=labels, index=labels)
>>> row_dist
```

Using the preceding code, we calculated the Euclidean distance between each pair of sample points in our dataset based on the features x, y, and z. We provided the condensed distance matrix—returned by pdist—as input to the squareform function to create a symmetrical matrix of the pair-wise distances as shown here:

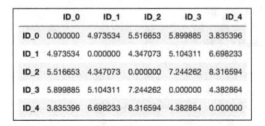

	ID_0	ID_1	ID_2	ID_3	ID_4
ID_0	0.000000	4.973534	5.516653	5.899885	3.835396
ID_1	4.973534	0.000000	4.347073	5.104311	6.698233
ID_2	5.516653	4.347073	0.000000	7.244262	8.316594
ID_3	5.899885	5.104311	7.244262	0.000000	4.382864
ID_4	3.835396	6.698233	8.316594	4.382864	0.000000

Next, we will apply the complete linkage agglomeration to our clusters using the linkage function from SciPy's cluster.hierarchy submodule, which returns a so-called **linkage matrix**.

However, before we call the linkage function, let us take a careful look at the function documentation:

```
>>> from scipy.cluster.hierarchy import linkage
>>> help(linkage)
[...]
Parameters:
  y : ndarray
      A condensed or redundant distance matrix. A condensed
      distance matrix is a flat array containing the upper
      triangular of the distance matrix. This is the form
      that pdist returns. Alternatively, a collection of m
      observation vectors in n dimensions may be passed as
      an m by n array.

  method : str, optional
      The linkage algorithm to use. See the Linkage Methods
      section below for full descriptions.

  metric : str, optional
      The distance metric to use. See the distance.pdist
      function for a list of valid distance metrics.
```

```
Returns:
  Z : ndarray
    The hierarchical clustering encoded as a linkage matrix.
[...]
```

Based on the function description, we conclude that we can use a condensed distance matrix (upper triangular) from the pdist function as an input attribute. Alternatively, we could also provide the initial data array and use the 'euclidean' metric as a function argument in linkage. However, we should not use the squareform distance matrix that we defined earlier, since it would yield different distance values than expected. To sum it up, the three possible scenarios are listed here:

- **Incorrect approach**: Using the squareform distance matrix shown in the following code snippet would lead to incorrect results:

```
>>> from scipy.cluster.hierarchy import linkage
>>> row_clusters = linkage(row_dist,
...                        method='complete',
...                        metric='euclidean')
```

- **Correct approach**: Using the condensed distance matrix as shown in the following code example yields the correct pairwise distance matrix:

```
>>> row_clusters = linkage(pdist(df, metric='euclidean'),
...                        method='complete')
```

- **Correct approach**: Using the complete input sample matrix as shown in the following code snippet also leads to a correct distance matrix similar to the preceding approach:

```
>>> row_clusters = linkage(df.values,
...                        method='complete',
...                        metric='euclidean')
```

To take a closer look at the clustering results, we can turn clustering results into a pandas DataFrame (best viewed in a Jupyter Notebook) as follows:

```
>>> pd.DataFrame(row_clusters,
...       columns=['row label 1',
...                'row label 2',
...                'distance',
...                'no. of items in clust.'],
...       index=['cluster %d' %(i+1) for i in
...              range(row_clusters.shape[0])])
```

As shown in the following screenshot, the linkage matrix consists of several rows where each row represents one merge. The first and second columns denote the most dissimilar members in each cluster, and the third column reports the distance between those members. The last column returns the count of the members in each cluster:

	row label 1	row label 2	distance	no. of items in clust.
cluster 1	0.0	4.0	3.835396	2.0
cluster 2	1.0	2.0	4.347073	2.0
cluster 3	3.0	5.0	5.899885	3.0
cluster 4	6.0	7.0	8.316594	5.0

Now that we have computed the linkage matrix, we can visualize the results in the form of a dendrogram:

```
>>> from scipy.cluster.hierarchy import dendrogram
# make dendrogram black (part 1/2)
# from scipy.cluster.hierarchy import set_link_color_palette
# set_link_color_palette(['black'])
>>> row_dendr = dendrogram(row_clusters,
...                        labels=labels,
...                        # make dendrogram black (part 2/2)
...                        # color_threshold=np.inf
...                        )
>>> plt.tight_layout()
>>> plt.ylabel('Euclidean distance')
>>> plt.show()
```

If you are executing the preceding code or reading an ebook version of this book, you will notice that the branches in the resulting dendrogram are shown in different colors. The coloring scheme is derived from a list of Matplotlib colors that are cycled for the distance thresholds in the dendrogram. For example, to display the dendrograms in black, you can uncomment the respective sections that I inserted in the preceding code:

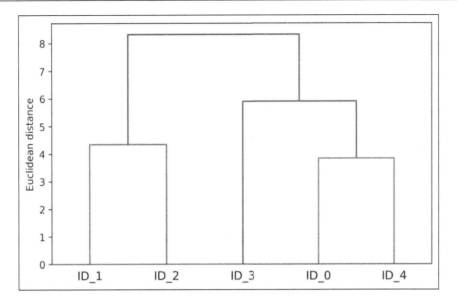

Such a dendrogram summarizes the different clusters that were formed during the agglomerative hierarchical clustering; for example, we can see that the samples `ID_0` and `ID_4`, followed by `ID_1` and `ID_2`, are the most similar ones based on the Euclidean distance metric.

Attaching dendrograms to a heat map

In practical applications, hierarchical clustering dendrograms are often used in combination with a **heat map**, which allows us to represent the individual values in the sample matrix with a color code. In this section, we will discuss how to attach a dendrogram to a heat map plot and order the rows in the heat map correspondingly.

However, attaching a dendrogram to a heat map can be a little bit tricky, so let's go through this procedure step by step:

1. We create a new `figure` object and define the *x* axis position, *y* axis position, width, and height of the dendrogram via the `add_axes` attribute. Furthermore, we rotate the dendrogram 90 degrees counter-clockwise. The code is as follows:

   ```
   >>> fig = plt.figure(figsize=(8,8), facecolor='white')
   >>> axd = fig.add_axes([0.09,0.1,0.2,0.6])
   >>> row_dendr = dendrogram(row_clusters, orientation='left')
   >>> # note: for matplotlib < v1.5.1, please use
   orientation='right'
   ```

2. Next, we reorder the data in our initial `DataFrame` according to the clustering labels that can be accessed from the dendrogram object, which is essentially a Python dictionary, via the `leaves` key. The code is as follows:

```
>>> df_rowclust = df.iloc[row_dendr['leaves'][::-1]]
```

3. Now, we construct the heat map from the reordered `DataFrame` and position it next to the dendrogram:

```
>>> axm = fig.add_axes([0.23,0.1,0.6,0.6])
>>> cax = axm.matshow(df_rowclust,
...                interpolation='nearest', cmap='hot_r')
```

4. Finally, we will modify the aesthetics of the dendrogram by removing the axis ticks and hiding the axis spines. Also, we will add a color bar and assign the feature and sample names to the *x* and *y* axis tick labels, respectively:

```
>>> axd.set_xticks([])
>>> axd.set_yticks([])
>>> for i in axd.spines.values():
...        i.set_visible(False)
>>> fig.colorbar(cax)
>>> axm.set_xticklabels([''] + list(df_rowclust.columns))
>>> axm.set_yticklabels([''] + list(df_rowclust.index))
>>> plt.show()
```

After following the previous steps, the heat map should be displayed with the dendrogram attached:

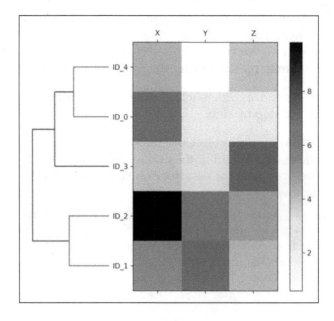

As we can see, the order of rows in the heat map reflects the clustering of the samples in the dendrogram. In addition to a simple dendrogram, the color-coded values of each sample and feature in the heat map provide us with a nice summary of the dataset.

Applying agglomerative clustering via scikit-learn

In the previous subsection, we saw how to perform agglomerative hierarchical clustering using SciPy. However, there is also an `AgglomerativeClustering` implementation in scikit-learn, which allows us to choose the number of clusters that we want to return. This is useful if we want to prune the hierarchical cluster tree. By setting the `n_cluster` parameter to 3, we will now cluster the samples into three groups using the same complete linkage approach based on the Euclidean distance metric, as before:

```
>>> from sklearn.cluster import AgglomerativeClustering
>>> ac = AgglomerativeClustering(n_clusters=3,
...                              affinity='euclidean',
...                              linkage='complete')
>>> labels = ac.fit_predict(X)
>>> print('Cluster labels: %s' % labels)
Cluster labels: [1 0 0 2 1]
```

Looking at the predicted cluster labels, we can see that the first and the fifth sample (`ID_0` and `ID_4`) were assigned to one cluster (label 1), and the samples `ID_1` and `ID_2` were assigned to a second cluster (label 0). The sample `ID_3` was put into its own cluster (label 2). Overall, the results are consistent with the results that we observed in the dendrogram. We shall note though that `ID_3` is more similar to `ID_4` and `ID_0` than to `ID_1` and `ID_2`, as shown in the preceding dendrogram figure; this is not clear from scikit-learn's clustering results. Let's now rerun the `AgglomerativeClustering` using `n_cluster=2` in the following code snippet:

```
>>> ac = AgglomerativeClustering(n_clusters=2,
...                              affinity='euclidean',
...                              linkage='complete')
>>> labels = ac.fit_predict(X)
>>> print('Cluster labels: %s' % labels)
Cluster labels: [0 1 1 0 0]
```

As we can see, in this *pruned* clustering hierarchy, label `ID_3` was assigned to the same cluster as `ID_0` and `ID_4`, as expected.

Locating regions of high density via DBSCAN

Although we can't cover the vast amount of different clustering algorithms in this chapter, let's at least introduce one more approach to clustering: **Density-based Spatial Clustering of Applications with Noise (DBSCAN)**, which does not make assumptions about spherical clusters like k-means, nor does it partition the dataset into hierarchies that require a manual cut-off point. As its name implies, density-based clustering assigns cluster labels based on dense regions of points. In DBSCAN, the notion of density is defined as the number of points within a specified radius ε.

According to the DBSCAN algorithm, a special label is assigned to each sample (point) using the following criteria:

- A point is considered a **core point** if at least a specified number (MinPts) of neighboring points fall within the specified radius ε
- A **border point** is a point that has fewer neighbors than MinPts within ε, but lies within the ε radius of a core point
- All other points that are neither core nor border points are considered **noise points**

After labeling the points as core, border, or noise, the DBSCAN algorithm can be summarized in two simple steps:

1. Form a separate cluster for each core point or connected group of core points (core points are connected if they are no farther away than ε).
2. Assign each border point to the cluster of its corresponding core point.

To get a better understanding of what the result of DBSCAN can look like before jumping to the implementation, let's summarize what we have just learned about core points, border points, and noise points in the following figure:

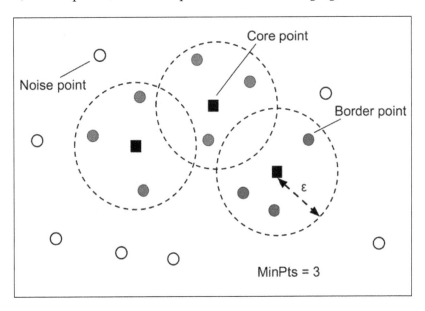

One of the main advantages of using DBSCAN is that it does not assume that the clusters have a spherical shape as in k-means. Furthermore, DBSCAN is different from k-means and hierarchical clustering in that it doesn't necessarily assign each point to a cluster but is capable of removing noise points.

For a more illustrative example, let's create a new dataset of half-moon-shaped structures to compare k-means clustering, hierarchical clustering, and DBSCAN:

```
>>> from sklearn.datasets import make_moons
>>> X, y = make_moons(n_samples=200,
...                   noise=0.05,
...                   random_state=0)
>>> plt.scatter(X[:,0], X[:,1])
>>> plt.show()
```

As we can see in the resulting plot, there are two visible, half-moon shaped groups consisting of 100 sample points each:

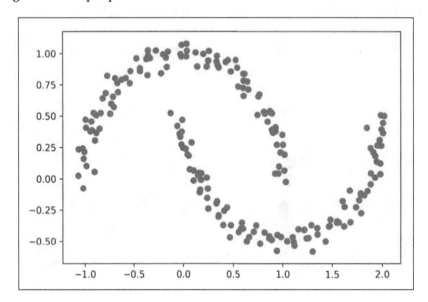

We will start by using the k-means algorithm and complete linkage clustering to see if one of those previously discussed clustering algorithms can successfully identify the half-moon shapes as separate clusters. The code is as follows:

```
>>> f, (ax1, ax2) = plt.subplots(1, 2, figsize=(8, 3))
>>> km = KMeans(n_clusters=2,
...             random_state=0)
>>> y_km = km.fit_predict(X)
>>> ax1.scatter(X[y_km==0,0],
...             X[y_km==0,1],
...             c='lightblue',
...             edgecolor='black',
...             marker='o',
...             s=40,
...             label='cluster 1')
>>> ax1.scatter(X[y_km==1,0],
...             X[y_km==1,1],
...             c='red',
...             edgecolor='black',
...             marker='s',
...             s=40,
...             label='cluster 2')
>>> ax1.set_title('K-means clustering')
```

```
>>> ac = AgglomerativeClustering(n_clusters=2,
...                              affinity='euclidean',
...                              linkage='complete')
>>> y_ac = ac.fit_predict(X)
>>> ax2.scatter(X[y_ac==0,0],
...             X[y_ac==0,1],
...             c='lightblue',
...             edgecolor='black',
...             marker='o',
...             s=40,
...             label='cluster 1')
>>> ax2.scatter(X[y_ac==1,0],
...             X[y_ac==1,1],
...             c='red',
...             edgecolor='black',
...             marker='s',
...             s=40,
...             label='cluster 2')
>>> ax2.set_title('Agglomerative clustering')
>>> plt.legend()
>>> plt.show()
```

Based on the visualized clustering results, we can see that the k-means algorithm is unable to separate the two cluster, and also the hierarchical clustering algorithm was challenged by those complex shapes:

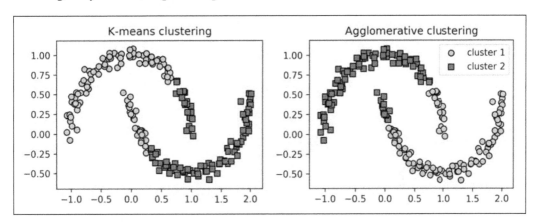

Finally, let us try the DBSCAN algorithm on this dataset to see if it can find the two half-moon-shaped clusters using a density-based approach:

```
>>> from sklearn.cluster import DBSCAN
>>> db = DBSCAN(eps=0.2,
...             min_samples=5,
...             metric='euclidean')
>>> y_db = db.fit_predict(X)
>>> plt.scatter(X[y_db==0,0],
...             X[y_db==0,1],
...             c='lightblue',
...             edgecolor='black',
...             marker='o',
...             s=40,
...             label='cluster 1')
>>> plt.scatter(X[y_db==1,0],
...             X[y_db==1,1],
...             c='red',
...             edgecolor='black',
...             marker='s',
...             s=40,
...             label='cluster 2')
>>> plt.legend()
>>> plt.show()
```

The DBSCAN algorithm can successfully detect the half-moon shapes, which highlights one of the strength of DBSCAN: clustering data of arbitrary shapes:

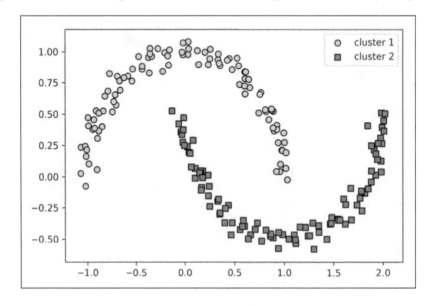

However, we shall also note some of the disadvantages of DBSCAN. With an increasing number of features in our dataset — assuming a fixed number of training examples — the negative effect of the **curse of dimensionality** increases. This is especially a problem if we are using the Euclidean distance metric. However, the problem of the *curse of dimensionality* is not unique to DBSCAN; it also affects other clustering algorithms that use the Euclidean distance metric, for example, k-means and hierarchical clustering algorithms. In addition, we have two hyperparameters in DBSCAN (MinPts and ε) that need to be optimized to yield good clustering results. Finding a good combination of MinPts and ε can be problematic if the density differences in the dataset are relatively large.

So far, we have seen three of the most fundamental categories of clustering algorithms: prototype-based clustering with k-means, agglomerative hierarchical clustering, and density-based clustering via DBSCAN. However, I also want to mention a fourth class of more advanced clustering algorithms that we have not covered in this chapter: **graph-based clustering**. Probably the most prominent members of the graph-based clustering family are the **spectral clustering** algorithms. Although there are many different implementations of spectral clustering, they all have in common that they use the eigenvectors of a similarity or distance matrix to derive the cluster relationships. Since spectral clustering is beyond the scope of this book, you can read the excellent tutorial by Ulrike von Luxburg to learn more about this topic. (*A tutorial on spectral clustering, U. Von Luxburg*, Statistics and Computing, 17(4): 395–416, 2007). It is freely available from arXiv at `http://arxiv.org/pdf/0711.0189v1.pdf`.

Note that, in practice, it is not always obvious which clustering algorithm will perform best on a given dataset, especially if the data comes in multiple dimensions that make it hard or impossible to visualize. Furthermore, it is important to emphasize that a successful clustering not only depends on the algorithm and its hyperparameters. Rather, the choice of an appropriate distance metric and the use of domain knowledge that can help guide the experimental setup can be even more important.

In the context of the curse of dimensionality, it is thus common practice to apply dimensionality reduction techniques prior to performing clustering. Such dimensionality reduction techniques for unsupervised datasets include principal component analysis and RBF kernel principal component analysis, which we covered in *Chapter 5, Compressing Data via Dimensionality Reduction*. Also, it is particularly common to compress datasets down to two-dimensional subspaces, which allows us to visualize the clusters and assigned labels using two-dimensional scatterplots, which are particularly helpful for evaluating the results.

Summary

In this chapter, you learned about three different clustering algorithms that can help us with the discovery of hidden structures or information in data. We started this chapter with a prototype-based approach, k-means, which clusters samples into spherical shapes based on a specified number of cluster centroids. Since clustering is an unsupervised method, we do not enjoy the luxury of ground truth labels to evaluate the performance of a model. Thus, we used intrinsic performance metrics such as the elbow method or silhouette analysis as an attempt to quantify the quality of clustering.

We then looked at a different approach to clustering: agglomerative hierarchical clustering. Hierarchical clustering does not require specifying the number of clusters up front, and the result can be visualized in a dendrogram representation, which can help with the interpretation of the results. The last clustering algorithm that we saw in this chapter was DBSCAN, an algorithm that groups points based on local densities and is capable of handling outliers and identifying non-globular shapes.

After this excursion into the field of unsupervised learning, it is now about time to introduce some of the most exciting machine learning algorithms for supervised learning: multilayer artificial neural networks. After their recent resurgence, neural networks are once again the hottest topic in machine learning research. Thanks to recently developed deep learning algorithms, neural networks are considered state-of-the-art for many complex tasks such as image classification and speech recognition. In *Chapter 12, Implementing a Multilayer Artificial Neural Network from Scratch*, we will construct our own multilayer neural network from scratch. In *Chapter 13, Parallelizing Neural Network Training with TensorFlow*, we will introduce powerful libraries that can help us to train complex network architectures most efficiently.

12
Implementing a Multilayer Artificial Neural Network from Scratch

As you may know, deep learning is getting a lot of attention from the press and is without any doubt the hottest topic in the machine learning field. Deep learning can be understood as a set of algorithms that were developed to train artificial neural networks with many layers most efficiently. In this chapter, you will learn the basic concepts of artificial neural networks so that you will be well-equipped for the following chapters, which will introduce advanced Python-based deep learning libraries and **Deep Neural Network** (**DNN**) architectures that are particularly well-suited for image and text analyses.

The topics that we will cover in this chapter are as follows:

- Getting a conceptual understanding of multilayer neural networks
- Implementing the fundamental backpropagation algorithm for neural network training from scratch
- Training a basic multilayer neural network for image classification

Modeling complex functions with artificial neural networks

At the beginning of this book, we started our journey through machine learning algorithms with artificial neurons in *Chapter 2, Training Simple Machine Learning Algorithms for Classification*. Artificial neurons represent the building blocks of the multilayer artificial neural networks that we will discuss in this chapter. The basic concept behind artificial neural networks was built upon hypotheses and models of how the human brain works to solve complex problem tasks. Although artificial neural networks have gained a lot of popularity in recent years, early studies of neural networks go back to the 1940s when Warren McCulloch and Walter Pitt first described how neurons could work.

However, in the decades that followed the first implementation of the **McCulloch-Pitt neuron** model—Rosenblatt's perceptron in the 1950s, many researchers and machine learning practitioners slowly began to lose interest in neural networks since no one had a good solution for training a neural network with multiple layers. Eventually, interest in neural networks was rekindled in 1986 when D.E. Rumelhart, G.E. Hinton, and R.J. Williams were involved in the (re)discovery and popularization of the backpropagation algorithm to train neural networks more efficiently, which we will discuss in more detail later in this chapter (*Learning representations by back-propagating errors, David E. Rumelhart, Geoffrey E. Hinton, Ronald J. Williams, Nature, 323* (6088): 533–536, *1986*). Readers who are interested in the history of **Artificial Intelligence** (**AI**), machine learning, and neural networks are also encouraged to read the Wikipedia article on *AI winter*, which are the periods of time where a large portion of the research community lost interest in the study of neural networks (`https://en.wikipedia.org/wiki/AI_winter`).

However, neural networks have never been as popular as they are today, thanks to the many major breakthroughs that have been made in the previous decade, which resulted in what we now call deep learning algorithms and architectures—neural networks that are composed of many layers. Neural networks are a hot topic not only in academic research but also in big technology companies such as Facebook, Microsoft, and Google, who invest heavily in artificial neural networks and deep learning research. As of today, complex neural networks powered by deep learning algorithms are considered state of the art when it comes to complex problem solving such as image and voice recognition. Popular examples of the products in our everyday life that are powered by deep learning are Google's image search and Google Translate—an application for smartphones that can automatically recognize text in images for real-time translation into more than 20 languages.

Many exciting applications of DNNs have been developed at major tech companies and the pharmaceutical industry as listed in the following, non-comprehensive list of examples:

- Facebook's DeepFace for tagging images (*DeepFace: Closing the Gap to Human-Level Performance in Face Verification, Y. Taigman, M. Yang, M. Ranzato, and L. Wolf*, IEEE Conference on **Computer Vision and Pattern Recognition (CVPR)**, pages 1701–1708, *2014*)

- Baidu's DeepSpeech, which is able to handle voice queries in Mandarin (*DeepSpeech: Scaling up end-to-end speech recognition, A. Hannun, C. Case, J. Casper, B. Catanzaro, G. Diamos, E. Elsen, R. Prenger, S. Satheesh, S. Sengupta, A. Coates,* and *Andrew Y. Ng*, arXiv preprint arXiv:1412.5567, *2014*)

- Google's new language translation service (*Google's Neural Machine Translation System: Bridging the Gap between Human and Machine Translation,* arXiv preprint arXiv:1412.5567, *2016*)

- Novel techniques for drug discovery and toxicity prediction (*Toxicity prediction using Deep Learning, T. Unterthiner, A. Mayr, G. Klambauer,* and *S. Hochreiter*, arXiv preprint arXiv:1503.01445, *2015*)

- A mobile application that can detect skin cancer with an accuracy similar to professionally trained dermatologists (*Dermatologist-level classification of skin cancer with deep neural networks, A. Esteva, B.Kuprel, R. A. Novoa, J. Ko, S. M. Swetter, H. M. Blau,* and *S.Thrun,* in *Nature 542,* no. *7639, 2017,* pages 115-118)

Single-layer neural network recap

This chapter is all about multilayer neural networks, how they work, and how to train them to solve complex problems. However, before we dig deeper into a particular multilayer neural network architecture, let's briefly reiterate some of the concepts of single-layer neural networks that we introduced in *Chapter 2*, *Training Simple Machine Learning Algorithms for Classification*, namely, the **ADAptive LInear NEuron (Adaline)** algorithm, which is shown in the following figure:

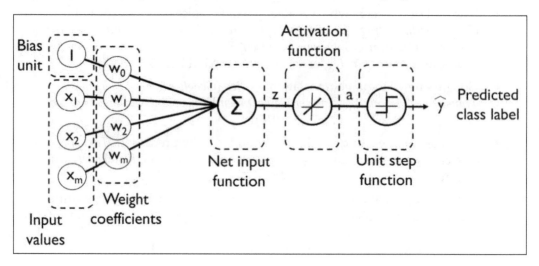

In *Chapter 2*, *Training Simple Machine Learning Algorithms for Classification*, we implemented the Adaline algorithm to perform binary classification, and we used the gradient descent optimization algorithm to learn the weight coefficients of the model. In every epoch (pass over the training set), we updated the weight vector w using the following update rule:

$$w := w + \Delta w, \quad \text{where } \Delta w = -\eta \nabla J(w)$$

In other words, we computed the gradient based on the whole training set and updated the weights of the model by taking a step into the opposite direction of the gradient $\nabla J(w)$. In order to find the optimal weights of the model, we optimized an objective function that we defined as the **Sum of Squared Errors (SSE)** cost function $J(w)$. Furthermore, we multiplied the gradient by a factor, the learning rate η, which we had to choose carefully to balance the speed of learning against the risk of overshooting the global minimum of the cost function.

In gradient descent optimization, we updated all weights simultaneously after each epoch, and we defined the partial derivative for each weight w_j in the weight vector **w** as follows:

$$\frac{\partial}{\partial w_j} J(\mathbf{w}) = -\sum_i \left(y^{(i)} - a^{(i)} \right) x_j^{(i)}$$

Here, $y^{(i)}$ is the target class label of a particular sample $x^{(i)}$, and $a^{(i)}$ is the activation of the neuron, which is a linear function in the special case of Adaline. Furthermore, we defined the activation function $\phi(\cdot)$ as follows:

$$\phi(z) = z = a$$

Here, the net input z is a linear combination of the weights that are connecting the input to the output layer:

$$z = \sum_j w_j x_j = \mathbf{w}^T \mathbf{x}$$

While we used the activation $\phi(z)$ to compute the gradient update, we implemented a threshold function to squash the continuous valued output into binary class labels for prediction:

$$\hat{y} = \begin{cases} 1 \ if \ g(z) \geq 0 \\ -1 \ \text{otherwise} \end{cases}$$

 Note that although Adaline consists of two layers, one input layer and one output layer, it is called single-layer network because of its single link between the input and output layers.

Also, we learned about a certain *trick* to accelerate the model learning, the so-called **stochastic gradient descent** optimization. Stochastic gradient descent approximates the cost from a single training sample (online learning) or a small subset of training samples (mini-batch learning). We will make use of this concept later in this chapter when we implement and train a multilayer perceptron. Apart from faster learning — due to the more frequent weight updates compared to gradient descent — its noisy nature is also regarded as beneficial when training multilayer neural networks with non-linear activation functions, which do not have a convex cost function. Here, the added noise can help to escape local cost minima, but we will discuss this topic in more detail later in this chapter.

Introducing the multilayer neural network architecture

In this section, you will learn how to connect multiple single neurons to a multilayer feedforward neural network; this special type of *fully connected* network is also called **Multilayer Perceptron (MLP)**. The following figure illustrates the concept of an MLP consisting of three layers:

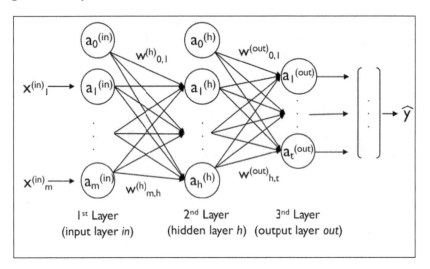

The MLP depicted in the preceding figure has one input layer, one hidden layer, and one output layer. The units in the hidden layer are fully connected to the input layer, and the output layer is fully connected to the hidden layer. If such a network has more than one hidden layer, we also call it a **deep artificial neural network**.

We can add an arbitrary number of hidden layers to the MLP to create deeper network architectures. Practically, we can think of the number of layers and units in a neural network as additional hyperparameters that we want to optimize for a given problem task using cross-validation techniques that we discussed in *Chapter 6, Learning Best Practices for Model Evaluation and Hyperparameter Tuning*.

However, the error gradients that we will calculate later via backpropagation will become increasingly small as more layers are added to a network. This vanishing gradient problem makes the model learning more challenging. Therefore, special algorithms have been developed to help train such deep neural network structures; this is known as **deep learning**.

As shown in the preceding figure, we denote the ith activation unit in the lth layer as $a_i^{(l)}$. To make the math and code implementations a bit more intuitive, we will not use numerical indices to refer to layers, but we will use the *in* superscript for the input layer, the *h* superscript for the hidden layer, and the *o* superscript for the output layer. For instance, $a_i^{(in)}$ refers to the ith value in the input layer, $a_i^{(h)}$ refers to the ith unit in the hidden layer, and $a_i^{(out)}$ refers to the ith unit in the output layer. Here, the activation units $a_0^{(in)}$ and $a_0^{(h)}$ are the **bias units**, which we set equal to 1. The activation of the units in the input layer is just its input plus the bias unit:

$$a^{(in)} = \begin{bmatrix} a_0^{(in)} \\ a_1^{(in)} \\ \vdots \\ a_m^{(in)} \end{bmatrix} = \begin{bmatrix} 1 \\ x_1^{(in)} \\ \vdots \\ x_m^{(in)} \end{bmatrix}$$

Later in this chapter, we will implement the multilayer perceptron using separate vectors for the bias unit, which makes the code implementation more efficient and easier to read. This concept is also used by TensorFlow, a deep learning library that we will introduce in *Chapter 13, Parallelizing Neural Network Training with TensorFlow*. However, the mathematical equations that will follow, would appear more complex or convoluted if we had to work with additional variables for the bias. However, note that the computation via appending 1s to the input vector (as shown previously) and using a weight variable as bias is exactly the same as operating with separate bias vectors; it is merely a different convention.

Each unit in layer l is connected to all units in layer $l+1$ via a weight coefficient. For example, the connection between the kth unit in layer l to the jth unit in layer $l+1$ will be written as $w_{k,j}^{(l+1)}$. Referring back to the previous figure, we denote the weight matrix that connects the input to the hidden layer as $W^{(h)}$, and we write the matrix that connects the hidden layer to the output layer as $W^{(out)}$.

While one unit in the output layer would suffice for a binary classification task, we saw a more general form of a neural network in the preceding figure, which allows us to perform multiclass classification via a generalization of the **One-versus-All** (**OvA**) technique. To better understand how this works, remember the one-hot representation of categorical variables that we introduced in *Chapter 4, Building Good Training Sets – Data Preprocessing*. For example, we can encode the three class labels in the familiar Iris dataset (*0=Setosa, 1=Versicolor, 2=Virginica*) as follows:

$$0 = \begin{bmatrix} 1 \\ 0 \\ 0 \end{bmatrix}, 1 = \begin{bmatrix} 0 \\ 1 \\ 0 \end{bmatrix}, 2 = \begin{bmatrix} 0 \\ 0 \\ 1 \end{bmatrix}$$

This one-hot vector representation allows us to tackle classification tasks with an arbitrary number of unique class labels present in the training set.

If you are new to neural network representations, the indexing notation (subscripts and superscripts) may look a little bit confusing at first. What may seem overly complicated at first will make much more sense in later sections when we vectorize the neural network representation. As introduced earlier, we summarize the weights that connect the input and hidden layers by a matrix $W^{(h)} \in \mathbb{R}^{m \times d}$, where d is the number of hidden units and m is the number of input units including the bias unit. Since it is important to internalize this notation to follow the concepts later in this chapter, let's summarize what we have just learned in a descriptive illustration of a simplified 3-4-3 multilayer perceptron:

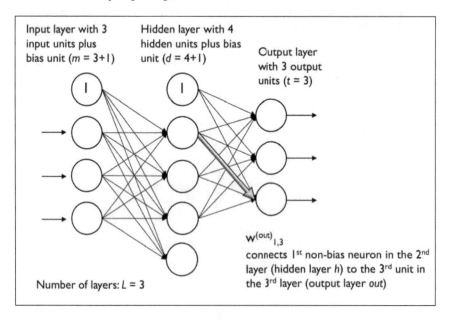

Activating a neural network via forward propagation

In this section, we will describe the process of **forward propagation** to calculate the output of an MLP model. To understand how it fits into the context of learning an MLP model, let's summarize the MLP learning procedure in three simple steps:

1. Starting at the input layer, we forward propagate the patterns of the training data through the network to generate an output.

2. Based on the network's output, we calculate the error that we want to minimize using a cost function that we will describe later.

3. We backpropagate the error, find its derivative with respect to each weight in the network, and update the model.

Finally, after we repeat these three steps for multiple epochs and learn the weights of the MLP, we use forward propagation to calculate the network output and apply a threshold function to obtain the predicted class labels in the one-hot representation, which we described in the previous section.

Now, let's walk through the individual steps of forward propagation to generate an output from the patterns in the training data. Since each unit in the hidden layer is connected to all units in the input layers, we first calculate the activation unit of the hidden layer $a_1^{(h)}$ as follows:

$$z_1^{(h)} = a_0^{(in)} w_{0,1}^{(h)} + a_1^{(in)} w_{1,1}^{(h)} + \cdots + a_m^{(in)} w_{m,1}^{(h)}$$

$$a_1^{(h)} = \phi\left(z_1^{(h)}\right)$$

Here, $z_1^{(h)}$ is the net input and $\phi(\cdot)$ is the activation function, which has to be differentiable to learn the weights that connect the neurons using a gradient-based approach. To be able to solve complex problems such as image classification, we need non-linear activation functions in our MLP model, for example, the sigmoid (logistic) activation function that we remember from the section about logistic regression in *Chapter 3, A Tour of Machine Learning Classifiers Using scikit-learn*:

$$\phi(z) = \frac{1}{1 + e^{-z}}$$

As we can remember, the sigmoid function is an S-shaped curve that maps the net input z onto a logistic distribution in the range 0 to 1, which cuts the y-axis at $z = 0$, as shown in the following graph:

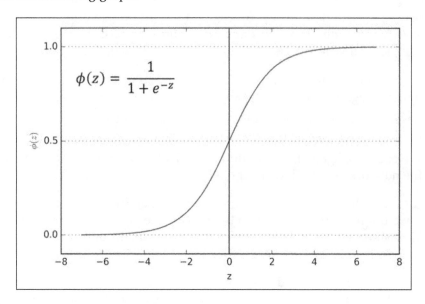

MLP is a typical example of a feedforward artificial neural network. The term **feedforward** refers to the fact that each layer serves as the input to the next layer without loops, in contrast to recurrent neural networks—an architecture that we will discuss later in this chapter and discuss in more detail in *Chapter 16, Modeling Sequential Data Using Recurrent Neural Networks*. The term *multilayer perceptron* may sound a little bit confusing since the artificial neurons in this network architecture are typically sigmoid units, not perceptrons. Intuitively, we can think of the neurons in the MLP as logistic regression units that return values in the continuous range between 0 and 1.

For purposes of code efficiency and readability, we will now write the activation in a more compact form using the concepts of basic linear algebra, which will allow us to vectorize our code implementation via NumPy rather than writing multiple nested and computationally expensive Python `for` loops:

$$z^{(h)} = a^{(in)}W^{(h)}$$

$$a^{(h)} = \phi\left(z^{(h)}\right)$$

Here, $a^{(in)}$ is our *1 x m* dimensional feature vector of a sample $x^{(in)}$ plus a bias unit. $W^{(h)}$ is an *m x d* dimensional weight matrix where *d* is the number of units in the hidden layer. After matrix-vector multiplication, we obtain the *1 x d* dimensional net input vector $z^{(h)}$ to calculate the activation $a^{(h)}$ (where $a^{(h)} \in \mathbb{R}^{1 \times d}$). Furthermore, we can generalize this computation to all *n* samples in the training set:

$$Z^{(h)} = A^{(in)}W^{(h)}$$

Here, $A^{(in)}$ is now an *n x m* matrix, and the matrix-matrix multiplication will result in an *n x d* dimensional net input matrix $Z^{(h)}$. Finally, we apply the activation function $\phi(\cdot)$ to each value in the net input matrix to get the *n x d* activation matrix $A^{(h)}$ for the next layer (here, the output layer):

$$A^{(h)} = \phi\left(Z^{(h)}\right)$$

Similarly, we can write the activation of the output layer in vectorized form for multiple samples:

$$Z^{(out)} = A^{(h)}W^{(out)}$$

Here, we multiply the *d x t* matrix $W^{(out)}$ (*t* is the number of output units) by the *n x d* dimensional matrix $A^{(h)}$ to obtain the *n x t* dimensional matrix $Z^{(out)}$ (the columns in this matrix represent the outputs for each sample).

Lastly, we apply the sigmoid activation function to obtain the continuous valued output of our network:

$$A^{(out)} = \phi\left(Z^{(out)}\right), \qquad A^{(out)} \in \mathbb{R}^{n \times t}$$

Classifying handwritten digits

In the previous section, we covered a lot of the theory around neural networks, which can be a little bit overwhelming if you are new to this topic. Before we continue with the discussion of the algorithm for learning the weights of the MLP model, backpropagation, let's take a short break from the theory and see a neural network in action.

The neural network theory can be quite complex, thus I want to recommend two additional resources, which cover some of the concepts that we discuss in this chapter in more detail:

- *Chapter 6, Deep Feedforward Networks, Deep Learning, I. Goodfellow, Y. Bengio*, and *A. Courville, MIT Press, 2016.* (Manuscripts freely accessible at `http://www.deeplearningbook.org`.)
- *Pattern Recognition and Machine Learning, C. M. Bishop and others, Volume 1. Springer New York, 2006.*

In this section, we will implement and train our first multilayer neural network to classify handwritten digits from the popular **Mixed National Institute of Standards and Technology (MNIST)** dataset that has been constructed by Yann LeCun and others, and serves as a popular benchmark dataset for machine learning algorithms (*Gradient-Based Learning Applied to Document Recognition, Y. LeCun, L. Bottou, Y. Bengio*, and *P. Haffner*, Proceedings of the IEEE, 86(11): 2278-2324, *November 1998*).

Obtaining the MNIST dataset

The MNIST dataset is publicly available at `http://yann.lecun.com/exdb/mnist/` and consists of the following four parts:

- **Training set images**: `train-images-idx3-ubyte.gz` (9.9 MB, 47 MB unzipped, and 60,000 samples)
- **Training set labels**: `train-labels-idx1-ubyte.gz` (29 KB, 60 KB unzipped, and 60,000 labels)
- **Test set images**: `t10k-images-idx3-ubyte.gz` (1.6 MB, 7.8 MB, unzipped and 10,000 samples)
- **Test set labels**: `t10k-labels-idx1-ubyte.gz` (5 KB, 10 KB unzipped, and 10,000 labels)

The MNIST dataset was constructed from two datasets of the US **National Institute of Standards and Technology (NIST)**. The training set consists of handwritten digits from 250 different people, 50 percent high school students, and 50 percent employees from the Census Bureau. Note that the test set contains handwritten digits from different people following the same split. After downloading the files, I recommend that you unzip the files using the Unix/Linux `gzip` tool from the Terminal for efficiency, using the following command in your local MNIST download directory:

```
gzip *ubyte.gz -d
```

Alternatively, you could use your favorite unzipping tool if you are working with a machine running on Microsoft Windows. The images are stored in byte format, and we will read them into NumPy arrays that we will use to train and test our MLP implementation. In order to do that, we will define the following helper function:

```python
import os
import struct
import numpy as np

def load_mnist(path, kind='train'):
    """Load MNIST data from `path`"""
    labels_path = os.path.join(path,
                               '%s-labels-idx1-ubyte' % kind)
    images_path = os.path.join(path,
                               '%s-images-idx3-ubyte' % kind)

    with open(labels_path, 'rb') as lbpath:
        magic, n = struct.unpack('>II',
                                 lbpath.read(8))
        labels = np.fromfile(lbpath,
                             dtype=np.uint8)

    with open(images_path, 'rb') as imgpath:
        magic, num, rows, cols = struct.unpack(">IIII",
                                               imgpath.read(16))
        images = np.fromfile(imgpath,
                             dtype=np.uint8).reshape(
                             len(labels), 784)
        images = ((images / 255.) - .5) * 2

    return images, labels
```

The load_mnist function returns two arrays, the first being an *n* x *m* dimensional NumPy array (images), where *n* is the number of samples and *m* is the number of features (here, pixels). The training dataset consists of 60,000 training digits and the test set contains 10,000 samples, respectively. The images in the MNIST dataset consist of 28 x 28 pixels, and each pixel is represented by a gray scale intensity value. Here, we unroll the 28 x 28 pixels into one-dimensional row vectors, which represent the rows in our images array (784 per row or image). The second array (labels) returned by the load_mnist function contains the corresponding target variable, the class labels (integers 0-9) of the handwritten digits.

The way we read in the image might seem a little bit strange at first:

```
>>> magic, n = struct.unpack('>II', lbpath.read(8))
>>> labels = np.fromfile(lbpath, dtype=np.int8)
```

To understand how those two lines of code work, let's take a look at the dataset description from the MNIST website:

```
[offset]  [type]           [value]            [description]
0000      32 bit integer   0x00000801(2049)   magic number (MSB first)
0004      32 bit integer   60000              number of items
0008      unsigned byte    ??                 label
0009      unsigned byte    ??                 label
........
xxxx      unsigned byte    ??                 label
```

Using the two preceding lines of code, we first read in the magic number, which is a description of the file protocol as well as the number of items (n) from the file buffer before we read the following bytes into a NumPy array using the `fromfile` method. The `fmt` parameter value `'>II'` that we passed as an argument to `struct.unpack` can be composed into the two following parts:

- `>`: This is big-endian — it defines the order in which a sequence of bytes is stored; if you are unfamiliar with the terms big-endian and little-endian, you can find an excellent article about *Endianness* on Wikipedia: `https://en.wikipedia.org/wiki/Endianness`

- `I`: This is an unsigned integer

Finally, we also normalized the pixels values in MNIST to the range -1 to 1 (originally 0 to 255) via the following code line:

```
images = ((images / 255.) - .5) * 2
```

The reason behind this is that gradient-based optimization is much more stable under these conditions as discussed in *Chapter 2, Training Simple Machine Learning Algorithms for Classification*. Note that we scaled the images on a pixel-by-pixel basis, which is different from the feature scaling approach that we took in previous chapters. Previously, we derived scaling parameters from the training set and used these to scale each column in the training set and test set. However, when working with image pixels, centering them at zero and rescaling them to a [-1, 1] range is also common and usually works well in practice.

Another recently developed trick to improve convergence in gradient-based optimization through input scaling is batch normalization, which is an advanced topic that we will not cover in this book. However, if you are interested in deep learning applications and research, I highly recommend that you read more about batch normalization in the excellent research article *Batch Normalization: Accelerating Deep Network Training by Reducing Internal Covariate Shift* by Sergey Ioffe and Christian Szegedy (2015, https://arxiv.org/abs/1502.03167).

By executing the following code, we will now load the 60,000 training instances as well as the 10,000 test samples from the local directory where we unzipped the MNIST dataset (in the following code snippet, it is assumed that the downloaded MNIST files were unzipped to the same directory in which this code was executed):

```
>>> X_train, y_train = load_mnist('', kind='train')
>>> print('Rows: %d, columns: %d'
...        % (X_train.shape[0], X_train.shape[1]))
Rows: 60000, columns: 784

>>> X_test, y_test = load_mnist('', kind='t10k')
>>> print('Rows: %d, columns: %d'
...        % (X_test.shape[0], X_test.shape[1]))
Rows: 10000, columns: 784
```

To get an idea of how those images in MNIST look, let's visualize examples of the digits 0-9 after reshaping the 784-pixel vectors from our feature matrix into the original 28 × 28 image that we can plot via Matplotlib's imshow function:

```
>>> import matplotlib.pyplot as plt

>>> fig, ax = plt.subplots(nrows=2, ncols=5,
...                        sharex=True, sharey=True)
>>> ax = ax.flatten()
>>> for i in range(10):
...     img = X_train[y_train == i][0].reshape(28, 28)
...     ax[i].imshow(img, cmap='Greys')

>>> ax[0].set_xticks([])
>>> ax[0].set_yticks([])
>>> plt.tight_layout()
>>> plt.show()
```

We should now see a plot of the 2 x 5 subfigures showing a representative image of each unique digit:

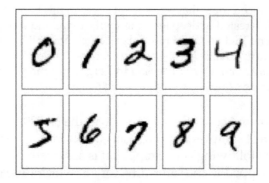

In addition, let's also plot multiple examples of the same digit to see how different the handwriting really is:

```
>>> fig, ax = plt.subplots(nrows=5,
...                         ncols=5,
...                         sharex=True,
...                         sharey=True)
>>> ax = ax.flatten()
>>> for i in range(25):
...     img = X_train[y_train == 7][i].reshape(28, 28)
...     ax[i].imshow(img, cmap='Greys')
>>> ax[0].set_xticks([])
>>> ax[0].set_yticks([])
>>> plt.tight_layout()
>>> plt.show()
```

After executing the code, we should now see the first 25 variants of the digit 7:

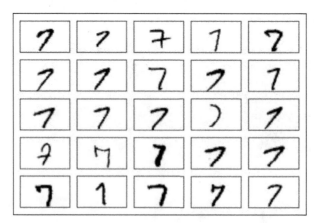

After we've gone through all the previous steps, it is a good idea to save the scaled images in a format that we can load more quickly into a new Python session to avoid the overhead of reading in and processing the data again. When we are working with NumPy arrays, an efficient yet most convenient method to save multidimensional arrays to disk is NumPy's `savez` function (the official documentation can be found here: `https://docs.scipy.org/doc/numpy/reference/generated/numpy.savez.html`).

In short, the `savez` function is analogous to Python's `pickle` module that we used in *Chapter 9, Embedding a Machine Learning Model into a Web Application*, but optimized for storing NumPy arrays. The `savez` function produces zipped archives of our data, producing `.npz` files that contain files in the `.npy` format; if you want to learn more about this format, you can find a nice explanation, including a discussion about advantages and disadvantages, in the NumPy documentation: `https://docs.scipy.org/doc/numpy/neps/npy-format.html`. Further, instead of using `savez`, we will use `savez_compressed`, which uses the same syntax as `savez`, but further compresses the output file down to substantially smaller file sizes (approximately 22 MB versus approximately 400 MB in this case). The following code snippet will save both the training and test datasets to the archive file `'mnist_scaled.npz'`:

```
>>> import numpy as np

>>> np.savez_compressed('mnist_scaled.npz',
...                      X_train=X_train,
...                      y_train=y_train,
...                      X_test=X_test,
...                      y_test=y_test)
```

After we created the `.npz` files, we can load the preprocessed MNIST image arrays using NumPy's `load` function as follows:

```
>>> mnist = np.load('mnist_scaled.npz')
```

The `mnist` variable now references to an object that can access the four data arrays as we provided them keyword arguments to the `savez_compressed` function, which are listed under the files attribute list of the `mnist` object:

```
>>> mnist.files
['X_train', 'y_train', 'X_test', 'y_test']
```

For instance, to load the training data into our current Python session, we will access the `'X_train'` array as follows (similar to a Python dictionary):

```
>>> X_train = mnist['X_train']
```

Using a list comprehension, we can retrieve all four data arrays as follows:

```
>>> X_train, y_train, X_test, y_test = [mnist[f] for
...                                     f in mnist.files]
```

Note that while the preceding `np.savez_compressed` and `np.load` examples are not essential for executing the code in this chapter, it serves as a demonstration of how to save and load NumPy arrays conveniently and efficiently.

Implementing a multilayer perceptron

In this subsection, we will now implement the code of an MLP with one input, one hidden, and one output layers to classify the images in the MNIST dataset. I have tried to keep the code as simple as possible. However, it may seem a little bit complicated at first, and I encourage you to download the sample code for this chapter from the Packt Publishing website or from GitHub (`https://github.com/rasbt/python-machine-learning-book-2nd-edition`) so that you can view this MLP implementation annotated with comments and syntax highlighting for better readability.

If you are not running the code from the accompanying Jupyter Notebook file or don't have access to the internet, I recommend that you copy the `NeuralNetMLP` code from this chapter into a Python script file in your current working directory, for example, `neuralnet.py`, which you can then import into your current Python session via the following command:

```
from neuralnet import NeuralNetMLP
```

The code will contain parts that we have not talked about yet, such as the backpropagation algorithm, but most of the code should look familiar to you based on the Adaline implementation in *Chapter 2*, *Training Simple Machine Learning Algorithms for Classification*, and the discussion of forward propagation in earlier sections.

Do not worry if not all of the code makes immediate sense to you; we will follow up on certain parts later in this chapter. However, going over the code at this stage can make it easier to follow the theory later.

The following is the implementation of a multilayer perceptron:

```
import numpy as np
import sys

class NeuralNetMLP(object):
    """ Feedforward neural network / Multi-layer perceptron
        classifier.
```

```
Parameters

------------

n_hidden : int (default: 30)
    Number of hidden units.
l2 : float (default: 0.)
    Lambda value for L2-regularization.
    No regularization if l2=0. (default)
epochs : int (default: 100)
    Number of passes over the training set.
eta : float (default: 0.001)
    Learning rate.
shuffle : bool (default: True)
    Shuffles training data every epoch
    if True to prevent circles.
minibatch_size : int (default: 1)
    Number of training samples per minibatch.
seed : int (default: None)
    Random seed for initializing weights and shuffling.

Attributes
-----------

eval_ : dict
  Dictionary collecting the cost, training accuracy,
  and validation accuracy for each epoch during training.

"""
def __init__(self, n_hidden=30,
             l2=0., epochs=100, eta=0.001,
             shuffle=True, minibatch_size=1, seed=None):

    self.random = np.random.RandomState(seed)
    self.n_hidden = n_hidden
    self.l2 = l2
    self.epochs = epochs
    self.eta = eta
    self.shuffle = shuffle
    self.minibatch_size = minibatch_size

def _onehot(self, y, n_classes):
    """Encode labels into one-hot representation

    Parameters
    -----------
```

```
        y : array, shape = [n_samples]
            Target values.

        Returns
        -----------
        onehot : array, shape = (n_samples, n_labels)


        """
        onehot = np.zeros((n_classes, y.shape[0]))
        for idx, val in enumerate(y.astype(int)):
            onehot[val, idx] = 1.
        return onehot.T

    def _sigmoid(self, z):
        """Compute logistic function (sigmoid)"""
        return 1. / (1. + np.exp(-np.clip(z, -250, 250)))

    def _forward(self, X):
        """Compute forward propagation step"""

        # step 1: net input of hidden layer
        # [n_samples, n_features] dot [n_features, n_hidden]
        # -> [n_samples, n_hidden]
        z_h = np.dot(X, self.w_h) + self.b_h

        # step 2: activation of hidden layer
        a_h = self._sigmoid(z_h)

        # step 3: net input of output layer
        # [n_samples, n_hidden] dot [n_hidden, n_classlabels]
        # -> [n_samples, n_classlabels]

        z_out = np.dot(a_h, self.w_out) + self.b_out

        # step 4: activation output layer
        a_out = self._sigmoid(z_out)

        return z_h, a_h, z_out, a_out

    def _compute_cost(self, y_enc, output):
        """Compute cost function.

        Parameters
        ----------
```

```
        y_enc : array, shape = (n_samples, n_labels)
            one-hot encoded class labels.
        output : array, shape = [n_samples, n_output_units]
            Activation of the output layer (forward propagation)

        Returns
        ---------
        cost : float
            Regularized cost

        """
        L2_term = (self.l2 *
                   (np.sum(self.w_h ** 2.) +
                    np.sum(self.w_out ** 2.)))

        term1 = -y_enc * (np.log(output))
        term2 = (1. - y_enc) * np.log(1. - output)
        cost = np.sum(term1 - term2) + L2_term
        return cost

    def predict(self, X):
        """Predict class labels

        Parameters
        ----------
        X : array, shape = [n_samples, n_features]
            Input layer with original features.

        Returns:
        ----------
        y_pred : array, shape = [n_samples]
            Predicted class labels.

        """
        z_h, a_h, z_out, a_out = self._forward(X)
        y_pred = np.argmax(z_out, axis=1)
        return y_pred

    def fit(self, X_train, y_train, X_valid, y_valid):
        """ Learn weights from training data.

        Parameters
        ----------
        X_train : array, shape = [n_samples, n_features]
```

```
        Input layer with original features.
    y_train : array, shape = [n_samples]
        Target class labels.
    X_valid : array, shape = [n_samples, n_features]
        Sample features for validation during training
    y_valid : array, shape = [n_samples]
        Sample labels for validation during training

    Returns:
    ----------
    self

    """
    n_output = np.unique(y_train).shape[0] # no. of class
                                           #labels

    n_features = X_train.shape[1]

    ########################
    # Weight initialization
    ########################

    # weights for input -> hidden
    self.b_h = np.zeros(self.n_hidden)
    self.w_h = self.random.normal(loc=0.0, scale=0.1,
                        size=(n_features,
                              self.n_hidden))

    # weights for hidden -> output
    self.b_out = np.zeros(n_output)
    self.w_out = self.random.normal(loc=0.0, scale=0.1,
                          size=(self.n_hidden,
                                n_output))

    epoch_strlen = len(str(self.epochs))  # for progr. format.
    self.eval_ = {'cost': [], 'train_acc': [], 'valid_acc': \
              []}

    y_train_enc = self._onehot(y_train, n_output)

    # iterate over training epochs
    for i in range(self.epochs):

        # iterate over minibatches
```

```
indices = np.arange(X_train.shape[0])

if self.shuffle:
    self.random.shuffle(indices)

for start_idx in range(0, indices.shape[0] -\
                      self.minibatch_size +\
                      1, self.minibatch_size):
    batch_idx = indices[start_idx:start_idx +\
                      self.minibatch_size]

    # forward propagation
    z_h, a_h, z_out, a_out = \
        self._forward(X_train[batch_idx])

    #################
    # Backpropagation
    #################

    # [n_samples, n_classlabels]
    sigma_out = a_out - y_train_enc[batch_idx]

    # [n_samples, n_hidden]
    sigmoid_derivative_h = a_h * (1. - a_h)

    # [n_samples, n_classlabels] dot [n_classlabels,
    #                                n_hidden]
    # -> [n_samples, n_hidden]
    sigma_h = (np.dot(sigma_out, self.w_out.T) *
              sigmoid_derivative_h)

    # [n_features, n_samples] dot [n_samples,
    #                                n_hidden]
    # -> [n_features, n_hidden]
    grad_w_h = np.dot(X_train[batch_idx].T, sigma_h)
    grad_b_h = np.sum(sigma_h, axis=0)

    # [n_hidden, n_samples] dot [n_samples,
    #                                n_classlabels]
    # -> [n_hidden, n_classlabels]
    grad_w_out = np.dot(a_h.T, sigma_out)
    grad_b_out = np.sum(sigma_out, axis=0)

    # Regularization and weight updates
```

```
            delta_w_h = (grad_w_h + self.l2*self.w_h)
            delta_b_h = grad_b_h # bias is not regularized
            self.w_h -= self.eta * delta_w_h
            self.b_h -= self.eta * delta_b_h

            delta_w_out = (grad_w_out + self.l2*self.w_out)
            delta_b_out = grad_b_out # bias is not regularized
            self.w_out -= self.eta * delta_w_out
            self.b_out -= self.eta * delta_b_out

        #############
        # Evaluation
        #############

        # Evaluation after each epoch during training
        z_h, a_h, z_out, a_out = self._forward(X_train)

        cost = self._compute_cost(y_enc=y_train_enc,
                                  output=a_out)

        y_train_pred = self.predict(X_train)
        y_valid_pred = self.predict(X_valid)

        train_acc = ((np.sum(y_train ==
                     y_train_pred)).astype(np.float) /
                     X_train.shape[0])
        valid_acc = ((np.sum(y_valid ==
                     y_valid_pred)).astype(np.float) /
                     X_valid.shape[0])

        sys.stderr.write('\r%0*d/%d | Cost: %.2f '
                         '| Train/Valid Acc.: %.2f%%/%.2f%% '
                         %
                         (epoch_strlen, i+1, self.epochs,
                          cost,
                          train_acc*100, valid_acc*100))
        sys.stderr.flush()

        self.eval_['cost'].append(cost)
        self.eval_['train_acc'].append(train_acc)
        self.eval_['valid_acc'].append(valid_acc)

    return self
```

Once you're done with executing this code, let's now initialize a new 784-100-10 MLP—a neural network with 784 input units (n_features), 100 hidden units (n_hidden), and 10 output units (n_output):

```
>>>nn = NeuralNetMLP(n_hidden=100,
...                  l2=0.01,
...                  epochs=200,
...                  eta=0.0005,
...                  minibatch_size=100,
...                  shuffle=True,
...                  seed=1)
```

If you read through the NeuralNetMLP code, you've probably already guessed what these parameters are for. Here, you find a short summary of these:

- l2: This is the λ parameter for L2 regularization to decrease the degree of overfitting.

- epochs: This is the number of passes over the training set.

- eta: This is the learning rate η.

- shuffle: This is for shuffling the training set prior to every epoch to prevent that the algorithm gets stuck in circles.

- seed: This is a random seed for shuffling and weight initialization.

- minibatch_size: This is the number of training samples in each mini-batch when splitting of the training data in each epoch for stochastic gradient descent. The gradient is computed for each mini-batch separately instead of the entire training data for faster learning.

Next, we train the MLP using 55,000 samples from the already shuffled MNIST training dataset and use the remaining 5,000 samples for validation during training. Note that training the neural network may take up to 5 minutes on standard desktop computer hardware.

As you may have noticed from the preceding code implementation, we implemented the fit method so that it takes four input arguments: training images, training labels, validation images, and validation labels. In neural network training, it is really useful to already compare training and validation accuracy during training, which helps us judge whether the network model performs well, given the architecture and hyperparameters.

In general, training (deep) neural networks is relatively expensive compared with the other models we discussed so far. Thus, we want to stop it early in certain circumstances and start over with different hyperparameter settings. Alternatively, if we find that it increasingly tends to overfit the training data (noticeable by an increasing gap between training and validation set performance), we may want to stop the training early as well.

Now, to start the training, we execute the following code:

```
>>> nn.fit(X_train=X_train[:55000],
...        y_train=y_train[:55000],
...        X_valid=X_train[55000:],
...        y_valid=y_train[55000:])
200/200 | Cost: 5065.78 | Train/Valid Acc.: 99.28%/97.98%
```

In our `NeuralNetMLP` implementation, we also defined an `eval_` attribute that collects the cost, training, and validation accuracy for each epoch so that we can visualize the results using Matplotlib:

```
>>> import matplotlib.pyplot as plt
>>> plt.plot(range(nn.epochs), nn.eval_['cost'])
>>> plt.ylabel('Cost')
>>> plt.xlabel('Epochs')
>>> plt.show()
```

The preceding code plots the cost over the 200 epochs, as shown in the following graph:

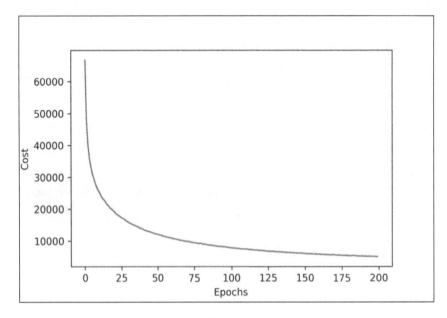

As we can see, the cost decreased substantially during the first 100 epochs and seems to slowly converge in the last 100 epochs. However, the small slope between epoch 175 and epoch 200 indicates that the cost would further decrease with a training over additional epochs.

Next, let's take a look at the training and validation accuracy:

```
>>> plt.plot(range(nn.epochs), nn.eval_['train_acc'],
...          label='training')
>>> plt.plot(range(nn.epochs), nn.eval_['valid_acc'],
...          label='validation', linestyle='--')
>>> plt.ylabel('Accuracy')
>>> plt.xlabel('Epochs')
>>> plt.legend()
>>> plt.show()
```

The preceding code examples plot those accuracy values over the 200 training epochs, as shown in the following figure:

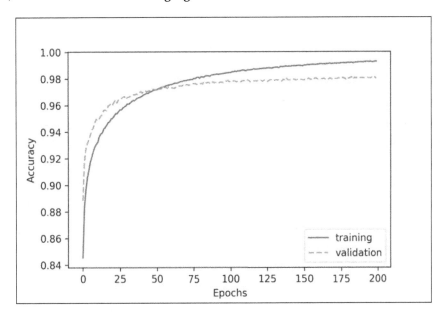

The plot reveals that the gap between training and validation accuracy increases the more epochs we train the network. At approximately the 50th epoch, the training and validation accuracy values are equal, and then, the network starts overfitting the training data.

Note that this example was chosen deliberately to illustrate the effect of overfitting and demonstrate why it is useful to compare the validation and training accuracy values during training. One way to decrease the effect of overfitting is to increase the regularization strength—for example, by setting `l2=0.1`. Another useful technique to tackle overfitting in neural networks, dropout, will be covered in *Chapter 15, Classifying Images with Deep Convolutional Neural Networks*.

Finally, let's evaluate the generalization performance of the model by calculating the prediction accuracy on the test set:

```
>>> y_test_pred = nn.predict(X_test)
>>> acc = (np.sum(y_test == y_test_pred)
...         .astype(np.float) / X_test.shape[0])
>>> print('Training accuracy: %.2f%%' % (acc * 100))
Test accuracy: 97.54%
```

Despite the slight overfitting on the training data, our relatively simple one-hidden layer neural network achieved a relatively good performance on the test dataset, similar to the validation set accuracy (97.98 percent).

To further fine-tune the model, we could change the number of hidden units, values of the regularization parameters, and the learning rate or use various other tricks that have been developed over the years but are beyond the scope of this book. In *Chapter 14, Going Deeper – The Mechanics of TensorFlow*, you will learn about a different neural network architecture that is known for its good performance on image datasets. Also, the chapter will introduce additional performance-enhancing tricks such as adaptive learning rates, momentum learning, and dropout.

Lastly, let's take a look at some of the images that our MLP struggles with:

```
>>> miscl_img = X_test[y_test != y_test_pred][:25]
>>> correct_lab = y_test[y_test != y_test_pred][:25]
>>> miscl_lab= y_test_pred[y_test != y_test_pred][:25]

>>> fig, ax = plt.subplots(nrows=5,
...                        ncols=5,
...                        sharex=True,
...                        sharey=True,)
>>> ax = ax.flatten()
>>> for i in range(25):
...     img = miscl_img[i].reshape(28, 28)
...     ax[i].imshow(img,
...             cmap='Greys',
...             interpolation='nearest')
...     ax[i].set_title('%d) t: %d p: %d'
```

```
    . . .                      % (i+1, correct_lab[i], miscl_lab[i]))

>>> ax[0].set_xticks([])
>>> ax[0].set_yticks([])
>>> plt.tight_layout()
>>> plt.show()
```

We should now see a 5 x 5 subplot matrix where the first number in the subtitles indicates the plot index, the second number represents the true class label (t), and the third number stands for the predicted class label (p):

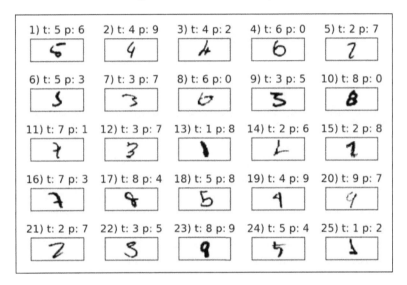

As we can see in the preceding figure, some of those images are even challenging for us humans to classify correctly. For example, the 6 in subplot 8 really looks like a carelessly drawn 0, and the 8 in subplot 23 could be a 9 due to the narrow lower part combined with the bold line.

Training an artificial neural network

Now that we have seen a neural network in action and have gained a basic understanding of how it works by looking over the code, let's dig a little bit deeper into some of the concepts, such as the logistic cost function and the backpropagation algorithm that we implemented to learn the weights.

Computing the logistic cost function

The logistic cost function that we implemented as the `_compute_cost` method is actually pretty simple to follow since it is the same cost function that we described in the logistic regression section in *Chapter 3, A Tour of Machine Learning Classifiers Using scikit-learn*:

$$J(w) = -\sum_{i=1}^{n} y^{[i]} \log\left(a^{[i]}\right) + \left(1 - y^{[i]}\right) \log\left(1 - a^{[i]}\right)$$

Here, $a^{[i]}$ is the sigmoid activation of the ith sample in the dataset, which we compute in the forward propagation step:

$$a^{[i]} = \phi\left(z^{[i]}\right)$$

Again, note that in this context, the superscript *[i]* is an index for training samples, not layers.

Now, let's add a regularization term, which allows us to reduce the degree of overfitting. As you recall from earlier chapters, the L2 regularization term is defined as follows (remember that we don't regularize the bias units):

$$L2 = \lambda \|w\|_2^2 = \lambda \sum_{j=1}^{m} w_j^2$$

By adding the L2 regularization term to our logistic cost function, we obtain the following equation:

$$J(w) = -\left[\sum_{i=1}^{n} y^{[i]} \log\left(a^{[i]}\right) + \left(1 - y^{[i]}\right) \log\left(1 - a^{[i]}\right)\right] + \frac{\lambda}{2} \|w\|_2^2$$

Since we implemented an MLP for multiclass classification that returns an output vector of t elements that we need to compare to the $t \times 1$ dimensional target vector in the one-hot encoding representation, for example, the activation of the third layer and the target class (here, class 2) for a particular sample may look like this:

$$a^{(out)} = \begin{bmatrix} 0.1 \\ 0.9 \\ \vdots \\ 0.3 \end{bmatrix}, \quad y = \begin{bmatrix} 0 \\ 1 \\ \vdots \\ 0 \end{bmatrix}$$

Thus, we need to generalize the logistic cost function to all t activation units in our network. Thus, the cost function (without the regularization term) becomes the following:

$$J(W) = -\sum_{i=1}^{n}\sum_{j=1}^{t} y_j^{[i]} log\left(a^{[i]}_j\right) + \left(1 - y_j^{[i]}\right) log\left(1 - a^{[i]}_j\right)$$

Here, again, the superscript *(i)* is the index of a particular sample in our training set.

The following generalized regularization term may look a little bit complicated at first, but here we are just calculating the sum of all weights of an l layer (without the bias term) that we added to the first column:

$$J(W) = -\left[\sum_{i=1}^{n}\sum_{j=1}^{t} y_j^{[i]} log\left(a^{[i]}_j\right) + \left(1 - y_j^{[i]}\right) log\left(1 - a^{[i]}_j\right)\right] + \frac{\lambda}{2}\sum_{l=1}^{L-1}\sum_{i=1}^{u_l}\sum_{j=1}^{u_{l+1}}\left(w_{j,i}^{(l)}\right)^2$$

Here, u_l refers to the number of units in a given layer l, and the following expression represents the penalty term:

$$\frac{\lambda}{2}\sum_{l=1}^{L-1}\sum_{i=1}^{u_l}\sum_{j=1}^{u_{l+1}}\left(w_{j,i}^{(l)}\right)^2$$

Remember that our goal is to minimize the cost function $J(W)$; thus we need to calculate the partial derivative of the parameters **W** with respect to each weight for every layer in the network:

$$\frac{\partial}{\partial w_{j,i}^{(l)}} J(W)$$

In the next section, we will talk about the backpropagation algorithm, which allows us to calculate those partial derivatives to minimize the cost function.

Note that W consists of multiple matrices. In a multilayer perceptron with one hidden unit, we have the weight matrix $W^{(h)}$, which connects the input to the hidden layer, and $W^{(out)}$, which connects the hidden layer to the output layer. An intuitive visualization of the three-dimensional tensor W is provided in the following figure:

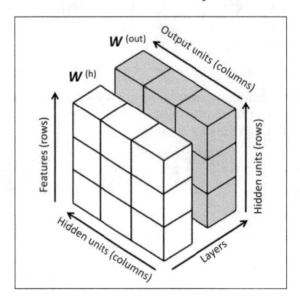

In this simplified figure, it may seem that both $W^{(h)}$ and $W^{(out)}$ have the same number of rows and columns, which is typically not the case unless we initialize an MLP with the same number of hidden units, output units, and input features.

If this sounds confusing, stay tuned for the next section, where we will discuss the dimensionality of $W^{(h)}$ and $W^{(out)}$ in more detail in the context of the backpropagation algorithm. Also, I want to encourage you to read through the code of the `NeuralNetMLP` again, which I annotated with helpful comments about the dimensionality with regard to the different matrices and vector transformations. You can obtain the annotated code either from Packt or the book's GitHub repository at `https://github.com/rasbt/python-machine-learning-book-2nd-edition`.

Developing your intuition for backpropagation

Although backpropagation was rediscovered and popularized more than 30 years ago (*Learning representations by back-propagating errors*, D. E. Rumelhart, G. E. Hinton, and R. J. Williams, Nature, 323: 6088, pages 533–536, 1986), it still remains one of the most widely used algorithms to train artificial neural networks very efficiently. If you are interested in additional references regarding the history of backpropagation, Juergen Schmidhuber wrote a nice survey article, *Who Invented Backpropagation?*, which you can find online at http://people.idsia.ch/~juergen/who-invented-backpropagation.html.

In this section, I intend to provide a short and intuitive summary and the bigger picture of how this fascinating algorithm works before we dive into more mathematical details. In essence, we can think of backpropagation as a very computationally efficient approach to compute the partial derivatives of a complex cost function in multilayer neural networks. Here, our goal is to use those derivatives to learn the weight coefficients for parameterizing such a multilayer artificial neural network. The challenge in the parameterization of neural networks is that we are typically dealing with a very large number of weight coefficients in a high-dimensional feature space. In contrast to cost functions of single-layer neural networks such as Adaline or logistic regression, which we have seen in previous chapters, the error surface of a neural network cost function is not convex or smooth with respect to the parameters. There are many bumps in this high-dimensional cost surface (local minima) that we have to overcome in order to find the global minimum of the cost function.

You may recall the concept of the chain rule from your introductory calculus classes. The chain rule is an approach to compute the derivative of a complex, nested function, such as $f(g(x))$, as follows:

$$\frac{d}{dx}\left[f\left(g\left(x\right)\right)\right] = \frac{df}{dg} \cdot \frac{dg}{dx}$$

Similarly, we can use the chain rule for an arbitrarily long function composition. For example, let's assume that we have five different functions, $f(x)$, $g(x)$, $h(x)$, $u(x)$, and $v(x)$, and let F be the function composition: $F(x) = f(g(h(u(v(x)))))$. Applying the chain rule, we can compute the derivative of this function as follows:

$$\frac{dF}{dx} = \frac{d}{dx}F\left(x\right) = \frac{d}{dx}f\left(g\left(h\left(u\left(v\left(x\right)\right)\right)\right)\right) = \frac{df}{dg} \cdot \frac{dg}{dh} \cdot \frac{dh}{du} \cdot \frac{du}{dv} \cdot \frac{dv}{dx}$$

In the context of computer algebra, a set of techniques has been developed to solve such problems very efficiently, which is also known as **automatic differentiation**. If you are interested in learning more about automatic differentiation in machine learning applications, I recommend that you read A. G. Baydin and B. A. Pearlmutter's article *Automatic Differentiation of Algorithms for Machine Learning*, arXiv preprint arXiv:1404.7456, 2014, which is freely available on arXiv at http://arxiv.org/pdf/1404.7456.pdf.

Automatic differentiation comes with two modes, the forward and reverse modes; backpropagation is simply just a special case of reverse mode automatic differentiation. The key point is that applying the chain rule in the forward mode can be quite expensive since we would have to multiply large matrices for each layer (Jacobians) that we eventually multiply by a vector to obtain the output. The trick of reverse mode is that we start from right to left: we multiply a matrix by a vector, which yields another vector that is multiplied by the next matrix and so on. Matrix-vector multiplication is computationally much cheaper than matrix-matrix multiplication, which is why backpropagation is one of the most popular algorithms used in neural network training.

To fully understand backpropagation, we need to borrow certain concepts from differential calculus, which is beyond the scope of this book. However, I have written a review chapter of the most fundamental concepts, which you might find useful in this context. It discusses function derivatives, partial derivatives, gradients, and the Jacobian. I made this text freely accessible at https://sebastianraschka.com/pdf/books/dlb/appendix_d_calculus.pdf. If you are unfamiliar with calculus or need a brief refresher, consider reading this text as an additional supporting resource before reading the next section.

Training neural networks via backpropagation

In this section, we will go through the math of backpropagation to understand how you can learn the weights in a neural network very efficiently. Depending on how comfortable you are with mathematical representations, the following equations may seem relatively complicated at first.

In a previous section, we saw how to calculate the cost as the difference between the activation of the last layer and the target class label. Now, we will see how the backpropagation algorithm works to update the weights in our MLP model from a mathematical perspective, which we implemented in the # Backpropagation section inside the fit method. As we recall from the beginning of this chapter, we first need to apply forward propagation in order to obtain the activation of the output layer, which we formulated as follows:

$$Z^{(h)} = A^{(in)}W^{(h)} \ \left(net\,input\,of\,the\,hidden\,layer \right)$$

$$A^{(h)} = \phi\left(Z^{(h)} \right) \left(activation\,of\,the\,hidden\,layer \right)$$

$$Z^{(out)} = A^{(h)}W^{(out)} \ \left(net\,input\,of\,the\,output\,layer \right)$$

$$A^{(out)} = \phi\left(Z^{(out)} \right) \left(activation\,of\,the\,output\,layer \right)$$

Concisely, we just forward-propagate the input features through the connection in the network, as shown in the following illustration:

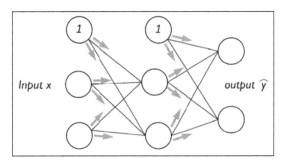

In backpropagation, we propagate the error from right to left. We start by calculating the error vector of the output layer:

$$\delta^{(out)} = a^{(out)} - y$$

Here, **y** is the vector of the true class labels (the corresponding variable in the NeuralNetMLP code is sigma_out).

Next, we calculate the error term of the hidden layer:

$$\delta^{(h)} = \delta^{(out)} \left(W^{(out)} \right)^{T} \odot \frac{\partial \phi \left(z^{(h)} \right)}{\partial z^{(h)}}$$

Here, $\frac{\partial \phi \left(z^{(h)} \right)}{\partial z^{(h)}}$ is simply the derivative of the sigmoid activation function, which we computed as `sigmoid_derivative_h = a_h * (1. - a_h)` in the `fit` method of the `NeuralNetMLP`:

$$\frac{\partial \phi(z)}{\partial z} = \left(a^{(h)} \odot \left(1 - a^{(h)} \right) \right)$$

Note that the $\odot$ symbol means element-wise multiplication in this context.

> Although it is not important to follow the next equations, you may be curious how I obtained the derivative of the activation function; I have summarized the derivation step by step here:
>
> $$\phi'(z) = \frac{\partial}{\partial z} \left(\frac{1}{1+e^{-z}} \right)$$
>
> $$= \frac{e^{-z}}{\left(1+e^{-z} \right)^{2}}$$
>
> $$= \frac{1+e^{-z}}{\left(1+e^{-z} \right)^{2}} - \left(\frac{1}{1+e^{-z}} \right)^{2}$$
>
> $$= \frac{1}{\left(1+e^{-z} \right)} - \left(\frac{1}{1+e^{-z}} \right)^{2}$$
>
> $$= \phi(z) - \left(\phi(z) \right)^{2}$$
>
> $$= \phi(z) \left(1 - \phi(z) \right)$$
>
> $$= a \left(1 - a \right)$$

Next, we compute the $\delta^{(h)}$ layer error matrix (`sigma_h`) as follows:

$$\delta^{(h)} = \delta^{(out)} \left(W^{(out)} \right)^T \odot \left(a^{(h)} \odot \left(1 - a^{(h)} \right) \right)$$

To better understand how we computed this $\delta^{(h)}$ term, let's walk through it in more detail. In the preceding equation, we used the transpose $\left(W^{(out)} \right)^T$ of the $h \times t$-dimensional matrix $W^{(out)}$. Here, t is the number of output class labels and h is the number of hidden units. The matrix multiplication between the $n \times t$-dimensional $\delta^{(out)}$ matrix and the $t \times h$-dimensional matrix $\left(W^{(out)} \right)^T$, results in an $n \times t$-dimensional matrix that we multiplied elementwise by the sigmoid derivative of the same dimension to obtain the $n \times t$-dimensional matrix $\delta^{(h)}$.

Eventually, after obtaining the δ terms, we can now write the derivation of the cost function as follows:

$$\frac{\partial}{\partial w_{i,j}^{(out)}} J\left(W \right) = a_j^{(h)} \delta_i^{(out)}$$

$$\frac{\partial}{\partial w_{i,j}^{(h)}} J\left(W \right) = a_j^{(in)} \delta_i^{(h)}$$

Next, we need to accumulate the partial derivative of every node in each layer and the error of the node in the next layer. However, remember that we need to compute $\Delta_{i,j}^{(l)}$ for every sample in the training set. Thus, it is easier to implement it as a vectorized version like in our `NeuralNetMLP` code implementation:

$$\Delta^{(h)} = \Delta^{(h)} + \left(A^{(in)} \right)^T \delta^{(h)}$$

$$\Delta^{(out)} = \Delta^{(out)} + \left(A^{(h)} \right)^T \delta^{(out)}$$

And after we have accumulated the partial derivatives, we can add the regularization term:

$$\Delta^{(l)} := \Delta^{(l)} + \lambda^{(l)} \left(except \ for \ the \ bias \ term \right)$$

The two previous mathematical equations correspond to the code variables `delta_w_h`, `delta_b_h`, `delta_w_out`, and `delta_b_out` in `NeuralNetMLP`.

Lastly, after we have computed the gradients, we can now update the weights by taking an opposite step towards the gradient for each layer *l*:

$$W^{(l)} := W^{(l)} - \eta \Delta^{(l)}$$

This is implemented as follows:

```
self.w_h -= self.eta * delta_w_h
self.b_h -= self.eta * delta_b_h
self.w_out -= self.eta * delta_w_out
self.b_out -= self.eta * delta_b_out
```

To bring everything together, let's summarize backpropagation in the following figure:

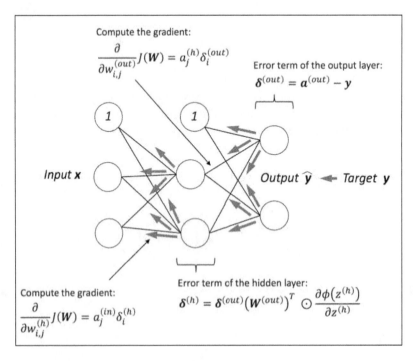

About the convergence in neural networks

You might be wondering why we did not use regular gradient descent but instead used mini-batch learning to train our neural network for the handwritten digit classification. You may recall our discussion on stochastic gradient descent that we used to implement online learning. In online learning, we compute the gradient based on a single training example ($k = 1$) at a time to perform the weight update. Although this is a stochastic approach, it often leads to very accurate solutions with a much faster convergence than regular gradient descent. Mini-batch learning is a special form of stochastic gradient descent where we compute the gradient based on a subset k of the n training samples with $1 < k < n$. Mini-batch learning has the advantage over online learning that we can make use of our vectorized implementations to improve computational efficiency. However, we can update the weights much faster than in regular gradient descent. Intuitively, you can think of mini-batch learning as predicting the voter turnout of a presidential election from a poll by asking only a representative subset of the population rather than asking the entire population (which would be equal to running the actual election).

Multilayer neural networks are much harder to train than simpler algorithms such as Adaline, logistic regression, or support vector machines. In multilayer neural networks, we typically have hundreds, thousands, or even billions of weights that we need to optimize. Unfortunately, the output function has a rough surface and the optimization algorithm can easily become trapped in local minima, as shown in the following figure:

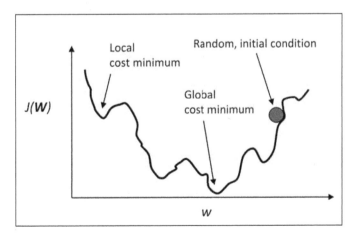

Note that this representation is extremely simplified since our neural network has many dimensions; it makes it impossible to visualize the actual cost surface for the human eye. Here, we only show the cost surface for a single weight on the x-axis. However, the main message is that we do not want our algorithm to get trapped in local minima. By increasing the learning rate, we can more readily escape such local minima. On the other hand, we also increase the chance of overshooting the global optimum if the learning rate is too large. Since we initialize the weights randomly, we start with a solution to the optimization problem that is typically hopelessly wrong.

A few last words about the neural network implementation

You may be wondering why we went through all of this theory just to implement a simple multilayer artificial network that can classify handwritten digits instead of using an open source Python machine learning library. In fact, we will introduce more complex neural network models in the next chapters, which we will train using the open source TensorFlow library (`https://www.tensorflow.org`). Although the from scratch implementation in this chapter seems a bit tedious at first, it was a good exercise for understanding the basics behind backpropagation and neural network training, and a basic understanding of algorithms is crucial for applying machine learning techniques appropriately and successfully.

Now that you have learned how feedforward neural networks work, we are ready to explore more sophisticated deep neural networks, such as TensorFlow and Keras (`https://keras.io`), which allow us to construct neural networks more efficiently, as we will see in *Chapter 13, Parallelizing Neural Network Training with TensorFlow*. Over the past two years, since its release in November 2015, TensorFlow has gained a lot of popularity among machine learning researchers, who use it to construct deep neural networks because of its ability to optimize mathematical expressions for computations on multi dimensional arrays utilizing **Graphical Processing Units (GPUs)**. While TensorFlow can be considered a low-level deep learning library, simplifying API such as Keras have been developed that make the construction of common deep learning models even more convenient, which we will see in *Chapter 13, Parallelizing Neural Network Training with TensorFlow*.

Summary

In this chapter, you have learned the basic concepts behind multilayer artificial neural networks, which are currently the hottest topics in machine learning research. In *Chapter 2, Training Simple Machine Learning Algorithms for Classification*, we started our journey with simple single-layer neural network structures and now we have connected multiple neurons to a powerful neural network architecture to solve complex problems such as handwritten digit recognition. We demystified the popular backpropagation algorithm, which is one of the building blocks of many neural network models that are used in deep learning. After learning about the backpropagation algorithm in this chapter, we are well-equipped for exploring more complex deep neural network architectures. In the remaining chapters, we will introduce TensorFlow, an open source library geared towards deep learning, which allows us to implement and train multilayer neural networks more efficiently.

13

Parallelizing Neural Network Training with TensorFlow

In this chapter, we'll move on from the mathematical foundations of machine learning and deep learning to introducing TensorFlow. TensorFlow is one of the most popular deep learning libraries currently available, and it can let us implement neural networks much more efficiently than any of our previous NumPy implementations. In this chapter, we'll start using TensorFlow and see how it brings significant benefits to training performance.

This chapter begins the next stage of our journey into training machine learning and deep learning, and we'll explore the following topics:

- How TensorFlow improves training performance
- Working with TensorFlow to write optimized machine learning code
- Using TensorFlow high-level APIs to build a multilayer neural network
- Choosing activation functions for artificial neural networks
- Introducing Keras, a high-level wrapper around TensorFlow, for implementing common deep learning architectures most conveniently

TensorFlow and training performance

TensorFlow can speed up our machine learning tasks significantly. To understand how it can do this, let's begin by discussing some of the performance challenges we typically run into when we run expensive calculations on our hardware.

The performance of computer processors has, of course, been improving continuously over recent years, and that's allowed us to train more powerful and complex learning systems, and so to improve the predictive performance of our machine learning models. Even the cheapest desktop computer hardware that's available right now comes with processing units that have multiple cores.

Also, in the previous chapters, we saw that many functions in scikit-learn allowed us to spread those computations over multiple processing units. However, by default, Python is limited to execution on one core due to the **Global Interpreter Lock** (**GIL**). So, although we, indeed, take advantage of its multiprocessing library to distribute our computations over multiple cores, we still have to consider that the most advanced desktop hardware rarely comes with more than 8 or 16 such cores.

If we recall from *Chapter 12, Implementing a Multilayer Artificial Neural Network from Scratch*, where we implemented a very simple multilayer perceptron with only one hidden layer consisting of 100 units, we had to optimize approximately 80,000 weight parameters (*[784*100 + 100] + [100 * 10] + 10 = 79,510*) to learn a model for a very simple image classification task. The images in MNIST are rather small (28 x 28 pixels), and we can only imagine the explosion in the number of parameters if we want to add additional hidden layers or work with images that have higher pixel densities.

Such a task would quickly become unfeasible for a single processing unit. The question then becomes — how can we tackle such problems more effectively?

The obvious solution to this problem is to use GPUs, which are real work horses. You can think of a graphics card as a small computer cluster inside your machine. Another advantage is that modern GPUs are relatively cheap compared to the state-of-the-art CPUs, as we can see in the following overview:

Specifications	Intel® Core™ i7-6900K Processor Extreme Ed.	NVIDIA GeForce® GTX™ 1080 Ti
Base Clock Frequency	3.2 GHz	< 1.5 GHz
Cores	8	3584
Memory Bandwidth	64 GB/s	484 GB/s
Floating-Point Calculations	409 GFLOPS	11300 GFLOPS
Cost	~ $1000.00	~ $700.00

The sources for the information in the table are the following websites:

- `https://www.intel.com/content/www/us/en/products/processors/`
  `core/x-series/i7-6900k.html`
- `https://www.nvidia.com/en-us/geforce/products/10series/geforce-`
  `gtx-1080-ti/`

(Date: August 2017)

At 70 percent of the price of a modern CPU, we can get a GPU that has 450 times more cores and is capable of around 30 times more floating-point calculations per second. So, what is holding us back from utilizing GPUs for our machine learning tasks?

The challenge is that writing code to target GPUs is not as simple as executing Python code in our interpreter. There are special packages, such as CUDA and OpenCL, that allow us to target the GPU. However, writing code in CUDA or OpenCL is probably not the most convenient environment for implementing and running machine learning algorithms. The good news is that this is what TensorFlow was developed for!

What is TensorFlow?

TensorFlow is a scalable and multiplatform programming interface for implementing and running machine learning algorithms, including convenience wrappers for deep learning.

TensorFlow was developed by the researchers and engineers of the Google Brain team; and while the main development is led by a team of researchers and software engineers at Google, its development also involves many contributions from the open source community. TensorFlow was initially built for only internal use at Google, but it was subsequently released in November 2015 under a permissive open source license.

To improve the performance of training machine learning models, TensorFlow allows execution on both CPUs and GPUs. However, its greatest performance capabilities can be discovered when using GPUs. TensorFlow supports CUDA-enabled GPUs officially. Support for OpenCL-enabled devices is still experimental. However, OpenCL will likely be officially supported in near future.

TensorFlow currently supports frontend interfaces for a number of programming languages. Lucky for us as Python users, TensorFlow's Python API is currently the most complete API, thereby attracting many machine learning and deep learning practitioners. Furthermore, TensorFlow has an official API in C++.

The APIs in other languages, such as Java, Haskell, Node.js, and Go, are not stable yet, but the open source community and TensorFlow developers are constantly improving them. TensorFlow computations rely on constructing a directed graph for representing the data flow. Even though building the graph may sound complicated, TensorFlow comes with high-level APIs that has made it very easy.

How we will learn TensorFlow

We'll learn first of all about the low-level TensorFlow API. While implementing models at this level can be a little bit cumbersome at first, the advantage of the low-level API is that it gives us more flexibility as programmers to combine the basic operations and develop complex machine learning models. Starting from TensorFlow version 1.1.0, high-level APIs are added on top of the low-level API (for instance, the so-called Layers and Estimators APIs), which allow building and prototyping models much faster.

After learning about the low-level API, we will move forward to explore two high-level APIs, namely TensorFlow **Layers** and **Keras**. However, let's begin by taking our first steps with TensorFlow low-level API, and ease ourselves into how everything works.

First steps with TensorFlow

In this section, we'll take our first steps in using the low-level TensorFlow API. Depending on how your system is set up, you can typically just use Python's `pip` installer and install TensorFlow from PyPI by executing the following from your Terminal:

```
pip install tensorflow
```

In case you want to use GPUs, the CUDA Toolkit as well as the NVIDIA cuDNN library need to be installed; then you can install TensorFlow with GPU support, as follows:

```
pip install tensorflow-gpu
```

TensorFlow is under active development; therefore, every couple of months, newer versions are released with significant changes. At the time of writing this chapter, the latest TensorFlow version is 1.3.0. You can verify your TensorFlow version from your Terminal, as follows:

```
python -c 'import tensorflow as tf; print(tf.__version__)'
```

If you should experience problems with the installation procedure, I recommend you to read more about system- and platform-specific recommendations that are provided at https://www.tensorflow.org/install/. Note that all the code in this chapter can be run on your CPU; using a GPU is entirely optional but recommended if you want to fully enjoy the benefits of TensorFlow. If you have a graphics card, refer to the installation page to set it up appropriately. In addition, you may find this TensorFlow-GPU setup guide helpful, which explains how to install the NVIDIA graphics card drivers, CUDA, and cuDNN on Ubuntu (not required but recommended requirements for running TensorFlow on a GPU): https://sebastianraschka.com/pdf/books/dlb/appendix_h_cloud-computing.pdf.

TensorFlow is built around a computation graph composed of a set of nodes. Each node represents an operation that may have zero or more input or output. The values that flow through the edges of the computation graph are called **tensors**.

Tensors can be understood as a generalization of scalars, vectors, matrices, and so on. More concretely, a scalar can be defined as a rank-0 tensor, a vector as a rank-1 tensor, a matrix as a rank-2 tensor, and matrices stacked in a third dimension as rank-3 tensors.

Once a computation graph is built, the graph can be launched in a TensorFlow Session for executing different nodes of the graph. In *Chapter 14, Going Deeper – The Mechanics of TensorFlow*, we will cover the steps in building the computation graph and launching the graph in a session in more detail.

As a warm-up exercise, we will start with the use of simple scalars from TensorFlow to compute a net input z of a sample point x in a one-dimensional dataset with weight w and bias b:

$$z = w \times x + b$$

The following code shows the implementation of this equation in the low-level TensorFlow API:

```
import tensorflow as tf

## create a graph
g = tf.Graph()
with g.as_default():
    x = tf.placeholder(dtype=tf.float32,
                       shape=(None), name='x')
    w = tf.Variable(2.0, name='weight')
```

```
        b = tf.Variable(0.7, name='bias')

        z = w*x + b

        init = tf.global_variables_initializer()
    ## create a session and pass in graph g
    with tf.Session(graph=g) as sess:
        ## initialize w and b:
        sess.run(init)
        ## evaluate z:
        for t in [1.0, 0.6, -1.8]:
            print('x=%4.1f --> z=%4.1f'%(
                    t, sess.run(z, feed_dict={x:t})))
```

After executing the previous code, you should see the following output:

```
x= 1.0 --> z= 2.7
x= 0.6 --> z= 1.9
x=-1.8 --> z=-2.9
```

This was pretty straightforward, right? In general, when we develop a model in the TensorFlow low-level API, we need to define placeholders for input data (x, y, and sometimes other tunable parameters); then, define the weight matrices and build the model from input to output. If this is an optimization problem, we should define the loss or cost function and determine which optimization algorithm to use. TensorFlow will create a graph that contains all the symbols that we have defined as nodes in this graph.

Here, we created a placeholder for x with `shape=(None)`. This allows us to feed the values in an element-by-element form and as a batch of input data at once, as follows:

```
>>> with tf.Session(graph=g) as sess:
...         sess.run(init)
...         print(sess.run(z, feed_dict={x:[1., 2., 3.]}))

[2.7 4.7 6.7]
```

Note that we are omitting Python's command-line prompt in several places in this chapter to improve the readability of long code examples by avoiding unnecessary text wrapping; this is because TensorFlow's function and method names can be very verbose.

Also, note that the official TensorFlow style guide (`https://www.tensorflow.org/community/style_guide`) recommends using two-character spacing for code indents. However, we chose four characters for indents as it is more consistent with the official Python style guide and also helps in displaying the code syntax highlighting in many text editors correctly as well as the accompanying Jupyter code notebooks at `https://github.com/rasbt/python-machine-learning-book-2nd-edition`.

Working with array structures

Let's discuss how to use array structures in TensorFlow. By executing the following code, we will create a simple rank-3 tensor of size $batchsize \times 2 \times 3$, reshape it, and calculate the column sums using TensorFlow's optimized expressions. Since we do not know the batch size a priori, we specify `None` for the batch size in the argument for the `shape` parameter of the placeholder `x`:

```
import tensorflow as tf
import numpy as np

g = tf.Graph()
with g.as_default():
    x = tf.placeholder(dtype=tf.float32,
                       shape=(None, 2, 3),
                       name='input_x')

    x2 = tf.reshape(x, shape=(-1, 6),
                    name='x2')

    ## calculate the sum of each column
    xsum = tf.reduce_sum(x2, axis=0, name='col_sum')

    ## calculate the mean of each column
    xmean = tf.reduce_mean(x2, axis=0, name='col_mean')

with tf.Session(graph=g) as sess:
    x_array = np.arange(18).reshape(3, 2, 3)

    print('input shape: ', x_array.shape)
    print('Reshaped:\n',
```

```
        sess.run(x2, feed_dict={x:x_array}))
    print('Column Sums:\n',
            sess.run(xsum, feed_dict={x:x_array}))
    print('Column Means:\n',
            sess.run(xmean, feed_dict={x:x_array}))
```

The output shown after executing the preceding code is given here:

```
input shape:   (3, 2, 3)
Reshaped:
 [[  0.   1.   2.   3.   4.   5.]
  [  6.   7.   8.   9.  10.  11.]
  [ 12.  13.  14.  15.  16.  17.]]

Column Sums:
 [ 18.  21.  24.  27.  30.  33.]

Column Means:
 [  6.   7.   8.   9.  10.  11.]
```

In this example, we worked with three functions — `tf.reshape`, `tf.reduce_sum`, and `tf.reduce_mean`. Note that for reshaping, we used the value `-1` for the first dimension. This is because we do not know the value of batch size; when reshaping a tensor, if you use `-1` for a specific dimension, the size of that dimension will be computed according to the total size of the tensor and the remaining dimension. Therefore, `tf.reshape(tensor, shape=(-1,))` can be used to flatten a tensor.

Feel free to explore other TensorFlow functions from the official documentation at `https://www.TensorFlow.org/api_docs/python/tf`.

Developing a simple model with the low-level TensorFlow API

Now that we have familiarized ourselves with TensorFlow, let's take a look at a really practical example and implement **Ordinary Least Squares** (**OLS**) regression. For a quick refresher on regression analysis, refer to *Chapter 10, Predicting Continuous Target Variables with Regression Analysis*.

Let's start by creating a small one-dimensional toy dataset with 10 training samples:

```
>>> import tensorflow as tf
>>> import numpy as np
>>>
>>> X_train = np.arange(10).reshape((10, 1))
>>> y_train = np.array([1.0, 1.3, 3.1,
```

```
  ...                        2.0,  5.0,  6.3,
  ...                        6.6,  7.4,  8.0,
  ...                        9.0])
```

Given this dataset, we want to train a linear regression model to predict the output y from the input x. Let's implement this model in a class, which we name `TfLinreg`. For this, we would need two placeholders—one for the input x and one for y for feeding the data into our model. Next, we need to define the trainable variables—weights w and bias b.

Then, we can define the linear regression model as $z = w \times x + b$, followed by defining the cost function to be the **Mean of Squared Error (MSE)**. To learn the weight parameters of the model, we use the gradient descent optimizer. The code is as follows:

```python
class TfLinreg(object):
    def __init__(self, x_dim, learning_rate=0.01,
                 random_seed=None):
        self.x_dim = x_dim
        self.learning_rate = learning_rate
        self.g = tf.Graph()
        ## build the model
        with self.g.as_default():
            ## set graph-level random-seed
            tf.set_random_seed(random_seed)

            self.build()
            ## create initializer
            self.init_op = tf.global_variables_initializer()

    def build(self):
        ## define placeholders for inputs
        self.X = tf.placeholder(dtype=tf.float32,
                                shape=(None, self.x_dim),
                                name='x_input')
        self.y = tf.placeholder(dtype=tf.float32,
                                shape=(None),
                                name='y_input')
        print(self.X)
        print(self.y)
        ## define weight matrix and bias vector
        w = tf.Variable(tf.zeros(shape=(1)),
                        name='weight')
        b = tf.Variable(tf.zeros(shape=(1)),
                        name="bias")
```

```
        print(w)
        print(b)

        self.z_net = tf.squeeze(w*self.X + b,
                                    name='z_net')
        print(self.z_net)

        sqr_errors = tf.square(self.y - self.z_net,
                                    name='sqr_errors')
        print(sqr_errors)
        self.mean_cost = tf.reduce_mean(sqr_errors,
                                        name='mean_cost')

        optimizer = tf.train.GradientDescentOptimizer(
                        learning_rate=self.learning_rate,
                        name='GradientDescent')
        self.optimizer = optimizer.minimize(self.mean_cost)
```

So far, we have defined a class to construct our model. We will create an instance of this class and call it `lrmodel`, as follows:

```
>>> lrmodel = TfLinreg(x_dim=X_train.shape[1], learning_rate=0.01)
```

The `print` statements that we wrote in the `build` method will display information about six nodes in the graph—X, y, w, b, z_net, and sqr_errors—with their names and shapes.

These `print` statements are optionally given for practice; however, inspecting the shapes of variables can be very helpful in debugging complex models. The following lines are printed when constructing the model:

```
Tensor("x_input:0", shape=(?, 1), dtype=float32)
Tensor("y_input:0", dtype=float32)
<tf.Variable 'weight:0' shape=(1,) dtype=float32_ref>
<tf.Variable 'bias:0' shape=(1,) dtype=float32_ref>
Tensor("z_net:0", dtype=float32)
Tensor("sqr_errors:0", dtype=float32)
```

The next step is to implement a training function to learn the weights of the linear regression model. Note that b is the bias unit (the *y*-axis intercept at *x* = *0*).

For training, we implement a separate function that needs a TensorFlow session, a model instance, training data, and the number of epochs as input arguments. In this function, first we initialize the variables in the TensorFlow session using the `init_op` operation defined in the model. Then, we iterate and call the `optimizer` operation of the model while feeding the training data. This function will return a list of training costs as a side product:

```
def train_linreg(sess, model, X_train, y_train, num_epochs=10):
    ## initialiaze all variables: W and b
    sess.run(model.init_op)

    training_costs = []
    for i in range(num_epochs):
        _, cost = sess.run([model.optimizer, model.mean_cost],
                        feed_dict={model.X:X_train,
                                    model.y:y_train})
        training_costs.append(cost)

    return training_costs
```

So, now we can create a new TensorFlow session to launch the `lrmodel.g` graph and pass all the required arguments to the `train_linreg` function for training:

```
>>> sess = tf.Session(graph=lrmodel.g)
>>> training_costs = train_linreg(sess, lrmodel, X_train, y_train)
```

Let's visualize the training costs after these 10 epochs to see whether the model is converged or not:

```
>>> import matplotlib.pyplot as plt
>>> plt.plot(range(1,len(training_costs) + 1), training_costs)
>>> plt.tight_layout()
>>> plt.xlabel('Epoch')
>>> plt.ylabel('Training Cost')
>>> plt.show()
```

As we can see in the following plot, this simple model converges very quickly after a few epochs:

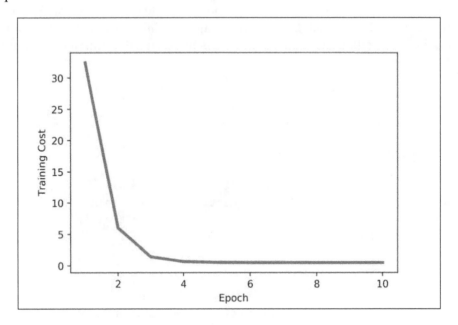

So far so good. Looking at the cost function, it seems that we built a working regression model from this particular dataset. Now, let's compile a new function to make predictions based on the input features. For this function, we need the TensorFlow session, the model, and the test dataset:

```
def predict_linreg(sess, model, X_test):
    y_pred = sess.run(model.z_net,
                      feed_dict={model.X:X_test})
    return y_pred
```

Implementing a predict function was pretty straightforward; just running `z_net` defined in the graph computes the predicted output values. Next, let's plot the linear regression fit on the training data:

```
>>> plt.scatter(X_train, y_train,
...             marker='s', s=50,
...             label='Training Data')
>>> plt.plot(range(X_train.shape[0]),
...          predict_linreg(sess, lrmodel, X_train),
...          color='gray', marker='o',
...          markersize=6, linewidth=3,
...          label='LinReg Model')
>>> plt.xlabel('x')
```

```
>>> plt.ylabel('y')
>>> plt.legend()
>>> plt.tight_layout()
>>> plt.show()
```

As we can see in the resulting plot, our model fits the training data points appropriately:

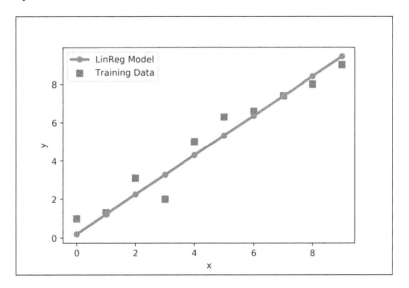

Training neural networks efficiently with high-level TensorFlow APIs

In this section, we will take a look at two high-level TensorFlow APIs — the Layers API (`tensorflow.layers` or `tf.layers`) and the Keras API (`tensorflow.contrib.keras`).

Keras can be installed as a separate package. It supports Theano or TensorFlow as backend (for more information, refer to the official website of Keras at `https://keras.io/`).

However, after the release of TensorFlow 1.1.0, Keras has been added to the TensorFlow `contrib` submodule. It is very likely that the Keras subpackage will be moved outside the experimental `contrib` submodule and become one of the main TensorFlow submodules soon.

Building multilayer neural networks using TensorFlow's Layers API

To see what neural network training via the `tensorflow.layers` (`tf.layers`) high-level API looks like, let's implement a multilayer perceptron to classify the handwritten digits from the MNIST dataset, which we introduced in the previous chapter. The MNIST dataset can be downloaded from `http://yann.lecun.com/exdb/mnist/` in four parts, as listed here:

- **Training set images**: `train-images-idx3-ubyte.gz` (9.5 MB)
- **Training set labels**: `train-labels-idx1-ubyte.gz` (32 KB)
- **Test set images**: `t10k-images-idx3-ubyte.gz` (1.6 MB)
- **Test set labels**: `t10k-labels-idx1-ubyte.gz` (8.0 KB)

Note that TensorFlow also provides the same dataset as follows:
```
import tensorflow as tf
from tensorflow.examples.tutorials.mnist import input_data
```
However, we work with the MNIST dataset as an external dataset to learn all the steps of data preprocessing separately. This way, you would learn what you need to do with your own dataset.

After downloading and unzipping the archives, we place the files in the `mnist` directory in our current working directory so that we can load the training as well as the test dataset, using the `load_mnist(path, kind)` function we implemented previously in *Chapter 12, Implementing a Multilayer Artificial Neural Network from Scratch*.

Then, the dataset will be loaded as follows:

```
>>> ## loading the data
>>> X_train, y_train = load_mnist('./mnist/', kind='train')
>>> print('Rows: %d,  Columns: %d' %(X_train.shape[0],
...                                   X_train.shape[1]))
Rows: 60000,  Columns: 784
>>> X_test, y_test = load_mnist('./mnist/', kind='t10k')
>>> print('Rows: %d,  Columns: %d' %(X_test.shape[0],
...                                   X_test.shape[1]))
Rows: 10000,  Columns: 784
>>> ## mean centering and normalization:
>>> mean_vals = np.mean(X_train, axis=0)
>>> std_val = np.std(X_train)
```

```
>>>
>>> X_train_centered = (X_train - mean_vals)/std_val
>>> X_test_centered = (X_test - mean_vals)/std_val
>>>
>>> del X_train, X_test
>>>
>>> print(X_train_centered.shape, y_train.shape)
(60000, 784) (60000,)
>>> print(X_test_centered.shape, y_test.shape)
(10000, 784) (10000,)
```

Now we can start building our model. We will start by creating two placeholders, named `tf_x` and `tf_y`, and then build a multilayer perceptron as in *Chapter 12, Implementing a Multilayer Artificial Neural Network from Scratch*, but with three fully connected layers.

However, we will replace the logistic units in the hidden layer with hyperbolic tangent activation functions (`tanh`), replace the logistic function in the output layer with `softmax`, and add an additional hidden layer.

 The `tanh` and `softmax` functions are new activation functions. We will learn more about these activation functions in the next section: *Choosing activation functions for multilayer neural networks*.

```
import tensorflow as tf

n_features = X_train_centered.shape[1]
n_classes = 10
random_seed = 123
np.random.seed(random_seed)

g = tf.Graph()
with g.as_default():
    tf.set_random_seed(random_seed)
    tf_x = tf.placeholder(dtype=tf.float32,
                          shape=(None, n_features),
                          name='tf_x')

    tf_y = tf.placeholder(dtype=tf.int32,
                          shape=None, name='tf_y')
    y_onehot = tf.one_hot(indices=tf_y, depth=n_classes)

    h1 = tf.layers.dense(inputs=tf_x, units=50,
                         activation=tf.tanh,
```

```
                                  name='layer1')

        h2 = tf.layers.dense(inputs=h1, units=50,
                                  activation=tf.tanh,
                                  name='layer2')

        logits = tf.layers.dense(inputs=h2,
                                  units=10,
                                  activation=None,
                                  name='layer3')

        predictions = {
            'classes' : tf.argmax(logits, axis=1,
                                  name='predicted_classes'),
            'probabilities' : tf.nn.softmax(logits,
                                  name='softmax_tensor')
        }
```

Next, we define the cost functions and add an operator for initializing the model variables as well as an optimization operator:

```
    ## define cost function and optimizer:
    with g.as_default():
        cost = tf.losses.softmax_cross_entropy(
                onehot_labels=y_onehot, logits=logits)

        optimizer = tf.train.GradientDescentOptimizer(
                learning_rate=0.001)

        train_op = optimizer.minimize(
                loss=cost)

        init_op = tf.global_variables_initializer()
```

Before we start training the network, we need a way to generate batches of data. For this, we implement the following function that returns a generator:

```
    def create_batch_generator(X, y, batch_size=128, shuffle=False):
        X_copy = np.array(X)
        y_copy = np.array(y)

        if shuffle:
            data = np.column_stack((X_copy, y_copy))
            np.random.shuffle(data)
            X_copy = data[:, :-1]
```

```
            y_copy = data[:, -1].astype(int)

        for i in range(0, X.shape[0], batch_size):
            yield (X_copy[i:i+batch_size, :], y_copy[i:i+batch_size])
```

Next, we can create a new TensorFlow session, initialize all the variables in our
network, and train it. We also display the average training loss after each epoch
monitors the learning process later:

```
>>> ## create a session to launch the graph
>>> sess =  tf.Session(graph=g)
>>> ## run the variable initialization operator
>>> sess.run(init_op)
>>>
>>> ## 50 epochs of training:
>>> for epoch in range(50):
...        training_costs = []
...        batch_generator = create_batch_generator(
...                X_train_centered, y_train,
...                batch_size=64)
...        for batch_X, batch_y in batch_generator:
...            ## prepare a dict to feed data to our network:
...            feed = {tf_x:batch_X, tf_y:batch_y}
...            _, batch_cost = sess.run([train_op, cost], feed_dict=feed)
...            training_costs.append(batch_cost)
...        print(' -- Epoch %2d  '
...            'Avg. Training Loss: %.4f' % (
...                epoch+1, np.mean(training_costs)
...        ))


 -- Epoch  1  Avg. Training Loss: 1.5573
 -- Epoch  2  Avg. Training Loss: 1.2532
 -- Epoch  3  Avg. Training Loss: 1.0854
 -- Epoch  4  Avg. Training Loss: 0.9738

 [...]
 -- Epoch 49  Avg. Training Loss: 0.3527
 -- Epoch 50  Avg. Training Loss: 0.3498
```

The training process may take a couple of minutes. Finally, we can use the trained model to do predictions on the test dataset:

```
>>> ## do prediction on the test set:
>>> feed = {tf_x : X_test_centered}
>>> y_pred = sess.run(predictions['classes'],
...                     feed_dict=feed)
>>>
>>> print('Test Accuracy: %.2f%%' % (
...         100*np.sum(y_pred == y_test)/y_test.shape[0]))

Test Accuracy: 93.89%
```

We can see that by leveraging high-level APIs, we can quickly build a model and test it. Therefore, a high-level API is very useful for prototyping our ideas and quickly checking the results.

Next, we will develop a similar classification model for MNIST using Keras, which is another high-level TensorFlow API.

Developing a multilayer neural network with Keras

The development of Keras started in the early months of 2015. As of today, it has evolved into one of the most popular and widely used libraries that is built on top of Theano and TensorFlow.

Similar to TensorFlow, the Keras allows us to utilize our GPUs to accelerate neural network training. One of its prominent features is that it has a very intuitive and user-friendly API, which allows us to implement neural networks in only a few lines of code.

Keras was first released as a standalone API that could leverage Theano as a backend, and the support for TensorFlow was added later. Keras is also integrated into TensorFlow from version 1.1.0. Therefore, if you have TensorFlow version 1.1.0, no more installation is needed for Keras. For more information about Keras, visit the official website at http://keras.io.

Currently, Keras is part of the contrib module (which contains packages developed by contributors to TensorFlow and is considered experimental code). In future releases of TensorFlow, it may be moved to become a separate module in the TensorFlow main API. For more information, visit the documentation on the TensorFlow website at https://www.tensorflow.org/api_docs/python/tf/contrib/keras.

Note that you may have to change the code from
`import tensorflow.contrib.keras as keras`
to `import tensorflow.keras as keras` in future
versions of TensorFlow in the following code examples.

On the following pages, we will walk through the code examples for using Keras
step by step. Using the same functions described in the previous section, we need to
load the data as follows:

```
>>> X_train, y_train = load_mnist('mnist/', kind='train')
>>> print('Rows: %d,  Columns: %d' %(X_train.shape[0],
...                                    X_train.shape[1]))
>>> X_test, y_test = load_mnist('mnist/', kind='t10k')
>>> print('Rows: %d,  Columns: %d' %(X_test.shape[0],
...                                    X_test.shape[1]))
Rows: 10000,  Columns: 784
>>>
>>> ## mean centering and normalization:
>>> mean_vals = np.mean(X_train, axis=0)
>>> std_val = np.std(X_train)
>>>
>>> X_train_centered = (X_train - mean_vals)/std_val
>>> X_test_centered = (X_test - mean_vals)/std_val
>>>
>>> del X_train, X_test
>>>
>>> print(X_train_centered.shape, y_train.shape)
(60000, 784) (60000,)
>>> print(X_test_centered.shape, y_test.shape)
(10000, 784) (10000,)
```

First, let's set the random seed for NumPy and TensorFlow so that we get consistent
results:

```
>>> import tensorflow as tf
>>> import tensorflow.contrib.keras as keras

# in Tf >= 1.4, use
# >>> import tensorflow.keras as keras
# instead of `import tensorflow.contrib.keras as keras
>>> np.random.seed(123)
>>> tf.set_random_seed(123)
```

To continue with the preparation of the training data, we need to convert the class labels (integers 0-9) into the one-hot format. Fortunately, Keras provides a convenient tool for this:

```
>>> y_train_onehot = keras.utils.to_categorical(y_train)
>>>
>>> print('First 3 labels: ', y_train[:3])
First 3 labels:  [5 0 4]
>>> print('\nFirst 3 labels (one-hot):\n', y_train_onehot[:3])
First 3 labels (one-hot):
 [[ 0.  0.  0.  0.  0.  1.  0.  0.  0.  0.]
  [ 1.  0.  0.  0.  0.  0.  0.  0.  0.  0.]
  [ 0.  0.  0.  0.  1.  0.  0.  0.  0.  0.]]
```

Now, we can get to the interesting part and implement a neural network. Briefly, we will have three layers, where the first two layers each have 50 hidden units with the `tanh` activation function and the last layer has 10 layers for the 10 class labels and uses `softmax` to give the probability of each class. Keras makes these tasks very simple, as you can see in the following code implementation:

```
model = keras.models.Sequential()

model.add(
    keras.layers.Dense(
        units=50,
        input_dim=X_train_centered.shape[1],
        kernel_initializer='glorot_uniform',
        bias_initializer='zeros',
        activation='tanh'))

model.add(
    keras.layers.Dense(
        units=50,
        input_dim=50,
        kernel_initializer='glorot_uniform',
        bias_initializer='zeros',
        activation='tanh'))

model.add(
    keras.layers.Dense(
        units=y_train_onehot.shape[1],
        input_dim=50,
        kernel_initializer='glorot_uniform',
```

```
                    bias_initializer='zeros',
                    activation='softmax'))


    sgd_optimizer = keras.optimizers.SGD(
            lr=0.001, decay=1e-7, momentum=.9)

    model.compile(optimizer=sgd_optimizer,
                    loss='categorical_crossentropy')
```

First, we initialize a new model using the `Sequential` class to implement a feedforward neural network. Then, we can add as many layers to it as we like. However, since the first layer that we add is the input layer, we have to make sure that the `input_dim` attribute matches the number of features (columns) in the training set (`784` features or pixels in the neural network implementation).

Also, we have to make sure that the number of output units (`units`) and input units (`input_dim`) of two consecutive layers match. In the preceding example, we added two hidden layers with 50 hidden units plus one bias unit each. The number of units in the output layer should be equal to the number of unique class labels—the number of columns in the one-hot-encoded class label array.

> Note that we used a new initialization algorithm for weight matrices by setting `kernel_initializer='glorot_uniform'`. Glorot initialization (also known as Xavier initialization) is a more robust way of initialization for deep neural networks (*Understanding the difficulty of training deep feedforward neural networks, Xavier Glorot* and *Yoshua Bengio*, in *Artificial Intelligence and Statistics*, volume 9, pages: 249-256. 2010). The biases are initialized to zero, which is more common, and in fact the default setting in Keras. We will discuss this weight initialization scheme in more detail in *Chapter 14, Going Deeper – The Mechanics of TensorFlow*.

Before we can compile our model, we also have to define an optimizer. In the preceding example, we chose a stochastic gradient descent optimization, which we are already familiar with from previous chapters. Furthermore, we can set values for the weight decay constant and momentum learning to adjust the learning rate at each epoch as discussed in *Chapter 12, Implementing a Multilayer Artificial Neural Network from Scratch*. Lastly, we set the cost (or loss) function to `categorical_crossentropy`.

The binary cross-entropy is just a technical term for the cost function in the logistic regression, and the categorical cross-entropy is its generalization for multiclass predictions via softmax, which we will cover in the section *Estimating class probabilities in multiclass classification via the softmax function* later in this chapter.

After compiling the model, we can now train it by calling the `fit` method. Here, we are using mini-batch stochastic gradient with a batch size of 64 training samples per batch. We train the MLP over 50 epochs, and we can follow the optimization of the cost function during training by setting `verbose=1`.

The `validation_split` parameter is especially handy since it will reserve 10 percent of the training data (here, 6,000 samples) for validation after each epoch so that we can monitor whether the model is overfitting during training:

```
>>> history = model.fit(X_train_centered, y_train_onehot,
...                     batch_size=64, epochs=50,
...                     verbose=1,
...                     validation_split=0.1)

Train on 54000 samples, validate on 6000 samples
Epoch 1/50
54000/54000 [==============================] - 3s - loss: 0.7247 -
val_loss: 0.3616
Epoch 2/50
54000/54000 [==============================] - 3s - loss: 0.3718 -
val_loss: 0.2815
Epoch 3/50
54000/54000 [==============================] - 3s - loss: 0.3087 -
val_loss: 0.2447

[...]
Epoch 50/50
54000/54000 [==============================] - 3s - loss: 0.0485 -
val_loss: 0.1174
```

Printing the value of the cost function is extremely useful during training. This is because we can quickly spot whether the cost is decreasing during training and stop the algorithm earlier, if otherwise, to tune the hyperparameter values.

To predict the class labels, we can then use the `predict_classes` method to return the class labels directly as integers:

```
>>> y_train_pred = model.predict_classes(X_train_centered, verbose=0)
>>> print('First 3 predictions: ', y_train_pred[:3])
First 3 predictions:  [5 0 4]
```

Finally, let's print the model accuracy on training and test sets:

```
>>> y_train_pred = model.predict_classes(X_train_centered,
...                                       verbose=0)
>>> correct_preds = np.sum(y_train == y_train_pred, axis=0)
>>> train_acc = correct_preds / y_train.shape[0]
>>>
>>> print('First 3 predictions: ', y_train_pred[:3])
First 3 predictions:  [5 0 4]
>>>
>>> print('Training accuracy: %.2f%%' % (train_acc * 100))
Training accuracy: 98.88%
>>>
>>> y_test_pred = model.predict_classes(X_test_centered,
...                                      verbose=0)
>>> correct_preds = np.sum(y_test == y_test_pred, axis=0)
>>> test_acc = correct_preds / y_test.shape[0]
>>> print('Test accuracy: %.2f%%' % (test_acc * 100))
Test accuracy: 96.04%
```

Note that this is just a very simple neural network without optimized tuning parameters. If you are interested in playing more with Keras, feel free to further tweak the learning rate, momentum, weight decay, and number of hidden units.

Choosing activation functions for multilayer networks

For simplicity, we have only discussed the sigmoid activation function in the context of multilayer feedforward neural networks so far; we used it in the hidden layer as well as the output layer in the multilayer perceptron implementation in *Chapter 12, Implementing a Multilayer Artificial Neural Network from Scratch*.

Although we referred to this activation function as a sigmoid function—as it is commonly called in literature—the more precise definition would be a *logistic function* or *negative log-likelihood function*. In the following subsections, you will learn more about alternative sigmoidal functions that are useful for implementing multilayer neural networks.

Technically, we can use any function as an activation function in multilayer neural networks as long as it is differentiable. We can even use linear activation functions, such as in Adaline (*Chapter 2, Training Simple Machine Learning Algorithms for Classification*). However, in practice, it would not be very useful to use linear activation functions for both hidden and output layers since we want to introduce nonlinearity in a typical artificial neural network to be able to tackle complex problems. The sum of linear functions yields a linear function after all.

The logistic activation function that we used in *Chapter 12, Implementing a Multilayer Artificial Neural Network from Scratch,* probably mimics the concept of a neuron in a brain most closely—we can think of it as the probability of whether a neuron fires or not.

However, logistic activation functions can be problematic if we have highly negative input since the output of the sigmoid function would be close to zero in this case. If the sigmoid function returns output that are close to zero, the neural network would learn very slowly and it becomes more likely that it gets trapped in the local minima during training. This is why people often prefer a hyperbolic tangent as an activation function in hidden layers.

Before we discuss what a hyperbolic tangent looks like, let's briefly recapitulate some of the basics of the logistic function and look at a generalization that makes it more useful for multilabel classification problems.

Logistic function recap

As we mentioned in the introduction to this section, the logistic function, often just called the sigmoid function, is in fact a special case of a sigmoid function. Recall from the section on logistic regression in *Chapter 3, A Tour of Machine Learning Classifiers Using scikit-learn,* that we can use a logistic function to model the probability that sample x belongs to the positive class (class 1) in a binary classification task. The given net input z is shown in the following equation:

$$z = w_0 x_0 + w_1 x_1 + \cdots + w_m x_m = \sum_{i=0}^{m} w_i x_i = w^T x$$

The logistic function will compute the following:

$$\phi_{logistic}(z) = \frac{1}{1 + e^{-z}}$$

Note that w_0 is the bias unit (*y*-axis intercept, which means $x_0 = 1$). To provide a more concrete example, let's assume a model for a two-dimensional data point *x* and a model with the following weight coefficients assigned to the *w* vector:

```
>>> import numpy as np

>>> X = np.array([1, 1.4, 2.5]) ## first value must be 1
>>> w = np.array([0.4, 0.3, 0.5])

>>> def net_input(X, w):
...     return np.dot(X, w)
...
>>> def logistic(z):
...     return 1.0 / (1.0 + np.exp(-z))
...
>>> def logistic_activation(X, w):
...     z = net_input(X, w)
...     return logistic(z)
...
>>> print('P(y=1|x) = %.3f' % logistic_activation(X, w))
P(y=1|x) = 0.888
```

If we calculate the net input and use it to activate a logistic neuron with those particular feature values and weight coefficients, we get a value of 0.888, which we can interpret as 88.8 percent probability that this particular sample *x* belongs to the positive class.

In *Chapter 12, Implementing a Multilayer Artificial Neural Network from Scratch*, we used the one-hot-encoding technique to compute the values in the output layer consisting of multiple logistic activation units. However, as we will demonstrate with the following code example, an output layer consisting of multiple logistic activation units does not produce meaningful, interpretable probability values:

```
>>> # W : array with shape = (n_output_units, n_hidden_units+1)
... #     note that the first column are the bias units
...
>>> W = np.array([[1.1, 1.2, 0.8, 0.4],
...               [0.2, 0.4, 1.0, 0.2],
...               [0.6, 1.5, 1.2, 0.7]])
>>>
>>> # A : data array with shape = (n_hidden_units + 1, n_samples)
... #     note that the first column of this array must be 1
...
>>> A = np.array([[1, 0.1, 0.4, 0.6]])
>>>
```

```
>>> Z = np.dot(W, A[0])
>>> y_probas = logistic(Z)
>>> print('Net Input: \n', Z)
Net Input:
 [ 1.78  0.76  1.65]
>>> print('Output Units:\n', y_probas)
Output Units:
 [ 0.85569687  0.68135373  0.83889105]
```

As we can see in the output, the resulting values cannot be interpreted as probabilities for a three-class problem. The reason for this is that they do not sum up to 1. However, this is in fact not a big concern if we only use our model to predict the class labels, not the class membership probabilities. One way to predict the class label from the output units obtained earlier is to use the maximum value:

```
>>> y_class = np.argmax(Z, axis=0)
>>> print('Predicted class label: %d' % y_class)
Predicted class label: 0
```

In certain contexts, it can be useful to compute meaningful class probabilities for multiclass predictions. In the next section, we will take a look at a generalization of the logistic function, the `softmax` function, which can help us with this task.

Estimating class probabilities in multiclass classification via the softmax function

In the previous section, we saw how we could obtain a class label using the `argmax` function. The `softmax` function is in fact a soft form of the `argmax` function; instead of giving a single class index, it provides the probability of each class. Therefore, it allows us to compute meaningful class probabilities in multiclass settings (multinomial logistic regression).

In `softmax`, the probability of a particular sample with net input z belonging to the ith class can be computed with a normalization term in the denominator, that is, the sum of all M linear functions:

$$p\left(y = i\middle|z\right) = \phi\left(z\right) = \frac{e^{z_i}}{\sum_{i=1}^{M} e^{z_j}}$$

To see `softmax` in action, let's code it up in Python:

```
>>> def softmax(z):
...     return np.exp(z) / np.sum(np.exp(z))
...
>>> y_probas = softmax(Z)
>>> print('Probabilities:\n', y_probas)
Probabilities:
 [ 0.44668973   0.16107406   0.39223621]

>>> np.sum(y_probas)
1.0
```

As we can see, the predicted class probabilities now sum up to 1, as we would expect. It is also notable that the predicted class label is the same as when we applied the `argmax` function to the logistic output. Intuitively, it may help to think of the `softmax` function as a *normalized* output that is useful to obtain meaningful class-membership predictions in multiclass settings.

Broadening the output spectrum using a hyperbolic tangent

Another sigmoid function that is often used in the hidden layers of artificial neural networks is the **hyperbolic tangent** (commonly known as **tanh**), which can be interpreted as a rescaled version of the logistic function:

$$\phi_{logistic}(z) = \frac{1}{1+e^{-z}}$$

$$\phi_{tanh}(z) = 2 \times \phi_{logistic}(2z) - 1 = \frac{e^z - e^{-z}}{e^z + e^{-z}}$$

The advantage of the hyperbolic tangent over the logistic function is that it has a broader output spectrum and ranges in the open interval (-1, 1), which can improve the convergence of the back propagation algorithm (*Neural Networks for Pattern Recognition, C. M. Bishop, Oxford University Press,* pages: 500-501, *1995*).

In contrast, the logistic function returns an output signal that ranges in the open interval (0, 1). For an intuitive comparison of the logistic function and the hyperbolic tangent, let's plot the two sigmoid functions:

```
>>> import matplotlib.pyplot as plt

>>> def tanh(z):
...        e_p = np.exp(z)
...        e_m = np.exp(-z)
...        return (e_p - e_m) / (e_p + e_m)

>>> z = np.arange(-5, 5, 0.005)
>>> log_act = logistic(z)
>>> tanh_act = tanh(z)
>>> plt.ylim([-1.5, 1.5])
>>> plt.xlabel('net input $z$')
>>> plt.ylabel('activation $\phi(z)$')
>>> plt.axhline(1, color='black', linestyle=':')
>>> plt.axhline(0.5, color='black', linestyle=':')
>>> plt.axhline(0, color='black', linestyle=':')
>>> plt.axhline(-0.5, color='black', linestyle=':')
>>> plt.axhline(-1, color='black', linestyle=':')
>>> plt.plot(z, tanh_act,
...          linewidth=3, linestyle='--',
...          label='tanh')
>>> plt.plot(z, log_act,
...          linewidth=3,
...          label='logistic')
>>> plt.legend(loc='lower right')
>>> plt.tight_layout()
>>> plt.show()
```

As we can see, the shapes of the two sigmoidal curves look very similar; however, the tanh function has 2× larger output space than the logistic function:

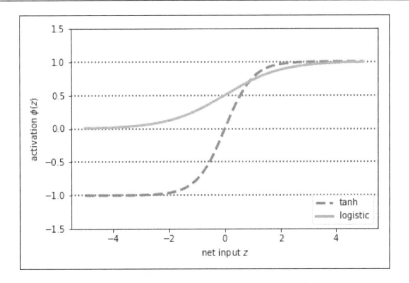

Note that we implemented the `logistic` and `tanh` functions verbosely for the purpose of illustration. In practice, we can use NumPy's `tanh` function to achieve the same results:

```
>>> tanh_act = np.tanh(z)
```

In addition, the logistic function is available in SciPy's special module:

```
>>> from scipy.special import expit
>>> log_act = expit(z)
```

Rectified linear unit activation

Rectified Linear Unit (ReLU) is another activation function that is often used in deep neural networks. Before we understand ReLU, we should step back and understand the vanishing gradient problem of tanh and logistic activations.

To understand this problem, let's assume that we initially have the net input $z_1 = 20$, which changes to $z_2 = 25$. Computing the tanh activation, we get $\phi(z_1) \approx 1.0$ and $\phi(z_2) \approx 1.0$, which shows no change in the output.

This means the derivative of activations with respect to net input diminishes as z becomes large. As a result, learning weights during the training phase become very slow because the gradient terms may be very close to zero. ReLU activation addresses this issue. Mathematically, ReLU is defined as follows:

$$\phi(z) = \max(0, z)$$

ReLU is still a nonlinear function that is good for learning complex functions with neural networks. Besides this, the derivative of ReLU, with respect to its input, is always 1 for positive input values. Therefore, it solves the problem of vanishing gradients, making it suitable for deep neural networks. We will use the ReLU activation function in the next chapter as an activation function for multilayer convolutional neural networks.

Now that we know more about the different activation functions that are commonly used in artificial neural networks, let's conclude this section with an overview of the different activation functions that we encountered in this book:

Activation Function	Equation	Example	1D Graph
Linear	$\phi(z) = z$	Adaline, linear regression	
Unit Step (Heaviside Function)	$\phi(z) = \begin{cases} 0 & z < 0 \\ 0.5 & z = 0 \\ 1 & z > 0 \end{cases}$	Perceptron variant	
Sign (signum)	$\phi(z) = \begin{cases} -1 & z < 0 \\ 0 & z = 0 \\ 1 & z > 0 \end{cases}$	Perceptron variant	
Piece-wise Linear	$\phi(z) = \begin{cases} 0 & z \leq -\frac{1}{2} \\ z + \frac{1}{2} & -\frac{1}{2} \leq z \leq \frac{1}{2} \\ 1 & z \geq \frac{1}{2} \end{cases}$	Support vector machine	
Logistic (sigmoid)	$\phi(z) = \dfrac{1}{1 + e^{-z}}$	Logistic regression, Multilayer NN	
Hyperbolic Tangent (tanh)	$\phi(z) = \dfrac{e^{z} - e^{-z}}{e^{z} + e^{-z}}$	Multilayer NN, RNNs	
ReLU	$\phi(z) = \begin{cases} 0 & z < 0 \\ z & z > 0 \end{cases}$	Multilayer NN, CNNs	

Summary

In this chapter, you learned how to use TensorFlow, an open source library for numerical computations with a special focus on deep learning. While TensorFlow is more inconvenient to use compared to NumPy, due to its additional complexity to support GPUs, it allows us to define and train large, multilayer neural networks very efficiently.

Also, you learned about the TensorFlow API to build complex machine learning and neural network models and run them efficiently. First, we explored programming in the low-level TensorFlow API. Implementing models at this level may be tedious when we have to program at the level of matrix-vector multiplications and define every detail of each operation. However, the advantage is that this allows us as developers to combine such basic operations and build more complex models. Furthermore, we discussed how TensorFlow allows us to utilize the GPUs for training and testing big neural networks to speed up the computations. Without the use of GPUs, training some networks would typically need months of computation!

We then explored two high-level APIs that make building neural network models a lot easier compared to the low-level API. Specifically, we used TensorFlow Layers and Keras to build the multilayer neural network and learned how to build models using those APIs.

Finally, you learned about different activation functions and understood their behaviors and applications. Specifically, in this chapter, we saw tanh, softmax, and ReLU. In *Chapter 12, Implementing a Multilayer Artificial Neural Network from Scratch*, we started with implementing a simple **Multilayer Perceptron** (**MLP**) to classify a handwritten image in the MNIST dataset. While the low-level implementation from scratch was helpful to illustrate the core concepts of a multilayer neural network, such as the forward pass and backpropagation, training neural networks using NumPy is very inefficient and impractical for large networks.

In the next chapter, we'll continue our journey and dive deeper into TensorFlow, and we'll find ourselves working with graph and session objects. Along the way, we'll learn many new concepts, such as placeholders, variables, and saving and restoring models in TensorFlow.

14

Going Deeper – The Mechanics of TensorFlow

In *Chapter 13*, *Parallelizing Neural Network Training with TensorFlow*, we trained a multilayer perceptron to classify MNIST digits, using various aspects of the TensorFlow Python API. That was a great way to dive us straight into some hands-on experience with TensorFlow neural network training and machine learning.

In this chapter, we'll now shift our focus squarely on to TensorFlow itself, and explore in detail the impressive mechanics and features that TensorFlow offers:

- Key features and advantages of TensorFlow
- TensorFlow ranks and tensors
- Understanding and working with TensorFlow graphs
- Working with TensorFlow variables
- TensorFlow operations with different scopes
- Common tensor transformations: working with ranks, shapes, and types
- Transforming tensors as multidimensional arrays
- Saving and restoring a model in TensorFlow
- Visualizing neural network graphs with TensorBoard

We'll stay hands-on in this chapter, of course, and implement graphs throughout the chapter to explore the main TensorFlow features and concepts. Along the way, we'll also revisit a regression model, explore neural network graph visualization with TensorBoard, and suggest some ways that you could explore visualizing more of the graphs that you'll make through this chapter.

Key features of TensorFlow

TensorFlow gives us a scalable, multiplatform programming interface for implementing and running machine learning algorithms. The TensorFlow API has been relatively stable and mature since its 1.0 release in 2017. There are other deep learning libraries available, but they are still very experimental by comparison.

A key feature of TensorFlow that we already noted in *Chapter 13*, *Parallelizing Neural Network Training with TensorFlow*, is its ability to work with single or multiple GPUs. This allows users to train machine learning models very efficiently on large-scale systems.

TensorFlow has strong growth drivers. Its development is funded and supported by Google, and so a large team of software engineers work on improvements continuously. TensorFlow also has strong support from open source developers, who avidly contribute and provide user feedback. This has made the TensorFlow library more useful to both academic researchers and developers in their industry. A further consequence of these factors is that TensorFlow has extensive documentation and tutorials to help new users.

Last but not least among these key features, TensorFlow supports mobile deployment, which makes it a very suitable tool for production.

TensorFlow ranks and tensors

The TensorFlow library lets users define operations and functions over tensors as computational graphs. Tensors are a generalizable mathematical notation for multidimensional arrays holding data values, where the dimensionality of a tensor is typically referred to as its **rank**.

We've worked mostly, so far, with tensors of rank zero to two. For instance, a scalar, a single number such as an integer or float, is a tensor of rank 0. A vector is a tensor of rank 1, and a matrix is a tensor of rank 2. But, it doesn't stop here. The tensor notation can be generalized to higher dimensions—as we'll see in the next chapter, when we work with an input of rank 3 and weight tensors of rank 4 to support images with multiple color channels.

To make the concept of a **tensor** more intuitive, consider the following figure, which represents tensors of ranks 0 and 1 in the first row, and tensors of ranks 2 and 3 in the second row:

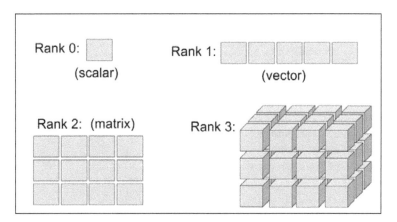

How to get the rank and shape of a tensor

We can use the tf.rank function to get the rank of a tensor. It is important to note that tf.rank will return a tensor as output, and in order to get the actual value, we will need to evaluate that tensor.

In addition to the tensor rank, we can also get the shape of a TensorFlow tensor (similar to the shape of a NumPy array). For example, if x is a tensor, we can get its shape using x.get_shape(), which will return an object of a special class called TensorShape.

We can print the shape and use it directly for the shape argument when creating other tensors. However, we **cannot** index or slice this object directly. If we want to index or slice different elements of this object, then we can convert it into a Python list, using the as_list method of the tensor class.

See the following examples on how to use the tf.rank function and the get_shape method of a tensor. The following code example illustrates how to retrieve the rank and shape of the tensor objects in a TensorFlow session:

```
>>> import tensorflow as tf
>>> import numpy as np
>>>
>>> g = tf.Graph()
>>>
>>> ## define the computation graph
>>> with g.as_default():
```

```
...        ## define tensors t1, t2, t3
...        t1 = tf.constant(np.pi)
...        t2 = tf.constant([1, 2, 3, 4])
...        t3 = tf.constant([[1, 2], [3, 4]])
...
...        ## get their ranks
...        r1 = tf.rank(t1)
...        r2 = tf.rank(t2)
...        r3 = tf.rank(t3)
...
...        ## get their shapes
...        s1 = t1.get_shape()
...        s2 = t2.get_shape()
...        s3 = t3.get_shape()
...        print('Shapes:', s1, s2, s3)
Shapes: [] (4,) (2, 2)
>>> with tf.Session(graph=g) as sess:
...        print('Ranks:',
...              r1.eval(),
...              r2.eval(),
...              r3.eval())

Ranks: 0 1 2
```

As we can see, the rank of the t1 tensor is 0 since it is just a scalar (corresponding to the [] shape). The rank of the t2 vector is 1, and since it has four elements, its shape is the one-element tuple (4,). Lastly, the shape of the 2 × 2 matrix t3 is 2; thus, its corresponding shape is given by the (2, 2) tuple.

Understanding TensorFlow's computation graphs

TensorFlow relies on building a computation graph at its core, and it uses this computation graph to derive relationships between tensors from the input all the way to the output. Let's say, we have rank 0 (scalar) tensors a, b, and c and we want to evaluate $z = 2 \times (a - b) + c$. This evaluation can be represented as a computation graph, as shown in the following figure:

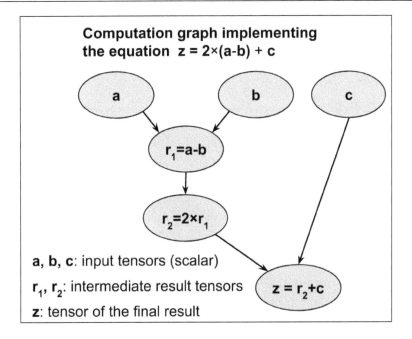

Computation graph implementing the equation $z = 2 \times (a-b) + c$

a, b, c: input tensors (scalar)

r_1, r_2: intermediate result tensors

z: tensor of the final result

As we can see, the computation graph is simply a network of nodes. Each node resembles an operation, which applies a function to its input tensor or tensors and returns zero or more tensors as the output.

TensorFlow builds this computation graph and uses it to compute the gradients accordingly. The individual steps for building and compiling such a computation graph in TensorFlow are as follows:

1. Instantiate a new, empty computation graph.
2. Add nodes (tensors and operations) to the computation graph.
3. Execute the graph:
    a. Start a new session
    b. Initialize the variables in the graph
    c. Run the computation graph in this session

So let's create a graph for evaluating $z = 2 \times (a - b) + c$, as shown in the previous figure, where a, b, and c are scalars (single numbers). Here, we define them as TensorFlow constants. A graph can be created by calling `tf.Graph()`, then nodes can be added to it as follows:

```
>>> g = tf.Graph()
>>>
>>> with g.as_default():
...     a = tf.constant(1, name='a')
...     b = tf.constant(2, name='b')
...     c = tf.constant(3, name='c')
...
...     z = 2*(a-b) + c
```

In this code, we added nodes to the g graph using `with g.as_default()`. If we do not explicitly create a graph, there is always a default graph, and therefore, all the nodes are added to the default graph. In this book, we try to avoid working with the default graph for clarity. This approach is especially useful when we are developing code in a Jupyter notebook, as we avoid piling up unwanted nodes in the default graph by accident.

A TensorFlow session is an environment in which the operations and tensors of a graph can be executed. A session object is created by calling `tf.Session` that can receive an existing graph (here, g) as an argument, as in `tf.Session(graph=g)`; otherwise, it will launch the default graph, which might be empty.

After launching a graph in a TensorFlow session, we can execute its nodes; that is, evaluating its tensors or executing its operators. Evaluating each individual tensor involves calling its `eval` method inside the current session. When evaluating a specific tensor in the graph, TensorFlow has to execute all the preceding nodes in the graph until it reaches that particular one. In case there are one or more placeholders, they would need to be fed, as we'll see later in the next section.

Quite similarly, we can also use a session's run method to execute operations that do not have any return types. An example of such an operation was introduced in *Chapter 13, Parallelizing Neural Network Training with TensorFlow*, for building multilayer perceptrons for MNIST, namely `train_op = optimizer.minimize(loss=cost)`. This operator can be executed as `train_op.run()`. Furthermore, there is a universal way of running both tensors and operators: `tf.Session().run()`. Using this method, as we'll see later on as well, multiple tensors and operators can be placed in a list or tuple. As a result, `tf.Session().run()` will return a list or tuple of the same size.

Here, we will launch the previous graph in a TensorFlow session and evaluate the tensor z as follows:

```
>>> with tf.Session(graph=g) as sess:
...     print('2*(a-b)+c => ', sess.run(z))
2*(a-b)+c =>   1
```

Remember that we define tensors and operations in a computation graph context within TensorFlow. A TensorFlow session is then used to execute the operations in the graph and fetch and evaluate the results.

In this section, we saw how to define a computation graph, how to add nodes to it, and how to evaluate the tensors in a graph within a TensorFlow session. We'll now take a deeper look into the different types of nodes that can appear in a computation graph, including placeholders and variables. Along the way, we'll see some other operators that do not return a tensor as the output.

Placeholders in TensorFlow

TensorFlow has special mechanisms for feeding data. One of these mechanisms is the use of placeholders, which are predefined tensors with specific types and shapes.

These tensors are added to the computation graph using the `tf.placeholder` function, and they do not contain any data. However, upon the execution of certain nodes in the graph, these placeholders need to be fed with data arrays.

In the following sections, we'll see how to define placeholders in a graph and how to feed them with data values upon execution.

Defining placeholders

As you now know, placeholders are defined using the `tf.placeholder` function. When we define placeholders, we need to decide what their shape and type should be, according to the shape and type of the data that will be fed through them upon execution.

Let's start with a simple example. In the following code, we will define the same graph that was shown in the previous section for evaluating $z = 2 \times (a-b) + c$. This time, however, we use placeholders for the scalars a, b, and c. Also, we store the intermediate tensors associated with r_1 and r_2, as follows:

```
>>> import tensorflow as tf
>>>
>>> g = tf.Graph()
```

```
>>> with g.as_default():
...     tf_a = tf.placeholder(tf.int32, shape=[],
...                         name='tf_a')
...     tf_b = tf.placeholder(tf.int32, shape=[],
...                         name='tf_b')
...     tf_c = tf.placeholder(tf.int32, shape=[],
...                         name='tf_c')
...
...     r1 = tf_a-tf_b
...     r2 = 2*r1
...     z  = r2 + tf_c
```

In this code, we defined three placeholders, named `tf_a`, `tf_b`, and `tf_c`, using type `tf.int32` (32-bit integers) and set their shape via `shape=[]` since they are scalars (tensors of rank 0). In the current book, we always precede the placeholder objects with `tf_` for clarity and to be able to distinguish them from other tensors.

Note that in the previous code example, we were dealing with scalars, and therefore, their shapes were specified as `shape=[]`. However, it is very straightforward to define placeholders of higher dimensions. For example, a rank 3 placeholder of type `float` and shape 3 x 4 x 5 can be defined as `tf.placeholder(dtype=tf.float32, shape=[3, 4, 5]`.

Feeding placeholders with data

When we execute a node in the graph, we need to create a python **dictionary** to feed the values of placeholders with data arrays. We do this according to the type and shape of the placeholders. This dictionary is passed as the input argument `feed_dict` to a session's `run` method.

In the previous graph, we added three placeholders of the type `tf.int32` to feed scalars for computing z. Now, in order to evaluate the result tensor z, we can feed arbitrary integer values (here, 1, 2, and 3) to the placeholders, as follows:

```
>>> with tf.Session(graph=g) as sess:
...     feed = {tf_a: 1,
...             tf_b: 2,
...             tf_c: 3}
...     print('z:',
...           sess.run(z, feed_dict=feed))
z: 1
```

This means that having extra arrays for placeholders does not cause any error; it is just redundant to do so. However, if a placeholder is needed for the execution of a particular node, and is not provided via the `feed_dict` argument, it will cause a runtime error.

Defining placeholders for data arrays with varying batchsizes

Sometimes, when we are developing a neural network model, we may deal with mini-batches of data that have different sizes. For example, we may train a neural network with a specific mini-batch size, but we want to use the network to make predictions on one or more data input.

A useful feature of placeholders is that we can specify None for the dimension that is varying in size. For example, we can create a placeholder of rank 2, where the first dimension is unknown (or may vary), as shown here:

```
>>> import tensorflow as tf
>>>
>>> g = tf.Graph()
>>>
>>> with g.as_default():
...     tf_x = tf.placeholder(tf.float32,
...                           shape=[None, 2],
...                           name='tf_x')
...
...     x_mean = tf.reduce_mean(tf_x,
...                             axis=0,
...                             name='mean')
```

Then, we can evaluate x_mean with two different input, x1 and x2, which are NumPy arrays of shape (5, 2) and (10, 2), as follows:

```
>>> import numpy as np
>>> np.random.seed(123)
>>> np.set_printoptions(precision=2)
>>> with tf.Session(graph=g) as sess:
...      x1 = np.random.uniform(low=0, high=1,
...                             size=(5, 2))
...      print('Feeding data with shape ', x1.shape)
...      print('Result:', sess.run(x_mean,
...                           feed_dict={tf_x: x1}))
...      x2 = np.random.uniform(low=0, high=1,
...                             size=(10,2))
...      print('Feeding data with shape', x2.shape)
...      print('Result:', sess.run(x_mean,
...                           feed_dict={tf_x: x2}))
```

This prints the following output:

```
Feeding data with shape (5, 2)
Result: [ 0.62   0.47]
Feeding data with shape (10, 2)
Result: [ 0.46   0.49]
```

Lastly, if we try printing the object tf_x, we will get Tensor("tf_x:0", shape=(?, 2), dtype=float32), which shows that the shape of this tensor is (?, 2).

Variables in TensorFlow

In the context of TensorFlow, variables are a special type of tensor objects that allow us to store and update the parameters of our models in a TensorFlow session during training. The following sections explain how we can define variables in a graph, initialize those variables in a session, organize variables via the so-called variable scope, and reuse existing variables.

Defining variables

TensorFlow variables store the parameters of a model that can be updated during training, for example, the weights in the input, hidden, and output layers of a neural network. When we define a variable, we need to initialize it with a tensor of values. Feel free to read more about TensorFlow variables at `https://www.tensorflow.org/programmers_guide/variables`.

TensorFlow provides two ways for defining variables:

- `tf.Variable(<initial-value>, name="variable-name")`
- `tf.get_variable(name, ...)`

The first one, `tf.Variable`, is a class that creates an object for a new variable and adds it to the graph. Note that `tf.Variable` does not have an explicit way to determine `shape` and `dtype`; the shape and type are set to be the same as those of the initial values.

The second option, `tf.get_variable`, can be used to **reuse** an existing variable with a given name (if the name exists in the graph) or create a new one if the name does not exist. In this case, the name becomes critical; that's probably why it has to be placed as the first argument to this function. Furthermore, `tf.get_variable` provides an explicit way to set `shape` and `dtype`; these parameters are only required when creating a new variable, not reusing existing ones.

The advantage of `tf.get_variable` over `tf.Variable` is twofold: `tf.get_variable` allows us to reuse existing variables, and it already uses the popular Xavier/Glorot initialization scheme by default.

Besides the initializer, the `get_variable` function provides other parameters to control the tensor, such as adding a regularizer for the variable. If you are interested in learning more about these parameters, feel free to read the documentation of `tf.get_variable` at `https://www.tensorflow.org/api_docs/python/tf/get_variable`.

Xavier (or Glorot) initialization

In the early development of deep learning, it was observed that random uniform or random normal weight initialization could often result in a poor performance of the model during training.

In 2010, Xavier Glorot and Yoshua Bengio investigated the effect of initialization and proposed a novel, more robust initialization scheme to facilitate the training of deep networks.

The general idea behind Xavier initialization is to roughly balance the variance of the gradients across different layers. Otherwise, one layer may get too much attention during training while the other layer lags behind.

According to the research paper by Glorot and Bengio, if we want to initialize the weights from uniform distribution, we should choose the interval of this uniform distribution as follows:

$$ W \sim Uniform\left(-\frac{\sqrt{6}}{\sqrt{n_{in} + n_{out}}}, \frac{\sqrt{6}}{\sqrt{n_{in} + n_{out}}} \right) $$

Here, n_{in} is the number of input neurons that are multiplied with the weights, and n_{out} is the number of output neurons that feed into the next layer. For initializing the weights from Gaussian (normal) distribution, the authors recommend choosing the standard deviation of this Gaussian to be $\sigma = \frac{\sqrt{2}}{\sqrt{n_{in} + n_{out}}}$.

TensorFlow supports Xavier initialization in both uniform and normal distributions of weights. The documentation provides detailed information about using Xavier initialization with TensorFlow: `https://www.tensorflow.org/api_docs/python/tf/contrib/layers/xavier_initializer`.

For more information about Glorot and Bengio's initialization scheme, including the mathematical derivation and proof, read their original paper (*Understanding the difficulty of deep feedforward neural networks, Xavier Glorot and Yoshua Bengio, 2010*), which is freely available at `http://proceedings.mlr.press/v9/glorot10a/glorot10a.pdf`.

In either initialization technique, it's important to note that the initial values are not set until we launch the graph in `tf.Session` and explicitly run the initializer operator in that session. In fact, the required memory for a graph is not allocated until we initialize the variables in a TensorFlow session.

Here is an example of creating a variable object where the initial values are created from a NumPy array. The `dtype` data type of this tensor is `tf.int64`, which is automatically **inferred** from its NumPy array input:

```
>>> import tensorflow as tf
>>> import numpy as np
>>>
>>> g1 = tf.Graph()
>>>
>>> with g1.as_default():
...     w = tf.Variable(np.array([[1, 2, 3, 4],
...                               [5, 6, 7, 8]]), name='w')
...     print(w)
<tf.Variable 'w:0' shape=(2, 4) dtype=int64_ref>
```

Initializing variables

Here, it is critical to understand that tensors defined as variables are not allocated in memory and contain no values until they are initialized. Therefore, before executing any node in the computation graph, we *must* initialize the variables that are within the path to the node that we want to execute.

This initialization process refers to allocating memory for the associated tensors and assigning their initial values. TensorFlow provides a function named `tf.global_variables_initializer` that returns an operator for initializing all the variables that exist in a computation graph. Then, executing this operator will initialize the variables as follows:

```
>>> with tf.Session(graph=g1) as sess:
...     sess.run(tf.global_variables_initializer())
...     print(sess.run(w))

[[1 2 3 4]
 [5 6 7 8]]
```

We can also store this operator in an object such as `init_op = tf.global_variables_initializer()` and execute this operator later using `sess.run(init_op)` or `init_op.run()`. However, we need to make sure that this operator is created after we define all the variables.

For example, in the following code, we define the variable w1, then we define the operator `init_op`, followed by the variable w2:

```
>>> import tensorflow as tf
>>>
>>> g2 = tf.Graph()
>>>
>>> with g2.as_default():
...     w1 = tf.Variable(1, name='w1')
...     init_op = tf.global_variables_initializer()
...     w2 = tf.Variable(2, name='w2')
```

Now, let's evaluate w1 as follows:

```
>>> with tf.Session(graph=g2) as sess:
...     sess.run(init_op)
...     print('w1:', sess.run(w1))
w1: 1
```

This works fine. Now, let's try evaluating w2:

```
>>> with tf.Session(graph=g2) as sess:
...     sess.run(init_op)
...     print('w2:', sess.run(w2))
FailedPreconditionError
Attempting to use uninitialized value w2
    [[Node: _retval_w2_0_0 = _Retval[T=DT_INT32, index=0, _device="/
job:localhost/replica:0/task:0/cpu:0"](w2)]]
```

As shown in the code example, executing the graph raises an error because w2 was not initialized via `sess.run(init_op)`, and therefore, couldn't be evaluated. The operator `init_op` was defined prior to adding w2 to the graph; thus, executing `init_op` will not initialize w2.

Variable scope

In this subsection, we're going to discuss *scoping*, which is an important concept in TensorFlow, and especially useful if we are constructing large neural network graphs.

With variable scopes, we can organize the variables into separate subparts. When we create a variable scope, the name of operations and tensors that are created within that scope are prefixed with that scope, and those scopes can further be nested. For example, if we have two subnetworks, where each subnetwork has several layers, we can define two scopes named `'net_A'` and `'net_B'`, respectively. Then, each layer will be defined within one of these scopes.

Let's see how the variable names will turn out in the following code example:

```
>>> import tensorflow as tf
>>>
>>> g = tf.Graph()
>>>
>>> with g.as_default():
...     with tf.variable_scope('net_A'):
...         with tf.variable_scope('layer-1'):
...             w1 = tf.Variable(tf.random_normal(
...                 shape=(10,4)), name='weights')
...         with tf.variable_scope('layer-2'):
...             w2 = tf.Variable(tf.random_normal(
...                 shape=(20,10)), name='weights')
...     with tf.variable_scope('net_B'):
...         with tf.variable_scope('layer-1'):
...             w3 = tf.Variable(tf.random_normal(
...                 shape=(10,4)), name='weights')
...
...     print(w1)
...     print(w2)
...     print(w3)


<tf.Variable 'net_A/layer-1/weights:0' shape=(10, 4) dtype=float32_
ref>
<tf.Variable 'net_A/layer-2/weights:0' shape=(20, 10) dtype=float32_
ref>
<tf.Variable 'net_B/layer-1/weights:0' shape=(10, 4) dtype=float32_
ref>
```

Notice that the variable names are now prefixed with their nested scopes, separated by the forward slash (/) symbol.

> For more information about variable scoping, read the documentation at https://www.tensorflow.org/programmers_guide/variable_scope and https://www.tensorflow.org/api_docs/python/tf/variable_scope.

Reusing variables

Let's imagine that we're developing a somewhat complex neural network model that has a classifier whose input data comes from more than one source. For example, we'll assume that we have data (X_A, y_A) coming from source A and data (X_B, y_B) comes from source B. In this example, we will design our graph in such a way that it will use the data from only one source as input tensor to build the network. Then, we can feed the data from the other source to the same classifier.

In the following example, we assume that data from source A is fed through a placeholder, and source B is the output of a generator network. We will build the generator network by calling the `build_generator` function within the `generator` scope, then we will add a classifier by calling `build_classifier` within the `classifier` scope:

```
>>> import tensorflow as tf
>>>
>>> ###########################
... ##    Helper functions    ##
... ###########################
>>>
>>> def build_classifier(data, labels, n_classes=2):
...     data_shape = data.get_shape().as_list()
...     weights = tf.get_variable(name='weights',
...                               shape=(data_shape[1],
...                                      n_classes),
...                               dtype=tf.float32)
...     bias = tf.get_variable(name='bias',
...                            initializer=tf.zeros(
...                                shape=n_classes))
...     logits = tf.add(tf.matmul(data, weights),
...                     bias,
...                     name='logits')
...     return logits, tf.nn.softmax(logits)
>>>
>>>
>>> def build_generator(data, n_hidden):
...     data_shape = data.get_shape().as_list()
...     w1 = tf.Variable(
...         tf.random_normal(shape=(data_shape[1],
...                                 n_hidden)),
...         name='w1')
...     b1 = tf.Variable(tf.zeros(shape=n_hidden),
...                      name='b1')
...     hidden = tf.add(tf.matmul(data, w1), b1,
```

```
...                         name='hidden_pre-activation')
...         hidden = tf.nn.relu(hidden, 'hidden_activation')
...
...         w2 = tf.Variable(
...             tf.random_normal(shape=(n_hidden,
...                                     data_shape[1])),
...             name='w2')
...         b2 = tf.Variable(tf.zeros(shape=data_shape[1]),
...                         name='b2')
...         output = tf.add(tf.matmul(hidden, w2), b2,
...                         name = 'output')
...         return output, tf.nn.sigmoid(output)
>>>
>>> ###########################
... ##  Build the graph      ##
... ###########################
>>>
>>> batch_size=64
>>> g = tf.Graph()
>>>
>>> with g.as_default():
...         tf_X = tf.placeholder(shape=(batch_size, 100),
...                               dtype=tf.float32,
...                               name='tf_X')
...
...         ## build the generator
...         with tf.variable_scope('generator'):
...             gen_out1 = build_generator(data=tf_X,
...                                        n_hidden=50)
...
...         ## build the classifier
...         with tf.variable_scope('classifier') as scope:
...             ## classifier for the original data:
...             cls_out1 = build_classifier(data=tf_X,
...                                         labels=tf.ones(
...                                             shape=batch_size))
...
...             ## reuse the classifier for generated data
...             scope.reuse_variables()
...             cls_out2 = build_classifier(data=gen_out1[1],
...                                         labels=tf.zeros(
...                                             shape=batch_size))
```

Notice that we have called the `build_classifier` function two times. The first call causes the building of the network. Then, we call `scope.reuse_variables()` and call that function again. As a result, the second call does not create new variables; instead, it reuses the same variables. Alternatively, we could reuse the variables by specifying the `reuse=True` parameter, as follows:

```
>>> g = tf.Graph()
>>>
>>> with g.as_default():
...     tf_X = tf.placeholder(shape=(batch_size, 100),
...                           dtype=tf.float32,
...                           name='tf_X')
...     ## build the generator
...     with tf.variable_scope('generator'):
...         gen_out1 = build_generator(data=tf_X,
...                                    n_hidden=50)
...
...     ## build the classifier
...     with tf.variable_scope('classifier'):
...         ## classifier for the original data:
...         cls_out1 = build_classifier(data=tf_X,
...                                     labels=tf.ones(
...                                         shape=batch_size))
...
...     with tf.variable_scope('classifier', reuse=True):
...         ## reuse the classifier for generated data
...         cls_out2 = build_classifier(data=gen_out1[1],
...                                     labels=tf.zeros(
...                                         shape=batch_size))
```

While we have discussed how to define computational graphs and variables in TensorFlow, a detailed discussion of how we can compute gradients in a computational graph is beyond the scope of this book, where we use TensorFlow's convenient optimizer classes that perform backpropagation automatically for us. If you are interested in learning more about the computation of gradients in computational graphs and the different ways to compute them in TensorFlow, please refer to the PyData talk by Sebastian Raschka at `https://github.com/rasbt/pydata-annarbor2017-dl-tutorial`.

Building a regression model

Since we've explored placeholders and variables, let's build an example model for regression analysis, similar to the one we created in *Chapter 13, Parallelizing Neural Network Training with TensorFlow*, where our goal is to implement a linear regression model: $\hat{y} = wx + b$.

In this model, w and b are the two parameters of this simple regression model that need to be defined as variables. Note that x is the input to the model, which we can define as a placeholder. Furthermore, recall that for training this model, we need to formulate a cost function. Here, we use the **Mean Squared Error (MSE)** cost function that we defined in *Chapter 10, Predicting Continuous Target Variables with Regression Analysis*, $MSE = \frac{1}{n}\sum_{i=1}^{n}\left(y^{(i)} - \hat{y}^{(i)}\right)^2$.

Here, y is the true value, which is given as the input to this model for training. Therefore, we need to define y as a placeholder as well. Finally, $\hat{y}$ is the prediction output, which will be computed using TensorFlow operations — tf.matmul and tf.add. Recall that TensorFlow operations return zero or more tensors; here, tf.matmul and tf.add return one tensor.

We can also use the overloaded operator + for adding two tensors; however, the advantage of tf.add is that we can provide an additional name for the resulting tensor via the name parameter.

So, let's summarize all our tensors with their mathematical notations and coding naming, as follows:

- Input x: tf_x defined as a placeholder
- Input y: tf_y defined as a placeholder
- Model parameter w: weight defined as a variable
- Model parameter b: bias defined as a variable
- Model output $\hat{y}$: y_hat returned by the TensorFlow operations to compute the prediction using the regression model

The code to implement this simple regression model is as follows:

```
>>> import tensorflow as tf
>>> import numpy as np
>>>
>>> g = tf.Graph()
>>>
>>> with g.as_default():
...        tf.set_random_seed(123)
```

```
...         ## placeholders
...         tf_x = tf.placeholder(shape=(None),
...                               dtype=tf.float32,
...                               name='tf_x')
...         tf_y = tf.placeholder(shape=(None),
...                               dtype=tf.float32,
...                               name='tf_y')
...
...         ## define the variable (model parameters)
...         weight = tf.Variable(
...             tf.random_normal(
...                 shape=(1, 1),
...                 stddev=0.25),
...             name='weight')
...         bias = tf.Variable(0.0, name='bias')
...
...         ## build the model
...         y_hat = tf.add(weight * tf_x, bias,
...                     name='y_hat')
...
...         ## compute the cost
...         cost = tf.reduce_mean(tf.square(tf_y - y_hat),
...                     name='cost')
...
...         ## train the model
...         optim = tf.train.GradientDescentOptimizer(
...             learning_rate=0.001)
...         train_op = optim.minimize(cost, name='train_op')
```

Now that we've built the graph, our next steps are to create a session to launch the graph and train the model. But before we go further, let's see how we can evaluate tensors and execute operations. We'll create a random regression data with one feature, using the `make_random_data` function and visualizing the data:

```
>>> ## create a random toy dataset for regression
>>>
>>> import numpy as np
>>> import matplotlib.pyplot as plt
>>> np.random.seed(0)
>>>
>>> def make_random_data():
...     x = np.random.uniform(low=-2, high=4, size=200)
...     y = []
...     for t in x:
```

```
...              r = np.random.normal(loc=0.0,
...                                   scale=(0.5 + t*t/3),
...                                   size=None)
...              y.append(r)
...          return x, 1.726*x -0.84 + np.array(y)
>>>
>>>
>>> x, y = make_random_data()
>>>
>>> plt.plot(x, y, 'o')
>>> plt.show()
```

The following figure shows the random regression data that we generated:

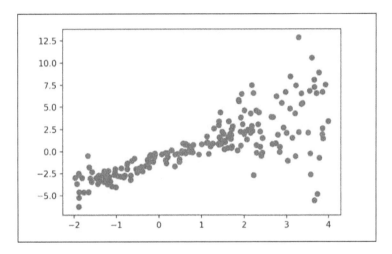

Now we're ready; let's train the previous model. Let's start by creating a TensorFlow session object called `sess`. Then, we want to initialize our variables which, as we saw, we can do with `sess.run(tf.global_variables_initializer())`. After this, we can create a `for` loop to execute the train operator and calculate the training cost at the same time.

So let's combine the two tasks, the first to execute an operator, and the second to evaluate a tensor, into one `sess.run` method call. The code for this is as follows:

```
>>> ## train/test splits
>>> x_train, y_train = x[:100], y[:100]
>>> x_test, y_test = x[100:], y[100:]
>>>
>>>
>>> n_epochs = 500
>>> training_costs = []
```

```
>>> with tf.Session(graph=g) as sess:
...        sess.run(tf.global_variables_initializer())
...
...        ## train the model for n_epochs
...        for e in range(n_epochs):
...            c, _ = sess.run([cost, train_op],
...                        feed_dict={tf_x: x_train,
...                                   tf_y: y_train})
...            training_costs.append(c)
...            if not e % 50:
...                print('Epoch %4d: %.4f' % (e, c))
Epoch    0: 12.2230
Epoch   50: 8.3876
Epoch  100: 6.5721
Epoch  150: 5.6844
Epoch  200: 5.2269
Epoch  250: 4.9725
Epoch  300: 4.8169
Epoch  350: 4.7119
Epoch  400: 4.6347
Epoch  450: 4.5742

>>> plt.plot(training_costs)
>>> plt.show()
```

The code generates the following graph that shows the training costs after each epoch:

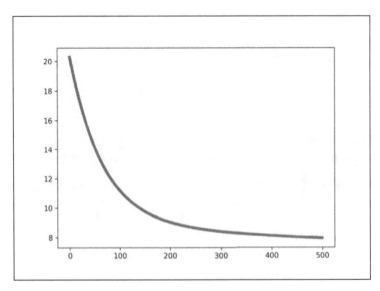

Executing objects in a TensorFlow graph using their names

Executing variables and operators by their names is very useful in many scenarios. For example, we may develop a model in a separate module; and thus the variables are not available in a different Python scope according to Python scoping rules. However, if we have a graph, we can execute the nodes of the graph using their names in the graph.

This can be done easily by changing the sess.run method from the previous code example, using the variable name of the **cost** in the graph rather than the Python variable cost by changing sess.run([cost, train_op], ...) to sess. run(['cost:0', 'train_op'], ...).

```
>>> n_epochs = 500
>>> training_costs = []
>>> with tf.Session(graph=g) as sess:
...        ## first, run the variables initializer
...        sess.run(tf.global_variables_initializer())
...
...        ## train the model for n_eopchs
...        for e in range(n_epochs):
...            c, _ = sess.run(['cost:0', 'train_op'],
...                        feed_dict={'tf_x:0':x_train,
...                                   'tf_y:0':y_train})
...            training_costs.append(c)
...            if e%50 == 0:
...                print('Epoch {:4d} : {:.4f}'
...                        .format(e, c))
```

Notice that we are evaluating the cost by its name, which is 'cost:0', and executing the train operator by its name: 'train_op'. Also, in feed_dict, instead of using tf_x: x_train, we are using 'tf_x:0': x_train.

If we pay attention to the names of the tensors, we will notice that TensorFlow adds a suffix `':0'` to the name of the tensors.

However, the names of operators do not have any suffix like that. When a tensor with a given name, such as `name='my_tensor'`, is created, TensorFlow appends `':0'`; so the name of this tensor will be `'my_tensor:0'`.

Then, if we try to create another tensor with the same name in the same graph, TensorFlow will append `'_1:0'` and so on to the name; therefore, the future tensors will be named `'my_tensor_1:0','my_tensor_2:0'`, and so on. This naming assumes that we are not trying to reuse the already created tensor.

Saving and restoring a model in TensorFlow

In the previous section, we built a graph and trained it. How about doing the actual prediction on the held out test set? The problem is that we did not save the model parameters; so, once the execution of the preceding statements are finished and we exit the `tf.Session` environment, all the variables and their allocated memories are freed.

One solution is to train a model, and as soon as the training is finished, we can feed it our test set. However, this is not a good approach since deep neural network models are typically trained over multiple hours, days, or even weeks.

The best approach is to save the trained model for future use. For this purpose, we need to add a new node to the graph, an instance of the `tf.train.Saver` class, which we call `saver`.

In the following statement, we can add more nodes to a particular graph. In this case, we are adding `saver` to the graph `g`:

```
>>> with g.as_default():
...     saver = tf.train.Saver()
```

Next, we can retrain the model with an additional call to `saver.save()` to save the model as follows:

```
>>> n_epochs = 500
>>> training_costs = []
>>> with tf.Session(graph=g) as sess:
...         sess.run(tf.global_variables_initializer())
...
...         ## train the model for n_epochs
...         for e in range(n_epochs):
...             c, _ = sess.run([cost, train_op],
...                         feed_dict={tf_x: x_train,
...                                    tf_y: y_train})
...             training_costs.append(c)
...             if not e % 50:
...                 print('Epoch %4d: %.4f' % (e, c))
...
...         saver.save(sess, './trained-model')
```

As a result of this new statement, three files are created with extensions `.data`, `.index`, and `.meta`. TensorFlow uses Protocol Buffers (`https://developers.google.com/protocol-buffers/`), which is a language-agnostic way, for serializing structured data.

Restoring a trained model requires two steps:

1. Rebuild the graph that has the same nodes and names as the saved model.
2. Restore the saved variables in a new `tf.Session` environment.

For the first step, we can run the statements, as we did in the first place, to build the graph g. But there is a much easier way to do this. Note that all of the information regarding the graph is saved as metadata in the file with the `.meta` extension. Using the following code, we rebuild the graph by importing it from the meta file:

```
>>> with tf.Session() as sess:
...         new_saver = tf.train.import_meta_graph(
...                             './trained-model.meta')
```

The `tf.train.import_meta_graph` function recreates the graph that is saved in the `'./trained-model.meta'` file. After recreating the graph, we can use the `new_saver` object to restore the parameters of the model in that session and execute it. The complete code to run the model on a test set is as follows:

```
>>> import tensorflow as tf
>>> import numpy as np
>>>
>>> g2 = tf.Graph()
>>> with tf.Session(graph=g2) as sess:
...      new_saver = tf.train.import_meta_graph(
...          './trained-model.meta')
...      new_saver.restore(sess, './trained-model')
...
...      y_pred = sess.run('y_hat:0',
...                       feed_dict={'tf_x:0': x_test})
```

Note that we evaluated the $\hat{y}$ tensor by its name that was given previously: `'y_hat:0'`. Also, we needed to feed the values for the `tf_x` placeholder, which is also done by its name: `'tf_x:0'`. In this case, there is no need to feed the values for the true y values. This is because executing the `y_hat` node does not depend on `tf_y` in the computation graph that we built.

Now, let's visualize the predictions, as follows:

```
>>> import matplotlib.pyplot as plt
>>>
>>> x_arr = np.arange(-2, 4, 0.1)
>>>
>>> g2 = tf.Graph()
>>> with tf.Session(graph=g2) as sess:
...      new_saver = tf.train.import_meta_graph(
...          './trained-model.meta')
...      new_saver.restore(sess, './trained-model')
...
...      y_arr = sess.run('y_hat:0',
```

```
...                             feed_dict={'tf_x:0' : x_arr})
>>>
>>> plt.figure()
>>> plt.plot(x_train, y_train, 'bo')
>>> plt.plot(x_test, y_test, 'bo', alpha=0.3)
>>> plt.plot(x_arr, y_arr.T[:, 0], '-r', lw=3)
>>> plt.show()
```

The result is shown in the following figure, where both the training data and test data are displayed:

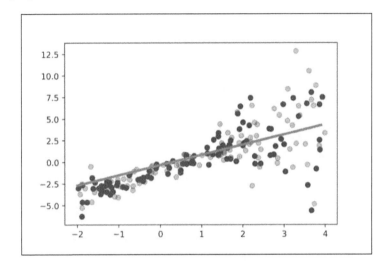

Saving and restoring a model is very often used during the training stage of large models as well. Since the training stage of large models can take several hours to days, we can break the training phase into smaller tasks. For example, if the intended number of epochs is 100, we can break it into 25 tasks, where each task would run four epochs one after the other. For this purpose, we can save the trained model and restore it in the next task.

Transforming Tensors as multidimensional data arrays

In this section, we explore a selection of operators that can be used to transform tensors. Note that some of these operators work very similar to NumPy array transformations. However, when we are dealing with tensors with ranks higher than 2, we need to be careful in using such transformations, for example, the transpose of a tensor.

First, as in NumPy, we can use the attribute `arr.shape` to get the shape of a NumPy array. In TensorFlow, we use the `tf.get_shape` function instead:

```
>>> import tensorflow as tf
>>> import numpy as np
>>>
>>> g = tf.Graph()
>>> with g.as_default():
...     arr = np.array([[1., 2., 3., 3.5],
...                     [4., 5., 6., 6.5],
...                     [7., 8., 9., 9.5]])
...     T1 = tf.constant(arr, name='T1')
...     print(T1)
...     s = T1.get_shape()
...     print('Shape of T1 is', s)
...     T2 = tf.Variable(tf.random_normal(
...         shape=s))
...     print(T2)
...     T3 = tf.Variable(tf.random_normal(
...         shape=(s.as_list()[0],)))
...     print(T3)
```

The output of the previous code example is as follows:

```
Tensor("T1:0", shape=(3, 4), dtype=float64)
Shape of T1 is (3, 4)
<tf.Variable 'Variable:0' shape=(3, 4) dtype=float32_ref>
<tf.Variable 'Variable_1:0' shape=(3,) dtype=float32_ref>
```

Notice that we used `s` to create `T2`, but we cannot slice or index `s` for creating `T3`. Therefore, we converted `s` into a regular Python list by `s.as_list()` and then used the usual indexing conventions.

Now, let's see how we can reshape tensors. Recall that in NumPy, we can use `np.reshape` or `arr.reshape` for this purpose. In TensorFlow, we use the function `tf.reshape` to reshape a tensor. As is the case for NumPy, one dimension can be set to `-1` so that the size of the new dimension will be inferred based on the total size of the array and the other remaining dimensions that are specified.

In the following code, we reshape the tensor T1 to T4 and T5, both of which have rank 3:

```
>>> with g.as_default():
...     T4 = tf.reshape(T1, shape=[1, 1, -1],
...                     name='T4')
...     print(T4)
...     T5 = tf.reshape(T1, shape=[1, 3, -1],
...                     name='T5')
...     print(T5)
```

The output is as follows:

```
Tensor("T4:0", shape=(1, 1, 12), dtype=float64)
Tensor("T5:0", shape=(1, 3, 4), dtype=float64)
```

Next, let's print the elements of T4 and T5:

```
>>> with tf.Session(graph = g) as sess:
...     print(sess.run(T4))
...     print()
...     print(sess.run(T5))

[[[ 1.    2.    3.    3.5   4.    5.    6.    6.5   7.    8.    9.    9.5]]]

[[[ 1.    2.    3.    3.5]
  [ 4.    5.    6.    6.5]
  [ 7.    8.    9.    9.5]]]
```

As we know, there are three ways to transpose an array in NumPy: arr.T, arr.transpose(), and np.transpose(arr). In TensorFlow, we use the tf.transpose function instead, and in addition to a regular transpose operation, we can change the order of dimensions in any way we want by specifying the order in perm=[...]. Here's an example:

```
>>> with g.as_default():
...     T6 = tf.transpose(T5, perm=[2, 1, 0],
...                     name='T6')
...     print(T6)
...     T7 = tf.transpose(T5, perm=[0, 2, 1],
...                     name='T7')
...     print(T7)

Tensor("T6:0", shape=(4, 3, 1), dtype=float64)
Tensor("T7:0", shape=(1, 4, 3), dtype=float64)
```

Next, we can also split a tensor into a list of subtensors using the `tf.split` function, as follows:

```
>>> with g.as_default():
...         t5_splt = tf.split(T5,
...                            num_or_size_splits=2,
...                            axis=2, name='T8')
...         print(t5_splt)

[<tf.Tensor 'T8:0' shape=(1, 3, 2) dtype=float64>,
 <tf.Tensor 'T8:1' shape=(1, 3, 2) dtype=float64>]
```

Here, it's important to note that the output is not a tensor object anymore; rather, it's a list of tensors. The name of these subtensors are `'T8:0'` and `'T8:1'`.

Lastly, another useful transformation is the concatenation of multiple tensors. If we have a list of tensors with the same shape and `dtype`, we can combine them into one big tensor using the `tf.concat` function. An example is given in the following code:

```
>>> g = tf.Graph()
>>> with g.as_default():
...         t1 = tf.ones(shape=(5, 1),
...                      dtype=tf.float32, name='t1')
...         t2 = tf.zeros(shape=(5, 1),
...                       dtype=tf.float32, name='t2')
...         print(t1)
...         print(t2)
>>> with g.as_default():
...         t3 = tf.concat([t1, t2], axis=0, name='t3')
...         print(t3)
...         t4 = tf.concat([t1, t2], axis=1, name='t4')
...         print(t4)

Tensor("t1:0", shape=(5, 1), dtype=float32)
Tensor("t2:0", shape=(5, 1), dtype=float32)

Tensor("t3:0", shape=(10, 1), dtype=float32)
Tensor("t4:0", shape=(5, 2), dtype=float32)
```

Let's print the values of these concatenated tensors:

```
>>> with tf.Session(graph=g) as sess:
...      print(t3.eval())
...      print()
...      print(t4.eval())

[[ 1.]
 [ 1.]
 [ 1.]
 [ 1.]
 [ 1.]
 [ 0.]
 [ 0.]
 [ 0.]
 [ 0.]
 [ 0.]]

[[ 1.  0.]
 [ 1.  0.]
 [ 1.  0.]
 [ 1.  0.]
 [ 1.  0.]]
```

Utilizing control flow mechanics in building graphs

Now let's learn about an interesting TensorFlow mechanic. TensorFlow provides a mechanism for making decisions when building a graph. However, there are some subtle differences when we use Python's control flow statements compared to TensorFlow's control flow functions, when constructing computation graphs.

To illustrate these differences with some simple code examples, let's consider implementing the following equation in TensorFlow:

$$res = \begin{cases} x+y & if \ x < y \\ x-y & otherwise \end{cases}$$

In the following code, we may naively use Python's `if` statement to build a graph that corresponds to the preceding equation:

```
>>> import tensorflow as tf
>>>
>>> x, y = 1.0, 2.0
>>>
>>> g = tf.Graph()
>>> with g.as_default():
...     tf_x = tf.placeholder(dtype=tf.float32,
...                           shape=None, name='tf_x')
...     tf_y = tf.placeholder(dtype=tf.float32,
...                           shape=None, name='tf_y')
...     if x < y:
...         res = tf.add(tf_x, tf_y, name='result_add')
...     else:
...         res = tf.subtract(tf_x, tf_y, name='result_sub')
...
...     print('Object:', res)
>>>
>>> with tf.Session(graph=g) as sess:
...     print('x < y: %s -> Result:' % (x < y),
...           res.eval(feed_dict={'tf_x:0': x,
...                               'tf_y:0': y}))
...     x, y = 2.0, 1.0
...     print('x < y: %s -> Result:' % (x < y),
...           res.eval(feed_dict={'tf_x:0': x,
...                               'tf_y:0': y}))
```

The result of this code will be as follows:

```
Object: Tensor("result_add:0", dtype=float32)
x < y: True -> Result: 3.0
x < y: False -> Result: 3.0
```

As you can see, the `res` object is a tensor named `'result_add:0'`. It is very important to understand that in the previous mechanism, the computation graph has only one branch associated with the addition operator, and the subtract operator has not been called.

The TensorFlow computation graph is static, which means that once the computation graph is built, it remains unchanged during the execution process. So, even when we change the values of x and y and feed the new values to the graph, these new tensors will go through the same path in the graph. Therefore, in both cases, we see the same output `3.0` for x=2, y=1 and for x=1, y=2.

Now, let's use the control flow mechanics in TensorFlow. In the following code, we implement the previous equation using the `tf.cond` function instead of Python's `if` statement:

```
>>> import tensorflow as tf
>>>
>>> x, y = 1.0, 2.0
>>>
>>> g = tf.Graph()
>>> with g.as_default():
...     tf_x = tf.placeholder(dtype=tf.float32,
...                           shape=None, name='tf_x')
...     tf_y = tf.placeholder(dtype=tf.float32,
...                           shape=None, name='tf_y')
...     res = tf.cond(tf_x < tf_y,
...                 lambda: tf.add(tf_x, tf_y,
...                                     name='result_add'),
...                 lambda: tf.subtract(tf_x, tf_y,
...                                     name='result_sub'))
...     print('Object:', res)
...
>>> with tf.Session(graph=g) as sess:
...     print('x < y: %s -> Result:' % (x < y),
...           res.eval(feed_dict={'tf_x:0': x,
...                               'tf_y:0': y}))
...     x, y = 2.0, 1.0
...     print('x < y: %s -> Result:' % (x < y),
...           res.eval(feed_dict={'tf_x:0': x,
...                               'tf_y:0': y}))
```

The result will be as follows:

```
Object: Tensor("cond/Merge:0", dtype=float32)
x < y: True -> Result: 3.0
x < y: False -> Result: 1.0
```

Here, we can see that the `res` object is named `"cond/Merge:0"`. In this case, the computation graph has two branches with a mechanism to decide which branch to follow at execution time. Therefore, when x=1, y=2, it follows the addition branch and the output will be 3.0, while for x=2, y=1, the subtraction branch is pursued and the result will be 1.0.

The following figure contrasts the differences in the computation graph of the previous implementation using the python `if` statement versus TensorFlow's `tf.cond` function;

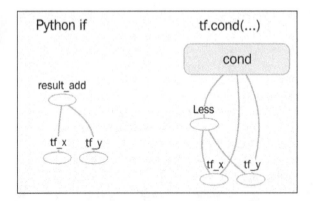

In addition to `tf.cond`, TensorFlow offers several other control flow operators, such as `tf.case` and `tf.while_loop`. For instance, `tf.case` is the TensorFlow control flow equivalent to a Python `if...else` statement. Consider the following Python expression:

```
if (x < y):
    result = 1
else:
    result = 0
```

The `tf.case` equivalent to the previous statement for conditional execution in a TensorFlow graph would then be implemented as follows:

```
f1 = lambda: tf.constant(1)
f2 = lambda: tf.constant(0)
result = tf.case([(tf.less(x, y), f1)], default=f2)
```

Similarly, we can add a `while` loop to a TensorFlow graph that increments the `i` variable by 1 until a threshold value (`threshold`) is reached, as follows:

```
i = tf.constant(0)
threshold = 100
c = lambda i: tf.less(i, 100)
b = lambda i: tf.add(i, 1)
r = tf.while_loop(cond=c, body=b, loop_vars=[i])
```

You can of course check out the official documentation for more information on the various control flow operators: https://www.tensorflow.org/api_guides/python/control_flow_ops.

You may have noticed that these computation graphs are built by TensorBoard, so now is a great time to take a good look at TensorBoard in the next section.

Visualizing the graph with TensorBoard

A great feature of TensorFlow is TensorBoard, which is a module for visualizing the graph as well as visualizing the learning of a model. Visualizing the graph allows us to see the connection between nodes, explore their dependencies, and debug the model if needed.

So let's visualize a network that we've already built, one which consists of a generator and a classifier part. We'll repeat some code that we previously used for defining the helper functions. So, revisit the *Reusing variables* section earlier in this chapter, for the function definitions of build_generator and build_classifier. Using these two helper functions, we will build the graph as follows:

```
>>> batch_size=64
>>> g = tf.Graph()
>>>
>>> with g.as_default():
...     tf_X = tf.placeholder(shape=(batch_size, 100),
...                           dtype=tf.float32,
...                           name='tf_X')
...
...     ## build the generator
...     with tf.variable_scope('generator'):
...         gen_out1 = build_generator(data=tf_X,
...                                    n_hidden=50)
...
...     ## build the classifier
...     with tf.variable_scope('classifier') as scope:
...         ## classifier for the original data:
...         cls_out1 = build_classifier(data=tf_X,
...                                     labels=tf.ones(
...                                         shape=batch_size))
...
...         ## reuse the classifier for generated data
...         scope.reuse_variables()
...         cls_out2 = build_classifier(data=gen_out1[1],
...                                     labels=tf.zeros(
...                                         shape=batch_size))
```

Note that no changes were needed so far for building the graph. So after building the graph, its visualization is straightforward. The following lines of code export the graph for visualization purposes:

```
>>> with tf.Session(graph=g) as sess:
...        sess.run(tf.global_variables_initializer())
...
...        file_writer = tf.summary.FileWriter(
...                              logdir='./logs/', graph=g)
```

This will create a new directory: `logs/`. Now, we just need to run the following command in a Linux or macOS Terminal:

`tensorboard --logdir logs/`

This command will print a message, which is a URL address. You can try launching TensorBoard by copying the link, for example, `http://localhost:6006/#graphs`, and pasting it into your browser's address bar. You should see the graph that corresponds to this model, as shown in the following figure:

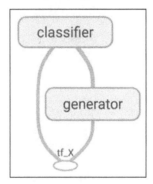

The large rectangular boxes indicate the two subnetworks that we built: generator and classifier. Since we used the `tf.variable_scope` function when we built this graph, all the components of each of these subnetworks are grouped into those rectangular boxes, as shown in the previous figure.

We can expand these boxes to explore their details: using your mouse, click on the plus sign on the top-right corner of these boxes to expand them. Doing this, we can see the details of the generator subnetwork, as shown in the following figure:

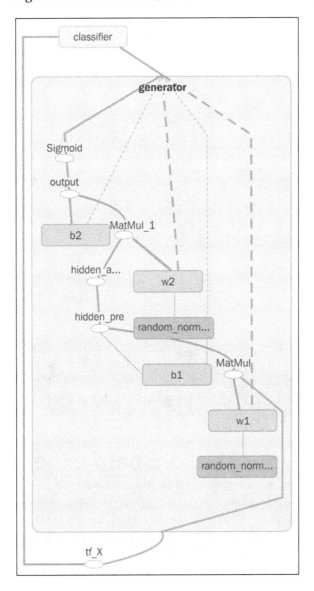

By exploring this graph, we can easily see that the generator has two weight tensors, named w1 and w2. Next, let's expand the classifier subnetwork, as shown in the following figure:

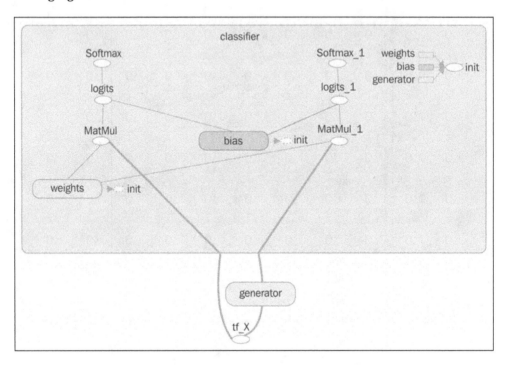

As you can see in this figure, the classifier has two sources of input, where one input comes from the tf_X placeholder and the other one is in fact the output of the generator subnetwork.

Extending your TensorBoard experience

As an interesting exercise, we suggest you use TensorBoard to visualize the different graphs we implemented throughout this chapter. For example, you could use similar steps for building the graphs, and then add extra lines for their visualization. You can also make graphs for the control flow section, which will show you the difference between graphs made by the Python if statement and the tf.cond function.

For more information and examples for graph visualization, visit the official TensorFlow tutorials page at https://www.tensorflow.org/get_started/graph_viz.

Summary

In this chapter, we covered in detail the key features and concepts of TensorFlow. We started with discussing TensorFlow's main features and advantages, and key TensorFlow concepts such as ranks and tensors. We then looked at TensorFlow's computation graphs, and discussed how to launch a graph in a session environment, and you learned about placeholders and variables. We then saw different ways to evaluate tensors and execute operators, using Python variables or by referring to them via their name in the graph.

We went further to explore some of the essential TensorFlow operators and functions for transforming tensors, such as `tf.transpose`, `tf.reshape`, `tf.split`, and `tf.concat`. Finally, we saw how to visualize a TensorFlow computation graph using TensorBoard. Visualizing computation graphs using this module can be very useful, especially when we are debugging complex models.

In the next chapter, we'll make use of this library to implement an advanced image classifier: a **Convolutional Neural Network** (**CNN**). CNNs are powerful models and have shown great performance in image classification and computer vision. We'll cover the basic operations in CNNs, and we'll implement deep convolutional networks for image classification using TensorFlow.

15

Classifying Images
with Deep Convolutional
Neural Networks

In the previous chapter, we looked in depth at different aspects of the TensorFlow API, became familiar with tensors, naming variables, and operators, and learned how to work with variable scopes. In this chapter, we'll now learn about **Convolutional Neural Networks (CNNs)**, and how we can implement CNNs in TensorFlow. We'll also take an interesting journey in this chapter as we apply this type of deep neural network architecture to image classification.

So we'll start by discussing the basic building blocks of CNNs, using a bottom-up approach. Then we'll take a deeper dive into the CNN architecture and how to implement deep CNNs in TensorFlow. Along the way we'll be covering the following topics:

- Understanding convolution operations in one and two dimensions
- Learning about the building blocks of CNN architectures
- Implementing deep convolutional neural networks in TensorFlow

Building blocks of convolutional neural networks

Convolutional neural networks, or CNNs, are a family of models that were inspired by how the visual cortex of human brain works when recognizing objects.

The development of CNNs goes back to the 1990's, when Yann LeCun and his colleagues proposed a novel neural network architecture for classifying handwritten digits from images (*Handwritten Digit Recognition with a Back-Propagation Network, Y LeCun, and others, 1989*, published at *Neural Information Processing Systems.(NIPS)* conference).

Due to the outstanding performance of CNNs for image classification tasks, they have gained a lot of attention and this led to tremendous improvements in machine learning and computer vision applications.

In the following sections, we next see how CNNs are used as feature extraction engines, and then we'll delve into the theoretical definition of convolution and computing convolution in one and two dimensions.

Understanding CNNs and learning feature hierarchies

Successfully extracting **salient (relevant) features** is key to the performance of any machine learning algorithm, of course, and traditional machine learning models rely on input features that may come from a domain expert, or are based on computational feature extraction techniques. Neural networks are able to automatically learn the features from raw data that are most useful for a particular task. For this reason, it's common to consider a neural network as a feature extraction engine: the early layers (those right after the input layer) extract **low-level features**.

Multilayer neural networks, and in particular, deep convolutional neural networks, construct a so-called **feature hierarchy** by combining the low-level features in a layer-wise fashion to form high-level features. For example, if we're dealing with images, then low-level features, such as edges and blobs, are extracted from the earlier layers, which are combined together to form high-level features – as object shapes like a building, a car, or a dog.

As you can see in the following image, a CNN computes **feature maps** from an input image, where each element comes from a local patch of pixels in the input image:

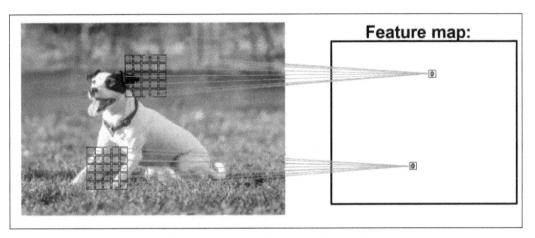

(Photo by Alexander Dummer on Unsplash)

This local patch of pixels is referred to as the **local receptive field**. CNNs will usually perform very well for image-related tasks, and that's largely due to two important ideas:

- **Sparse-connectivity**: A single element in the feature map is connected to only a small patch of pixels. (This is very different from connecting to the whole input image, in the case of perceptrons. You may find it useful to look back and compare how we implemented a fully connected network that connected to the whole image, in *Chapter 12, Implementing a Multilayer Artificial Neural Network from Scratch.*)
- **Parameter-sharing**: The same weights are used for different patches of the input image.

As a direct consequence of these two ideas, the number of weights (parameters) in the network decreases dramatically, and we see an improvement in the ability to capture **salient** features. Intuitively, it makes sense that nearby pixels are probably more relevant to each other than pixels that are far away from each other.

Typically, CNNs are composed of several **Convolutional (conv)** layers and subsampling (also known as **Pooling (P)**) layers that are followed by one or more **Fully Connected (FC)** layers at the end. The fully connected layers are essentially a multilayer perceptron, where every input unit i is connected to every output unit j with weight w_{ij} (which we learned about in *Chapter 12, Implementing a Multilayer Artificial Neural Network from Scratch*).

Please note that subsampling layers, commonly known as **pooling layers**, do not have any learnable parameters; for instance, there are no weights or bias units in pooling layers. However, both convolution and fully connected layers have such weights and biases.

In the following sections, we'll study convolutional and pooling layers in more detail and see how they work. To understand how convolution operations work, let's start with a convolution in one dimension before working through the typical two-dimensional cases as applications for two-dimensional images later.

Performing discrete convolutions

A **discrete convolution** (or simply **convolution**) is a fundamental operation in a CNN. Therefore, it's important to understand how this operation works. In this section, we'll learn the mathematical definition and discuss some of the **naive** algorithms to compute convolutions of two one-dimensional vectors or two two-dimensional matrices.

Please note that this description is solely for understanding how a convolution works. Indeed, much more efficient implementations of convolutional operations already exist in packages such as TensorFlow, as we will see later in this chapter.

Mathematical notation

In this chapter, we will use subscripts to denote the size of a multidimensional array; for example, $A_{n_1 \times n_2}$ is a two-dimensional array of size $n_1 \times n_2$. We use brackets $[.]$ to denote the indexing of a multidimensional array. For example, $A[i, j]$ means the element at index i, j of matrix A. Furthermore, note that we use a special symbol $*$ to denote the convolution operation between two vectors or matrices, which is not to be confused with the multiplication operator $*$ in Python.

Performing a discrete convolution in one dimension

Let's start with some basic definitions and notations we are going to use. A discrete convolution for two one-dimensional vectors **x** and **w** is denoted by $y = x * w$, in which vector **x** is our input (sometimes called **signal**) and **w** is called the **filter** or **kernel**. A discrete convolution is mathematically defined as follows:

$$y = x * w \rightarrow y[i] = \sum_{k=-\infty}^{+\infty} x[i-k]w[k]$$

Here, the brackets [] are used to denote the indexing for vector elements. The index *i* runs through each element of the output vector **y**. There are two odd things in the preceding formula that we need to clarify: $-\infty$ to $+\infty$ indices and negative indexing for **x**.

Cross-correlation

Cross-correlation (or simply correlation) between an input vector and a filter is denoted by $y = x * w$ and is very much like a sibling for a convolution with a small difference; the difference is that in cross-correlation, the multiplication is performed in the same direction. Therefore, it is not required to rotate the filter matrix **w** in each dimension. Mathematically, cross-correlation is defined as follows:

$$y = x * w \rightarrow y[i] = \sum_{k=-\infty}^{+\infty} x[i+k]w[k]$$

The same rules for padding and stride may be applied to cross-correlation as well. Note that most deep learning frameworks (including TensorFlow) implement cross-correlation but refer to it as convolution.

The first issue where the sum runs through indices from $-\infty$ to $+\infty$ seems odd mainly because in machine learning applications, we always deal with finite feature vectors. For example, if **x** has 10 features with indices $0,1,2,...,8,9$, then indices $-\infty:-1$ and $10:+\infty$ are out of bounds for **x**. Therefore, to correctly compute the summation shown in the preceding formula, it is assumed that **x** and **w** are filled with zeros. This will result in an output vector **y** that also has infinite size with lots of zeros as well. Since this is not useful in practical situations, **x** is padded only with a finite number of zeros.

This process is called **zero-padding** or simply **padding**. Here, the number of zeros padded on each side is denoted by *p*. An example padding of a one-dimensional vector **x** is shown in the following figure:

Original **x**:

| 3 | 2 | 1 | 7 | 1 | 2 | 5 | 4 |

Padding with p=2

| 0 | 0 | 3 | 2 | 1 | 7 | 1 | 2 | 5 | 4 | 0 | 0 |

Let's assume that the original input **x** and filter **w** have n and m elements, respectively, where $m \leq n$. Therefore, the padded vector x^p has size $n + 2p$. Then, the practical formula for computing a discrete convolution will change to the following:

$$y = x * w \rightarrow y[i] = \sum_{k=0}^{k=m-1} x^p[i + m - k]w[k]$$

Now that we have solved the infinite index issue, the second issue is indexing **x** with $i + m - k$. The important point to notice here is that **x** and **w** are indexed in different directions in this summation. For this reason, we can flip one of those vectors, **x** or **w**, after they are padded. Then, we can simply compute their dot product.

Let's assume we flip the filter **w** to get the rotated filter w^r. Then, the dot product $x[i:i+m].w^r$ is computed to get one element $y[i]$, where $x[i:i+m]$ is a patch of **x** with size m.

This operation is repeated like in a sliding window approach to get all the output elements. The following figure provides an example with $x = (3,2,1,7,1,2,5,4)$ and $w = \left(\frac{1}{2}, \frac{3}{4}, 1, \frac{1}{4}\right)$ so that the first three output elements are computed:

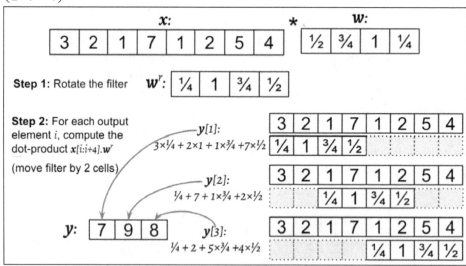

You can see in the preceding example that the padding size is zero ($p = 0$). Notice that the rotated filter w^r is shifted by two cells each time we shift. This **shift** is another hyperparameter of a convolution, the **stride** s. In this example, the stride is two, $s = 2$. Note that the stride has to be a positive number smaller than the size of the input vector. We'll talk more about padding and strides in the next section!

The effect of zero-padding in a convolution

So far here, we've used zero-padding in convolutions to compute finite-sized output vectors. Technically, padding can be applied with any $p \geq 0$. Depending on the choice p, boundary cells may be treated differently than the cells located in the middle of **x**.

Now consider an example where $n = 5$, $m = 3$. Then, $p = 0$, **x**[0] is only used in computing one output element (for instance, **y**[0]), while **x**[1] is used in the computation of two output elements (for instance, **y**[0] and **y**[1]). So, you can see that this different treatment of elements of **x** can artificially put more emphasis on the middle element, **x**[2], since it has appeared in most computations. We can avoid this issue if we choose $p = 2$, in which case, each element of x will be involved in computing three elements of **y**.

Furthermore, the size of the output **y** also depends on the choice of the padding strategy we use. There are three modes of padding that are commonly used in practice: **full**, **same**, and **valid**:

- In the **full** mode, the padding parameter p is set to $p = m - 1$. Full padding increases the dimensions of the output; thus, it is rarely used in convolutional neural network architectures.

- **Same** padding is usually used if you want to have the size of the output the same as the input vector **x**. In this case, the padding parameter p is computed according to the filter size, along with the requirement that the input size and output size are the same.

- Finally, computing a convolution in the **valid** mode refers to the case where $p = 0$ (no padding).

The following figure illustrates the three different padding modes for a simple 5 x 5 pixel input with a kernel size of 3 x 3 and a stride of 1:

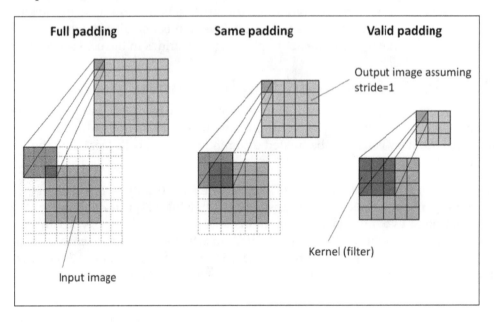

The most commonly used padding mode in convolutional neural networks is **same** padding. One of its advantages over the other padding modes is that same padding preserves the height and width of the input images or tensors, which makes designing a network architecture more convenient.

One big disadvantage of the **valid** padding versus **full** and **same** padding, for example, is that the volume of the tensors would decrease substantially in neural networks with many layers, which can be detrimental to the network performance.

In practice, it is recommended that you preserve the spatial size using same padding for the convolutional layers and decrease the spatial size via pooling layers instead. As for the full padding, its size results in an output larger than the input size. Full padding is usually used in signal processing applications where it is important to minimize boundary effects. However, in deep learning context, boundary effect is not usually an issue, so we rarely see full padding.

Determining the size of the convolution output

The output size of a convolution is determined by the total number of times that we shift the filter **w** along the input vector. Let's assume that the input vector has size n and the filter is of size m. Then, the size of the output resulting from $x * w$ with padding p and stride s is determined as follows:

$$o = \left\lfloor \frac{n + 2p - m}{s} \right\rfloor + 1$$

Here, $\lfloor . \rfloor$ denotes the floor operation:

The floor operation returns the largest integer that is equal or smaller to the input, for example:

$$floor(1.77) = \lfloor 1.77 \rfloor = 1$$

Consider the following two cases:

- Compute the output size for an input vector of size 10 with a convolution kernel of size 5, padding 2, and stride 1:

$$n - 10, m = 5, p = 2, s = 1 \rightarrow o = \left\lfloor \frac{10 + 2 \times 2 - 5}{1} \right\rfloor + 1 = 10$$

  (Note that in this case, the output size turns out to be the same as the input; therefore, we conclude this as **mode='same'**)

- How can the output size change for the same input vector, but have a kernel of size 3, and stride 2?

$$n = 10, m = 3, p = 2, s = 2 \rightarrow o = \left\lfloor \frac{10 + 2 \times 2 - 3}{2} \right\rfloor + 1 = 6$$

If you are interested to learn more about the size of the convolution output, we recommend the manuscript *A guide to convolution arithmetic for deep learning*, *Vincent Dumoulin and Francesco Visin, 2016*, which is freely available at https://arxiv.org/abs/1603.07285.

Finally, in order to learn how to compute convolutions in one dimension, a naïve implementation is shown in the following code block, and the results are compared with the `numpy.convolve` function. The code is as follows:

```
>>> import numpy as np
>>> def conv1d(x, w, p=0, s=1):
...        w_rot = np.array(w[::-1])
...        x_padded = np.array(x)
...        if p > 0:
...             zero_pad = np.zeros(shape=p)
...             x_padded = np.concatenate([zero_pad,
                                           x_padded,
                                           zero_pad])
...        res = []
...        for i in range(0, int(len(x)/s),s):
...             res.append(np.sum(x_padded[i:i+w_rot.shape[0]] *
                                  w_rot))
...        return np.array(res)

>>> ## Testing:
>>> x = [1, 3, 2, 4, 5, 6, 1, 3]
>>> w = [1, 0, 3, 1, 2]

>>> print('Conv1d Implementation:',
... conv1d(x, w, p=2, s=1))
Conv1d Implementation: [   5.  14.  16.  26.  24.  34.  19.  22.]

>>> print('Numpy Results:',
... np.convolve(x, w, mode='same'))
Numpy Results: [ 5 14 16 26 24 34 19 22]
```

So far, here, we have explored the convolution in 1D. We started with 1D case to make the concepts easier to understand. In the next section, we will extend this to two dimensions.

Performing a discrete convolution in 2D

The concepts you learned in the previous sections are easily extendible to two dimensions. When we deal with two-dimensional input, such as a matrix $X_{n_1 \times n_2}$ and the filter matrix $W_{m_1 \times m_2}$, where $m_1 \le n_1$ and $m_2 \le n_2$, then the matrix $Y = X * W$ is the result of 2D convolution of X with W. This is mathematically defined as follows:

$$Y = X * W \rightarrow Y[i,j] = \sum_{k_1=-\infty}^{+\infty} \sum_{k_2=-\infty}^{+\infty} X[i-k_1, j-k_2] W[k_1, k_2]$$

Notice that if you omit one of the dimensions, the remaining formula is exactly the same as the one we used previously to compute the convolution in 1D. In fact, all the previously mentioned techniques, such as zero-padding, rotating the filter matrix, and the use of strides, are also applicable to 2D convolutions, provided that they are extended to both the dimensions independently. The following example illustrates the computation of a 2D convolution between an input matrix $X_{3\times3}$, a kernel matrix $W_{3\times3}$, padding $p = (1, 1)$, and stride $s = (2, 2)$. According to the specified padding, one layer of zeros are padded on each side of the input matrix, which results in the padded matrix $X_{5\times5}^{padded}$, as follows:

With the preceding filter, the rotated filter will be:

$$W^r = \begin{bmatrix} 0.5 & 1 & 0.5 \\ 0.1 & 0.4 & 0.3 \\ 0.4 & 0.7 & 0.5 \end{bmatrix}$$

Note that this rotation is *not* the same as the transpose matrix. To get the rotated filter in NumPy, we can write `W_rot=W[::-1,::-1]`. Next, we can shift the rotated filter matrix along the padded input matrix X^{padded} like a sliding window and compute the sum of the element-wise product, which is denoted by the $\odot$ operator in the following figure:

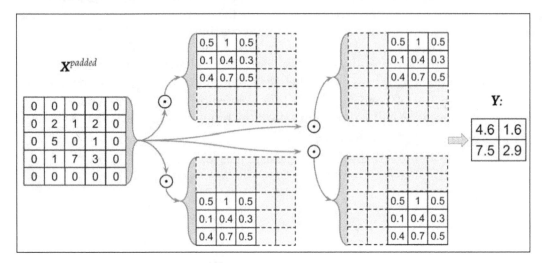

The result will be the 2 x 2 matrix **Y**.

Let's also implement the 2D convolution according to the **naïve** algorithm described. The `scipy.signal` package provides a way to compute 2D convolution via the `scipy.signal.convolve2d` function:

```
>>> import numpy as np
>>> import scipy.signal

>>> def conv2d(X, W, p=(0, 0), s=(1, 1)):
...         W_rot = np.array(W)[::-1,::-1]
...         X_orig = np.array(X)
...         n1 = X_orig.shape[0] + 2*p[0]
...         n2 = X_orig.shape[1] + 2*p[1]
...         X_padded = np.zeros(shape=(n1, n2))
...         X_padded[p[0]:p[0]+X_orig.shape[0],
...                  p[1]:p[1]+X_orig.shape[1]] = X_orig
...
...         res = []
...         for i in range(0, int((X_padded.shape[0] - \
...                          W_rot.shape[0])/s[0])+1, s[0]):
...             res.append([])
...             for j in range(0, int((X_padded.shape[1] - \
```

```
...                             W_rot.shape[1])/s[1])+1, s[1]):
...                  X_sub = X_padded[i:i+W_rot.shape[0],
...                                   j:j+W_rot.shape[1]]
...              res[-1].append(np.sum(X_sub * W_rot))
...        return(np.array(res))

>>> X = [[1, 3, 2, 4], [5, 6, 1, 3], [1, 2, 0, 2], [3, 4, 3, 2]]
>>> W = [[1, 0, 3], [1, 2, 1], [0, 1, 1]]

>>> print('Conv2d Implementation:\n',
...        conv2d(X, W, p=(1, 1), s=(1, 1)))
Conv2d Implementation:
 [[ 11.   25.   32.   13.]
 [ 19.   25.   24.   13.]
 [ 13.   28.   25.   17.]
 [ 11.   17.   14.    9.]]


>>> print('SciPy Results:\n',
...        scipy.signal.convolve2d(X, W, mode='same'))
SciPy Results:
 [[11 25 32 13]
 [19 25 24 13]
 [13 28 25 17]
 [11 17 14  9]]
```

We provided a naïve implementation to compute a 2D convolution for the purpose of understanding the concepts. However, this implementation is very inefficient in terms of memory requirements and computational complexity. Therefore, it should not be used in real-world neural network applications.

In recent years, much more efficient algorithms have been developed that use the Fourier transformation for computing convolutions. It is also important to note that in the context of neural networks, the size of a convolution kernel is usually much smaller than the size of the input image. For example, modern CNNs usually use kernel sizes such as 1 x 1, 3 x 3, or 5 x 5, for which efficient algorithms have been designed that can carry out the convolutional operations much more efficiently, such as the **Winograd's Minimal Filtering** algorithm. These algorithms are beyond the scope of this book, but if you are interested to learn more, you can read the manuscript: *Fast Algorithms for Convolutional Neural Networks, Andrew Lavin and Scott Gray, 2015*, which is freely available at (https://arxiv.org/abs/1509.09308).

In the next section, we will discuss subsampling, which is another important operation often used in CNNs.

Subsampling

Subsampling is typically applied in two forms of pooling operations in convolutional neural networks: **max-pooling** and **mean-pooling** (also known as **average-pooling**). The pooling layer is usually denoted by $P_{n_1 \times n_2}$. Here, the subscript determines the size of the neighborhood (the number of adjacent pixels in each dimension), where the max or mean operation is performed. We refer to such a neighborhood as the **pooling size**.

The operation is described in the following figure. Here, max-pooling takes the maximum value from a neighborhood of pixels, and mean-pooling computes their average:

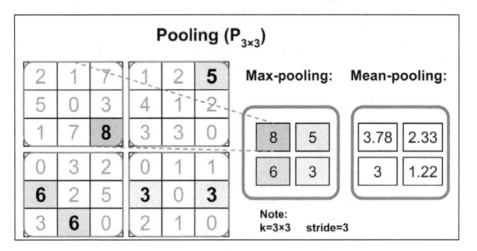

The advantage of pooling is twofold:

- Pooling (max-pooling) introduces some sort of local invariance.
  This means that small changes in a local neighborhood do not change the result of max-pooling. Therefore, it helps generate features that are more robust to noise in the input data. See the following example that shows max-pooling of two different input matrices X_1 and X_2 results in the same output:

$$X_1 = \begin{bmatrix} 10 & 255 & 125 & 0 & 170 & 100 \\ 70 & 255 & 105 & 25 & 25 & 70 \\ 255 & 0 & 150 & 0 & 10 & 10 \\ 0 & 255 & 10 & 10 & 150 & 20 \\ 70 & 15 & 200 & 100 & 95 & 0 \\ 35 & 25 & 100 & 20 & 0 & 60 \end{bmatrix}$$

$$X_2 = \begin{bmatrix} 100 & 100 & 100 & 50 & 100 & 50 \\ 95 & 255 & 100 & 125 & 125 & 170 \\ 80 & 40 & 10 & 10 & 125 & 150 \\ 255 & 30 & 150 & 20 & 120 & 125 \\ 30 & 30 & 150 & 100 & 70 & 70 \\ 70 & 30 & 100 & 200 & 70 & 95 \end{bmatrix}$$

$$\xrightarrow{\text{max-pooling } P_{2\times2}} \begin{bmatrix} 255 & 125 & 170 \\ 255 & 150 & 150 \\ 70 & 200 & 95 \end{bmatrix}$$

- Pooling decreases the size of features, which results in higher computational efficiency. Furthermore, reducing the number of features may reduce the degree of overfitting as well.

Traditionally, pooling is assumed to be nonoverlapping. Pooling is typically performed on nonoverlapping neighborhoods, which can be done by setting the stride parameter equal to the pooling size. For example, a nonoverlapping pooling layer $P_{n_1 \times n_2}$ requires a stride parameter $s = (n_1, n_2)$.

On the other hand, overlapping pooling occurs if the stride is smaller than pooling size. An example where overlapping pooling is used in a convolutional network is described in *ImageNet Classification with Deep Convolutional Neural Networks, A. Krizhevsky, I. Sutskever, and G. Hinton, 2012*, which is freely available as a manuscript at https://papers.nips.cc/paper/4824-imagenet-classification-with-deep-convolutional-neural-networks.

Putting everything together to build a CNN

So far, we've learned about the basic building blocks of convolutional neural networks. The concepts illustrated in this chapter are not really more difficult than traditional multilayer neural networks. Intuitively, we can say that the most important operation in a traditional neural network is the matrix-vector multiplication.

For instance, we use matrix-vector multiplications to pre-activations (or net input) as in $a = Wx + b$. Here, x is a column vector representing pixels, and W is the weight matrix connecting the pixel inputs to each hidden unit. In a convolutional neural network, this operation is replaced by a convolution operation, as in $A = W * X + b$, where X is a matrix representing the pixels in a height x width arrangement. In both cases, the pre-activations are passed to an activation function to obtain the activation of a hidden unit $H = \phi(A)$, where ϕ is the activation function. Furthermore, recall that subsampling is another building block of a convolutional neural network, which may appear in the form of pooling, as we described in the previous section.

Working with multiple input or color channels

An input sample to a convolutional layer may contain one or more 2D arrays or matrices with dimensions $N_1 \times N_2$ (for example, the image height and width in pixels). These $N_1 \times N_2$ matrices are called **channels**. Therefore, using multiple channels as input to a convolutional layer requires us to use a rank-3 tensor or a three-dimensional array: $X_{N_1 \times N_2 \times C_{in}}$, where C_{in} is the number of input channels.

For example, let's consider images as input to the first layer of a CNN. If the image is colored and uses the RGB color mode, then $C_{in} = 3$ (for the red, green, and blue color channels in RGB). However, if the image is in grayscale, then we have $C_{in} = 1$ because there is only one channel with the grayscale pixel intensity values.

When we work with images, we can read images into NumPy arrays using the `'uint8'` (unsigned 8-bit integer) data type to reduce memory usage compared to 16-bit, 32-bit, or 64-bit integer types, for example. Unsigned 8-bit integers take values in the range [0, 255], which are sufficient to store the pixel information in RGB images, which also take values in the same range.

Next, let's look at an example of how we can read in an image into our Python session using SciPy. However, please note that reading images with SciPy requires that you have the **Python Imaging Library** (**PIL**) package installed. We can install Pillow (https://python-pillow.org), a more user-friendly fork of PIL, to satisfy those requirements, as follows:

pip install pillow

Once Pillow is installed, we can use the `imread` function from the `scipy.misc` module to read an RGB image (this example image is located in the code bundle folder that is provided with this chapter at https://github.com/rasbt/python-machine-learning-book-2nd-edition/tree/master/code/ch15):

```
>>> import scipy.misc
>>> img = scipy.misc.imread('./example-image.png',
...                          mode='RGB')
>>> print('Image shape:', img.shape)
Image shape: (252, 221, 3)
>>> print('Number of channels:', img.shape[2])
Number of channels: 3
>>> print('Image data type:', img.dtype)
Image data type: uint8
>>> print(img[100:102, 100:102, :])
  [[[179 134 110]
   [182 136 112]]

  [[180 135 111]
   [182 137 113]]]
```

Now that we have familiarized ourselves with the structure of input data, the next question is how can we incorporate multiple input channels in the convolution operation that we discussed in the previous sections?

Please note that the `imread` function, as well as other image processing utilities from `scipy.misc`, have been outsourced into a separate library, `imageio`. Hence, in future versions of SciPy, `scipy.misc.imread` might not work anymore. In this case, you can use the equivalent `imageio.imread` function after installing `imageio` via pip and importing it into your current Python session.

The answer is very simple: we perform the convolution operation for each channel separately and then add the results together using the matrix summation. The convolution associated with each channel (c) has its own kernel matrix as $W[:,:,c]$. The total pre-activation result is computed in the following formula:

$$
\begin{aligned}
&\text{Given a sample } \mathbf{X}_{n_1 \times n_2 \times c_{in}}, \\
&\text{a kernel matrix } \mathbf{W}_{m_1 \times m_2 \times c_{in}}, \\
&\text{and bias value } b
\end{aligned}
\Rightarrow
\begin{cases}
Y^{Conv} = \sum_{c=1}^{C_{in}} W[:,:,c] * X[:,:,c] \\
\text{pre-activation:} \quad \mathbf{A} = \mathbf{Y}^{Conv} + b \\
\text{Feature map:} \quad \mathbf{H} = \phi(\mathbf{A})
\end{cases}
$$

The final result, **h**, is called a **feature map**. Usually, a convolutional layer of a CNN has more than one feature map. If we use multiple feature maps, the kernel tensor becomes four-dimensional: $width \times height \times C_{in} \times C_{out}$. Here, width x height is the kernel size, C_{in} is the number of input channels, and C_{out} is the number of output feature maps. So, now let's include the number of output feature maps in the preceding formula and update it as follows:

$$
\begin{aligned}
&\text{Given a sample } \ \mathbf{X}_{n_1 \times n_2 \times C_{in}} \\
&\text{kernel matrix } \mathbf{W}_{m_1 \times m_2 \times C_{in} \times C_{out}} \\
&\text{and bias vector } \ \mathbf{b}_{C_{out}}
\end{aligned}
\Rightarrow
\begin{cases}
Y^{Conv}[:,:,k] = \sum_{c=1}^{C_{in}} W[:,:,c,k] * X[:,:,c] \\
A[:,:,k] = Y^{Conv}[:,:,k] + b[k] \\
H[:,:,k] = \phi(A[:,:,k])
\end{cases}
$$

To conclude our discussion of computing convolutions in the context of neural networks, let's look at the example in the following figure that shows a convolutional layer, followed by a pooling layer.

In this example, there are three input channels. The kernel tensor is four-dimensional. Each kernel matrix is denoted as $m_1 \times m_2$, and there are three of them, one for each input channel. Furthermore, there are five such kernels, accounting for five output feature maps. Finally, there is a pooling layer for subsampling the feature maps, as shown in the following figure:

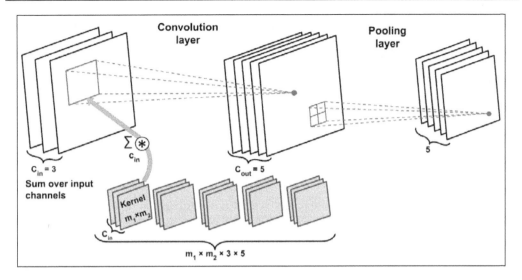

How many trainable parameters exist in the preceding example?

To illustrate the advantages of convolution, **parameter-sharing** and **sparse-connectivity**, let's work through an example. The convolutional layer in the network shown in the preceding figure is a four-dimensional tensor. So, there are $m_1 \times m_2 \times 3 \times 5$ parameters associated with the kernel. Furthermore, there is a bias vector for each output feature map of the convolutional layer. Thus, the size of the bias vector is 5. Pooling layers do not have any (trainable) parameters; therefore, we can write the following:

$$m_1 \times m_2 \times 3 \times 5 + 5$$

If input tensor is of size $n_1 \times n_2 \times 3$, assuming that the convolution is performed with **mode='same'**, then the output feature maps would be of size $n_1 \times n_2 \times 5$.

Note that this number is much smaller than the case if we wanted to have a fully connected layer instead of the convolution layer. In the case of a fully connected layer, the number of parameters for the weight matrix to reach the same number of output units would have been as follows:

$$\left(n_1 \times n_2 \times 3 \right) \times \left(n_1 \times n_2 \times 5 \right) = \left(n_1 \times n_2 \right)^2 \times 3 \times 5$$

Given that $m_1 < n_1$ and $m_2 < n_2$, we can see that the difference in the number of trainable parameters is huge.

In the next section, we will talk about how to regularize a neural network.

Regularizing a neural network with dropout

Choosing the size of a network, whether we are dealing with a traditional (fully connected) neural network or a CNN, has always been a challenging problem. For instance, the size of a weight matrix and the number of layers need to be tuned to achieve a reasonably good performance.

The **capacity** of a network refers to the level of complexity of the function that it can learn. Small networks, networks with a relatively small number of parameters, have a low capacity and are therefore likely to be **under fit**, resulting in poor performance since they cannot learn the underlying structure of complex datasets.

Yet, very large networks may more easily result in **overfitting**, where the network will memorize the training data and do extremely well on the training set while achieving poor performance on the held-out test set. When we deal with real-world machine learning problems, we do not know how large the network should be **a priori**.

One way to address this problem is to build a network with a relatively large capacity (in practice, we want to choose a capacity that is slightly larger than necessary) to do well on the training set. Then, to prevent overfitting, we can apply one or multiple regularization schemes to achieve good generalization performance on new data, such as the held-out test set. A popular choice for regularization is L2 regularization, which we discussed previously in this book.

In recent years, another popular regularization technique called **dropout** has emerged that works amazingly well for regularizing (deep) neural networks (*Dropout: a simple way to prevent neural networks from overfitting, Nitish Srivastava and. others, Journal of Machine Learning Research 15.1*, pages 1929-1958, 2014, http://www.jmlr.org/papers/volume15/srivastava14a/srivastava14a.pdf).

Intuitively, dropout can be considered as the consensus (averaging) of an ensemble of models. In ensemble learning, we train several models independently. During prediction, we then use the consensus of all the trained models. However, both training several models and collecting and averaging the output of multiple models is computationally expensive. Here, dropout offers a workaround with an efficient way to train many models at once and compute their average predictions at test or prediction time.

Dropout is usually applied to the hidden units of higher layers. During the training phase of a neural network, a fraction of the hidden units is **randomly** dropped at every iteration with probability p_{drop} (or the keep probability $p_{keep} = 1 - p_{drop}$).

This dropout probability is determined by the user and the common choice is $p = 0.5$, as discussed in the previously mentioned article by *Nitish Srivastava and others*, 2014. When dropping a certain fraction of input neurons, the weights associated with the remaining neurons are rescaled to account for the missing (dropped) neurons.

The effect of this random dropout forces the network to learn a redundant representation of the data. Therefore, the network cannot rely on an activation of any set of hidden units since they may be turned off at any time during training and is forced to learn more general and robust patterns from the data.

This random dropout can effectively prevent overfitting. The following figure shows an example of applying dropout with probability $p = 0.5$ during the training phase, thereby half of the neurons become inactive randomly. However, during prediction, all neurons will contribute to computing the pre-activations of the next layer.

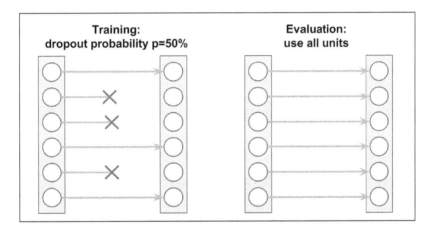

As shown here, one important point to remember is that units may drop randomly during training only, while for the evaluation phase, all the hidden units must be active (for instance, $p_{drop} = 0$ or $p_{keep} = 1$). To ensure that the overall activations are on the same scale during training and prediction, the activations of the active neurons have to be scaled appropriately (for example, by halving the activation if the dropout probability was set to $p = 0.5$).

However, since it is inconvenient to always scale activations when we make predictions in practice, TensorFlow and other tools scale the activations during training (for example, by doubling the activations if the dropout probability was set to $p = 0.5$).

So, what is the relationship between dropout and ensemble learning? Since we drop different hidden neurons at each iteration, effectively we are training different models. When all these models are finally trained, we set the keep probability to 1 and use all the hidden units. This means we are taking the average activation from all the hidden units.

Implementing a deep convolutional neural network using TensorFlow

In *Chapter 13, Parallelizing Neural Network Training with TensorFlow*, you may recall that we implemented a multilayer neural network for handwritten digit recognition problems, using different API levels of TensorFlow. You may also recall that we achieved about 97 percent accuracy.

So now, we want to implement a CNN to solve this same problem and see its predictive power in classifying handwritten digits. Note that the fully connected layers that we saw in the *Chapter 13, Parallelizing Neural Network Training with TensorFlow* were able to perform well on this problem. However, in some applications, such as reading bank account numbers from handwritten digits, even tiny mistakes can be very costly. Therefore, it is crucial to reduce this error as much as possible.

The multilayer CNN architecture

The architecture of the network that we are going to implement is shown in the following figure. The input is 28 x 28 grayscale images. Considering the number of channels (which is 1 for grayscale images) and a batch of input images, the input tensor's dimensions will be batchsize x 28 x 28 x 1.

The input data goes through two convolutional layers that have a kernel size of 5 x 5. The first convolution has 32 output feature maps, and the second one has 64 output feature maps. Each convolution layer is followed by a subsampling layer in the form of a max-pooling operation.

Then a fully-connected layer passes the output to a second fully-connected layer, which acts as the final *softmax* output layer. The architecture of the network that we are going to implement is shown in the following figure:

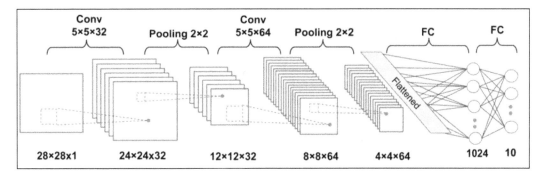

The dimensions of the tensors in each layer are as follows:

- **Input**: $[batchsize \times 28 \times 28 \times 1]$
- **Conv_1**: $[batchsize \times 24 \times 24 \times 32]$
- **Pooling_1**: $[batchsize \times 12 \times 12 \times 32]$
- **Conv_2**: $[batchsize \times 8 \times 8 \times 64]$
- **Pooling_2**: $[batchsize \times 4 \times 4 \times 64]$
- **FC_1**: $[batchsize \times 1024]$
- **FC_2 and softmax layer**: $[batchsize \times 10]$

We'll implement this network using two APIs: the low-level TensorFlow API and the TensorFlow Layers API. But first, let's define some helper functions at the beginning of the next section.

Loading and preprocessing the data

If you'll recall again from *Chapter 13, Parallelizing Neural Network Training with TensorFlow*, we used a function called `load_mnist` to read the MNIST handwritten digit dataset. Now we need to repeat the same procedure here as well, as follows:

```
>>> #### Loading the data
>>> X_data, y_data = load_mnist('./mnist/', kind='train')
>>> print('Rows: {},  Columns: {}'.format(
...            X_data.shape[0], X_data.shape[1]))
>>> X_test, y_test = load_mnist('./mnist/', kind='t10k')
>>> print('Rows: {},  Columns: {}'.format(
...            X_test.shape[0], X_test.shape[1]))

>>> X_train, y_train = X_data[:50000,:], y_data[:50000]
>>> X_valid, y_valid = X_data[50000:,:], y_data[50000:]

>>> print('Training:   ', X_train.shape, y_train.shape)
>>> print('Validation: ', X_valid.shape, y_valid.shape)
>>> print('Test Set:   ', X_test.shape, y_test.shape)
```

We are splitting the data into a training, a validation, and a test sets. The following result shows the shape of each set:

```
Rows: 60000,  Columns: 784
Rows: 10000,  Columns: 784
Training:    (50000, 784) (50000,)
Validation:  (10000, 784) (10000,)
Test Set:    (10000, 784) (10000,)
```

After we've loaded the data, we need a function for iterating through mini-batches of data, as follows:

```
>>> def batch_generator(X, y, batch_size=64,
...                     shuffle=False, random_seed=None):
...
...        idx = np.arange(y.shape[0])
...
...        if shuffle:
...            rng = np.random.RandomState(random_seed)
...            rng.shuffle(idx)
...            X = X[idx]
...            y = y[idx]
...
...        for i in range(0, X.shape[0], batch_size):
...            yield (X[i:i+batch_size, :], y[i:i+batch_size])
```

This function returns a generator with a tuple for a match of samples, for instance, data *X* and labels *y*. We then need to normalize the data (mean centering and division by the standard deviation) for better training performance and convergence.

We compute the mean of each feature using the training data (X_train) and calculate the standard deviation across all features. The reason why we don't compute the standard deviation for each feature individually is because some features (pixel positions) in image datasets such as MNIST have a constant value of 255 across all images corresponding to white pixels in a grayscale image.

A constant value across all samples indicates no variation, and therefore, the standard deviation of those features will be zero, and a result would yield the division-by-zero error, which is why we compute the standard deviation from the X_train array using np.std without specifying an axis argument:

```
>>> mean_vals = np.mean(X_train, axis=0)
>>> std_val = np.std(X_train)

>>> X_train_centered = (X_train - mean_vals)/std_val
>>> X_valid_centered = (X_valid - mean_vals)/std_val
>>> X_test_centered = (X_test - mean_vals)/std_val
```

Now we are ready to implement the CNN we just described. We will proceed by implementing the CNN model in TensorFlow.

Implementing a CNN in the TensorFlow low-level API

For implementing a CNN in TensorFlow, first we define two wrapper functions to make the process of building the network simpler: a wrapper function for a convolutional layer and a function for building a fully connected layer.

The first function for a convolution layer is as follows:

```
import tensorflow as tf
import numpy as np

def conv_layer(input_tensor, name,
               kernel_size, n_output_channels,
               padding_mode='SAME', strides=(1, 1, 1, 1)):
    with tf.variable_scope(name):
        ## get n_input_channels:
        ##   input tensor shape:
        ##   [batch x width x height x channels_in]
```

```
    input_shape = input_tensor.get_shape().as_list()
    n_input_channels = input_shape[-1]

    weights_shape = list(kernel_size) + \
                    [n_input_channels, n_output_channels]

    weights = tf.get_variable(name='_weights',
                              shape=weights_shape)
    print(weights)
    biases = tf.get_variable(name='_biases',
                             initializer=tf.zeros(
                                 shape=[n_output_channels]))
    print(biases)
    conv = tf.nn.conv2d(input=input_tensor,
                        filter=weights,
                        strides=strides,
                        padding=padding_mode)
    print(conv)
    conv = tf.nn.bias_add(conv, biases,
                          name='net_pre-activation')
    print(conv)
    conv = tf.nn.relu(conv, name='activation')
    print(conv)

    return conv
```

This wrapper function will do all the necessary work for building a convolutional layer, including defining the weights, biases, initializing them, and the convolution operation using the `tf.nn.conv2d` function. There are four required arguments:

- `input_tensor`: The tensor given as input to the convolutional layer
- `name`: The name of the layer, which is used as the scope name
- `kernel_size`: The dimensions of the kernel tensor provided as a tuple or list
- `n_output_channels`: The number of output feature maps

Notice that the weights are initialized using the Xavier (or Glorot) initialization method by default when using tf.get_variable (we discussed the Xavier/Glorot initialization scheme in *Chapter 14, Going Deeper – The Mechanics of TensorFlow*), while the biases are initialized to zeros using the `tf.zeros` function. The net pre-activations are passed to the ReLU activation function. We can print the operations and TensorFlow graph nodes to see the shape and type of tensors. Let's test this function with a simple input by defining a placeholder, as follows:

```
>>> g = tf.Graph()
>>> with g.as_default():
...      x = tf.placeholder(tf.float32, shape=[None, 28, 28, 1])
...      conv_layer(x, name='convtest',
...                 kernel_size=(3, 3),
...                 n_output_channels=32)
>>>
>>> del g, x

<tf.Variable 'convtest/_weights:0' shape=(3, 3, 1, 32) dtype=float32_
ref>
<tf.Variable 'convtest/_biases:0' shape=(32,) dtype=float32_ref>
Tensor("convtest/Conv2D:0", shape=(?, 28, 28, 32), dtype=float32)
Tensor("convtest/net_pre-activaiton:0", shape=(?, 28, 28, 32),
dtype=float32)
Tensor("convtest/activation:0", shape=(?, 28, 28, 32), dtype=float32)
```

The next wrapper function is for defining our fully connected layers:

```
def fc_layer(input_tensor, name,
             n_output_units, activation_fn=None):
    with tf.variable_scope(name):
        input_shape = input_tensor.get_shape().as_list()[1:]
        n_input_units = np.prod(input_shape)
        if len(input_shape) > 1:
            input_tensor = tf.reshape(input_tensor,
                                      shape=(-1, n_input_units))

        weights_shape = [n_input_units, n_output_units]
        weights = tf.get_variable(name='_weights',
                                  shape=weights_shape)
        print(weights)
        biases = tf.get_variable(name='_biases',
                                 initializer=tf.zeros(
                                     shape=[n_output_units]))
```

```
            print(biases)
            layer = tf.matmul(input_tensor, weights)
            print(layer)
            layer = tf.nn.bias_add(layer, biases,
                                   name='net_pre-activaiton')
            print(layer)
            if activation_fn is None:
                return layer

            layer = activation_fn(layer, name='activation')
            print(layer)
            return layer
```

The wrapper function `fc_layer` also builds the weights and biases, initializes them similar to the `conv_layer` function, and then performs a matrix multiplication using the `tf.matmul` function. The `fc_layer` function has three required arguments:

- `input_tensor`: The input tensor
- `name`: The name of the layer, which is used as the scope name
- `n_output_units`: The number of output units

We can test this function for a simple input tensor as follows:

```
>>> g = tf.Graph()
>>> with g.as_default():
...      x = tf.placeholder(tf.float32,
...                          shape=[None, 28, 28, 1])
...      fc_layer(x, name='fctest', n_output_units=32,
...               activation_fn=tf.nn.relu)
>>>
>>> del g, x
<tf.Variable 'fctest/_weights:0' shape=(784, 32) dtype=float32_ref>
<tf.Variable 'fctest/_biases:0' shape=(32,) dtype=float32_ref>
Tensor("fctest/MatMul:0", shape=(?, 32), dtype=float32)
Tensor("fctest/net_pre-activaiton:0", shape=(?, 32), dtype=float32)
Tensor("fctest/activation:0", shape=(?, 32), dtype=float32)
```

The behavior of this function is a bit different for the two fully connected layers in our model. The first fully connected layer gets its input right after a convolutional layer; therefore, the input is still a 4D tensor. For the second fully connected layer, we need to flatten the input tensor using the `tf.reshape` function. Furthermore, the net pre-activations from the first FC layer are passed to the ReLU activation function, but the second one corresponds to the `logits`, and therefore, a linear activation must be used.

Now we can utilize these wrapper functions to build the whole convolutional network. We define a function called `build_cnn` to handle the building of the CNN model, as shown in the following code:

```
def build_cnn(learning_rate=1e-4)
    ## Placeholders for X and y:
    tf_x = tf.placeholder(tf.float32, shape=[None, 784],
                          name='tf_x')
    tf_y = tf.placeholder(tf.int32, shape=[None],
                          name='tf_y')

    # reshape x to a 4D tensor:
    # [batchsize, width, height, 1]
    tf_x_image = tf.reshape(tf_x, shape=[-1, 28, 28, 1],
                            name='tf_x_reshaped')
    ## One-hot encoding:
    tf_y_onehot = tf.one_hot(indices=tf_y, depth=10,
                             dtype=tf.float32,
                             name='tf_y_onehot')

    ## 1st layer: Conv_1
    print('\nBuilding 1st layer:')
    h1 = conv_layer(tf_x_image, name='conv_1',
                    kernel_size=(5, 5),
                    padding_mode='VALID',
                    n_output_channels=32)
    ## MaxPooling
    h1_pool = tf.nn.max_pool(h1,
                             ksize=[1, 2, 2, 1],
                             strides=[1, 2, 2, 1],
                             padding='SAME')
    ## 2n layer: Conv_2
    print('\nBuilding 2nd layer:')
    h2 = conv_layer(h1_pool, name='conv_2',
                    kernel_size=(5, 5),
                    padding_mode='VALID',
                    n_output_channels=64)
    ## MaxPooling
    h2_pool = tf.nn.max_pool(h2,
                             ksize=[1, 2, 2, 1],
                             strides=[1, 2, 2, 1],
                             padding='SAME')

    ## 3rd layer: Fully Connected
```

```
print('\nBuilding 3rd layer:')
h3 = fc_layer(h2_pool, name='fc_3',
              n_output_units=1024,
              activation_fn=tf.nn.relu)

## Dropout
keep_prob = tf.placeholder(tf.float32, name='fc_keep_prob')
h3_drop = tf.nn.dropout(h3, keep_prob=keep_prob,
                        name='dropout_layer')

## 4th layer: Fully Connected (linear activation)
print('\nBuilding 4th layer:')
h4 = fc_layer(h3_drop, name='fc_4',
              n_output_units=10,
              activation_fn=None)

## Prediction
predictions = {
    'probabilities': tf.nn.softmax(h4, name='probabilities'),
    'labels': tf.cast(tf.argmax(h4, axis=1), tf.int32,
                      name='labels')
}


## Loss Function and Optimization
cross_entropy_loss = tf.reduce_mean(
    tf.nn.softmax_cross_entropy_with_logits(
        logits=h4, labels=tf_y_onehot),
    name='cross_entropy_loss')

## Optimizer
optimizer = tf.train.AdamOptimizer(learning_rate)
optimizer = optimizer.minimize(cross_entropy_loss,
                               name='train_op')
## Computing the prediction accuracy
correct_predictions = tf.equal(
    predictions['labels'],
    tf_y, name='correct_preds')

accuracy = tf.reduce_mean(
    tf.cast(correct_predictions, tf.float32),
    name='accuracy')
```

In order to get stable results, we need to use a random seed for both NumPy and TensorFlow. Setting the TensorFlow random seed can be done at the graph level by placing the `tf.set_random_seed` function within the graph scope, which we will see later. The following figure shows the TensorFlow graph related to our multilayer CNN as visualized by TensorBoard:

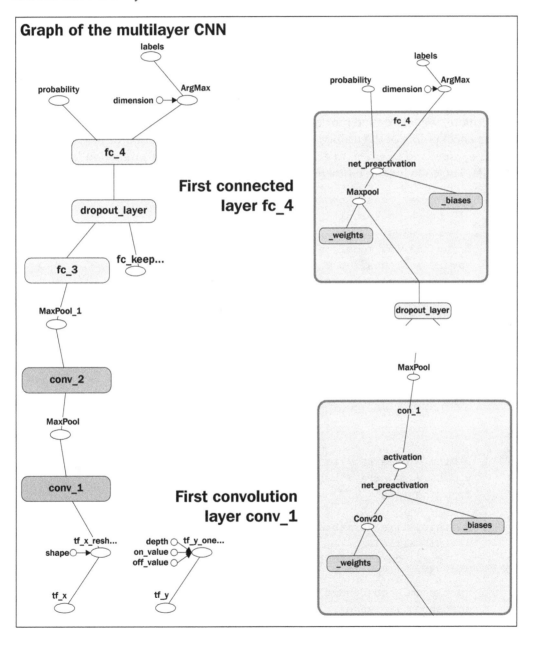

Note that in this implementation, we used the `tf.train.AdamOptimizer` function for training the CNN model. The Adam optimizer is a robust gradient-based optimization method suited for nonconvex optimization and machine learning problems. Two popular optimization methods inspired Adam: `RMSProp` and `AdaGrad`.

The key advantage of Adam is in the choice of update step size derived from the running average of gradient moments. Please feel free to read more about the Adam optimizer in the manuscript, *Adam: A Method for Stochastic Optimization, Diederik P. Kingma and Jimmy Lei Ba, 2014*. The article if freely available at `https://arxiv.org/abs/1412.6980`.

Furthermore, we will define four other functions: `save` and `load` for saving and loading checkpoints of the trained model, `train` for training the model using `training_set`, and `predict` to get prediction probabilities or prediction labels of the test data. The code for these functions is as follows:

```python
def save(saver, sess, epoch, path='./model/'):
    if not os.path.isdir(path):
        os.makedirs(path)
    print('Saving model in %s' % path)
    saver.save(sess, os.path.join(path,'cnn-model.ckpt'),
               global_step=epoch)


def load(saver, sess, path, epoch):
    print('Loading model from %s' % path)
    saver.restore(sess, os.path.join(
            path, 'cnn-model.ckpt-%d' % epoch))


def train(sess, training_set, validation_set=None,
          initialize=True, epochs=20, shuffle=True,
          dropout=0.5, random_seed=None):

    X_data = np.array(training_set[0])
    y_data = np.array(training_set[1])
    training_loss = []

    ## initialize variables
    if initialize:
        sess.run(tf.global_variables_initializer())

    np.random.seed(random_seed) # for shuflling in batch_generator
    for epoch in range(1, epochs+1):
        batch_gen = batch_generator(
```

```
                            X_data, y_data,
                            shuffle=shuffle)
            avg_loss = 0.0
            for i,(batch_x,batch_y) in enumerate(batch_gen):
                feed = {'tf_x:0': batch_x,
                        'tf_y:0': batch_y,
                        'fc_keep_prob:0': dropout}
                loss, _ = sess.run(
                        ['cross_entropy_loss:0', 'train_op'],
                        feed_dict=feed)
                avg_loss += loss

            training_loss.append(avg_loss / (i+1))
            print('Epoch %02d Training Avg. Loss: %7.3f' % (
                epoch, avg_loss), end=' ')
            if validation_set is not None:
                feed = {'tf_x:0': validation_set[0],
                        'tf_y:0': validation_set[1],
                        'fc_keep_prob:0': 1.0}
                valid_acc = sess.run('accuracy:0', feed_dict=feed)
                print(' Validation Acc: %7.3f' % valid_acc)
            else:
                print()

    def predict(sess, X_test, return_proba=False):
        feed = {'tf_x:0': X_test,
                'fc_keep_prob:0': 1.0}
        if return_proba:
            return sess.run('probabilities:0', feed_dict=feed)
        else:
            return sess.run('labels:0', feed_dict=feed)
```

Now we can create a TensorFlow graph object, set the graph-level random seed, and build the CNN model in that graph, as follows:

```
>>> ## Define random seed
>>> random_seed = 123
>>>
>>>
>>> ## create a graph
>>> g = tf.Graph()
>>> with g.as_default():
...     tf.set_random_seed(random_seed)
```

```
...         ## build the graph
...         build_cnn()
...
...         ## saver:
...         saver = tf.train.Saver()
```

Note that in the preceding code, after we built the model by calling the `build_cnn` function, we created a saver object from the `tf.train.Saver` class for saving and restoring trained models, as we saw in *Chapter 14, Going Deeper – The Mechanics of TensorFlow*.

The next step is to train our CNN model. For this, we need to create a TensorFlow session to launch the graph; then, we call the `train` function. To train the model for the first time, we have to initialize all the variables in the network.

For this purpose, we have defined an argument named `initialize` that will take care of the initialization. When `initialize=True`, we will execute `tf.global_variables_initializer` through `session.run`. This initialization step should be avoided in case you want to train additional epochs; for example, you can restore an already trained model and train further for additional 10 epochs. The code for training the model for the first time is as follows:

```
>>> ## create a TF session
>>> ## and train the CNN model
>>>
>>> with tf.Session(graph=g) as sess:
...     train(sess,
...         training_set=(X_train_centered, y_train),
...         validation_set=(X_valid_centered, y_valid),
...         initialize=True,
...         random_seed=123)
...     save(saver, sess, epoch=20)

Epoch 01 Training Avg. Loss: 272.772  Validation Acc:    0.973
Epoch 02 Training Avg. Loss:  76.053  Validation Acc:    0.981
Epoch 03 Training Avg. Loss:  51.309  Validation Acc:    0.984
Epoch 04 Training Avg. Loss:  39.740  Validation Acc:    0.986
Epoch 05 Training Avg. Loss:  31.508  Validation Acc:    0.987
...
Epoch 19 Training Avg. Loss:   5.386  Validation Acc:    0.991
Epoch 20 Training Avg. Loss:   3.965  Validation Acc:    0.992
Saving model in ./model/
```

After the 20 epochs are finished, we save the trained model for future use so that we do not have to retrain the model every time, and therefore, save computational time. The following code shows how to restore a saved model. We delete the graph g, then create a new graph g2, and reload the trained model to do prediction on the test set:

```
>>> ### Calculate prediction accuracy
>>> ### on test set
>>> ### restoring the saved model
>>>
>>> del g
>>>
>>> ## create a new graph
>>> ## and build the model
>>> g2 = tf.Graph()
>>> with g2.as_default():
...     tf.set_random_seed(random_seed)
...     ## build the graph
...     build_cnn()
...
...     ## saver:
...     saver = tf.train.Saver()
>>>
>>> ## create a new session
>>> ## and restore the model
>>> with tf.Session(graph=g2) as sess:
...     load(saver, sess,
...             epoch=20, path='./model/')
...
...     preds = predict(sess, X_test_centered,
...                     return_proba=False)
...
...     print('Test Accuracy: %.3f%%' % (100*
...             np.sum(preds == y_test)/len(y_test)))

Building 1st layer:
..
Building 2nd layer:
..
Building 3rd layer:
..
Building 4th layer:
..
Test Accuracy: 99.310%
```

The output contains several extra lines from the `print` statements in the `build_cnn` function, but they are not shown here for brevity. As you can see, the prediction accuracy on the test set is already better than what we achieved using the multilayer perceptron in *Chapter 13, Parallelizing Neural Network Training with TensorFlow*.

Please, make sure you use `X_test_centered`, which is the preprocessed version of the test data; you will get lower accuracy if you try using `X_test` instead.

Now, let's look at the predicted labels as well as their probabilities on the first 10 test samples. We already have the predictions stored in `preds`; however, in order to have more practice in using the session and launching the graph, we repeat those steps here:

```
>>> ## run the prediction on
>>> ##   some test samples
>>> np.set_printoptions(precision=2, suppress=True)
>>>
>>> with tf.Session(graph=g2) as sess:
...     load(saver, sess,
...          epoch=20, path='./model/')
...
...     print(predict(sess, X_test_centered[:10],
...             return_proba=False))
...
...     print(predict(sess, X_test_centered[:10],
...             return_proba=True))

Loading model from ./model/
INFO:tensorflow:Restoring parameters from ./model/cnn-model.ckpt-20
[7 2 1 0 4 1 4 9 5 9]
[[ 0.    0.    0.    0.    0.    0.    0.    1.    0.    0.  ]
 [ 0.    0.    1.    0.    0.    0.    0.    0.    0.    0.  ]
 [ 0.    1.    0.    0.    0.    0.    0.    0.    0.    0.  ]
 [ 1.    0.    0.    0.    0.    0.    0.    0.    0.    0.  ]
 [ 0.    0.    0.    0.    1.    0.    0.    0.    0.    0.  ]
 [ 0.    1.    0.    0.    0.    0.    0.    0.    0.    0.  ]
 [ 0.    0.    0.    0.    1.    0.    0.    0.    0.    0.  ]
 [ 0.    0.    0.    0.    0.    0.    0.    0.    0.    1.  ]
 [ 0.    0.    0.    0.    0.    0.99  0.01  0.    0.    0.  ]
 [ 0.    0.    0.    0.    0.    0.    0.    0.    0.    1.  ]]
```

Finally, let's see how we can train the model further to reach a total of 40 epochs. Since, we have already trained 20 epochs from the initialized weights and biases. We can save time by restoring the already trained model and continue training for 20 additional epochs. This will be very easy to do with our setup. We need to call the `train` function again, but this time, we set `initialize=False` to avoid the initialization step. The code is as follows:

```
## continue training for 20 more epochs
## without re-initializing :: initialize=False
## create a new session
## and restore the model
with tf.Session(graph=g2) as sess:
    load(saver, sess,
         epoch=20, path='./model/')

    train(sess,
          training_set=(X_train_centered, y_train),
          validation_set=(X_valid_centered, y_valid),
          initialize=False,
          epochs=20,
          random_seed=123)

    save(saver, sess, epoch=40, path='./model/')

    preds = predict(sess, X_test_centered,
                    return_proba=False)

    print('Test Accuracy: %.3f%%' % (100*
                np.sum(preds == y_test)/len(y_test)))
```

The result shows that training for 20 additional epochs slightly improved the performance to get 99.37 percent prediction accuracy on the test set.

In this section, we saw how to implement a multilayer convolutional neural network in the low-level TensorFlow API. In the next section, we'll now implement the same network but we'll use the TensorFlow Layers API.

Implementing a CNN in the TensorFlow Layers API

For the implementation in the TensorFlow Layers API, we need to repeat the same process of loading the data and preprocessing steps to get X_train_centered, X_valid_centered, and X_test_centered. Then, we can implement the model in a new class, as follows:

```python
import tensorflow as tf
import numpy as np


class ConvNN(object):
    def __init__(self, batchsize=64,
                 epochs=20, learning_rate=1e-4,
                 dropout_rate=0.5,
                 shuffle=True, random_seed=None):
        np.random.seed(random_seed)
        self.batchsize = batchsize
        self.epochs = epochs
        self.learning_rate = learning_rate
        self.dropout_rate = dropout_rate
        self.shuffle = shuffle

        g = tf.Graph()
        with g.as_default():
            ## set random-seed:
            tf.set_random_seed(random_seed)

            ## build the network:
            self.build()

            ## initializer
            self.init_op = \
                tf.global_variables_initializer()

            ## saver
            self.saver = tf.train.Saver()

        ## create a session
```

```
        self.sess = tf.Session(graph=g)

def build(self):

    ## Placeholders for X and y:
    tf_x = tf.placeholder(tf.float32,
                          shape=[None, 784],
                          name='tf_x')
    tf_y = tf.placeholder(tf.int32,
                          shape=[None],
                          name='tf_y')
    is_train = tf.placeholder(tf.bool,
                          shape=(),
                          name='is_train')

    ## reshape x to a 4D tensor:
    ##   [batchsize, width, height, 1]
    tf_x_image = tf.reshape(tf_x, shape=[-1, 28, 28, 1],
                          name='input_x_2dimages')
    ## One-hot encoding:
    tf_y_onehot = tf.one_hot(indices=tf_y, depth=10,
                            dtype=tf.float32,
                            name='input_y_onehot')

    ## 1st layer: Conv_1
    h1 = tf.layers.conv2d(tf_x_image,
                          kernel_size=(5, 5),
                          filters=32,
                          activation=tf.nn.relu)
    ## MaxPooling
    h1_pool = tf.layers.max_pooling2d(h1,
                          pool_size=(2, 2),
                          strides=(2, 2))
    ## 2n layer: Conv_2
    h2 = tf.layers.conv2d(h1_pool, kernel_size=(5, 5),
                          filters=64,
                          activation=tf.nn.relu)
    ## MaxPooling
    h2_pool = tf.layers.max_pooling2d(h2,
                          pool_size=(2, 2),
                          strides=(2, 2))

    ## 3rd layer: Fully Connected
```

```
input_shape = h2_pool.get_shape().as_list()
n_input_units = np.prod(input_shape[1:])
h2_pool_flat = tf.reshape(h2_pool,
                          shape=[-1, n_input_units])
h3 = tf.layers.dense(h2_pool_flat, 1024,
                     activation=tf.nn.relu)

## Dropout
h3_drop = tf.layers.dropout(h3,
                            rate=self.dropout_rate,
                            training=is_train)

## 4th layer: Fully Connected (linear activation)
h4 = tf.layers.dense(h3_drop, 10,
                     activation=None)

## Prediction
predictions = {
    'probabilities': tf.nn.softmax(h4,
                        name='probabilities'),
    'labels': tf.cast(tf.argmax(h4, axis=1),
                        tf.int32, name='labels')
}

## Loss Function and Optimization
cross_entropy_loss = tf.reduce_mean(
    tf.nn.softmax_cross_entropy_with_logits(
        logits=h4, labels=tf_y_onehot),
    name='cross_entropy_loss')

## Optimizer
optimizer = tf.train.AdamOptimizer(self.learning_rate)
optimizer = optimizer.minimize(cross_entropy_loss,
                        name='train_op')

## Finding accuracy
correct_predictions = tf.equal(
    predictions['labels'],
    tf_y, name='correct_preds')

accuracy = tf.reduce_mean(
```

```
            tf.cast(correct_predictions, tf.float32),
            name='accuracy')

def save(self, epoch, path='./tflayers-model/'):
    if not os.path.isdir(path):
        os.makedirs(path)
    print('Saving model in %s' % path)
    self.saver.save(self.sess,
                    os.path.join(path, 'model.ckpt'),
                    global_step=epoch)

def load(self, epoch, path):
    print('Loading model from %s' % path)
    self.saver.restore(self.sess,
        os.path.join(path, 'model.ckpt-%d' % epoch))

def train(self, training_set,
          validation_set=None,
          initialize=True):
    ## initialize variables
    if initialize:
        self.sess.run(self.init_op)

    self.train_cost_ = []
    X_data = np.array(training_set[0])
    y_data = np.array(training_set[1])

    for epoch in range(1, self.epochs+1):
        batch_gen = \
            batch_generator(X_data, y_data,
                            shuffle=self.shuffle)
        avg_loss = 0.0
        for i, (batch_x,batch_y) in \
            enumerate(batch_gen):
            feed = {'tf_x:0': batch_x,
                    'tf_y:0': batch_y,
                    'is_train:0': True} ## for dropout
            loss, _ = self.sess.run(
                ['cross_entropy_loss:0', 'train_op'],
                feed_dict=feed)
            avg_loss += loss

        print('Epoch %02d: Training Avg. Loss: '
              '%7.3f' % (epoch, avg_loss), end=' ')
```

```
        if validation_set is not None:
            feed = {'tf_x:0': batch_x,
                    'tf_y:0': batch_y,
                    'is_train:0' : False} ## for dropout
            valid_acc = self.sess.run('accuracy:0',
                    feed_dict=feed)
            print('Validation Acc: %7.3f' % valid_acc)
        else:
            print()

    def predict(self, X_test, return_proba=False):
        feed = {'tf_x:0' : X_test,
                'is_train:0' : False} ## for dropout
        if return_proba:
            return self.sess.run('probabilities:0',
                                  feed_dict=feed)
        else:
            return self.sess.run('labels:0',
                                  feed_dict=feed)
```

The structure of this class is very similar to the previous section with the low-level TensorFlow API. The class has a constructor that sets the training parameters, creates a graph g, and builds the model. Besides the constructor, there are five major methods:

- `.build`: Builds the model
- `.save`: To save a trained model
- `.load`: To restore a saved model
- `.train`: Trains the model
- `.predict`: To do prediction on a test set

Similar to the implementation in the previous section, we've used a dropout layer after the first fully connected layer. In the previous implementation that used the low-level TensorFlow API, we used the `tf.nn.dropout` function, but here we used `tf.layers.dropout`, which is a wrapper for the `tf.nn.dropout` function. There are two major differences between these two functions that we need to be careful about:

- `tf.nn.dropout`: This has an argument called `keep_prob` that indicates the probability of keeping the units, while `tf.layers.dropout` has a `rate` parameter, which is the rate of dropping units—therefore `rate = 1 - keep_prob`.

- In the `tf.nn.dropout` function, we fed the `keep_prob` parameter using a placeholder so that during the training, we will use `keep_prob=0.5`. Then, during the inference (or prediction) mode, we used `keep_prob=1`. However, in `tf.layers.dropout`, the value of `rate` is provided upon the creation of the dropout layer in the graph, and we cannot change it during the training or the inference modes. Instead, we need to provide a Boolean argument called `training` to determine whether we need to apply dropout or not. This can be done using a placeholder of type `tf.bool`, which we will feed with the value `True` during the training mode and `False` during the inference mode.

We can create an instance of the `ConvNN` class, train it for 20 epochs, and save the model. The code for this is as follows:

```
>>> cnn = ConvNN(random_seed=123)
>>>
>>> ## train the model
>>> cnn.train(training_set=(X_train_centered, y_train),
...           validation_set=(X_valid_centered, y_valid),
...           initialize=True)
>>> cnn.save(epoch=20)
```

After the training is finished, the model can be used to do prediction on the test dataset, as follows:

```
>>> del cnn
>>>
>>> cnn2 = ConvNN(random_seed=123)
>>> cnn2.load(epoch=20, path='./tflayers-model/')
>>>
>>> print(cnn2.predict(X_test_centered[:10, :]))

Loading model from ./tflayers-model/
INFO:tensorflow:Restoring parameters from ./tflayers-model/model.ckpt-20
[7 2 1 0 4 1 4 9 5 9]
```

Finally, we can measure the accuracy of the test dataset as follows:

```
>>> preds = cnn2.predict(X_test_centered)
>>>
>>> print('Test Accuracy: %.2f%%' % (100*
...         np.sum(y_test == preds)/len(y_test)))

Test Accuracy: 99.32%
```

The obtained prediction accuracy is 99.32 percent, which means there are only 68 misclassified test samples!

This concludes our discussion on implementing convolutional neural networks using the TensorFlow low-level API and TensorFlow Layers API. We defined some wrapper functions for the first implementation using the low-level API. The second implementation was more straightforward since we could use the `tf.layers.conv2d` and `tf.layers.dense` functions to build the convolutional and the fully connected layers.

Summary

In this chapter, we learned about CNNs, or convolutional neural networks, and explored the building blocks that form different CNN architectures. We started by defining the convolution operation, then we learned about its fundamentals by discussing 1D as well as 2D implementations.

We also covered subsampling by discussing two forms of pooling operations: max-pooling and average-pooling. Then, putting all these blocks together, we built a deep convolutional neural network and implemented it using the TensorFlow core API as well as the TensorFlow **Layers** API to apply CNNs for image classification.

In the next chapter, we'll move on to **Recurrent Neural Networks (RNN)**. RNNs are used for learning the structure of sequence data, and they have some fascinating applications, including language translation and image captioning!

16

Modeling Sequential Data Using Recurrent Neural Networks

In the previous chapter, we focused on **Convolutional Neural Networks** (**CNNs**) for image classification. In this chapter, we will explore **Recurrent Neural Networks** (**RNNs**) and see their application in modeling sequential data and a specific subset of sequential data—time-series data. As an overview, in this chapter, we will cover the following topics:

- Introducing sequential data
- RNNs for modeling sequences
- **Long Short-Term Memory (LSTM)**
- **Truncated Backpropagation Through Time (T-BPTT)**
- Implementing a multilayer RNN for sequence modeling in TensorFlow
- Project one – RNN sentiment analysis of the IMDb movie review dataset
- Project two – RNN character-level language modeling with LSTM cells, using text data from Shakespeare's Hamlet
- Using gradient clipping to avoid exploding gradients

Since this chapter is the last in our *Python Machine Learning* journey, we'll conclude with a summary of what we've learned about RNNs, and an overview of all the machine learning and deep learning topics that led us to RNNs across the journey of the book. We'll then sign off by sharing with you links to some of our favorite people and initiatives in this wonderful field so that you can continue your journey into machine learning and deep learning.

Introducing sequential data

Let's begin our discussion of RNNs by looking at the nature of sequential data, more commonly known as **sequences**. We'll take a look at the unique properties of sequences that make them different from other kinds of data. We'll then see how we can represent sequential data, and explore the various categories of models for sequential data, which are based on the input and output of a model. This will help us explore the relationship between RNNs and sequences a little bit later on in the chapter.

Modeling sequential data – order matters

What makes sequences unique, from other data types, is that elements in a sequence appear in a certain order, and are not independent of each other.

If you recall from *Chapter 6, Learning Best Practices for Model Evaluation and Hyperparameter Tuning*, we discussed that typical machine learning algorithms for supervised learning assume that the input data is **Independent and Identically Distributed** (IID). For example, if we have n data samples, $x^{(1)}, x^{(2)}, \ldots, x^{(n)}$, the order in which we use the data for training our machine learning algorithm does not matter.

However, this assumption is not valid anymore when we deal with sequences—by definition, order matters.

Representing sequences

We've established that sequences are a nonindependent order in our input data; we next need to find ways to leverage this valuable information in our machine learning model.

Throughout this chapter, we will represent sequences as $\left(x^{(1)}, x^{(2)}, \ldots, x^{(T)}\right)$. The superscript indices indicate the order of the instances, and the length of the sequence is T. For a sensible example of sequences, consider time-series data, where each sample point $x^{(t)}$ belongs to a particular time t.

The following figure shows an example of time-series data where both x's and y's naturally follow the order according to their time axis; therefore, both x's and y's are sequences:

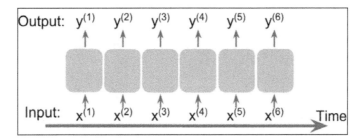

The standard neural network models that we have covered so far, such as MLPs and CNNs, are not capable of handling *the order* of input samples. Intuitively, one can say that such models do not have a *memory* of the past seen samples. For instance, the samples are passed through the feedforward and backpropagation steps, and the weights are updated independent of the order in which the sample is processed.

RNNs, by contrast, are designed for modeling sequences and are capable of remembering past information and processing new events accordingly.

The different categories of sequence modeling

Sequence modeling has many fascinating applications, such as language translation (perhaps from English to German), image captioning, and text generation.

However, we need to understand the different types of sequence modeling tasks to develop an appropriate model. The following figure, based on the explanations in the excellent article *The Unreasonable Effectiveness of Recurrent Neural Networks* by Andrej Karpathy (http://karpathy.github.io/2015/05/21/rnn-effectiveness/), shows several different relationship categories of input and output data:

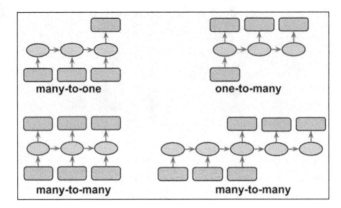

So, let's consider the input and output data here. If neither the input or output data represents sequences, then we are dealing with standard data, and we can use any of the previous methods to model such data. But if either the input or output is a sequence, the data will form one of the following three different categories:

- **Many-to-one**: The input data is a sequence, but the output is a fixed-size vector, not a sequence. For example, in sentiment analysis, the input is text-based and the output is a class label.

- **One-to-many**: The input data is in standard format, not a sequence, but the output is a sequence. An example of this category is image captioning—the input is an image; the output is an English phrase.

- **Many-to-many**: Both the input and output arrays are sequences. This category can be further divided based on whether the input and output are synchronized or not. An example of a **synchronized** many-to-many modeling task is video classification, where each frame in a video is labeled. An example of a **delayed** many-to-many would be translating a language into another. For instance, an entire English sentence must be read and processed by a machine before producing its translation into German.

Now, since we know about the categories of sequence modeling, we can move forward to discuss the structure of an RNN.

RNNs for modeling sequences

In this section, now that we understand sequences, we can look at the foundations of RNNs. We'll start by introducing the typical structure of an RNN, and we'll see how the data flows through it with one or more hidden layers. We'll then examine how the neuron activations are computed in a typical RNN. This will create a context for us to discuss the common challenges in training RNNs, and explore the modern solution to these challenges — LSTM.

Understanding the structure and flow of an RNN

Let's start by introducing the architecture of an RNN. The following figure shows a standard feedforward neural network and an RNN, in a side by side for comparison:

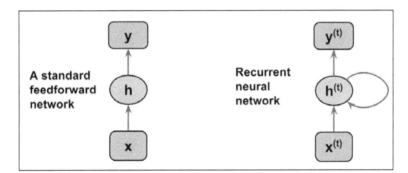

Both of these networks have only one hidden layer. In this representation, the units are not displayed, but we assume that the input layer (**x**), hidden layer (**h**), and output layer (**y**) are vectors which contain many units.

This generic RNN architecture could correspond to the two sequence modeling categories where the input is a sequence. Thus, it could be either many-to-many if we consider $y^{(t)}$ as the final output, or it could be many-to-one if, for example, we only use the last element of $y^{(t)}$ as the final output.

Later, we will see how the output sequence $y^{(t)}$ can be converted into standard, nonsequential output.

In a standard feedforward network, information flows from the input to the hidden layer, and then from the hidden layer to the output layer. On the other hand, in a recurrent network, the hidden layer gets its input from both the input layer and the hidden layer from the previous time step.

The flow of information in adjacent time steps in the hidden layer allows the network to have a memory of past events. This flow of information is usually displayed as a loop, also known as a **recurrent edge** in graph notation, which is how this general architecture got its name.

In the following figure, the single hidden layer network and the multilayer network illustrate two contrasting architectures:

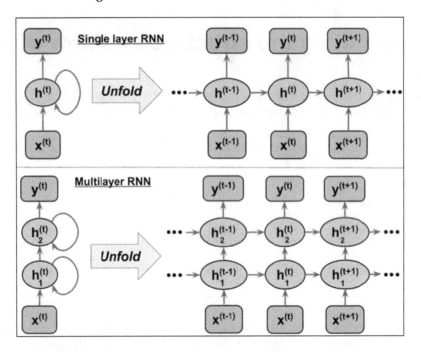

In order to examine the architecture of RNNs and the flow of information, a compact representation with a recurrent edge can be unfolded, which you can see in the preceding figure.

As we know, each hidden unit in a standard neural network receives only one input—the net preactivation associated with the input layer. Now, in contrast, each hidden unit in an RNN receives two *distinct* sets of input—the preactivation from the input layer and the activation of the same hidden layer from the previous time step t-1.

At the first time step $t = 0$, the hidden units are initialized to zeros or small random values. Then, at a time step where t > 0, the hidden units get their input from the data point at the current time $x^{(t)}$ and the previous values of hidden units at $t - 1$, indicated as $h^{(t-1)}$.

Similarly, in the case of a multilayer RNN, we can summarize the information flow as follows:

- *layer* $= 1$: Here, the hidden layer is represented as $h_1^{(t)}$ and gets its input from the data point $x^{(t)}$ and the hidden values in the same layer, but the previous time step $h_1^{(t-1)}$

- *layer* $= 2$: The second hidden layer, $h_2^{(t)}$ receives its inputs from the hidden units from the layer below at the current time step ($h_1^{(t)}$) and its own hidden values from the previous time step $h_2^{(t-1)}$

Computing activations in an RNN

Now that we understand the structure and general flow of information in an RNN, let's get more specific and compute the actual activations of the hidden layers as well as the output layer. For simplicity, we'll consider just a single hidden layer; however, the same concept applies to multilayer RNNs.

Each directed edge (the connections between boxes) in the representation of an RNN that we just looked at is associated with a weight matrix. Those weights do not depend on time t; therefore, they are shared across the time axis. The different weight matrices in a single layer RNN are as follows:

- W_{xh}: The weight matrix between the input $x^{(t)}$ and the hidden layer **h**
- W_{hh}: The weight matrix associated with the recurrent edge
- W_{hy}: The weight matrix between the hidden layer and output layer

You can see these weight matrices in the following figure:

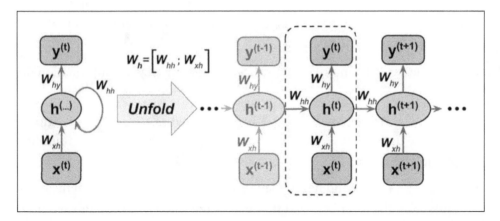

In certain implementations, you may observe that weight matrices W_{xh} and W_{hh} are concatenated to a combined matrix $W_h = [W_{xh}; W_{hh}]$. Later on, we'll make use of this notation as well.

Computing the activations is very similar to standard multilayer perceptrons and other types of feedforward neural networks. For the hidden layer, the net input z_h (preactivation) is computed through a linear combination. That is, we compute the sum of the multiplications of the weight matrices with the corresponding vectors and add the bias unit $- z_h^{(t)} = W_{xh} x^{(t)} + W_{hh} h^{(t-1)} + b_h$. Then, the activations of the hidden units at the time step t are calculated as follows:

$$h^{(t)} = \phi_h\left(z_h^{(t)}\right) = \phi_h\left(W_{xh} x^{(t)} + W_{hh} h^{(t-1)} + b_h\right)$$

Here, b_h is the bias vector for the hidden units and $\phi_h(\cdot)$ is the activation function of the hidden layer.

In case you want to use the concatenated weight matrix $W_h = [W_{xh}; W_{hh}]$, the formula for computing hidden units will change as follows:

$$h^{(t)} = \phi_h \left([W_{xh}; W_{hh}] \begin{bmatrix} x^{(t)} \\ h^{(t-1)} \end{bmatrix} + b_h \right)$$

Once the activations of hidden units at the current time step are computed, then the activations of output units will be computed as follows:

$$y^{(t)} = \phi_y \left(W_{hy} h^{(t)} + b_y \right)$$

To help clarify this further, the following figure shows the process of computing these activations with both formulations:

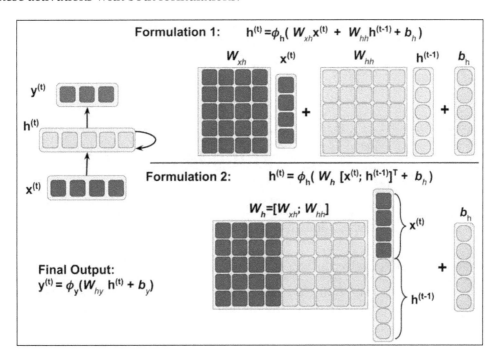

Training RNNs using BPTT

The learning algorithm for RNNs was introduced in 1990s
*Backpropagation Through Time: What It Does and How to Do It (Paul Werbos,
Proceedings of IEEE, 78(10):1550-1560, 1990).*

The derivation of the gradients might be a bit complicated, but the basic
idea is that the overall loss L is the sum of all the loss functions at times
$t = 1$ to $t = T$:

$$L = \sum_{t=1}^{T} L^{(t)}$$

Since the loss at time $1:t$ is dependent on the hidden units at all
previous time steps $1:t$, the gradient will be computed as follows:

$$\frac{\partial L^{(t)}}{\partial W_{hh}} = \frac{\partial L^{(t)}}{\partial y^{(t)}} \times \frac{\partial y^{(t)}}{\partial h^{(t)}} \times \left(\sum_{k=1}^{t} \frac{\partial h^{(t)}}{\partial h^{(k)}} \times \frac{\partial h^{(k)}}{\partial W_{hh}} \right)$$

Here, $\frac{\partial h^{(t)}}{\partial h^{(k)}}$ is computed as a multiplication of adjacent time steps:

$$\frac{\partial h^{(t)}}{\partial h^{(k)}} = \prod_{i=k+1}^{t} \frac{\partial h^{(i)}}{\partial h^{(i-1)}}$$

The challenges of learning long-range interactions

Backpropagation through time, or BPTT, which we briefly mentioned in the previous
information box, introduces some new challenges.

Because of the multiplicative factor $\frac{\partial h^{(t)}}{\partial h^{(k)}}$ in the computing gradients of a loss
function, the so-called **vanishing** or **exploding** gradient problem arises. This
problem is explained through the examples in the following figure, which shows an
RNN with only one hidden unit for simplicity:

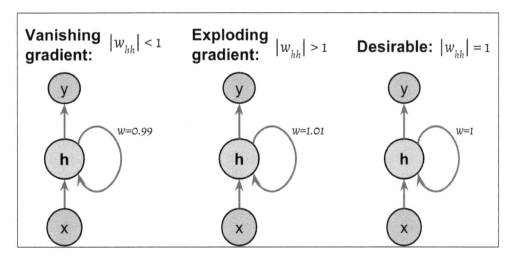

Basically, $\dfrac{\partial \boldsymbol{h}^{(t)}}{\partial \boldsymbol{h}^{(k)}}$ has $t-k$ multiplications; therefore, multiplying the w weight $t-k$ times results in a factor $- w^{t-k}$. As a result, if $|w|<1$, this factor becomes very small when $t-k$ is large. On the other hand, if the weight of the recurrent edge is $|w|>1$, then w^{t-k} becomes very large when $t-k$ is large. Note that large $t-k$ refers to long-range dependencies.

Intuitively, we can see that a naïve solution to avoid vanishing or exploding gradient can be accomplished by ensuring $|w|=1$. If you are interested and would like to investigate this in more detail, I encourage you to read *On the difficulty of training recurrent neural networks* by R. Pascanu, T. Mikolov, and Y. Bengio, 2012 (`https://arxiv.org/pdf/1211.5063.pdf`).

In practice, there are two solutions to this problem:

- Truncated backpropagation through time (TBPTT)
- Long short-term memory (LSTM)

TBPTT clips the gradients above a given threshold. While TBPTT can solve the exploding gradient problem, the truncation limits the number of steps that the gradient can effectively flow back and properly update the weights.

On the other hand, LSTM, designed in 1997 by Hochreiter and Schmidhuber, has been more successful in modeling long-range sequences by overcoming the vanishing gradient problem. Let's discuss LSTM in more detail.

LSTM units

LSTMs were first introduced to overcome the vanishing gradient problem (*Long Short-Term Memory*, S. *Hochreiter* and J. *Schmidhuber*, *Neural Computation*, 9(8): 1735-1780, *1997*). The building block of an LSTM is a **memory cell**, which essentially represents the hidden layer.

In each memory cell, there is a recurrent edge that has the desirable weight $w = 1$, as we discussed previously, to overcome the vanishing and exploding gradient problems. The values associated with this recurrent edge is called **cell state**. The unfolded structure of a modern LSTM cell is shown in the following figure:

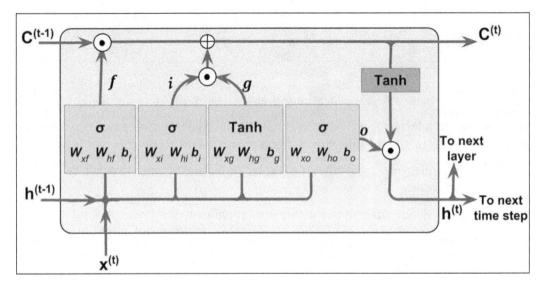

Notice that the cell state from the previous time step, $C^{(t-1)}$, is modified to get the cell state at the current time step, $C^{(t)}$, without being multiplied directly with any weight factor.

The flow of information in this memory cell is controlled by some units of computation that we'll describe here. In the previous figure, $\odot$ refers to the **element-wise product** (element-wise multiplication) and $\oplus$ means **element-wise summation** (element-wise addition). Furthermore, $x^{(t)}$ refers to the input data at time t, and $h^{(t-1)}$ indicates the hidden units at time $t-1$.

Four boxes are indicated with an activation function, either the sigmoid function (σ) or hyperbolic tangent (tanh), and a set of weights; these boxes apply linear combination by performing matrix-vector multiplications on their input. These units of computation with sigmoid activation functions, whose output units are passed through $\odot$, are called **gates**.

In an LSTM cell, there are three different types of gates, known as the forget gate, the input gate, and the output gate:

- The **forget gate** (f_t) allows the memory cell to reset the cell state without growing indefinitely. In fact, the forget gate decides which information is allowed to go through and which information to suppress. Now, f_t is computed as follows:

$$f_t = \sigma\left(W_{xf}x^{(t)} + W_{hf}h^{(t-1)} + b_f\right)$$

   Note that the forget gate was not part of the original LSTM cell; it was added a few years later to improve the original model (*Learning to Forget: Continual Prediction with LSTM, F. Gers, J. Schmidhuber, and F. Cummins, Neural Computation 12, 2451-2471, 2000*).

- The **input gate** (i_t) and input node (g_t) are responsible for updating the cell state. They are computed as follows:

$$i_t = \sigma\left(W_{xi}x^{(t)} + W_{hi}h^{(t-1)} + b_i\right)$$

$$g_t = \tanh\left(W_{xg}x^{(t)} + W_{hg}h^{(t-1)} + b_g\right)$$

   The cell state at time t is computed as follows:

$$C^{(t)} = \left(C^{(t-1)} \odot f_t\right) \oplus \left(i_t \odot g_t\right)$$

- The **output gate** (o_t) decides how to update the values of hidden units:

$$o_t = \sigma\left(W_{xo}x^{(t)} + W_{ho}h^{(t-1)} + b_o\right)$$

Given this, the hidden units at the current time step are computed as follows:

$$h^{(t)} = o_t \odot \tanh\left(C^{(t)}\right)$$

The structure of an LSTM cell and its underlying computations might seem too complex. However, the good news is that TensorFlow has already implemented everything in wrapper functions that allows us to define our LSTM cells easily. We'll see the real application of LSTMs in action when we use TensorFlow later in this chapter.

We have introduced LSTMs in this section, which provide a basic approach for modeling long-range dependencies in sequences. Yet, it is important to note that there are many variations of LSTMs described in literature (*An Empirical Exploration of Recurrent Network Architectures, Rafal Jozefowicz, Wojciech Zaremba,* and *Ilya Sutskever, Proceedings of ICML, 2342-2350, 2015*).

Also, worth noting is a more recent approach, called **Gated Recurrent Unit (GRU)**, which was proposed in 2014. GRUs have a simpler architecture than LSTMs; therefore, they are computationally more efficient while their performance in some tasks, such as polyphonic music modeling, is comparable to LSTMs. If you are interested in learning more about these modern RNN architectures, refer to the paper, *Empirical Evaluation of Gated Recurrent Neural Networks on Sequence Modeling* by *Junyoung Chung and others 2014* (`https://arxiv.org/pdf/1412.3555v1.pdf`).

Implementing a multilayer RNN for sequence modeling in TensorFlow

Now that we introduced the underlying theory behind RNNs, we are ready to move on to the more practical part to implement RNNs in TensorFlow. During the rest of this chapter, we will apply RNNs to two common problems tasks:

1. Sentiment analysis
2. Language modeling

These two projects, which we'll build together in the following pages, are both fascinating but also quite involved. Thus, instead of providing all the code all at once, we will break the implementation up into several steps and discuss the code in detail. If you like to have a big picture overview and see all the code at once before diving into the discussion, we recommend you to take a look at the code implementation first, which you can view at `https://github.com/rasbt/python-machine-learning-book-2nd-edition/blob/master/code/ch16/ch16.ipynb`.

Note, before we start coding in this chapter, that since we're using a very modern build of TensorFlow, we'll be using code from the `contrib` submodule of TensorFlow's Python API, in the latest version of TensorFlow (1.3.0) from August 2017. These `contrib` functions and classes, as well as their documentation references used in this chapter, may change in the future versions of TensorFlow, or they may be integrated into the `tf.nn` submodule. We therefore advise you to keep an eye on the TensorFlow API documentation (`https://www.tensorflow.org/api_docs/python/`) to be updated with the latest version details, in particular, if you have any problems using the `tf.contrib` code described in this chapter.

Project one – performing sentiment analysis of IMDb movie reviews using multilayer RNNs

You may recall from *Chapter 8, Applying Machine Learning to Sentiment Analysis*, that sentiment analysis is concerned with analyzing the expressed opinion of a sentence or a text document. In this section and the following subsections, we will implement a multilayer RNN for sentiment analysis using a many-to-one architecture.

In the next section, we will implement a many-to-many RNN for an application language modeling. While the chosen examples are purposefully simple to introduce the main concepts of RNNs, language modeling has a wide range of interesting applications such as building chatbot — giving computers the ability to directly talk and interact with a human.

Preparing the data

In the preprocessing steps in *Chapter 8, Applying Machine Learning to Sentiment Analysis*, we created a clean dataset named `movie_data.csv`, which we'll use again now. So, first let's import the necessary modules and read the data into a `DataFrame` pandas, as follows:

```
>>> import pyprind
>>> import pandas as pd
>>> from string import punctuation
>>> import re
>>> import numpy as np
>>>
>>> df = pd.read_csv('movie_data.csv', encoding='utf-8')
```

Recall that this `df` data frame has two columns, namely `'review'` and `'sentiment'`, where `'review'` contains the text of movie reviews and `'sentiment'` contains the `0` or `1` labels. The text component of these movie reviews are sequences of words; therefore, we want to build an RNN model to process the words in each sequence, and at the end, classify the entire sequence to `0` or `1` classes.

To prepare the data for input to a neural network, we need to encode it into numeric values. To do this, we first find the unique words in the entire dataset, which can be done using sets in Python. However, I found that using sets for finding unique words in such a large dataset is not efficient. A more efficient way is to use `Counter` from the collections package. If you want to learn more about `Counter`, refer to its documentation at `https://docs.python.org/3/library/collections. html#collections.Counter`.

In the following code, we will define a `counts` object from the `Counter` class that collects the counts of occurrence of each unique word in the text. Note that in this particular application (and in contrast to the bag-of-words model), we are only interested in the set of unique words and won't require the word counts, which are created as a side product.

Then, we create a mapping in the form of a dictionary that maps each unique word, in our dataset, to a unique integer number. We call this dictionary `word_to_int`, which can be used to convert the entire text of a review into a list of numbers. The unique words are sorted based on their counts, but any arbitrary order can be used without affecting the final results. This process of converting a text into a list of integers is performed using the following code:

```
>>> ## Preprocessing the data:
>>> ## Separate words and
>>> ## count each word's occurrence
```

```
>>>
>>> from collections import Counter

>>> counts = Counter()
>>> pbar = pyprind.ProgBar(len(df['review']), \
...                         title='Counting words occurrences')
>>> for i,review in enumerate(df['review']):
...     text = ''.join([c if c not in punctuation else ' '+c+' ' \
...                     for c in review]).lower()
...     df.loc[i,'review'] = text
...     pbar.update()
...     counts.update(text.split())
>>>
>>> ## Create a mapping
>>> ## Map each unique word to an integer
>>> word_counts = sorted(counts, key=counts.get, reverse=True)
>>> print(word_counts[:5])
>>> word_to_int = {word: ii for ii, word in \
...                enumerate(word_counts, 1)}
>>>
>>>
>>> mapped_reviews = []
>>> pbar = pyprind.ProgBar(len(df['review']), \
...                         title='Map reviews to ints')
>>> for review in df['review']:
...     mapped_reviews.append([word_to_int[word] \
...                           for word in review.split()])
...     pbar.update()
```

So far, we've converted sequences of words into sequences of integers. However, there is one issue that we still need to solve — the sequences currently have different lengths. In order to generate input data that is compatible with our RNN architecture, we will need to make sure that all the sequences have the same length.

For this purpose, we define a parameter called `sequence_length` that we set to 200. Sequences that have fewer than 200 words will be left-padded with zeros. Vice versa, sequences that are longer than 200 words are cut such that only the last 200 corresponding words will be used. We can implement this preprocessing step in two steps:

1. Create a matrix of zeros, where each row corresponds to a sequence of size 200.

2. Fill the index of words in each sequence from the right-hand side of the matrix. Thus, if a sequence has a length of 150, the first 50 elements of the corresponding row will stay zero.

These two steps are shown in the following figure, for a small example with eight sequences of sizes 4, 12, 8, 11, 7, 3, 10, and 13:

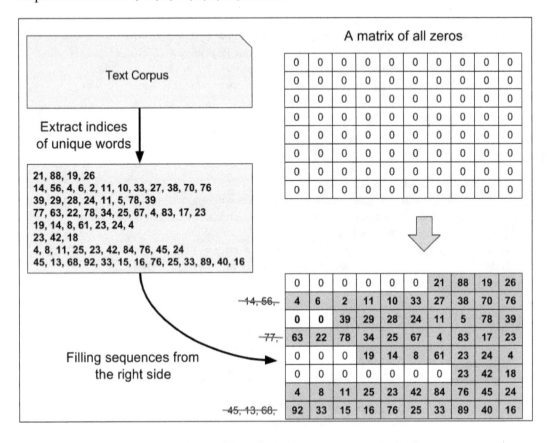

Note that `sequence_length` is, in fact, a hyperparameter and can be tuned for optimal performance. Due to page limitations, we did not optimize this hyperparameter further, but we encourage you to try this with different values for `sequence_length`, such as 50, 100, 200, 250, and 300.

Check out the following code for the implementation of these steps to create sequences of the same length:

```
>>> ## Define same-length sequences
>>> ## if sequence length < 200: left-pad with zeros
>>> ## if sequence length > 200: use the last 200 elements
>>>
>>> sequence_length = 200  ## (Known as T in our RNN formulas)
```

```
>>> sequences = np.zeros((len(mapped_reviews), sequence_length),
...                       dtype=int)
>>>
>>> for i, row in enumerate(mapped_reviews):
...     review_arr = np.array(row)
...     sequences[i, -len(row):] = review_arr[-sequence_length:]
```

After we preprocess the dataset, we can proceed with splitting the data into separate training and test sets. Since the dataset was already shuffled, we can simply take the first half of the dataset for training and the second half for testing, as follows:

```
>>> X_train = sequences[:25000,:]
>>> y_train = df.loc[:25000, 'sentiment'].values
>>> X_test = sequences[25000:,:]
>>> y_test = df.loc[25000:, 'sentiment'].values
```

Now if we want to separate the dataset for cross-validation, we can further split the second half of the data further to generate a smaller test set and a validation set for hyperparameter optimization.

Finally, we define a helper function that breaks a given dataset (which could be a training set or test set) into chunks and returns a generator to iterate through these chunks (also known as **mini-batches**):

```
>>> np.random.seed(123) # for reproducibility

>>> ## Define a function to generate mini-batches:
>>> def create_batch_generator(x, y=None, batch_size=64):
...     n_batches = len(x)//batch_size
...     x = x[:n_batches*batch_size]
...     if y is not None:
...         y = y[:n_batches*batch_size]
...     for ii in range(0, len(x), batch_size):
...         if y is not None:
...             yield x[ii:ii+batch_size], y[ii:ii+batch_size]
...         else:
...             yield x[ii:ii+batch_size]
```

Using generators, as we've done in this code, is a very useful technique for handling memory limitations. This is the recommended approach for splitting the dataset into mini-batches for training a neural network, rather than creating all the data splits upfront and keeping them in memory during training.

Embedding

During the data preparation in the previous step, we generated sequences of the same length. The elements of these sequences were integer numbers that corresponded to the *indices* of unique words.

These word indices can be converted into input features in several different ways. One naïve way is to apply one-hot encoding to convert indices into vectors of zeros and ones. Then, each word will be mapped to a vector whose size is the number of unique words in the entire dataset. Given that the number of unique words (the size of the vocabulary) can be in the order of 20,000, which will also be the number of our input features, a model trained on such features may suffer from the **curse of dimensionality**. Furthermore, these features are very sparse, since all are zero except one.

A more elegant way is to map each word to a vector of fixed size with real-valued elements (not necessarily integers). In contrast to the one-hot encoded vectors, we can use finite-sized vectors to represent an infinite number of real numbers (in theory, we can extract infinite real numbers from a given interval, for example [-1, 1]).

This is the idea behind the so-called **embedding**, which is a feature-learning technique that we can utilize here to automatically learn the salient features to represent the words in our dataset. Given the number of unique words *unique_words*, we can choose the size of the embedding vectors to be much smaller than the number of unique words (*embedding_size << unique_words*) to represent the entire vocabulary as input features.

The advantages of embedding over one-hot encoding are as follows:

- A reduction in the dimensionality of the feature space to decrease the effect of the curse of dimensionality

- The extraction of salient features since the embedding layer in a neural network is trainable

The following schematic representation shows how embedding works by mapping vocabulary indices to a trainable embedding matrix:

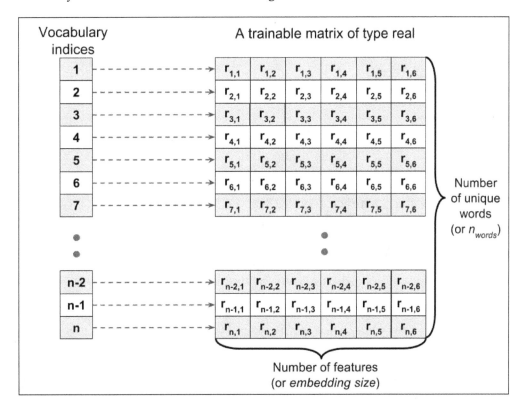

TensorFlow implements an efficient function, `tf.nn.embedding_lookup`, that maps each integer that corresponds to a unique word, to a row of this trainable matrix. For example, integer 1 is mapped to the first row, integer 2 is mapped to the second row, and so on. Then, given a sequence of integers, such as <0, 5, 3, 4, 19, 2...>, we need to look up the corresponding rows for each element of this sequence.

Now let's see how we can create an embedding layer in practice. If we have `tf_x` as the input layer where the corresponding vocabulary indices are fed with type `tf.int32`, then creating an embedding layer can be done in two steps, as follows:

1. We start by creating a matrix of size $[n\_words \times embedding\_size]$ as a tensor variable, which we call `embedding`, and we initialize its elements randomly with floats between [-1, 1]:

```
embedding = tf.Variable(
                tf.random_uniform(
                    shape=(n_words, embedding_size),
                    minval=-1, maxval=1)
            )
```

2. Then, we use the `tf.nn.embedding_lookup` function to look up the row in the embedding matrix associated with each element of `tf_x`:

```
embed_x = tf.nn.embedding_lookup(embedding, tf_x)
```

As you may have observed in these steps, to create an embedding layer, the `tf.nn.embedding_lookup` function requires two arguments: the embedding tensor and the lookup IDs.

The `tf.nn.embedding_lookup` function has a few optional arguments that allow you to tweak the behavior of the embedding layer, such as applying L2 normalization. Feel free to read more about this function from its official documentation at `https://www.tensorflow.org/api_docs/python/tf/nn/embedding_lookup`.

Building an RNN model

Now we're ready to build an RNN model. We'll implement a `SentimentRNN` class that has the following methods:

- A constructor to set all the model parameters and then create a computation graph and call the `self.build` method to build the multilayer RNN model.

- A `build` method that declares three placeholders for input data, input labels, and the keep-probability for the dropout configuration of the hidden layer. After declaring these, it creates an embedding layer, and builds the multilayer RNN using the embedded representation as input.

- A `train` method that creates a TensorFlow session for launching the computation graph, iterates through the mini-batches of data, and runs for a fixed number of epochs, to minimize the cost function defined in the graph. This method also saves the model after 10 epochs for checkpointing.

- A `predict` method that creates a new session, restores the last checkpoint saved during the training process, and carries out the predictions for the test data.

In the following code, we'll see the implementation of this class and its methods broken into separate code sections.

The SentimentRNN class constructor

Let's start with the constructor of our `SentimentRNN` class, which we'll code as follows:

```python
import tensorflow as tf

class SentimentRNN(object):
    def __init__(self, n_words, seq_len=200,
                 lstm_size=256, num_layers=1, batch_size=64,
                 learning_rate=0.0001, embed_size=200):
        self.n_words = n_words
        self.seq_len = seq_len
        self.lstm_size = lstm_size  ## number of hidden units
        self.num_layers = num_layers
        self.batch_size = batch_size
        self.learning_rate = learning_rate
        self.embed_size = embed_size

        self.g = tf.Graph()
        with self.g.as_default():
            tf.set_random_seed(123)
            self.build()
            self.saver = tf.train.Saver()
            self.init_op = tf.global_variables_initializer()
```

Here, the n_words parameter must be set equal to the number of unique words (plus 1 since we use zero to fill sequences whose size is less than 200) and it's used while creating the embedding layer along with the embed_size hyperparameter. Meanwhile, the seq_len variable must be set according to the length of the sequences that were created in the preprocessing steps we went through previously. Note that lstm_size is another hyperparameter that we've used here, and it determines the number of hidden units in each RNN layer.

The build method

Next, let's discuss the `build` method for our `SentimentRNN` class. This is the longest and most critical method in our sequence, so we'll be going through it in plenty of detail. First, we'll look at the code in full, so we can see everything together, and then we'll analyze each of its main parts:

```python
def build(self):
    ## Define the placeholders
    tf_x = tf.placeholder(tf.int32,
                shape=(self.batch_size, self.seq_len),
                name='tf_x')
    tf_y = tf.placeholder(tf.float32,
                shape=(self.batch_size),
                name='tf_y')
    tf_keepprob = tf.placeholder(tf.float32,
                name='tf_keepprob')

    ## Create the embedding layer
    embedding = tf.Variable(
                tf.random_uniform(
                    (self.n_words, self.embed_size),
                    minval=-1, maxval=1),
                name='embedding')
    embed_x = tf.nn.embedding_lookup(
                embedding, tf_x,
                name='embeded_x')

    ## Define LSTM cell and stack them together
    cells = tf.contrib.rnn.MultiRNNCell(
            [tf.contrib.rnn.DropoutWrapper(
                tf.contrib.rnn.BasicLSTMCell(self.lstm_size),
                output_keep_prob=tf_keepprob)
             for i in range(self.num_layers)])

    ## Define the initial state:
    self.initial_state = cells.zero_state(
            self.batch_size, tf.float32)
    print('  << initial state >> ', self.initial_state)

    lstm_outputs, self.final_state = tf.nn.dynamic_rnn(
            cells, embed_x,
            initial_state=self.initial_state)

    ## Note: lstm_outputs shape:
```

```
##  [batch_size, max_time, cells.output_size]
print('\n  << lstm_output   >> ', lstm_outputs)
print('\n  << final state   >> ', self.final_state)

logits = tf.layers.dense(
        inputs=lstm_outputs[:, -1],
        units=1, activation=None,
        name='logits')

logits = tf.squeeze(logits, name='logits_squeezed')
print ('\n  << logits        >> ', logits)

y_proba = tf.nn.sigmoid(logits, name='probabilities')
predictions = {
    'probabilities': y_proba,
    'labels' : tf.cast(tf.round(y_proba), tf.int32,
        name='labels')
}
print('\n  << predictions   >> ', predictions)

## Define the cost function
cost = tf.reduce_mean(
        tf.nn.sigmoid_cross_entropy_with_logits(
        labels=tf_y, logits=logits),
        name='cost')

## Define the optimizer
optimizer = tf.train.AdamOptimizer(self.learning_rate)
train_op = optimizer.minimize(cost, name='train_op')
```

So first of all in our `build` method here, we created three placeholders, namely `tf_x`, `tf_y`, and `tf_keepprob`, which we need for feeding the input data. Then we added the embedding layer, which builds the embedded representation `embed_x`, as we discussed earlier.

Next, in our `build` method, we built the RNN network with LSTM cells. We did this in three steps:

1. First, we defined the multilayer RNN cells.

2. Next, we defined the initial state for these cells.

3. Finally, we created an RNN specified by the RNN cells and their initial states.

Let's break these three steps out in detail in the following three sections, so we can examine in depth how we built the RNN network in our `build` method.

Step 1 – defining multilayer RNN cells

To examine how we coded our `build` method to build the RNN network, the first step was to define our multilayer RNN cells.

Fortunately, TensorFlow has a very nice wrapper class to define LSTM cells — the `BasicLSTMCell` class — which can be stacked together to form a multilayer RNN using the `MultiRNNCell` wrapper class. The process of stacking RNN cells with a dropout has three nested steps; these three nested steps can be described from inside out as follows:

1. First, create the RNN cells using `tf.contrib.rnn.BasicLSTMCell`.

2. Apply the dropout to the RNN cells using `tf.contrib.rnn.DropoutWrapper`.

3. Make a list of such cells according to the desired number of RNN layers and pass this list to `tf.contrib.rnn.MultiRNNCell`.

In our `build` method code, this list is created using Python list comprehension. Note that for a single layer, this list has only one cell.

You can read more about these functions at the following links:

- `tf.contrib.rnn.BasicLSTMCell`:https://www.tensorflow.org/api_docs/python/tf/contrib/rnn/BasicLSTMCell

- `tf.contrib.rnn.DropoutWrapper`: https://www.tensorflow.org/api_docs/python/tf/contrib/rnn/DropoutWrapper

- `tf.contrib.rnn.MultiRNNCell`: https://www.tensorflow.org/api_docs/python/tf/contrib/rnn/MultiRNNCell

Step 2 – defining the initial states for the RNN cells

The second step that our `build` method takes to build the RNN network was to define the initial states for the RNN cells.

You'll recall from the architecture of LSTM cells, there are three types of inputs in an LSTM cell — input data $x^{(t)}$, activations of hidden units from the previous time step $h^{(t-1)}$, and the cell state from the previous time step $C^{(t-1)}$.

So, in our `build` method implementation, $x^{(i)}$ is the embedded `embed_x` data tensor. However, when we evaluate the `cells`, we also need to specify the previous state of the cells. So, when we start processing a new input sequence, we initialize the cell states to zero state; then after each time step, we need to store the updated state of the cells to use for the next time step.

Once our multilayer RNN object is defined (`cells` in our implementation), we define its initial state in our `build` method using the `cells.zero_state` method.

Step 3 – creating the RNN using the RNN cells and their states

The third step to creating the RNN in our `build` method, used the `tf.nn.dynamic_rnn` function to pull together all our components.

The `tf.nn.dynamic_rnn` function therefore pulls the embedded data, the RNN cells, and their initial states, and creates a pipeline for them according to the unrolled architecture of LSTM cells.

The `tf.nn.dynamic_rnn` function returns a tuple containing the activations of the RNN cells, `outputs`; and their final states, `state`. The output is a three-dimensional tensor with this shape— (`batch_size, num_steps, lstm_size`). We pass `outputs` to a fully connected layer to get `logits` and we store the final state to use as the initial state of the next mini-batch of data.

 Feel free to read more about the `tf.nn.dynamic_rnn` function at its official documentation page at https://www.tensorflow.org/api_docs/python/tf/nn/dynamic_rnn.

Finally, in our `build` method, after setting up the RNN components of the network, the cost function and optimization schemes can be defined like any other neural network.

The train method

The next method in our `SentimentRNN` class is `train`. This method call is quite similar to the train methods we created in *Chapter 14, Going Deeper – The Mechanics of TensorFlow* and *Chapter 15, Classifying Images with Deep Convolutional Neural Networks* except that we have an additional tensor, `state`, that we feed into our network.

The following code shows the implementation of the `train` method:

```
def train(self, X_train, y_train, num_epochs):
    with tf.Session(graph=self.g) as sess:
        sess.run(self.init_op)
        iteration = 1
        for epoch in range(num_epochs):
            state = sess.run(self.initial_state)

            for batch_x, batch_y in create_batch_generator(
                        X_train, y_train, self.batch_size):
                feed = {'tf_x:0': batch_x,
                        'tf_y:0': batch_y,
                        'tf_keepprob:0': 0.5,
                        self.initial_state : state}
                loss, _, state = sess.run(
                        ['cost:0', 'train_op',
                        self.final_state],
                        feed_dict=feed)

                if iteration % 20 == 0:
                    print("Epoch: %d/%d Iteration: %d "
                        "| Train loss: %.5f" % (
                        epoch + 1, num_epochs,
                        iteration, loss))

                iteration +=1
            if (epoch+1)%10 == 0:
                self.saver.save(sess,
                    "model/sentiment-%d.ckpt" % epoch)
```

In this implementation of our `train` method, at the beginning of each epoch, we start from the zero states of RNN cells as our current state. Running each mini-batch of data is performed by feeding the current state along with the data `batch_x` and their labels `batch_y`. Upon finishing the execution of a mini-batch, we update the state to be the final state, which is returned by the `tf.nn.dynamic_rnn` function. This updated state will be used toward execution of the next mini-batch. This process is repeated and the current state is updated throughout the epoch.

The predict method

Finally, the last method in our SentimentRNN class is the predict method, which keeps updating the current state similar to the train method, shown in the following code:

```
def predict(self, X_data, return_proba=False):
    preds = []
    with tf.Session(graph = self.g) as sess:
        self.saver.restore(
            sess, tf.train.latest_checkpoint('./model/'))
        test_state = sess.run(self.initial_state)
        for ii, batch_x in enumerate(
            create_batch_generator(
                X_data, None, batch_size=self.batch_size), 1):
            feed = {'tf_x:0' : batch_x,
                    'tf_keepprob:0' : 1.0,
                    self.initial_state : test_state}
            if return_proba:
                pred, test_state = sess.run(
                    ['probabilities:0', self.final_state],
                    feed_dict=feed)
            else:
                pred, test_state = sess.run(
                    ['labels:0', self.final_state],
                    feed_dict=feed)

            preds.append(pred)

    return np.concatenate(preds)
```

Instantiating the SentimentRNN class

We've now coded and examined all four parts of our SentimentRNN class, which were the class constructor, the build method, the train method, and the predict method.

We are now ready to create an object of the class SentimentRNN, with parameters as follows:

```
>>> n_words = max(list(word_to_int.values())) + 1
>>>
>>> rnn = SentimentRNN(n_words=n_words,
...                    seq_len=sequence_length,
...                    embed_size=256,
```

```
...                         lstm_size=128,
...                         num_layers=1,
...                         batch_size=100,
...                         learning_rate=0.001)
```

Notice here that we use `num_layers=1` to use a single RNN layer. Although our implementation allows us to create multilayer RNNs, by setting `num_layers` greater than 1. Here we should consider the small size of our dataset, and that a single RNN layer may generalize better to unseen data, since it is less likely to overfit the training data.

Training and optimizing the sentiment analysis RNN model

Next, we can train the RNN model by calling the `rnn.train` function. In the following code, we train the model for `40` epochs using the input from `X_train` and the corresponding class labels stored in `y_train`:

```
>>> rnn.train(X_train, y_train, num_epochs=40)
Epoch: 1/40 Iteration: 20 | Train loss: 0.70637
Epoch: 1/40 Iteration: 40 | Train loss: 0.60539
Epoch: 1/40 Iteration: 60 | Train loss: 0.66977
Epoch: 1/40 Iteration: 80 | Train loss: 0.51997
...
```

The trained model is saved using TensorFlow's checkpointing system, which we discussed in *Chapter 14, Going Deeper – The Mechanics of TensorFlow*. Now, we can use the trained model for predicting the class labels on the test set, as follows:

```
>>> preds = rnn.predict(X_test)
>>> y_true = y_test[:len(preds)]
>>> print('Test Acc.: %.3f' % (
...        np.sum(preds == y_true) / len(y_true)))
```

The result will show an accuracy of 86 percent. Given the small size of this dataset, this is comparable to the test prediction accuracy obtained in *Chapter 8, Applying Machine Learning to Sentiment Analysis*.

We can optimize this further by changing the hyperparameters of the model, such as `lstm_size`, `seq_len`, and `embed_size`, to achieve better generalization performance. However, for hyperparameter tuning, it is recommended that we create a separate validation set and that we don't repeatedly use the test set for evaluation to avoid introducing bias through test data leakage, which we discussed in *Chapter 6, Learning Best Practices for Model Evaluation and Hyperparameter Tuning*.

Also, if you're interested in the prediction probabilities on the test set rather than the class labels, then you can set `return_proba=True` as follows:

```
>>> proba = rnn.predict(X_test, return_proba=True)
```

So this was our first RNN model for sentiment analysis. We'll now go further and create an RNN for character-by-character language modeling in TensorFlow, as another popular application of sequence modeling.

Project two – implementing an RNN for character-level language modeling in TensorFlow

Language modeling is a fascinating application that enables machines to perform human-language-related tasks, such as generating English sentences. One of the interesting efforts in this area is the work done by Sutskever, Martens, and Hinton (*Generating Text with Recurrent Neural Networks, Ilya Sutskever, James Martens*, and *Geoffrey E. Hinton, Proceedings of the 28th International Conference on Machine Learning (ICML-11), 2011* https://pdfs.semanticscholar.org/93c2/0e38c85b69fc2d2eb3 14b3c1217913f7db11.pdf).

In the model that we'll build now, the input is a text document, and our goal is to develop a model that can generate new text similar to the input document. Examples of such an input can be a book or a computer program in a specific programming language.

In character-level language modeling, the input is broken down into a sequence of characters that are fed into our network one character at a time. The network will process each new character in conjunction with the memory of the previously seen characters to predict the next character. The following figure shows an example of character-level language modeling:

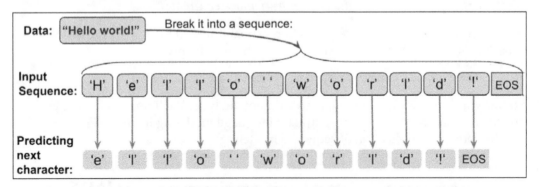

We can break this implementation down into three separate steps — preparing the data, building the RNN model, and performing next-character prediction and sampling to generate new text.

If you recall from the previous sections of this chapter, we mentioned the exploding gradient problem. In this application, we'll also get a chance to play with a gradient clipping technique to avoid this exploding gradient problem.

Preparing the data

In this section, we prepare the data for character-level language modeling.

To get the input data, visit the Project Gutenberg website at `https://www.gutenberg.org/`, which provides thousands of free e-books. For our example, we can get the book *The Tragedie of Hamlet* by William Shakespeare in plain text format from `http://www.gutenberg.org/cache/epub/2265/pg2265.txt`.

Note that this link will directly take you to the download page. If you are using macOS or a Linux operating system, you can download the file with the following command in the Terminal:

```
curl http://www.gutenberg.org/cache/epub/2265/pg2265.txt > pg2265.txt
```

If this resource becomes unavailable in future, a copy of this text is also included in this chapter's code directory in the book's code repository at `https://github.com/rasbt/python-machine-learning-book-2nd-edition`.

Once we have some data, we can read it into a Python session as plain text. In the following code, the Python variable `chars` represents the set of *unique* characters observed in this text. We then create a dictionary that maps each character to an integer, `char2int`, and a dictionary that performs reverse mapping, for instance, mapping integers to those unique characters— `int2char`. Using the `char2int` dictionary, we convert the text into a NumPy array of integers. The following figure shows an example of converting characters into integers and the reverse for the words `"Hello"` and `"world"`:

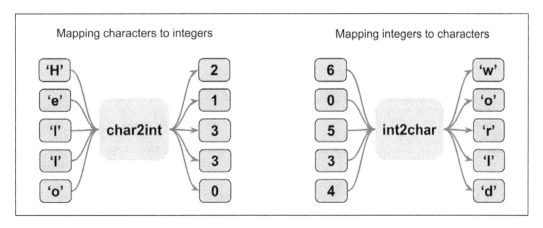

This code reads the text from the downloaded link, removes the beginning portion of the text that contains some legal description of the Gutenberg project, and then constructs the dictionaries based on the text:

```
>>> import numpy as np
>>> ## Reading and processing text
>>> with open('pg2265.txt', 'r', encoding='utf-8') as f:
...       text=f.read()
>>> text = text[15858:]
>>> chars = set(text)
>>> char2int = {ch:i for i,ch in enumerate(chars)}
>>> int2char = dict(enumerate(chars))
>>> text_ints = np.array([char2int[ch] for ch in text],
...                        dtype=np.int32)
```

Now, we should reshape the data into batches of sequences, the most important step in preparing data. As we know, the goal is to predict the next character based on the sequence of characters that we have observed so far. Therefore, we shift the input (**x**) and output (**y**) of the neural network by one character. The following figure shows the preprocessing steps, starting from a text corpus to generating data arrays for **x** and **y**:

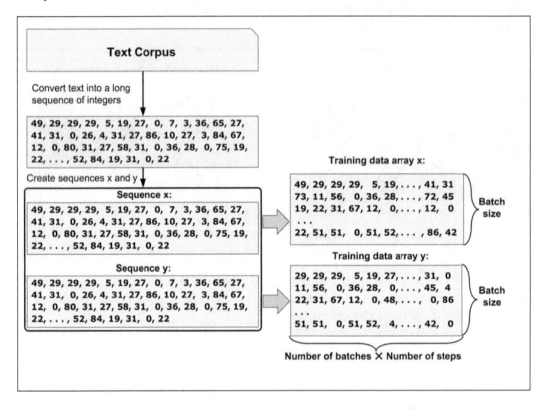

As you can see in this figure, the training arrays **x** and **y** have the same shapes or dimensions, where the number of rows is equal to the *batch size* and the number of columns is *number of batches × number of steps* .

Given the input array `data` that contains the integers that correspond to the characters in the text corpus, the following function will generate x and y with the same structure shown in the previous figure:

```
>>> def reshape_data(sequence, batch_size, num_steps):
...         mini_batch_length = batch_size * num_steps
...         num_batches = int(len(sequence) / mini_batch_length)
...         if num_batches*mini_batch_length + 1 > len(sequence):
...             num_batches = num_batches - 1
```

```
...         ## Truncate the sequence at the end to get rid of
...         ## remaining charcaters that do not make a full batch
...         x = sequence[0: num_batches*mini_batch_length]
...         y = sequence[1: num_batches*mini_batch_length + 1]
...         ## Split x & y into a list batches of sequences:
...         x_batch_splits = np.split(x, batch_size)
...         y_batch_splits = np.split(y, batch_size)
...         ## Stack the batches together
...         ## batch_size x mini_batch_length
...         x = np.stack(x_batch_splits)
...         y = np.stack(y_batch_splits)
...
...         return x, y
```

The next step is to split the arrays **x** and **y** into mini-batches where each row is a sequence with length equal to the *number of steps*. The process of splitting the data array **x** is shown in the following figure:

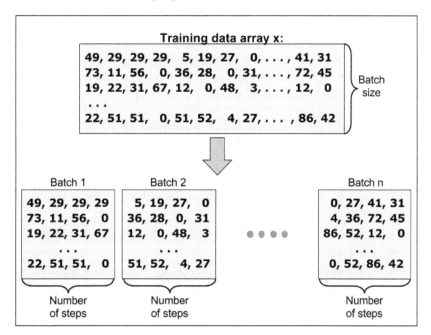

In the following code, we define a function named `create_batch_generator` that splits the data arrays **x** and **y**, as shown in the previous figure, and outputs a batch generator. Later, we will use this generator to iterate through the mini-batches during the training of our network:

```
>>> def create_batch_generator(data_x, data_y, num_steps):
...        batch_size, tot_batch_length = data_x.shape
...        num_batches = int(tot_batch_length/num_steps)
...        for b in range(num_batches):
...            yield (data_x[:, b*num_steps:(b+1)*num_steps],
...                    data_y[:, b*num_steps:(b+1)*num_steps])
```

At this point, we've now completed the data preprocessing steps, and we have the data in the proper format. In the next section, we'll implement the RNN model for character-level language modeling.

Building a character-level RNN model

To build a character-level neural network, we'll implement a class called `CharRNN` that constructs the graph of the RNN in order to predict the next character, after observing a given sequence of characters. From the classification perspective, the number of classes is the total number of unique characters that exists in the text corpus. The `CharRNN` class has four methods, as follows:

- A constructor that sets up the learning parameters, creates a computation graph, and calls the `build` method to construct the graph based on the sampling mode versus the training mode.

- A `build` method that defines the placeholders for feeding the data, constructs the RNN using LSTM cells, and defines the output of the network, the cost function, and the optimizer.

- A `train` method to iterate through the mini-batches and train the network for the specified number of epochs.

- A `sample` method to start from a given string, calculate the probabilities for the next character, and choose a character randomly according to these probabilities. This process will be repeated, and the sampled characters will be concatenated together to form a string. Once the size of this string reaches the specified length, it will return the string.

We'll break these four methods into separate code sections and explain each one. Note that implementing the RNN part of this model is very similar to the implementation in the *Project one – performing sentiment analysis of IMDb movie reviews using multilayer RNNs* section. So, we'll skip the description of building the RNN components here.

The constructor

In contrast to our previous implementation for sentiment analysis, where the same computation graph was used for both training and prediction modes, this time our computation graph is going to be different for the training versus the sampling mode.

Therefore we need to add a new Boolean type argument to the constructor, to determine whether we're building the model for the training mode or the sampling mode. The following code shows the implementation of the constructor enclosed in the class definition:

```python
import tensorflow as tf
import os

class CharRNN(object):
    def __init__(self, num_classes, batch_size=64,
                 num_steps=100, lstm_size=128,
                 num_layers=1, learning_rate=0.001,
                 keep_prob=0.5, grad_clip=5,
                 sampling=False):
        self.num_classes = num_classes
        self.batch_size = batch_size
        self.num_steps = num_steps
        self.lstm_size = lstm_size
        self.num_layers = num_layers
        self.learning_rate = learning_rate
        self.keep_prob = keep_prob
        self.grad_clip = grad_clip

        self.g = tf.Graph()
        with self.g.as_default():
            tf.set_random_seed(123)

            self.build(sampling=sampling)

            self.saver = tf.train.Saver()

            self.init_op = tf.global_variables_initializer()
```

As we planned earlier, the Boolean `sampling` argument is used to determine whether the instance of `CharRNN` is for building the graph in the training mode (`sampling=False`) or the sampling mode (`sampling=True`).

In addition to the `sampling` argument, we've introduced a new argument called `grad_clip`, which is used for clipping the gradients to avoid the exploding gradient problem that we mentioned earlier.

Then, similar to the previous implementation, the constructor creates a computation graph, sets the graph-level random seed for consistent output, and builds the graph by calling the `build` method.

The build method

The next method of the `CharRNN` class is `build`, which is very similar to the `build` method in the *Project one – performing sentiment analysis of IMDb movie reviews using multilayer RNNs* section, except for some minor differences. The `build` method first defines two local variables, `batch_size` and `num_steps`, based on the mode, as follows:

$$in\ sampling\ mode: \begin{cases} batch\_size = 1 \\ num\_steps = 1 \end{cases}$$

$$in\ training\ mode: \begin{cases} batch\_size = self.batch\_size \\ num\_steps = self.num\_steps \end{cases}$$

Recall that in the sentiment analysis implementation, we used an embedding layer to create a salient representation for the unique words in the dataset. In contrast, here we are using the one-hot encoding scheme for both x and y with `depth=num_classes`, where `num_classes` is in fact the total number of characters in the text corpus.

Building a multilayer RNN component of the model is exactly the same as in our sentiment analysis implementation, using the `tf.nn.dynamic_rnn` function. However, `outputs` from the `tf.nn.dynamic_rnn` function is a three-dimensional tensor with this shape—`batch_size, num_steps, lstm_size`. Next, this tensor will be reshaped into a two-dimensional tensor with the `batch_size*num_steps, lstm_size` shape, which is passed to the `tf.layers.dense` function to make a fully connected layer and obtain `logits` (net inputs). Finally, the probabilities for the next batch of characters are obtained and the cost function is defined. In addition, here, we apply gradient clipping using the `tf.clip_by_global_norm` function to avoid the exploding gradient problem.

The following code shows the implementation of what we've just described for our new `build` method:

```
def build(self, sampling):
    if sampling == True:
        batch_size, num_steps = 1, 1
    else:
        batch_size = self.batch_size
        num_steps = self.num_steps

    tf_x = tf.placeholder(tf.int32,
                          shape=[batch_size, num_steps],
                          name='tf_x')
    tf_y = tf.placeholder(tf.int32,
                          shape=[batch_size, num_steps],
                          name='tf_y')
    tf_keepprob = tf.placeholder(tf.float32,
                          name='tf_keepprob')

    # One-hot encoding:
    x_onehot = tf.one_hot(tf_x, depth=self.num_classes)
    y_onehot = tf.one_hot(tf_y, depth=self.num_classes)

    ### Build the multi-layer RNN cells
    cells = tf.contrib.rnn.MultiRNNCell(
        [tf.contrib.rnn.DropoutWrapper(
            tf.contrib.rnn.BasicLSTMCell(self.lstm_size),
            output_keep_prob=tf_keepprob)
        for _ in range(self.num_layers)])

    ## Define the initial state
    self.initial_state = cells.zero_state(
                batch_size, tf.float32)

    ## Run each sequence step through the RNN
    lstm_outputs, self.final_state = tf.nn.dynamic_rnn(
                cells, x_onehot,
                initial_state=self.initial_state)

    print('  << lstm_outputs  >>', lstm_outputs)

    seq_output_reshaped = tf.reshape(
                lstm_outputs,
```

```
                    shape=[-1, self.lstm_size],
                    name='seq_output_reshaped')

    logits = tf.layers.dense(
                    inputs=seq_output_reshaped,
                    units=self.num_classes,
                    activation=None,
                    name='logits')

    proba = tf.nn.softmax(
                    logits,
                    name='probabilities')

    y_reshaped = tf.reshape(
                    y_onehot,
                    shape=[-1, self.num_classes],
                    name='y_reshaped')
    cost = tf.reduce_mean(
                    tf.nn.softmax_cross_entropy_with_logits(
                        logits=logits,
                        labels=y_reshaped),
                    name='cost')

    # Gradient clipping to avoid "exploding gradients"
    tvars = tf.trainable_variables()
    grads, _ = tf.clip_by_global_norm(
                    tf.gradients(cost, tvars),
                    self.grad_clip)
    optimizer = tf.train.AdamOptimizer(self.learning_rate)
    train_op = optimizer.apply_gradients(
                    zip(grads, tvars),
                    name='train_op')
```

The train method

The next method of the `CharRNN` class is the `train` method, which is very similar
to the `train` method described in the *Project one – performing sentiment analysis of
IMDb movie reviews using multilayer RNNs* section. Here is the `train` method code,
which will look very familiar to the sentiment analysis version we built earlier in this
chapter:

```
def train(self, train_x, train_y,
          num_epochs, ckpt_dir='./model/'):
    ## Create the checkpoint directory
```

```
## if it does not exists
if not os.path.exists(ckpt_dir):
    os.mkdir(ckpt_dir)

with tf.Session(graph=self.g) as sess:
    sess.run(self.init_op)

    n_batches = int(train_x.shape[1]/self.num_steps)
    iterations = n_batches * num_epochs
    for epoch in range(num_epochs):

        # Train network
        new_state = sess.run(self.initial_state)
        loss = 0
        ## Mini-batch generator:
        bgen = create_batch_generator(
                train_x, train_y, self.num_steps)
        for b, (batch_x, batch_y) in enumerate(bgen, 1):
            iteration = epoch*n_batches + b

            feed = {'tf_x:0': batch_x,
                    'tf_y:0': batch_y,
                    'tf_keepprob:0' : self.keep_prob,
                    self.initial_state : new_state}
            batch_cost, _, new_state = sess.run(
                    ['cost:0', 'train_op',
                        self.final_state],
                    feed_dict=feed)
            if iteration % 10 == 0:
                print('Epoch %d/%d Iteration %d'
                        '| Training loss: %.4f' % (
                        epoch + 1, num_epochs,
                        iteration, batch_cost))

        ## Save the trained model
        self.saver.save(
                sess, os.path.join(
                    ckpt_dir, 'language_modeling.ckpt'))
```

The sample method

The final method in our `CharRNN` class is the `sample` method. The behavior of this `sample` method is similar to that of the `predict` method that we implemented in the *Project one – performing sentiment analysis of IMDb movie reviews using multilayer RNNs* section. However, the difference here is that we calculate the probabilities for the next character from an observed sequence—`observed_seq`. Then, these probabilities are passed to a function named `get_top_char`, which randomly selects one character according to the obtained probabilities.

Initially, the observed sequence starts from `starter_seq`, which is provided as an argument. When new characters are sampled according to their predicted probabilities, they are appended to the observed sequence, and the new observed sequence is used for predicting the next character.

The implementation of the `sample` method is as follows:

```
def sample(self, output_length,
        ckpt_dir, starter_seq="The "):
    observed_seq = [ch for ch in starter_seq]
    with tf.Session(graph=self.g) as sess:
        self.saver.restore(
            sess,
            tf.train.latest_checkpoint(ckpt_dir))
        ## 1: run the model using the starter sequence
        new_state = sess.run(self.initial_state)
        for ch in starter_seq:
            x = np.zeros((1, 1))
            x[0, 0] = char2int[ch]
            feed = {'tf_x:0': x,
                    'tf_keepprob:0': 1.0,
                    self.initial_state: new_state}
            proba, new_state = sess.run(
                    ['probabilities:0', self.final_state],
                    feed_dict=feed)

        ch_id = get_top_char(proba, len(chars))
        observed_seq.append(int2char[ch_id])

        ## 2: run the model using the updated observed_seq
        for i in range(output_length):
            x[0,0] = ch_id
            feed = {'tf_x:0': x,
                    'tf_keepprob:0': 1.0,
```

```
                        self.initial_state: new_state}
            proba, new_state = sess.run(
                    ['probabilities:0', self.final_state],
                    feed_dict=feed)

            ch_id = get_top_char(proba, len(chars))
            observed_seq.append(int2char[ch_id])

        return ''.join(observed_seq)
```

So here, the `sample` method calls the `get_top_char` function to choose a character ID randomly (`ch_id`) according to the obtained probabilities.

In this `get_top_char` function, the probabilities are first sorted, then the `top_n` probabilities are passed to the `numpy.random.choice` function to randomly select one out of these top probabilities. The implementation of the `get_top_char` function is as follows:

```
def get_top_char(probas, char_size, top_n=5):
    p = np.squeeze(probas)
    p[np.argsort(p)[:-top_n]] = 0.0
    p = p / np.sum(p)
    ch_id = np.random.choice(char_size, 1, p=p)[0]
    return ch_id
```

Note, of course, that this function should be defined *before* the definition of the `CharRNN` class; we've explained it in this order here so that we can explain the concepts in order. Browse through the code notebook that accompanies this chapter to get a better overview of the order in which the functions are defined.

Creating and training the CharRNN Model

Now we're ready to create an instance of the `CharRNN` class to build the RNN model, and to train it with the following configurations:

```
>>> batch_size = 64
>>> num_steps = 100
>>> train_x, train_y = reshape_data(text_ints,
...                                 batch_size,
...                                 num_steps)
>>>
>>> rnn = CharRNN(num_classes=len(chars), batch_size=batch_size)
>>> rnn.train(train_x, train_y,
...           num_epochs=100,
...           ckpt_dir='./model-100/')
```

The trained model will be saved in a directory called `./model-100/` so that we can reload it later for prediction or for continuing the training.

The CharRNN model in the sampling mode

Next up, we can create a new instance of the `CharRNN` class in the sampling mode by specifying that `sampling=True`. We'll call the `sample` method to load the saved model in the `./model-100/` folder, and generate a sequence of 500 characters:

```
>>> del rnn
>>>
>>> np.random.seed(123)
>>> rnn = CharRNN(len(chars), sampling=True)
>>> print(rnn.sample(ckpt_dir='./model-100/',
...                   output_length=500))
```

The generated text will look like the following:

```
The stall soues tay and the hates,
The perse in there is that so the meanes this made there

    Ham. Ile teath thes are this makere of a driane,
Why shis mestend the Casst of is singe,
In this to this, to mers it is for marth,
Ase hinees sim thig tald ow a tore andere,
In histhene tistere shere this wile and my Lord:
And tit mighes the secleer allost heruen, and that hash to sall and hears,
If you his moses tonger and mout ofr mesting a forte tis at

    Pomin. Where in you dist and sintere shan shall
```

You can see that in the resulting output, that some English words are mostly preserved. It's also important to note that this is from an old English text; therefore, some words in the original text may be unfamiliar. To get a better result, we would need to train the model for higher number of epochs. Feel free to repeat this with a much larger document and train the model for more epochs.

Chapter and book summary

We hope you enjoyed this last chapter of *Python Machine Learning* and our exciting tour of machine learning and deep learning. Through the journey of this book, we've covered the essential topics that this field has to offer, and you should now be well equipped to put those techniques into action to solve real-world problems.

We started our journey with a brief overview of the different types of learning tasks: supervised learning, reinforcement learning, and unsupervised learning. We then discussed several different learning algorithms that you can use for classification, starting with simple single-layer neural networks in *Chapter 2, Training Simple Machine Learning Algorithms for Classification.*

We continued to discuss advanced classification algorithms in *Chapter 3, A Tour of Machine Learning Classifiers Using scikit-learn,* and we learned about the most important aspects of a machine learning pipeline in *Chapter 4, Building Good Training Sets – Data Preprocessing* and *Chapter 5, Compressing Data via Dimensionality Reduction.*

Remember that even the most advanced algorithm is limited by the information in the training data that it gets to learn from. So in *Chapter 6, Learning Best Practices for Model Evaluation and Hyperparameter Tuning,* we learned about the best practices to build and evaluate predictive models, which is another important aspect in machine learning applications.

If one single learning algorithm does not achieve the performance we desire, it can be sometimes helpful to create an ensemble of experts to make a prediction. We explored this in *Chapter 7, Combining Different Models for Ensemble Learning.*

Then in *Chapter 8, Applying Machine Learning to Sentiment Analysis,* we applied machine learning to analyze one of the most popular and interesting forms of data in the modern age that's dominated by social media platforms on the internet — text documents.

Next, we reminded ourselves that machine learning techniques are not limited to offline data analysis, and in *Chapter 9, Embedding a Machine Learning Model into a Web Application,* we saw how to embed a machine learning model into a web application to share it with the outside world.

For the most part, our focus was on algorithms for classification, which is probably the most popular application of machine learning. However, this is not where our journey ended! In *Chapter 10, Predicting Continuous Target Variables with Regression Analysis,* we explored several algorithms for regression analysis to predict continuous valued output values.

Another exciting subfield of machine learning is clustering analysis, which can help us find hidden structures in the data, even if our training data does not come with the right answers to learn from. We worked with this in *Chapter 11, Working with Unlabeled Data – Clustering Analysis.*

We then shifted our attention to one of one of the most exciting algorithms in the whole machine learning field — artificial neural networks. We started by implementing a multilayer perceptron from scratch with NumPy in *Chapter 12, Implementing a Multilayer Artificial Neural Network from Scratch.*

The power of TensorFlow became obvious in *Chapter 13, Parallelizing Neural Network Training with TensorFlow*, where we used TensorFlow to facilitate the process of building neural network models and make use of GPUs to make the training of multilayer neural networks more efficient.

We delved deeper into the mechanics of TensorFlow in *Chapter 14, Going Deeper – The Mechanics of TensorFlow*, and discussed the different aspects and mechanics of TensorFlow, including variables and operators in a TensorFlow computation graph, variable scopes, launching graphs, and different ways of executing nodes.

In *Chapter 15, Classifying Images with Deep Convolutional Neural Networks*, we dived into convolutional neural networks, which are widely used in computer vision at the moment, due to their great performance in image classification tasks.

Finally, here in *Chapter 16, Modeling Sequential Data Using Recurrent Neural Networks*, we learned about sequence modeling using RNNs. While a comprehensive study of deep learning is well beyond the scope of this book, we hope that we've kindled your interest enough to follow the most recent advancements in this field of deep learning.

If you're considering a career in machine learning, or you just want to keep up to date with the current advancements in this field, I can recommend to you the works of the following leading experts in the machine learning field:

- Geoffry Hinton (`http://www.cs.toronto.edu/~hinton/`)
- Andrew Ng (`http://www.andrewng.org/`)
- Yann LeCun (`http://yann.lecun.com`)
- Juergen Schmidhuber (`http://people.idsia.ch/~juergen/`)
- Yoshua Bengio (`http://www.iro.umontreal.ca/~bengioy/yoshua_en/`)

Just to name a few!

And of course, don't hesitate to join the scikit-learn, TensorFlow, and Keras mailing lists to participate in interesting discussions around these libraries and machine learning in general. Lastly, you can find out what we, the authors, are up at `http://sebastianraschka.com` and `http://vahidmirjalili.com`. You're always welcome to contact us if you have any questions about this book, or need some general tips about machine learning.

Index

explained variance 147, 148
explanatory variable 310
Exploratory data analysis (EDA) 314

F

False negative (FN) 206
False positive (FP) 206, 208
feature extraction 130
feature hierarchy 494
feature importance
  assessing, with random forests 136-138
feature maps 495, 510
features
  eliminating, with missing values 109, 110
feature scaling
  about 120-122
  gradient descent, improving through 42-44
feature selection 130
feature space
  samples, projecting onto 162
feature transformation 148-151
feature vectors
  words, transforming into 259, 260
feed forward neural net 388
fitted scikit-learn estimators
  serializing 282-284
Flask
  about 287
  reference 287
  web application, developing with 287
Flask web application
  creating 288-290
  directory structure, setting up 291
  form validation 290, 291
  Jinja2 templating engine, used for
    implementing macro 292
  rendering 290, 291
  result page, creating 294
  style, adding via CSS 293
forward propagation
  neural network, activating via 387-389
fuzzifier 356
fuzziness coefficient 356
fuzzy clustering 354
fuzzy C-means (FCM) algorithm 354
fuzzy k-means 354

G

Gated Recurrent Unit (GRU) 550
gates 549
Gaussian kernel 85
geometric interpretation
  of L2 regularization 124, 125
Gini impurity 90
Global Interpreter Lock (GIL) 422
Glorot initialization 464
Google Developers portal
  reference 265
gradient descent
  about 36
  cost functions, minimizing with 35-37
  improving, through feature scaling 42-44
  regression for regression parameters,
    solving with 319-323
gradient descent learning algorithm
  for logistic regression 69
gradient descent optimization
    algorithm 120
graph
  building, control flow mechanics
    used 483-486
  visualizing, with TensorBoard 487-490
graph-based clustering 377
Graphical Processing Units (GPUs) 418
greedy algorithms 130
grid search
  about 201
  hyperparameters, tuning via 201, 202
  machine leaning models,
    fine-tuning via 201

H

half-moon shapes separation
    example 173-176
handwritten digits
  classifying 389, 390
hard clustering
  versus soft clustering 354-357
heat map
  dendrograms, attaching to 369-371
hidden structures
  discovering, with unsupervised learning 7